Ernst Mohr
The Production of Consumer Society

Dedicated to Hans-Christoph Binswanger (1929-2018)

Ernst Mohr is Professor emeritus of Economics at the University of St. Gallen, Switzerland. His research interests concern the interrelation between culture and consumption, addressing, among others, stylistic innovation, aesthetics and the economy, and taste as a driver of the consumer industry.

Ernst Mohr

The Production of Consumer Society

Cultural-Economic Principles of Distinction

[transcript]

Bibliographic information published by the Deutsche Nationalbibliothek

The Deutsche Nationalbibliothek lists this publication in the Deutsche National-bibliografie; detailed bibliographic data are available in the Internet at http://dnb.d-nb.de

© 2021 transcript Verlag, Bielefeld

Cover layout: Kordula Röckenhaus, Bielefeld
Copy-editing: Ben Stowers
Typeset: Jan Gerbach, Bielefeld
Printed by Majuskel Medienproduktion GmbH, Wetzlar
Print-ISBN 978-3-8376-5703-6
PDF-ISBN 978-3-8394-5703-0
https://doi.org/10.14361/9783839457030

Content

PART 2: THE PRODUCTIVE CONSUMER

PART 3: THE STYLISH PRESENT DAY

Preface

Economics leads us to believe that the consumption of large quantities benefits us – more of everything is the source of our happiness. That's why we strive for ever more of the same, and more of all that's new. And that's why we are expected to be buying like mad for ever greater satisfaction – in absolute or relative terms. No branch of economics is more mistaken than consumer theory. At its core, it remains a theory of the relationship between things and people (via the relationship between quantities and prices), and not one between people.

Of course, we also consume quantities: however many calories of food, square metres of our homes – just as people in hunter-gatherer economies did, whose consumption remains the blueprint for economics to this day. But today we are deriving less and less utility from quantities consumed per se. Instead, and increasingly so, the consumption of social differences – of social distance and social proximity – generates utility for us. We strive for more of the same, only as far as it helps create that social distance or proximity – as today we seldom succeed at this by merely striving for this goal. Much more conducive to utility is the consumption of quality: "Yes to this, no to that!". This is the point of departure in this book.

We consume in ways that certain people are not consuming, and consume roughly the same as others. In this way we produce social distance and proximity, distance from one and proximity to the other. This is the source of our happiness. We use consumer goods for our benefit – here I agree with economic orthodoxy. But we don't succeed by piling up mountains of them, which we then devour and otherwise exploit, but rather by opening up divides between people and thereby manifesting distance, as well as building bridges to other people and thereby expressing proximity to them. This production view of social distance and proximity opens up a consumer theory, the core of which is not the relationship between things and people, but between people and people, a view that is presented here.

But how exactly do we produce social distance and proximity as we consume? Non-trivial answers beyond "Yes to this, no to that!" are not evident. The economic orthodoxy remains silent here, except perhaps for the assertion that "Yes to this, no to that!" depends on which goods convey information a consumer wants other consumers to know. But what the desired information should be remains obscure or a communicative primitive (like 'being rich', understood as communicable simply by high consumer spending). Sociology is hardly doing any better. There, "Yes to this, no to that!" is understood as being the consequence of interpersonal differences in financial and non-financial (human and social) capital stocks. Although these are regarded as the source of social distance and proximity, sociology has little more to offer than a tautology as to how the latter are created: social distance and proximity are created by (the production of) social distance and proximity. Psychology, on the other hand, lacks the systematic consideration of the material, and material culture research lacks the broader view. And semiotics concerns itself with the relationship between symbols, but it remains all the more silent on the relationship between distance and proximity, which are themselves also symbols. And as a result, it also remains silent on the relationship between people, who with their "Yes to this, no to that!", move closer to some and further away from others. The goal of the following is to close these gaps a bit.

It will be shown how social distance and proximity are communicated by consumption and produced by communication. The approach taken can be regarded as a (material) cultural-economic one. The world of things (augmented by matching behaviours) provides the 'material' for opening up interpersonal divides on the one hand and building bridges on the other. Culture provides the classification system that turns "Yes to this, no to that!" into a communicative activity, and the economy opens up the sphere of activity for consumers, confronting them with the consequences of their actions. Consumption, understood as the consumption of social distance and proximity rather than quantities of goods, closes the production-consumption circuit. But not, as in economic orthodoxy, in a self-referential economic system, but rather via culture. Culture is not an addendum to the economic circuit, but central to it.

Part 1: Culture of Dissimilarity

Chapter 1
Material

"We speak through our clothes."
Umberto Eco[1]

Singletons: *Piña*

Piña is a textile that represents the Philippines in a singular way.[2] In a complicated, time-consuming process, fibres are extracted from pineapple leaves and woven into an airy, semi-transparent, very expensive whitish fabric. Piña was worn in the 19th century by the Philippine *Ilustrado* class. *Ilustrados* – the enlightened ones – were Spanish mestizos born in the Philippines, who had received their higher education in Europe and enhanced their wealth with overseas trade. The wearing of piña was synonymous with the command of the Spanish language, wealth, refined European manners and urbanity. Even before the indigenous population (*Indios*) did so, and in spite of their close economic and cultural ties to Spain, the *Ilustrados* developed the idea of an independent (national) identity separate from Spanish colonial rule. Piña was the textile of choice of the wealthy male Filipino for his *barong tagalog*, the wide, long-sleeved, embroidered shirt worn over his trousers.

Later, in the first half of the 20th century, having shifted from Spanish to American colonial influence, the country's elite displayed the American tastes of the time. The western suit with shirt and tie became the clothing of a man of the world and piña became passé, now a sign of the Spanish-European past. The national Filipino identity was simultaneously migrating into lower social strata, and in 1953, after the country had gained its independence, the man of the

---

1   Quoted from Kidder 2005, p. 345.

2   Roces 2013.

masses, Ramon Magsaysay, won the presidential election against his America-leaning predecessor, Manuel Quezon. Piña then rose through a symbolic act of the newly-elected president to a symbol of the new nation: for his inauguration Magsaysay preferred a barong tagalog in sinfully expensive piña over a western suit. Piña thus became a symbol of national identity, from having been the symbol of the Spanish-European past, and having been still earlier a symbol of a cultivated way of life.[3]

Its manufacturing technique combined with the history of its use made piña an incomparable fabric. It belongs within the world of objects, the superset of all objects, to the class of singular pieces separated from all other objects – piña is a singleton, an object in a set of its own, without comparable relatives.[4] In the following, a singleton is represented by the symbol ∘.[5]*

Piña impressively demonstrates the non-verbal communicative power of objects. A fibre obtained from the pineapple plant and woven into a textile conveys distance and proximity over a long period of time; distance between the *Ilustrados* and the *Indios* as well as in relation to the colonial rulers, and proximity to one

---

3   Today piña belongs to the Filipiniana and is the romanticised symbol of a refined urban Filipino past.

4   Proceeding from objects usually with a plurality of characteristics (material, colour, cut, etc.), a singleton can be defined as an object identical to its sole characteristic (for example, the textile piña). Thus, a singleton object is a mathematical unit set, a set with exactly one member, its characteristic, because the set of its characteristics is by definition (tautologically) a unit set. Defined as a singleton, all garments made from piña are therefore identical and the set of all objects with this characteristic is a unit set. Another example: kitsch is one of several characteristics of certain paintings and therefore there exist different kitschy paintings, hence the set of kitschy paintings contains more than one member. However, as a painterly category 'kitsch', all kitschy pictures are identical and the set of objects with this property shrinks to a unit set. It is already clear from these examples that the mathematical properties of sets of objects are not exogenous, giving reliable orientation to cultural and social scientific analysis. Rather, they are culturally-made variables. We will encounter this complication throughout the book. The derivation of properties from sets of objects is the main analytical task in the following. The use of mathematical language is unproblematic as long as it is understood as the means of an author – and the author is culture.

5   In the following footnotes marked with *, generic terms and concepts used in the main text are translated into the language of set theory. If not explicitly defined, the mathematical notation follows that of Basili and Vannucci (2013), as this source is also used for the further specification of the terms 'distance' and 'proximity'. The reader disinterested in the later formal modelling may simply skip the *footnotes.

another. Piña is exemplary of two important properties of the entire world of objects. Firstly, an object not only creates distance *or* proximity, but both simultaneously – it acts as a separator and a cement in tandem. One can hardly be separated from the other, almost as if distance creates proximity and proximity creates distance. Secondly, with piña, distance and proximity were not created within a group or in between groups, but distance was created towards *other* groups, and at the same time proximity was created *within* a group. The world of objects thus renders the social space visible. Objects are socially distinguishing features *vis-à-vis* the outside world, and at the same time means for identification and the characteristics of identity within a group.

0/+Consumption

Piña is quintessential for the understanding of consumption. Although the fabric itself is a typical consumer good, it does not offer utility by way of positive quantities consumed. *Ceteris paribus* – the more, the better, but through an ordered "Yes to this, no to that!" of at least two consumers, who answer "Yes to what, no to what?" each in a different way.

For understanding this claim, it is helpful to distinguish the consumption goods basket from the goods *type* basket. In the orthodoxy[6], the utility-generating consumption goods basket contains *positive* quantities of each type of goods that the consumer consumes. Types not consumed are not contained in it – in line with the shrewd motto, 'You can't do something with nothing'. In the orthodoxy, this reduction of the sources of utility to positive quantities of goods is also motivated by the fact that zero quantities are irrelevant for compliance with the consumer's budget restriction. The consumed quantity zero of a type of good, for example, of piña by the Spanish colonial masters or later the 'Americanists', is budget-neutral, no matter how expensive the good may be – just as the consumption of positive quantities of goods whose market price is zero is budget neutral. Solely focused on the analysis of scarcity, the orthodoxy treats goods with a positive price that the consumer does not consume in the same way as it treats goods consumed in positive quantities that cost nothing – both are ignored or dismissed as economically irrelevant.

This is a grave omission. For it obscures the view of another source of consumer utility: the utility that consumer A, for example, the Philippine 'Americanist', obtains precisely by *not* consuming positive quantities, i.e. shunning that

---

6   Orthodoxy in the following refers to neoclassical consumer economics.

good (piña), which consumer B, in the example of the Philippine nationalist, is consuming in positive quantities, i.e. is surrounding himself with it, and shunning instead a different good (the Western suit). Avoiding different *types* of goods in each case brings about utility for both consumers because it establishes their identities.

Therefore, a more general definition of economic behaviour than that commonly used in orthodoxy is called for. There, economic activity requires an input of resources. Consequently, that which does not cost any (finite) resources, however defined, is not an economically relevant action. Utility is thus the sole derivative of the availability of scarce resources (nature, money, time, knowledge, network). Zero-quantity consumption, because it's budget neutral, remains economically indeterminate – and implicitly economically irrelevant – however rational it may be.

Here, 'rational' is to be understood in Popper's sense (being consensual across the social sciences) as behaviour appropriate in a concrete situation. In the orthodoxy, zero-quantity consumption is rationalised as the case whereby the first unit of the good that the consumer actually consumes in zero quantity, would provide a lower marginal utility than the last unit of each good that they consume in positive quantities. The resulting conclusion that zero-quantity consumption must then provide a still smaller utility is implicit in the orthodoxy. But it is a false conclusion. For in the identity-forming context, discontinuities at the zero-point of consumption must be taken into account. The first piña barong tagalog consumed might give the Philippine 'Americanist' a lower marginal utility than the last unit of every good he consumes in positive quantities. Nonetheless, his zero-quantity consumption gives him greater utility than the first unit consumed – and perhaps even greater utility than the first unit of a good he actually consumes in positive quantity. The 'Americanist's' specific rationale is thus completely different from that of the orthodox model: the Philippine 'Americanist' doesn't consume piña because the first unit gives him (too) little marginal utility. But instead, because the transition from one unit of piña to zero-unit consumption gives him a large utility increase. Nothing would make him consume piña if it's consumed by the nationalist. This zero-consumption utility, however, would disappear if piña were not worn by the Filipino nationalist, then it would've lost its identity-generating capacity for both consumers.

The crosswise asymmetric zero and positive-quantity consumption of two consumers and two goods is therefore highly relevant for happiness or utility. It is an economically relevant activity, if economic relevance is viewed in terms of seeking happiness or utility, rather than from scarce resources. To this end, economic activity must be understood in more general terms as whatever contributes to happiness or utility, regardless of whether it costs scarce resources or not. To leave it open until the question is settled whether it is the one or the other, I will use the terms *happiness/utility*.

Consumption here is therefore defined as the way in which humans use the world of objects – the culturally laden world of things that partly can and partly cannot be bought – including related consumer behaviours. Then the consumer can also consume an object, if firstly, they don't consume any of its *specimens*, and secondly, if the crossing from the first unit consumed to zero-quantity consumption yields a discreet positive utility increase. Consumption that meets these two conditions is referred to as zero-quantity consumption.[7] In the following, it is assumed that this increase in utility is due to the existence of other consumers who consume the object in positive quantities, and therefore zero-quantity consumption makes a difference to these consumers.

Positive-quantity consumption of an object is defined as consumption of at least one unit. Note that positive-quantity consumption makes no distinction between different positive quantities of specimens of an object. The consumption of ten piña-tailored barong tagalog is the same as the consumption of one. Zero-quantity consumption by a consumer of an object presupposes the existence of a positive-quantity consumer of that same object. For at least two consumers and for at least one object, consumption is asymmetrical: one avoids the object – piña no! – and the other exhibits it – piña yes! I refer to this relationship between consumers as zero/positive-quantity consumption, in short *0/+consumption*.

Identity, Quality, Motivation

In the following, *social identity* is understood as being mediated by *0/+consumption*: as a consequence of 'one avoids an object and the other surrounds himself with it'. In extreme cases, a single object can convey the different identities of two consumers as a minimum requirement. Umberto Eco's "We speak through our clothes" (which we wear) can therefore be extended to include "...and those we do not wear". The 'piña yes!' of the nationalist and the 'piña no!' of the 'Americanist' lead to different identities only when they are jointly at work.

In the real world we find multiple *0/+consumption*: two consumers with different identities surround themselves asymmetrically with a larger number of

---

7   Note that the second condition of this definition means that not any decision not to consume a
     unit of an object is necessarily an act of consumption. In the case of objects for which it is not
     fulfilled, the orthodox "You can't do something with nothing" continues to apply.

objects, and avoid a larger number of other objects – identity, so to speak, as the result of whole communication salvos from the world of objects. I will use the term consumer *style* for that kind of *0/+consumption*.

In this interpretation, social identity is exclusively conveyed by the world of objects. Without the use of the object world – the position taken here – there is no identity, and putting it simply, nothing more than the world of objects is needed for creating identity. So, the presumption is that consumers' styles are a necessary and sufficient means for creating their identity.

Here the difference between identity and identification is already evident. Identification is a psychological process of assigning oneself to other persons (self-categorisation) with the desire of belonging and for inclusion. Identity, on the other hand, is the result of successful inclusion in a group and thus something social, which in turn presupposes that there must be at least one alternative. Although the Filipino can identify with the entire population of the Philippines, they can only be a Filipino nationalist if there is at least one alternative, in this case the Filipino 'Americanist', and vice versa. This means that piña can only convey identity to the Filipino nationalist if it also conveys the different identity of the Filipino 'Americanist'. *0/+consumption* thus becomes the central social nexus.

The view conveyed here moves the consumption of *quantities* of objects into the background and the consumption of *types* into the foreground. The consumer goods basket full of specimens is replaced by the goods *type* basket, which contains no more than one specimen of the goods types consumed in positive quantities, regardless of the number of units consumed. The consumer goods type baskets therefore differ in *quality* – regardless of how many units of a differentiating product type are actually consumed. That is why I refer to this view as the *Quality Theory of Consumption* (QTC). With regard to utility generated by an object, the only important question in QTC is the binary one: zero or positive-quantity consumption – yes or no?[8*]

Consumption theory thus undergoes a transformation from a theory of the relationship between thing and human (quantity theory of consumption of the orthodoxy), to a theory of the relationship between human and human (QTC). In

---

[8*] Define x_i as a specimen of object type i that can be used for the production of social distance and proximity. Let $X := \{x_1, \ldots, x_h\}$ be the finite population of one specimen for each existing object type in the world of objects. Let $A \in X$ and $B \in X$ be the goods type baskets of two consumers a and b. The set difference of A and B, $A \backslash B := \{x \mid (x \in A) \wedge (x \notin B)\}$, and of B and A, $B \backslash A := \{x \mid (x \in B) \wedge (x \notin A)\}$ are the utility generating object types. Utility generating for both consumers is the symmetrical difference $(A \backslash B) \cup (B \backslash A)$.

the orthodoxy's quantity theory, the central relationship is established via quantities and prices, in QTC via the quality of objects. In other words, in QTC consumer utility is created by the difference between consumers. These differences are comprised of visible distinguishing patterns in consumption, which is why utility arises only from collective consumption. The idea of consumption of social distance and proximity intuitively captures these relationships.

Which motives for consumption does this QTC assume? Individual consumption exclusively serves social manipulation with the simultaneously pursued goals:

i.   Proximity: the sublimation of one's own individuality within the social in-group (elective affinity), whose membership the individual attains.
ii. Distance: the sublimation of the differences between one's in-group and (all) out-groups.

The collectivist (Eastern) society is not modelled this way, but rather the individualistic (Western) society. The individual does not strive to fuse with their social in-group (or its prototype), does not strive to disappear in it, but to curate and display their individuality therein. But they're not so individualistic as to have no need whatsoever of belonging to a group, they seek to belong to an in-group, and also to demarcate themself with this group from the rest of society. The individual thus attains a dual identity, an *individual identity* arising from differences *vis-à-vis* all other members of their in-group, and a *collective identity* arising from differences between this in-group and the out-groups.

Chains: Purple, Titian, Uniform

The world of objects, by which social difference is created, is made up not only of singletons. One of the distinguishing features are the shades of colours consumers wear. For example, the colour purple is a blend of the primary colours blue and red, different blending ratios result in different shades. Every shade can be assigned to a certain proportion of the colour red (alternatively to the colour blue), and be compared using this mapping. Any shade of purple has either a larger or smaller proportion of red than any other shade. A finite number of purple shades can therefore be thought of as arranged in a chain with the two extremes 'almost red' and 'almost blue'.

In the world of objects many chains exist of at least ordinally comparable objects. They can be compared by criteria such as 'more or less ornamental', 'more or less colourful', 'authentic', 'modern', 'French', 'perfect', 'complete', etc. One question in need of further clarification is how to treat elements of chains as opposed to singletons regarding the creation of social distance and proximity. By intuition, differently! If one consumer wears red and the other blue (which can be thought of as two singletons among colours), then this makes for a different distance between the two than if they wear shades of purple in order to convey the common affiliation to a group. But also by way of their different shades, convey their belonging to different hierarchical levels in it. For a deeper understanding of the production of social distance and proximity by way of the world of objects, it is therefore helpful to distinguish chains from singletons.[9] Chains are represented in the following by the symbol $|$.[10*]

In art history chains can be traced in painting styles, for example of Titian. As an exponent of High Renaissance painting, Titian's complete oeuvre does not show a 'finished' style of this epoch, but a style that evolved.[11] Young Titian was called to Padua to paint frescoes for the Scuola del Santo. Dedicated to the miracles of Saint Anthony (Miracle of the Newborn Infant, Miracle of the Jealous Husband, and Miracle of the Irascible Son), the frescoes are the first works attributable to him. Their subjects resemble earlier frescoes painted by Paduan painters for the Scuola. This resemblance, however, and the fact that all these frescoes were created for the same principal, are precisely where Titian's stylistic autonomy manifests itself. His style shows fewer human figures, but instead more monumental ones. They are arranged in the foreground, the depicted landscape merely forms the background. The eye's focus is thus led towards the foreground, where the interactions of the figures show narrative clarity, classical drama and previously unknown dynamics. This way, the style is radically different from the typical 15th century painterly narrative style, where figures are depicted as minor additions in a decorative architectural and scenic splendour. It is likely, though, that Titian's break with the painterly style typical of the time, and his independent tendency towards the classical were inspired by sculptures in the Basilica of

---

9   The reservation made in footnote 4 regarding the mathematical property of singletons applies mutatis mutandis also to chains: Whether a subset of objects is a chain is determined by culture. Elements of a subset of, for example, purple shades can be equated with their common characteristic 'purple', which makes the chain a unit set and their elements identical specimens of the singleton purple.

10* A chain of X is a set $C \in X$, so each pair of elements $(x, y) \in C \times C$ is a total, transitive and antisymmetric binary relation on C.

11   Wilk 1983.

Saint Anthony of Padua. Many of his later works sublimate the style of his Paduan frescoes.

Titian's oeuvre is an example of a chain in art brought to light by art history (culture). The radical break with the traditional painterly narrative style has created a new subset of artworks that possess the uniqueness of a singleton as a whole (Titian's entire oeuvre), but can also be treated as non-identical objects of the object type 'by Titian'. Chains of artworks have extremes, as 'almost red' and 'almost blue' are the extremes for the purple shades. The extreme that marks the beginning of Titian's style lies in sculpture, not painting, another extreme for instance in his Bacchanal of 1518/19,[12] a work that consummately displays his style.

As we consume art in our collections, as we visit museums, indulging in some and shunning other forms of art, we show our individual taste in it. Being part of the world of objects, art generates utility, helping create social distance and proximity. But this also applies to objects of crafts, the oriental carpet as well as the nativity scene. Art, as used for the production of social distance and proximity, is not a class of objects of its own, though its potential to achieve this in a subtle way may be greater than that of nativity scenes, for example.

At first glance, the soldier's uniform appears as the stark opposite of art. In art, subtle distinguishing features make the difference; in uniforms, uniformity reigns. But to think of them in the o/+consumption model as if pars pro toto applies would still be wrong. The uniform separates the military from civilians, but it is also a distinguishing feature within the military. The uniform too has characteristics of the chain.

The emergence of the Danish military uniform in the 18th century is a case in point.[13] Uniforms brought about both social distance and proximity in a complicated way. In its basic uniformity, the garb had to be adjusted to the military hierarchy, and the rules for its use had to be also compatible with the lifestyle of the military ranks. In the 18th century, Denmark was a military state with a bigger army than Prussia in terms of population. As in Prussia, the Danish officer corps was recruited exclusively from the aristocracy. The earlier military organisation of the mercenary army established and demanded loyalty only towards the regiment and its colonel, a war entrepreneur, whose loyalty to his clients depended variably on the amount and regularity of payments received. The nascent idea of the territorial state, and the total subordination of everyone under the kingship,

---

12 Sometimes artists change their style in the course of their work. The extremes of their oeuvre therefore need not lie in the chronological beginning and ending of their work.

13 Lind, 2010.

now required a military with loyalty to king and state that could be deployed against both the outside world and the civilian population within.

The standardisation of the soldiers' garb and the introduction of a Danish officer class, whose members down to the lieutenant ranked above every civilian in the Danish hierarchy, served that purpose. The officer corps had to wear their uniform permanently, including during non-military practices in their aristocratic lifestyle. The fact that the officer corps of the former mercenary armies had not even worn uniforms in battle, as a sign of their aristocratic lifestyle, was an obstacle to this standardisation. The Danish king needed to take this into account if he was to win the loyalty of his officers. The new Danish uniform thus had to convey distance from the civilian (and thus proximity between all members of the military) and avoid too close a proximity within the military, between officers and common soldiers.

All over Europe, the stylistic language of the military garb, and thus the material with which social distance and proximity had to be 'tailored', consisted of a practical woollen coat, the renouncement of printed textile material, a bold choice of colours, sturdy shoes, and more or less bizarre headgear. The uniform made up of this material, although remaining receptive to civilian fashion trends, had to always convey three deviations from the civilian: I am a warrior (always ready to be deployed to the field), I belong (to the state) and I serve (my king). For the officer corps there was a further deviation from the civilian, which expressed: I am in command. Besides the distance of the entire organisation to the civilian world, officers' uniforms also had to convey the hierarchy of command within.

Communicating the warrior status was the simple part of this combined task. Extravagant cut of garment and choice of colours sufficed. The communication of serving and belonging was a more difficult task to achieve. In Denmark it was tried with the colour grey for the coat and distinguishing colours on cuffs and other garments, which transformed the uniform from a regimental costume into an emblem of royal service. Subordination under the absolutist king was made palatable to the officer corps with the introduction of a rank register (and all officers were soon listed in it): no civilian in Denmark ranked higher than those in the register, no matter how rich, or how old their aristocratic family was. In Denmark, as throughout Europe, the refinement of officers' uniforms with elements of aristocratic garb manifested the corps' elevated hierarchical status: the sash, silver and gold clasps and embroidery, plumes, cockades and other insignia, etc. But nothing marked the officers' status more than the portepee, the sword loop, which in Denmark was hued in the heraldic colours of the ruling dynasty, red and gold. An unmistakable sign of the officer corps, the warrior, obedience to the Danish state, service to the king, and power of command.

Here, too, intuition tells us that uniform variants contribute to social distance and proximity differently to singletons. Viewing uniforms as a chain of objects, ordinally marking varying degrees of combativeness, zeal for service, belonging to and commanding power, will do more justice to their social distance and proximity-producing capacity than treating them simply as 'one and the same'. Uniforms of the police, and formerly that of the post office, the railway, the clergy, as well as that of present day's 'corporate world', is material for the creation of social distance and proximity, which can be treated as chains.

Excursion into Nature

Chains order objects as though on a string. Consider the subset of the world of objects which consists of four purple shades (objects), A (almost blue), B (purple with a blue component of ¾), C (with a blue component of ½), D (with ¼). Figure 1 (left side), shows this subset as a chain, ordered such that an object differs from its upper (or lower) neighbour by a portion of blue that is 25 percentage points lower (or higher). The chain conveys three items of information. First, purple shades are distinguished by larger or smaller portions of blue; second, shade A has the largest portion; and third, the difference in the portions of all 'neighbouring' shades is 25 percentage points. The first two items of information are necessary and sufficient for a total ordinal ranking, where total means 'all objects in the set': C is bluer than D, B is bluer than C (and thus D), and A is bluer than B (and thus C and D). All chains are a total order.

The third, cardinal information gives the exact difference in the portions of blue of two shades. It can be used in chemistry to define colour formulae which produce, for example, exactly shades A, B, C and D. To create a total order in a subset, however, a metric is redundant, an ordinal scale is sufficient.

Figure 1: Chain and phylogram.

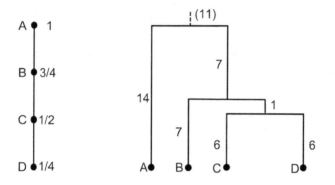

Left: chain of four purple shades, A, B, C, D, with the proportion of blue as a fraction of one. Right: phylogram of the great apes, A orangutan, B gorilla, C chimpanzee/bonobo, D human. Numbers next to the vertical branches indicate the genetic distance between these species as lengths. But biologists do not convey any information in the horizontal width of their phylograms. The dashed branch at the very top represents the rooting of the phylogram of the great apes in the (larger and not depicted) evolutionary tree of Old World monkeys.

With these properties of the chain, it is now possible to identify some of culture's peculiarities. Firstly, the world of cultural objects should not be thought of as being ordered in a single chain. For this would amount to a culture aligning the whole world of objects towards a single referential point, as, for example, scholasticism tried to align everything earthly in the direction of God. Instead, we must be prepared for finding multiple chains. For example, chains of artworks that are more or less attributed to a painting style, chains of drinks more or less hip. The order of every single chain is total, but the order across all chains is not.

Secondly, this does not imply that different chains have nothing to do with each other. They can have an intersection of (common) objects, as branches of a tree have a common stem. Chains that are bundled at one end make a tree. A tree made of chains, in contrast to any chain in it, is not a total, but only a partial order of objects, because the free ends of the chains are not ordinally comparable. The hippest drink and the hippest painting remain (until further notice) incomparable.

Waiting for us is a fragmented order of the world of objects with a plethora of singletons that are not comparable to anything else, ∘, a plethora of detached chains that are not comparable to anything else, but where the objects in each are totally ordered, |, and a plethora of partially ordered trees, which are incomparable to other trees. Trees are represented here by the symbol ⋔ .[14*] A material for the production of social distance and proximity awaits you, which is not only voluminous, but also heterogeneous. This material of singletons, chains and trees are symbolised by {∘,|,⋔} when it comes to focusing on the heterogeneity of the orderings in the world of objects.

Thirdly, the shades A, B, C and D in Figure 1 illustrate a special case. Only in exceptional cases can you expect more than ordinal rankings of cultural objects: bluer, older, more beautiful, more modern, more authentic, fresher, more picturesque, more ascetic (or their antonyms) are the scales with which you frequently have to settle for. The typical case in Figure 1 (left side) is a chain with no numbers marking the distances.

A difference between culture and nature emerges: order in nature is greater than that to be found in culture. Evolutionary biologists hope to eventually determine the complete tree of life that unites all smaller trees of organisms in a single stem. In other words, they are convinced that it exists. Only the computational capacity of computers stand in the way of its decoding. The stepwise decoding of the genomes of more and more species (natural objects) allows for the ever more frequent use of a metric to determine genetic dissimilarity.[15] The world of objects used for the production of social distance and proximity is less ordered than nature. Evolutionary biology is nevertheless a good starting point from which to further consider the upcoming issues, not least because it has concerned itself with the dissimilarity of objects for longer than social sciences have.

Figure 1 (right side) shows a phylogram used in evolutionary biology, depicting a partial order in a selected set of reproductive communities (species). A phylogram is a tree with special properties. First: the partial order is defined as the cardinally measurable degree of genetic kinship of two species from the set of species considered. Second: objects are placed at the ends of the branches only – human (D), chimpanzee/ bonobo (C), gorilla (B) and orangutan (A). Third: the node connecting, for example, human with chimpanzee/bonobo marks the last common ancestor of both. The next node up marks the last common ancestor of gorilla and chimpanzee/bonobo/human. The top horizontal line marks the last common ancestor of orangutan/gorilla/chimpanzee/bonobo/human (perhaps not yet discovered as a fossil) as the common link of all species of this subset. Fourth: fossils do not belong in the subset of objects considered and hence have

---

14* A tree $Z, Z \in X$, is a set, so that for each $x \in Z$ the set $x \downarrow = \{y \in Z\}$ of 'preceding' elements is a total, transitive and antisymmetric binary relation in Z.

15 Dawkins 2005.

no place in the phylogram. Fifth: the cardinal measure (in millions of years, Myr) is the time passed since a common last ancestor. There are 6 Myr since the separation of chimpanzee/bonobo from human, 7 Myr since the separation of chimpanzee/bonobo and human from gorilla, and 14 Myr since their joint separation from orangutan. The phylogram of the great apes depicts their genetic kinship metrically. In evolutionary biology, such precision is achieved by means of the triangulation technique: from the genetic distance measured between two living species as the base of an isosceles triangle, the apex of the triangle is calculated from the known average mutation rate of the genetic material per Myr. The wider the base of the triangle, the further back the division into different species.

Figure 2 shows the kinship between the great apes as a cladogram. In the cladogram, the branch length conveys no information, as the only information that can be retrieved is from the relative positions of nodes. Both C and D are more closely related to one another than either one to B or A, and C/D are more closely related to B than to A. In contrast to the phylogram, however, the cladogram does not say exactly how closely two species are related. The cladogram has been the appropriate way of depicting kinship in nature before the decoding of genomes.

Figure 2: Cladogram of the great apes.

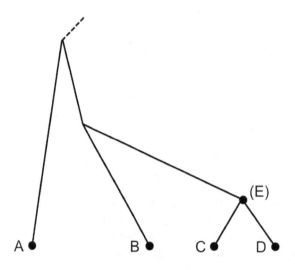

Orangutan (A), gorilla (B), chimpanzee/bonobo (C), human (D). The cladogram shows no information about the kinship of two species by the lengths of branches, but only by the relative positions of the nodes. C is more closely related to D than B is.

A Glimpse at the Peculiarities of Culture

It would be illusory to think that we could find metric scales for cultural objects, the way biology has found the genetic distance between species in nature. So, I will continue my analysis starting with ordinal scales: more or less of what is blue, new, authentic, Japanese, aggressive, young, modern, etc. Evolutionary biologists (now) use a metric scale because it was gifted to them by nature. So far, culture has not been that generous. I am left only with those findings from social and cultural sciences to work with that can be obtained. And they initially amount to an ordinal scale. Yet, I must separate the wheat from the chaff by modelling in the spirit of emic field research, i.e., take into account only those ordinal distinguishing features that consumers are able and accustomed to recognise and consider as such. This requires them sharing a prior cultural knowledge. The analyst's intuition is a crude yet conductive method to remove the chaff – depending on whether you trust the consumer to recognise, for example, not only the baroque as a style (though they may not necessarily be able to designate it as such), but also some gradations of it. The experts' sophisticated etic deliberations, though, can be left in their libraries.

A second difference between biology and culture concerns the method of discovering order in subsets, be it reproductive communities or consumer goods. Evolutionary biologists have discovered order in nature for the sake of their specific interests and developed appropriate methods. When it comes to consumption, you have yet to discover (invent) methods appropriate for your specific interests.

Biologists have found the difference between two objects, A and B, in the genome. For example, A has the genome $a_1b_1c_1d_1$ and B the genome $a_2b_1c_1d_2$. They differ in a and d (for example, a_1 are fins, a_2 are four-toed feet, d_1 are baleen and d_2 are teeth); however, they have the same features b_1 (pulmonary respiration) and c_1 (a vertically mobile spinal column). The genetic distance between A and B in this example is therefore 2, and the two objects are the close relatives, whale (A) and hippopotamus (B). The cardinality of their dissimilarity is a gift of nature, because functional genes (for example, a and d) are taxa-independent causes of a particular pheno-typicality (as a is causal for body parts suitable for locomotion, and d for those in the mouth). The alternatives are, however, available only in 'pure' form, for example, in form either a_1 or a_2, and not as a mixed form a_{1-2}. Fins and toed feet match body mass, but they are always fixed to either fin or toed foot; we never find 'fin-toed' feet in live species. This gift of nature allows the dissimilarity of two species to be measured cardinally by numbering (and depicting these numbers in the phylogram as vertical lengths). In culture, we can also think of the 'genome' of an object, abcd, the same way to begin with, for example, a being colour, b plasticity, c impudence, d nostalgia. But for good reason it is difficult to think a,b,c,d merely in binary terms. In the world of cultural objects of interest to us, there are not only fins or toed feet, but also many gradations of 'fin-toed' feet.

The Lascaux prehistoric cave art, for example, is a mixture of painting and sculpture; depending on your viewpoint they have more of one or the other. Titian's inspiration from the sculptures at the basilica in Padua has been mentioned already. And what hair length exactly marks the boundary between ECT and 'perker' hairstyles? All that is left for cultural objects is the possibility of mixed forms with varying shades.

The phylogenetic species concept in evolutionary biology has defined dissimilarity between two species to be the vertical length of two branches up to the node that unites them in the phylogram. But if you deal with the production of social distance and proximity instead, you first must find a precise meaning for dissimilarity in the world of objects. What this means is not crystal clear and I will address it in chapter 3. For the time being, social science is more complex than biology.

As fossils can no longer reproduce and lost their genetic material long ago, we find only subsets of live species in the phylograms and cladograms of biology. The Lucy fossil from the East African Rift has no place in Figure 1 (right side) and Figure 2. In culture another principle applies: everything usable for the production of social distance and proximity must be taken into account in cladograms of the world of objects. So, when consumers create social distance and proximity by visiting museums, exhibits aren't 'fossils' (as old as they may be), but just as 'alive' as the drink consumed in the museum café. Culture is availing us with almost all of its objects ever created. They hardly lose their 'cultural genes'. Nearly everything that has ever been created is still culturally alive.

To biologists, the claim that humans descended from gorillas is absurd. Since gorillas are a living reproductive community, this would mean that humans are more advanced in evolutionary terms than gorillas, who've been standing on the evolutionarily spot for the last seven million years, leaving evolution to humans. For biologists, the gorilla is as much a current expression of the evolution of nature as the human is. We therefore do not find live species in phylograms or cladograms positioned on top of each other in a branch. There is no species E in Figure 2 in biology. Species are always positioned side by side. Applying this to culture would require that no object be positioned on top of another in cladograms. I will maintain this practice as a mere convention until it becomes advantageous to deviate from it and consider objects such as E in Figure 2; when it becomes important to consider shades in one dimension of the objects' features, such as purple shades in a chain belonging to a tree of objects, which differ in more than one dimension.

In biology, a reproductive community is seen as a *dichotomous* diversification from the tree of life. A group is separated from its fellow specimens (for example, by the break-up of a continent or by driftwood crossing the sea) and transforms into a new reproductive community. A convention among biologists lets the group left behind to also become a new reproductive community, parallel to the emigrants. So, one is turning into two, but the crucial point is, always into *only* two. The tree of life is thus made of nodes, from each of which exactly two branches grow (evolutionary dichotomy). From the biological point of view, this is a plausible assumption, because evolutionary polytomies – the branching of more than two reproduction communities from a common ancestor – are hard to imagine. How unlikely is it that a group of Old World monkeys drifted on a mangrove raft from what is now West Africa to South America, and another group to India from the same place? But in the cultural sphere we cannot rule out multiple splits (cultural polytomies). For now though, I will maintain the dichotomy of splits as a mere convention.

As mentioned, evolutionary biology always leaves living reproductive communities at the very same stage of evolution. This is reflected in the phylogram by the constantly identical length of each branch up to the common origin.[16*] This property is not mandatory for cultural trees. The lengths above objects to their common origin can vary. A branch of cultural history can end while another goes on. Much like cultural objects that find their place in the 'interior' of cultural trees (for example, E in Figure 2), sooner or later branches may cease to lengthen. The Moai Maea of Easter Island, for example, are as much a part of the world of cultural objects as Henry Moore's sculptures. But the further evolution of these stone heads came to an abrupt end in the 16th century, while Moore's oeuvre continues to produce new successors. I will adopt the longitudinal equality of branches of trees from evolutionary biology, remaining aware that it is a pure convention, to be broken when deemed necessary.

16* To this end, ultrametric scales are used in evolutionary biology for determining the lengths in evolutionary trees.

Cultural Trees: Oriental Carpet, Traditional Costume, Archaic Style

You can barely determine how many types of oriental carpets there are. Carpets have many characteristics: the material quality of wool and dyes, the knot density per square centimetre, the manufacturing technique (hand-made, mechanically), age and origin, the symbols shown, the previous owner(s), the dealer. Its characteristics allow a carpet to belong to the subset of authentic oriental carpets, or not. However, the presence of multiple characteristics in a single piece of textile complicates the aggregation of different assessments (place of origin, manufacturing technique, material type, ornamentation etc.) into an overall score of authenticity. For example, when you disagree on the weight given to different characteristics. What's considered authentic and what's not is a matter of cultural negotiation.[17]

The authentic oriental carpet illustrates the difficulty of trying to define a non-ordered cultural subset *per se*. Counterfeiting is a contributing cause of this difficulty. The complete oeuvre of the avant-garde artist Kazimir Malevich is hard to define, because counterfeits are circulated time and again. Although with artists like Titian, the definition of the subset of their entire oeuvre poses little problem.

Titian's oeuvre is a tree. A part consists of the type of works described above, call it type A. Its overwhelming dynamic of figurative interaction differs from later works, such as the *Venus of Urbino* (1538), with its calmer characteristics rather resembling a still life. Call these paintings type B. What both types A and B have in common and set them apart from pre-Titian painting style, is the dominance of figure(s) in the foreground with architecture and landscape as decorative background. Another type in Titian's oeuvre, emanating from his still-life painting in type B, is his portrait painting. Call it type C. It largely dispenses with narratives from the background, but instead reveals grandeur, tragedy, or be it the cunning of the person portrayed. Yet another type, call it type D, is his later work and revisits the early figurative dynamics of type A, but with mythological instead of religious subjects, such as the *Robbery of Europe* (1559–62).

But how can these four types of works be placed in a tree of Titian's oeuvre? It's obvious now that the definition of the non-ordered subset is not the only complication cultural trees pose. This is because one can always transform a non-ordered subset of cultural objects into differently ordered sets. Figure 3 illustrates this by way of Titian's example.

---

17   Spooner 2010.

Figure 3: Cladograms of Titian's oeuvre.

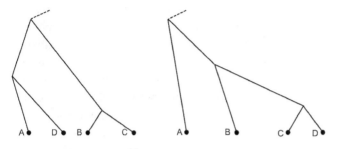

Left: cladogram of the semantic variety of his oeuvre (simplification). Right: cladogram of the chronological variety of his oeuvre (simplification). Depending on the ordering principle, semantically or chronologically, different cladograms result from the same non-ordered subset of his oeuvre types (A, B, C, D).

To the right, Titian's richness of stylistic variations is depicted, resulting from a chronological ordering principle. The chronological origin lies in Paduan sculpture, from which the dynamic style of his frescoes (type A) emerged, followed by still-life painting (type B) and portrait painting (type C), and the painting of mythological subjects (type D).

But why should the chronological order of Titian's style be the 'correct' one? Almost typical of culture is its plethora of competing orders. So here too. Though art historians have developed the chronological order, there are also those who focus on the syntactical and semantic order of artworks. Figure 3 (left side) shows the simplified semantic order of Titian's oeuvre: Titian's late, mythological phase (D) is semantically more closely akin to his Paduan, early phase (A) than to the portrait painting (C) that preceded it. Which, in turn, is semantically more closely akin to his still-lifes (B) than to the Paduan frescoes (A).

What determines which ordering principle applies? As I will argue in the second part of the book, culture itself as 'crystallised history' determines this, although human agency also exerts a limited influence in the form of style leadership.

Now, returning to the issue of separating the wheat from the chaff: what is the 'correct' order of cultural objects used for producing social distance and proximity? It is not the Titian experts in their etic approach who can answer this for you. Instead, in an emic manner you must take into account whichever order consumers find for themselves: syntax, semantics, chronology, or simply 'beautiful' versus 'ugly', or 'old stuff' versus 'new stuff'.

Traditional costume is yet another tree in the world of objects. With exceptions such as the Oktoberfest, traditional costume is a distinctive and differentiating feature of ethnic and autochthonous groups. It evokes social distance outwards and proximity inwards. The traditional costume is available in different nuances, moderating proximity inwards. The Appenzell women's costume, for example, distinguishes between unmarried, married women and widows. Another example is the historical costume of Turkish peoples.[18] Over a long period of time, its basic components, indistinguishable between the sexes, consisted of a long, bag-like pair of trousers pleated at the hips and ankles (şalvar), a shirt (gömlek) over which a long-sleeved garment (entari) was worn, which in turn was covered by a caftan, a short jacket (cepken) and a wide, body-length cape (ferace). For centuries, these components remained largely fashion-resistant in being an adaptation to the climatic conditions of the Eurasian steppe. Fashion only showed itself at a few stylistic turning points, for example in the way the garments were closed, right over left or in front, and in westernisation through the introduction of gender-specific costumes. Costumes display substantial similarity in material, cut and pieces among the nomadic peoples of the Huns, Sakassas, Kirghizes and other Turkish peoples. However, different clans have displayed influence from their respective neighbouring cultures in their regional variations. The traditional costumes of Turkish peoples are a wide-branching stylistic tree of complementary individual objects, which at the same time convey the social distance between and proximity within subgroups.

Trees in the arts are not confined to the oeuvre of single artists. The most impressive example is perhaps the archaic style.[19] Originating in the Upper Palaeolithic age by unnamed artists and shown to this day in the paintings of schoolchildren and in tribal art, its traces can be found, for example, in the potteries of Josiah Wedgewood, the sketches of the architect Étienne-Louis Boullée, paintings by Jean-Auguste-Dominique Ingres, Georges Seurat and Kazimir Malevich. And it appears in a plethora of refinements in the paintings of Paul Klee, Joan Miró, Karel Appel, in the paintings and sculptures of Pablo Picasso, in the sculptures of Alberto Giacometti and Jene Highstein, and in the buildings of Ludwig Mies van der Rohe. The archaic style sublimates the most visible features of things and behaviours through elementary figuration: sequential, explanatory narration; linear, processional composition of asynchronous elements of the same size; different perspectives on figures; the optical creation of space by means of a grid of lines; and monochromatic colouration of planar areas. In a

---

18   Koç and Koca 2011.

19   Howard 1981.

large tree, the archaic style unites a vast number of scattered artworks from a wide variety of artistic genres, dating back thousands of years, and created by a large number of known and anonymous artists. A multitude of such trees, large and small, can be found in the world of objects.

The Illusion of Total Cultural Order

Evolutionary biology entertains a belief in the existence of a tree uniting the whole animal world, which combines with that of flora to form the tree of life.[20] To believe the consumers' world of objects as a whole were such a tree would be illusory.

Such illusion is already evident when looking at art alone, the object category best explored in its internal structure. While there are styles that transcend artistic genres and artists' oeuvres such as the archaic style, there are also the many styles that can be strictly separated from one another according to form and content. For example, John F. Moffitt, art historian and painter, has systematised art by extracting the artist's philosophical motivation from the visual experience of artwork.[21] For this purpose, he divides visual experience into two overarching categories, the experience of depicted shapes and that of presentation of content. These broad categories he then breaks down into more specific experiential principles. The archaic style, for example, conveys the experience of its shapes through the principles of abstraction, anonymity, frontality, planarity, typologisation, and areal colouration. And it conveys content idealistically, showing philosophical or ideological concepts by figurative symbolism, sacrificing the beauty of appearance for a didactic program, working with repetition and showing the human being as an undifferentiated abstraction lacking a recognisable psyche. This way, Moffitt identifies four clearly distinguishable styles in 18th–20th century painting: the classical style in the tradition of the High Renaissance (from Titian to, in his analysis, Henry Moore's sculptures); baroque, including abstract expressionism (Caravaggio to Wassily Kandinsky); mannerism including pop-art (Giorgio Vasari to Robert Rauschenberg), and the archaic style. In Moffitt's understanding, the painting of this period consists of four separate trees.

So, you'd best give up the illusion of a total order of the world of cultural objects, noticing instead that it may better be characterised as a set of different types of subsets, {○, |, ⋔}, of singletons, chains and trees, existing in different

---

20   Dawkins 2005.

21   Moffitt 1979.

variants.[22*] Such is the material by which social distance and proximity are produced and consumed. With such material, the orthodox marginal utility concept cannot be analytically expressed. Nor can consumer behaviour be predicted in the epistemological 'as-if' manner, now so familiar to economics.

Qualitative considerations are to replace quantitative ones: the non-identity, but comparability of objects in chains is one such qualitative aspect. Others are the comparability of objects in a branch of a tree, the commonality of a common origin of all its branches, but also the incomparability that is hidden in the set of objects at the end of its branches. And not least, the incomparability from tree to tree and chain to chain and from trees, chains and singletons to one another. Such material calls for a qualitative analysis. In the face of this, quantities have become a rather crude analytical side of consumption. Instead, qualitative aspects come to the fore, to be dealt with in the *o/+consumption* perspective.

A Glimpse at a Colourful World

It is only by taking a qualitative approach that the analyst can access consumers' wealth of options for consumer decisions, a wealth less and less reflected by their economic resources alone – nature (beauty, intelligence), money, time, education, and networks. In combination with the budget-neutral consumability of the world of objects (*o-consumption*), money, though not yet redundant in practice, is losing both its unchallenged status as the source of consumption and its predictive accuracy.

Which is why I am pretending here that its effect has completely fizzled out. In what follows I conceive the social realm devoid of money (and all other economic resources), because the full scope of *o/+consumption* for the social realm can only be grasped this way. Even if in reality it is of course also moderated by beauty, intelligence, money, time, education and personal networks.

This way, you can perform an interesting thought experiment: suppose everyone had the exact same resources, the same consumption space, and identical preferences over consumption alternatives. How diverse – how colourful – would society be after consumers have made their choices? The orthodox forecast is this: everyone consumes the same, because everyone starts out the same; society remains as it began, even after consumption, it is still lacking any social diversity. In the orthodox view, a colourful society is predictable only by

---

22* $X = \left\{ \{o_1, ..., o_h\}, \{l_1, ..., l_i\}, \{m_1, ..., m_j\} \right\}$

assumption: society becomes colourful only if its members are already endowed with differences in economic resources upfront.

With the *0/+consumption* approach, you arrive at a radically different conclusion: *0/+consumption* turns a society that was completely homogeneous to begin with, into a colourful bouquet of different social groups, that both constitute themselves in society and show themselves in it. Part 2 of the book is dedicated to this. Here I claim for later reflection that QTC's *0/+consumption* approach, but not the orthodoxy, allows for the prediction of a colourful society without taking it as a given.

Beyond the World of Things

This radical point of analytical departure from a uniform society prior to consumption, is further motivated by the fact that social distance and proximity are not only produced by the world of things. Behaviours as distinguishing individual characteristics can also convey social distance and proximity. This further augments the redundancy of money as a social vehicle.

In the late 18th century, the fad of the living (Greek) statue appeared in Naples, a hotspot of romantic-intellectual Europe.[23] In the salons of Neapolitan society, ladies – dressed in high-waisted, white, semi-transparent muslin (which later became the French empirical style, the *robe à la grecque*) – presented themselves in touching poses as 'living classicism'. The tambourine striking Bacchante and Pygmalion's Galatea were popular subjects.

It was Emma Hart, an Englishwoman of lower pedigree, who by mastery of this self-staging became the star of Neapolitan salons. Her marriage to the rich art connoisseur William Hamilton took her from maiden to Lady Hamilton. Her posing was even the precursor for high aristocratic imitators, such as Lady Charlotte Campbell, whom Tischbein painted in the style of a living Greek statue. Goethe, by contrast, in his *Elective Affinities*, infers with Luciane's immature posing a different, derogative meaning to the living statue. Today, Emma Hart would post selfies on the internet.

George 'Beau' Brummell, 'King of the Dandies', since the time of the British Regency is still unrivalled in his virtuoso frolicking with social distance and proximity.[24] Bestowed with boldness more than wealth, the 'style entrepreneur' Beau Brummell became sovereign of the most exclusive salons, adored by all of London

23   Rauser 2015.

24   Smith 1974.

(including the ruling Prince of Wales). After having detached himself from his petty bourgeois family, he entered the upper echelons of society in a style of ceremony, audience orientation, contempt, and exclusivity. Beau's ceremony was both aggressive and defensive, dragging a protective trench between him and others that could only be bridged with taste and finesse. By plastering over the superficiality and banality of his socialisation with formal dignity, he brought matters of taste and conduct to the fore while turning substance (e.g., of lineage and wealth) into a minor issue, and interpersonal relationships into the mere celebration of norms. Brummel's audience orientation was evident to his regular visitors, including the Prince Regent himself, attending his morning dress-up ceremony. Or when at the salons or opera he delivered his devastating judgments of taste with cutting irony, inhaled by the audience like sharp tobacco smoke. Brummell displayed contempt towards everything and everyone, all the way to absurdity – nothing was worth being taken seriously, no one from fine society could've ever hoped to be on equal footing with him. His exclusivity marked an impassable distance to those he regarded inferior. To let himself be carried out of the house into his coach to save his shoes from the dirt of the gutter was part of this game. Brummell thus epitomised dandyism, which was later to influence Baudelaire's anti-aesthetic and Wilde's preoccupation with the thoroughly ritualised upper class.

Brummell had access to fine society by means of a small inheritance, but his rise was first and foremost due to his well-calculated behaviour. Resources such as money, wealth, or an exclusive family background were of secondary importance. The dandy existence was hard work, and above all it cost a lot of time, which someone who was just rich enough that he needed not earn a living from work – like the members of the leisure class – had plenty of. All relevant actors were endowed with the same amount of time.

Ironically, in today's high-performance society, availability of time in the societal strata is reversed, yet showing the same need for an alternative theory of consumption: the champs of high-performance society, much like the past leisure class, do have plenty of money, but now are short of time. The unemployed are short of money, but they have plenty of time. Celebrating that one has no time now serves the same social distance and proximity-producing aspiration as the former demonstration of an abundance of time. The production of social distance and proximity with conspicuous behaviour remains as pertinent today as ever.

The neo-tribe of bike couriers is not part of the modern 'leisure class' of the (full-time) unemployed.[25] Professionally, its members never have time, but they still have enough left that they can waste in distance and proximity-creating behaviour.[26] Their style unfolds in three dimensions: behaviour, appearance, jargon. The most respected couriers show the riskiest style when riding their bikes – 'Ride it like you stole it!' – fearlessly riding on a wave of flowing traffic, sacrificing their safety and ignoring traffic rules. The archetype of the bike courier does without a helmet and has a track bike without gears and brakes, which is difficult to handle on the road and risky for the rider. Over functional sports clothes, filthy-looking street clothes are worn. Just as in other neo-tribes, for example free climbers, the jargon is full of idioms unfamiliar to outsiders. Such as *fix* for a track bike, *wave* for fluid motion, or *line* for the (mostly curved) path through (stationary) traffic. *Alleycats* – organised, illegal, breakneck bicycle races through urban traffic – offer the ideal opportunity to spurn danger. Alleycats prove that couriers' appetite for risk is not (only) owed to commercial pressure, but (also) to a desire for social distance and proximity. This style manifests an urban group of 'rebels without brakes', which creates distance from the rest of society and proximity to each other without the input of money, wealth, or formal human capital, but rather with creative behaviour.

We and the Others and We Amongst Ourselves

For clarification of the concepts of social distance and proximity, one can think of their relationship in social space in one of two ways. First, with the exclusive view of the external differentiation of a group, distance and proximity could be regarded as synonyms for the dissimilarity of two social groups (just as the distance between two villages, measured as the crow flies, can be considered equally close and distant). Alternatively, regarding external *and* internal dissimilarity, one can take an orthogonal understanding of distance and proximity. External dissimilarity is understood as dissimilarity between two social groups that produces social distance between them. Internal dissimilarity is understood as dissimilarity of two individuals within a social group, producing social proximity, albeit without letting the group members become identical. I will always use the terms distance and proximity in this second sense: distance in the sense of dissimilarity between groups, and proximity in the sense of dissimilarity of

---

25   A neo-tribe differs from a subculture in its voluntary membership (Maffesoli 2007).

26   Kidder 2005.

members of a group. In the following, distance and proximity are not synonyms, but stand in an *orthogonal* relationship.

Orthogonal social distance and proximity, as my modelling has it, are the determinants of human identity. Consumer utility derived from the identity of a member of society hinges on both, distance and proximity. Well-planned consumption, the choice of *o/+consumption* from the ordered world of objects, {o, |, ⋔}, is correspondingly complex. This complexity is dealt with in the second part of the book.

What is typical about the orthogonality of distance and proximity can be seen in the (semi) criminal youth milieu.[27] The *juvenile gangster style* features the 'perker' hairstyle (short on the sides and back, longer on top), designer sports hoody and jacket, tank-top, baseball cap, low-waisted tubular jeans, sneakers, silver and gold chains – all of which make up an expensive outfit for the young. Group behaviour presents 'bad guys', ready to answer the smallest sign of disrespect with (the threat of) immediate violence. The jargon is a mix of both black rap and mother tongue. This style does not distance itself from an abstract opposite, but rebels against the prevailing mainstream in a provocative aesthetic: what the mainstream avoids, it displays, what the mainstream displays, it avoids. Social distance thrives upon *o/+consumption*, for which a concrete opposite, here the mainstream, is targeted. This is what the 'gangster' style has in common with piña, with which the Philippine 'Americanists' were targeted. This is the one dimension of orthogonality, that of social distance to the out-group.

But at the same time the juvenile gangster style also performs in the second dimension, proximity inside the group. Therewith, the production of social distance goes hand in hand with the production of social proximity – 'we and the others' goes together with 'we amongst ourselves'. It is trivial that distance to out-groups bonds a group together. However, what is not trivial is that the production of proximity does not lead to total proximity, to the fusion of the group members' identities. Limited proximity is the case at hand in individualistic societies. In the juvenile gangster style it is having 'done time' that makes a 'gangster' authentic. No other elements of his style suffice for that. Newcomers and those who were never caught or were repeatedly released by police have a lower internal standing. Even kids stemming from the local population find it hard to gain respect in this milieu, assumed to lack an innate talent for crime. So it is (the glorification of) crime that creates – simultaneously and orthogonally – distance from the mainstream and limited proximity within the milieu.

---

27 Bengtsson 2012.

The orthogonality of social distance and proximity will be further clarified in chapter 3. Here is a preview of it: in the phylogram, proximity is visible in a portion of the vertical lengths of the branches, and distance in a portion of the horizontal width of the phylogram. In the graphical representation of the phylogram, the orthogonality of distance and proximity is thus shown in the expansion of the tree in two-dimensional space.

Fluid Society

Of the examples from the world of objects dealt with so far, several share the factor of their appearances occurring at a time of social change and instability. Piña became a sign of Filipino identity from the end of American rule to the liberation from American influence. The Italian Renaissance flourished when the Papal, Milanese and Habsburg powers were at odds. The Danish military uniform was born when the feudal system was gradually abandoned in favour of the territorial state. The living Greek statues emerged at a time of romantic liberalisation, and Beau Brummel's dandyism appeared in the Regency era, when the continuity of the old order was unsure. This commonality is no coincidence. The more fluid society is, i.e., the less crystalline social structure it contains, the more fertile is the soil for the enlargement of the world of objects. Because the world of objects brings order back into fluid society, as the following examples show.

Westminster Abbey houses four floor mosaics in the Roman Cosmati style. In the abbey's stylistic language, they take the special status of a singleton.[28] Why did the abbey, the coronation site and mausoleum of the English kings, break with the Anglo-French early gothic style it was otherwise built in? The Cosmati mosaics are located right at the coronation ceremony's traditional site within the abbey. The abbey and mosaics were commissioned by Henry III, King of England and Duke of Aquitaine, at a time of declining English influence on the continent. A desire arose for an independent, purely English identity, detached from France, as the nucleus of a new ideology of dominion. The Cosmati mosaics at the coronation site helped articulate this growing need for distance and establish a new relationship with the continent.[29]

Japanese urban youth styles show many contrasting features to western ones. *Kogyaru*, a very trashy style, is a good example. The term is derogatory for a

---

28 When interpreted as a singleton, the four non-identical mosaics must be treated as specimens of a single object. For the logic of this interpretation, see footnote 4.

29 Binski 1990.

young, infantilised girl. The kogyaru look includes deeply tanned skin, obtained in tanning studios or by applying chemicals. This contrasts starkly with the historical ideal of the noble Japanese woman, pale from avoiding the sun (to which peasant women are exposed), and further whitened from additional application of make-up. Instead, kogyaru adapts to the Western ideal of skin, expressing the luxury of quality time spent in the sun. How did this 'cultural rupture' come about? When Japan ended its isolationist course of the shoguns, it suffered humiliating experiences with the West which increasingly called its national identity into question. The need for modernisation grew into Western-style modernisation – 'datsu a nyo o' (from East to West) – including imitation of Western colonialism. Colonialism demanded a hierarchical demarcation of the Japanese race from the rest of Asia, with the Japanese in the lead. At the turn of the 20th century, this notion of distance from Asia found support in the West, with the construction of proximity to the Japanese (as opposed to other Asians) as 'honorary whites' by Nazi Germany and in South African apartheid. A Japanese *McDonald's* franchise owner's statement, "If we eat McDonald's hamburgers…we will become taller, our skin become white, and our hair blonde" is only understandable against this historical background of a nation in search of its racial identity. This search arose from the belief that race could be manipulated, or at least disguised. Kogyaru is a stylistic offshoot thereof. It targets race as a supposedly innate attribute of humans, by depicting Western racial attributes in an ironic, camp way, thereby holding up a mirror to the artificiality of Japan's westernisation. Besides tanning, the kogyaru style features brown or blonde coloured hair and hazel or blue coloured contact lenses. The trashy kogyaru youth style owes its existence to a deeply rooted identity crisis of the Japanese nation.[30]

In the late 17th century, the dilution of traditional English social structure had reached the provincial town. While pedigree and land ownership still exclusively shaped social structure in the countryside, this no longer applied in cities. The pathway into cities' upper echelons was also widened by commercial success, by profession, or by election to magisterial positions. The urban upper echelons of society came to be a mix of people with very different histories. However, the need for proximity amongst each other, and for distance from the socially inferior urban population remained. Yet this now had to be done in a way conducive to the increasing disparity of resources, controlled by the urban elite. The *English gentleman* performed this task by showing his prosperity (rather than exorbitant riches), demonstrating refinement and selectivity in his attire and home, as well as with his pronounced 'liberal upbringing', courtesy and sensitivity (also

---

30   Black 2009.

towards the less well-off). The *English gentleman* is a product of a period of disso-
lution of traditional society and a need for a new order, which he helped to create.[31]

When the multi-ethnic Habsburg Empire neared its end, the Vienna Secession artists' group broke away from the Viennese court's official style of historicism. It addressed the fragility, morbidity and hypocrisy of the old system and
proposed a new one. The oeuvre of Gustav Klimt, founding president of the Secession, exemplifies the agenda in its treatment of sexuality. Natural sexuality
was taboo in official Vienna. In historicism, the naked female body was deper-
sonalised and transfigured by mythological narratives, for example the figurine
of Eve. Klimt's paintings replaced historicism's Eve with the Nini of the Viennese
demimonde: with pubic hair as opposed to without, and with lively faces, his
women show a natural sexuality, and therein, the artificiality of the official ideology. Klimt's work, revolving around the castrating *femme fatale*, grew from a
time of an obsolete order, offering a new one containing natural sexuality.[32]

Feminism was born from the fluidity of society and, in rejecting the traditional gender role, has itself contributed to it. The *New Woman* had to illustrate
her new role within the world of objects. Smoking in public was one of her means.
The *Marlboro* man of the second half of the 20th century was preceded by the
'Marlboro' woman in its first half: the modern, smoking woman, co-opted by advertising. Earlier, in Victorian times, the pioneers of the women's movement distanced themselves from women in their traditional role by rejecting impractical
garb, with hoop skirt and corsage, repositioning themselves as trendy and fashionable. The Orient's stylistic inventory was ideally suited for this purpose, as it
left the body with every freedom under a wide cover, also serving as a symbol for
a simpler romantic life and women's natural beauty. The oriental style embodied
these ideals well into the 20th century, promoting the ideology of the *New
Woman*.[33] New objects – adopted as old ones from the Orient, but given new
meaning – found their way into the world of objects of a society that had become
more fluid.[34]

---

31   Stobart 2011.

32   Néret 2007.

33   Rabinovitch-Fox 2015.

34   Indigenisation of objects from foreign cultures can sometimes be reciprocal in meaning, as the
example of the armchair impressively shows (Cevik 2010). The growing predilection for the oriental in the Victorian West brought forth the Turkish armchair (Ottoman) in America, a thing
given the term American-style in the Ottoman world, in response to its growing interest in the
West. Not only can the same thing acquire a different meaning in different cultures (Coca-Cola),

The fluid society and its novel creations in the world of objects can also be seen in small details. *Hip hop*, a variant of the American black ghetto style, presents itself as a tough style for the hyper-masculine identity. Its dress code is gender-specific: head to toe, he is wrapped in wide, closed textiles – the mystified 'big black dick' is hidden in wide pants with a deep crotch. She presents her black body as the object of male desire in close-fitting attire. This hip hop dress code reflects the traditional division of labour in Western mainstream clothing: men hide, women show. Only since the 1980s did the man begin to wear close-fitting garb. First for homosexual wearers who began advertising the male body as a sexual object – a new opportunity in the course of sexual liberation. The *0/+consumption* of the hip hopper's wide pants and the homosexual's tight jeans produced, in the simplest way possible, the distance and proximity that the prudery of the male hip hop identity was in need of. However, that liberation also created a new audience for hip hop music, rejecting the examples of the old prudery. Some rappers began adapting their garb to this audience, their tight pants now becoming an irritation for the traditional hip hop identity. The fluidity of (American) society thus created the necessity and the opportunity for a stylistic differentiation within hip hop, between traditional hip hoppers and, from their point of view, the 'emasculated'.[35] Distance within all of hip hop increased with it.

Occasionally, objects are exported from one fluid society to another one. The European *refugee/pyjama style* is an example. The term refers to the neglect of etiquette and self-stylisation owing to necessity and to the bricolage of clothing under the pressure of a sudden flight. This style displays unpretentious comfort (plus sizes), second-hand appearance (faded colours), mid-length garments devoid of neckline, untailored, worn sloppily. It has already entered the Western mainstream. Fluidity of one society, Syria (war), brings fluidity to Europe (refugee crisis) and with it the necessity to restore order with new material for new social encounters. Today, not all refugees have arrived in European labour markets, but all are already productive in the supermarket of style.

The overall findings of this chapter are: the world of objects conveys social distance and proximity – distance between groups and proximity within groups. It consists of comparable and incomparable elements and subsets – of singletons, chains and trees, {○, |, ⋔}. The key for the creation of social distance and proximity is a qualitative one, *0/+consumption*. It is through it that order in society is created. The fluidity of society creates the necessity for new material in the

---

but as the armchair shows, it can be endowed symmetrically with the meaning 'from the (respective) other culture'.

35   Penney 2012.

world of objects. This way, a lost order in society is replaced by a new one. Now the question is how the world of objects obtains its ordering capacity.

Chapter 2
Style

"Every apparition can be experienced in two ways. The two ways are not at random, but they are attached to the apparitions – they are derived from the nature of the apparition, from two of their characteristics: exterior – interior."
Wassily Kandinsky[1]

"Le style c'est l'homme même."
Georges-Louis Leclerc, Comte de Buffon[2]

Although people find it difficult to define the concept of style spontaneously, they classify each other as belonging or not belonging together by respective styles. They always do so when they see others as punk, nerd, hipster, hippie, yuppie, emo, or belonging to hip hop or the mainstream. Which succeeds more frequently than not! Yet, the question is how this works and why.

Sociology asserts style to be either representative or constitutive of social groups, or else both.[3] However, there is consensus in all of sociology that social

---

1   Kandinsky 1973 (1926), p. 13, my translation.

2   Cited after Saisselin 1958.

3   Modernist sociology regards differences in endowment (financial and cultural capital) as being constitutive for forming social groups; style is merely representative of social groups (for example, the Birmingham School in its analysis of British youth cultures [Hebdige 1988]). In contrast, in the postmodern variant of sociology, the group style is understood as the constituent characteristic of the group; it is only by showing a style, that groups can come into being and are able to persist; other socio-cultural characteristics, for example the endowment with capital, play no or only a secondary role. Bourdieu (1982) marks the transition from modernism to postmodernism,

groups and their style form an inseparable entity. Group identities possess group-specific styles; and social distance between groups manifests itself in such differences. I will refer to the group-specific style as the *common style* (of a group).

If social distance between groups is established by means of different group-specific styles, how then will proximity be established within a group? As I will argue in chapter 3, this is achieved by means of the *individual style* of the group members. The more similar individual styles are, the greater proximity is within the group; the more dissimilar they are, the less proximity there is. Individual style and individual identity form an entity.

Collective identity and common style form a corresponding pair, and individual identity forms one with individual style. So, the very core of the production of social distance and proximity is affected by the question of exactly how and why human beings recognise social groups and individuals by their style. To answer this question I need to clarify the concept of style, which is the aim of this chapter.

In science, style is addressed at different levels of aggregation. Sociology addresses it at the aggregate level of object ensembles. The ensemble as a whole, a subset from the world of objects, is defined as a style, freed from its constituent components, and assigned to a social group. At this level of aggregation, the style has lost the material substance of its empirical evidence, 'anything goes' as an ensemble as long as it differs from the ensembles of other groups.

Archaeology and art history search for style on the disaggregated level of the particular object, e.g., an (antique) vase, or a painting. There, characteristics are found which are subsequently searched for in other objects. The subset of objects with these characteristics, remaining variable in number, is then seen as consisting of elements made in their shared style. Objects are thus assigned to different cultural taxa, referred to as a style. For example, ceramic fragment may belong to the cultural taxon of the Ionic style and another to the Corinthian style. Or a painting may belong to the cultural taxon of the High Renaissance and another to mannerism. The assignment of human beings to a style is done eclectically: be they those known by name, painting in a certain style (e.g., abstract expressionism), or the artistic avant-garde of a time and place (for example, the Vienna

---

postulating that their outward signals are as representative of social groups as they are constitutive for them.

Secession), or members of a style who will never be identified (e.g., Funnelbeaker culture), showing up in history only through association with that style.[4]

The following considerations remain in the tradition of art history and archaeology if we start from the analysis of style in the world of things. However, from a sociological point of view, I perceive this material style as being interwoven with the social. In this context, I will define the term 'style' more precisely, step by step.

Beauty versus the Aesthetic

Beauty is a value and a quality, aesthetics is merely a quality.[5] In the following, style is understood as an aesthetic concept: a style can be, but isn't necessarily beautiful. A punk wearing a safety pin in his or her ear and a representative of goth, pale as death, also show style – no matter how ugly they may be perceived to be. The aesthetics of a style is reflected in the quality of the ensemble of objects that constitute it. In this interpretation, style is a neutral concept. So, when I refer to the style of one group and that of another, I am referring to the different qualities as they are shown in their *0/+consumption*.

As a concept of aesthetics and not a term for beauty, style has an important implication for all that follows: two styles cannot be ordinally ranked. As a style is not a value but merely a quality, it defies ordinal comparisons such as: more or less beautiful than another style, more or less accomplished, more or less appealing, more or less contemporary. Two styles are incomparable in this normative sense, they are economic substitutes for "Yes to this, no to that!", or alternatively, 'No to this, yes to that!' As they are merely different qualities, styles lend themselves to the production of social distance and proximity without imposing hierarchies themselves.

Style, understood as being aesthetic, is therefore equally suitable for the analysis of stratified and non-stratified societies. As the object of scientific investigation, the human being may be admiring or pejorative of other people's 'styles', but the sentiment of beauty cannot be the issue here. Instead I take both the individual and the common style as the fundamental scientific concept for the analysis of stratified and non-stratified society.

---

4   Much like archaeology, material culture starts from the analysis of individual objects, but it further investigates their systematic connection to the human. Ensembles of objects are, however, not in its focus, and therefore not the style.

5   Costello 2004.

Individual versus Common

Art historians define the style of objects using the *signature model*. They look for the artist's 'hallmark' in an object. The origin of the word style, *stylus* – the pen of the writer – already points to this. In the signature model, the style of an object is the unmistakable hallmark of its creator. Knowing his individual style, the art historian accredits a newly discovered fresco, previously concealed under a coat of paint, to Titian. Or the art historian exposes a painting previously attributed to Kazimir Malevich as a fake. Or they attribute a newly discovered object to a particular but unknown artist, whose hallmark has already become visible in other works. One such artist is the fifth century B.C. Greek known as 'The Master of the Berlin Amphora', whose stylistic signature is evident on over 300 vases.[6] The signature model is also used in archaeology. However, there the aim is not to identify a creator as an individual, but rather to assign, for example, the finds of a certain area to a culture defined only by its style, such as the Funnelbeaker culture.[7]

Thus, in the signature model, the origin of a thing or a subset of the world of things is determined by means of style, regardless of whether the origin is an individual, a group, or an epoch. In doing so, intentionality is always assumed. As a result, things from nature cannot be of a style, only artificial things can. Their style makes them part of culture. Intentionality may refer to the thing as a whole, as is the case with Joseph Beuys' *Fat Corner* (1982), which he intended to be seen as a whole. It can also refer to the use of a manufacturing technique alone, such as the potter's wheel, which leads to common characteristics of the things produced on it.

Analysts in the tradition of the art historian Heinrich Wölfflin and the philosopher Richard Wollheim, further refine the concept of 'signature' by distinguishing between two basic concepts of style. A work that shows, for example, Titian's individual style, is created by him. A work in the *common style* of Titian is not by him, but shows (as do all paintings of the High Renaissance) characteristics which are exemplary in Titian's individual style. In other words, the individual style of an artist, whether they're known by name or not, is causal for their output. The common style, on the other hand, has a purely taxonomic function; it is a way of classifying objects and thus ordering them into subsets of the world of objects. The individual style is associated with a proper name (of an artist) or

---

6   Lezzi-Hafter 2017.

7   Neer 2005.

pseudonym (of a graffiti sprayer), the common style groups objects into subsets with no proper name/pseudonym.

Nevertheless, even the concept of common style cannot do without the idea of a creator: behind their objects too, people invariably exist. Such as the painters of the High Renaissance known by name, the architects, stonemasons and scribes of the gothic period, some unknown by name, the creators of the Funnelbeaker style of the distant past, who remain forever in obscurity. The further back archaeologists and art historians turn their gaze, the less knowledge they can hope to gain from anything other than the styles of things they're dealing with.

The creators of punk, nerd, hipster, hippie, yuppie, emo, hip hop styles, even those of the mainstream, are unknown by name, and these styles cannot be attributed to an unnamed, but particular individual as creator. The styles of social groups form the distinguishing features of cultural taxa, in much the same way as shape, size, but also behaviour form distinguishing features in the morphological species concept of biology. And in the same way that the morphological species concept equates the physical appearance of an arbitrary animal *pars pro toto* to the species it belongs to, regardless of individual differences between its specimens, the individual style of any particular person can be equated *pars pro toto* to the group it belongs to, despite differences in all its members' individual styles. Consequently, the common style made up of these individual styles cannot be attributed to any one of the group's members alone.

That is, the common styles of social groups are the cultural taxa of society. Postmodern sociology's claim that people are no longer separated from one another by socio-economic and socio-cultural differences[8] leaves their collective style as the only distinguishing feature of social grouping – unless you entertain the extreme idea of a totally individualised society that is completely void of group membership. The *0/+consumption* creates social distance in society by means of clear-cut common styles in which it manifests itself. Punk, nerd, hipster, hippie, yuppie, emo, hip hop and mainstream styles are the taxa of postmodern society, for all of which *0/+consumption* is constitutive.

The common style in culture and the genome of reproductive communities in nature are found at the same taxonomic level, namely that where groups of individuals are clustered by their common characteristics. At the lower, more disaggregated level of specimens, there is the individual style in culture and the alleles in nature, which are responsible for individual characteristics within a species (including, e.g., eye and hair colour, lactose and sucrose tolerance in

---

8   Müller 1992.

humans). The common style establishes distance between social groups, the individual style the (imperfect) proximity within a group.

So, the consumer always harbours two styles: the individual one, with which they establish themselves within a group, and the common one, which they share with that group. The individual style is nested within the common one, like the alleles are nested within the genome of the species. But unlike the latter, the individual style is not nature's gift, but the result of the individual's stylistic volition, exploiting the freedom granted by the group. In turn, the common style is the result of the collective freedom that the group enjoys within society, and in which the individual styles find their limits.

The distinction between individual and common style casts new light on Georg Simmel's consumer dilemma, the quest for both individuality and conformity.[9] Simmel's dilemma is a communicative one: the more individual someone is, the less their consumer language is understood – the more conformist someone is, the better it is understood. In QTC, the dilemma reoccurs, not as a communicative dilemma, but a social one. It's not about the need that one's individual style must still be understood in non-verbal communication, but rather that one's individual style must not imperil their group's distance to other groups. This limits the subset of the world of objects with which the individual style can be crafted, if the individual wants to remain in their group.

Original versus Mutation

This raises the issues of the relation between an original and its mutations in a common style, and of the authenticity of an object and the individual style. The original is the origin of a cultural tree, ᛗ. In object art, for example, the *objets trouvés* by Marcel Duchamp, such as the urinal staged for the artwork *Fontaine* (1917), are at the origin of the tree. In its branches are Joseph Beuys' *Fat Corner* (1982) and Alex Van Gelder's *Meat Portraits* (2012) as their mutations. Which end of the chains, |, of a cultural tree is more authentic, the original or the mutation?

Often, the original is deemed more authentic: Leonardo's *Last Supper* (1494–1498) prevails over its thousands of mutations (including those created for mere advertising). Applied to the style of social groups, the English provincial gentleman (as a specific behavioural style) is more authentic than the (thing-oriented) German mutations from the *Hubertus* hunter catalogue. The costume of Appenzell Innerrhoden is also more authentic than the mutations at the Oktoberfest.

---

9   Simmel 1905.

Steve Jobs embodies the Silicon Valley creative class more authentically than his present-day epigones and is therefore their iconic figure.

Yet, authenticity is a socially constructed reality, which both the Oriental carpet and the juvenile gangster style show. That is why the original is not automatically the most authentic. The mutation can also be authentic from case to case. Stylistically, Lascaux's cave paintings from the last glacial period belong in the same stylistic tree, the archaic style, as Picasso's cubist painting *Les Demoiselles d'Avignon* (1907). *Lascaux* is older, but *Avignon* is the seminal work of cubism, and more authentic to it than *Lascaux*. Which end of the chain displays the authentic is not clear from the outset. In Figure 1 (left side) it is either A or D.

Authentic objects are style-specific: almost all styles of social groups express a finished identity, while treating the unfinished one as taboo.[10] In contrast, the gay style *camp* exposes the artificiality of the finished identity, and thereby its changeability. This calls for consistently new, innovative, often provocative means to counteract the solidification of the illusion of the 'natural' finished identity. The latest mutation in camp is therefore more authentic than all its forerunners.

Signature versus Expression

For art critics, style is not the same as it is for art historians. Art critics work with an expression model of style, as opposed to the signature model used by art historians. In both models, only artificial objects can have style. But according to the expression model, the intention of the artist is always found in an artwork. This idea of style is therefore not founded on there being a joint origin of artworks, but on commonalities in expression – two pieces are in the same style when they express the same thing or something similar. For example, gothic pieces share the same intention of expressing the almightiness and glory of God. The expression model of style is tailor-made for the analysis of social groups; individuals and groups express their individual and collective identity by means of their style.

But do the signature and expression models share more than style's artificiality? For the philosopher Nelson Goodman, the stylistic signature is merely a metaphorical one. The art historian is speaking metaphorically when saying that an artwork shows the 'signature' of this or that epoch. But the metaphor is in itself a familiar code for expression. Titian's Paduan frescoes are filled with meta-

---

10   Mohr 2016.

phors. In distinguishing between these two models, the finer aspects still need to be worked out.[11]

You cannot think of style as affecting the relationship between people if, ontologically, style is mere signature. Because then styles would be nothing but placeholders for people. Although people are distinguishable by them, they would otherwise remain interchangeable. Apart from their signature, punks would have nothing in common with one another and would be no different from bankers. Then the styles called punk, goth and banker could just as well be given the serial numbers 1, 2 and 3, without loss of information. If serial numbers were the sole epistemological contribution of the concept of style – as formulated by the philosopher Judith Genova regarding the question of literary style – it would be hard to see why style should be of any interest at all.

However, it's another story if style's ontology is expressive instead. In that case, different styles express different ideas, including conflict-ridden ones. Punk, nerd, hipster, hippie, yuppie, emo and hip hop styles can then be understood by the mainstream as social criticisms, which contradict one' s own style. It is only by virtue of an expressive ontology that style can produce social distance. And it suffices if this ontology is construed, for example, by one group simply believing that another group's style sets the tone for social unrest. For these reasons, I define style as an ensemble of objects whose ontology is expression.

There is an almost unlimited number of codes available for expression[12], but this does not mean that style is an arbitrary collection of codes. After all, styles also differ in the codes they like to have. Those codes that occur frequently in a style are referred to as the *symbol system* of style.[13] Wassily Kandinsky's symbol system, for example, which is found in his entire oeuvre, comprises little more than dots, lines, and primary colours. Symbol systems can also be found in styles of social groups. The tattoos popular in youth styles are coded differently from prisoner and sailor tattoos.[14] So, in different styles different tools are used to (non-verbally) express social distance and proximity. The language in which different styles speak is, however, a shared one, otherwise one group would not be able to understand what another wants to express. The symbol system of a style is comparable to the speech style of a clergyman, which differs from that of a sports reporter, although both understand each other when they talk about God and sports.

---

11   Jacquette 2000.

12   Mick, Burroughs, Hetzel and Brannen 2004.

13   Hellman 1977.

14   Irwin 2001.

Representation versus Exemplification

Two modes of expression exist: representation and exemplification. Titian's Paduan frescoes represent the miracles of Saint Anthony. And yet, some art is not
about something else but about itself. As representation, such an artwork would
represent itself, which would not be a helpful construct, as René Magritte's *The
Treachery of Images* demonstrates. It is a naturalistic depiction of a pipe captioned
'Ceci n'est pas une pipe', expressing that what you see in a naturalistic painting
of a thing is not the thing itself, but its representation. Yet the painting itself –
here *The Treachery of Images* – is not a representation but rather, in Nelson Goodman's tradition, an exemplification of how the brain's processing of stimuli can
produce something that was not previously there. So, *The Treachery of Images* is
better understood in Goodman's tradition as 'exemplification'. The means of this
exemplification is style, prompting Judith Genova to say: "A piece of work with
style, as opposed to one without, not only shows but also says what it is all
about."[15]

Put simply, the common style of a group not only shows something, but it
frankly exclaims, "We are collectively one-of-a-kind, incomparable!" Punk even
yells this. But this is exactly the message needed for the production of social distance. Common style is what creates social distance, what shows and what de-
clares it. Likewise, individual style, which creates social proximity, exclaims, "I
am one of you, but cannot be mistaken for any of you!"

In his aesthetics of art, Arthur Danto draws a radical distinction between representation and exemplification. All art, he says, is open to interpretation and so
has the semiotic structure of a metaphor. However, he goes on, one can only interpret a metaphor if one understands not only its meaning, but also why exactly
this and no other piece of art can embody this metaphor. Hence, while the artist
is free in *what* they want to say (what is to be exemplified), they are bound without
alternative in *how* it is to be said. There is only one way to represent (the way the
ambassador alone represents his/her country). So for Danto, the *how* of an artwork is representation, barred from all alternatives.

---

15   Genova 1979, p. 322.

What versus How

An expressive ontology of style is about which style expresses what and how. The *what* ultimately concerns social positioning, the range of which Dick Hebdige has mapped out for British youth cultures. The object of expression can be crude, like that of the hyper-masculine hip hopper. Or it can be subtle, like that of the post-revolutionary, neo-classical American style, which, to set itself apart from the Rococo of the English colonial masters, made visible the values of the new era, purified of absolutism.[16]

Much like Danto's, an alternative approach assigns style not to the *what*, but to the *how*. Style is then the way something was made, and has nothing to do with what it is. A painting's style thus shows itself in the artist's painting technique (*how*), and not in *what* it expresses. With this ontology of style, the ensuing tasks are clearly divided between art history and archaeology on the one hand, and art criticism on the other. Art history and archaeology deal with facts (the *how*), art criticism evaluates and thereby also *constructs* expression (the *what*) – and is, *NB*, forever busy legitimising its judgments.[17] If you followed the approach of art criticism strictly, artistic style would lose its status as fact. Transferring this to the style of social groups, what o/+consumption then produced would not be fact but merely owing to the imagination of *homo sociologicus*. Would style in society then just be smoke and mirrors?

So, how can empirical substance be restored in the ontology of style as expression? You have two options. First, from a constructivist perspective, the social distance or proximity that two people construct are facts if their behaviour reflects this distance or proximity. But then the world of things is essentially redundant. Secondly, the neat separability of the *what* and *how*, and of art history and art criticism, is to be relativised.[18] In this way, style does not only encompass the *how* of painting, for example with Kandinsky's dots, lines and primary colours. Because in art, *how* something is made can hardly be appreciated without an idea of *what*. Magritte's *Treachery of Images*, for example, shows the *how* only in the *what*: only in the naturalistically painted pipe and the caption 'Ceci n'est pas une pipe' (*what*), the *how* of the contradiction in the *Treachery of Images* becomes

---

16   Prown 1980.

17   The fact-based approach of art history and archaeology obviously also addresses the who of the signature model. The surviving Paduan records of instalments paid in 1510 to a Ticiano Vecellio for work done in the *Scuola del Santo*, are proof not only of when the frescoes were made but also by whom.

18   Robinson 1981, Wartovsky 1993.

transparent. Art history that disregards art criticism is therefore doomed to failure. Stylistically, the *how* cannot be separated from the *what*, fact and construct
fuse into a joint reality. And, empirically, the different styles of *Harley* bikers and
bicycle couriers, for example, can be experienced directly by participatory observation of the joint workings of the *how* and *what*.[19] It is precisely in this experience
of the human being by the human being that style produces social distance and
proximity.

The Material versus the Personal

How many sheets of paper fit between the individual and their style? How closely
does the individual let their style approach themself? How do others see the individual in relation to their style? Separate from it or fused with it?

From an extreme standpoint, style is an artificial pose, manner devoid of substance. If you lean toward this view, it is difficult to imagine the subset of the
world of objects, visible in style, to credibly produce and communicate identity.
Then, you are essentially assuming 0/+*consumption* has no impact on utility. From
this perspective, the orthodox consumption theory is the right one for you.

The pragmatist philosopher Richard Shusterman's somatic style concept
(*somaesthetics*), which is inspired by Eastern philosophy, offers the opposite
view.[20] Somatic style is habitus fed by spirit.[21] It manifests itself in the individual's behaviour. The artificial gait of the fashion model on the catwalk does not
belong to it. Rather, somatic style shows who we are. It is the natural expression
of our personality. It may be understood as the spiritual base of our identity. Our
spirit reveals itself to others through our body and is recognised by them in our
physicality. The somatic side of our style grants or denies authenticity to our
overall style. In a coherent overall style, the superficial world of things is anchored in the depth of our spirit; in an incoherent overall style, the somatic style
mercilessly reveals the artificiality of our material style – the 'gentleman' I may
wish to be is downgraded to a mere wearer of tweed jackets.

If you agree with Shusterman, style is the human being itself – in contrast to
Comte de Buffon's own understanding of his *Le style c'est l'homme même*, where the

---

19   Schouten and McAlexander 1995, Kidder 2005.

20   Shusterman 2011.

21   This contrasts with Bourdieu's habitus, which to a greater extent is fed by the social via parental
      upbringing.

writing style is the result of role play by the author.[22] Style, according to Shuster-man, demands an intentionality that comes from the spirit, animating our feelings, desires, thoughts, actions and expression. Our animating spirit, which underlies all our exterior appearance, helps others recognise us. Our individual style is therefore not so much a bold creation, but rather slowly comes about by our constantly working on and developing ourselves. The somatic stylisation of our exterior serves one purpose only: the strengthening of our spirit. Our somatic style is thus as much our character as it is our corpuscle, as much our inner subjectivity as it is our outer form, connecting inside with outside, depth with surface. It remains malleable as a variable, but it cannot be changed by us on a whim; we can't change it the way we can change our shirt.

In Shusterman's understanding, the dark complexion in kogyaru's outer appearance is not part of a coherent somatic style, nor is the theatricality of pro wrestlers, nor are the crocodile tears shed by figure skaters in the 'kiss and cry' area, bodies pumped full of anabolic steroids, nor is Beau Brummel's posing. But Emma Hart's posing, expressing a classical ideal, can be part of a coherent somatic style, as can be parkour acrobatics, as a physical expression of the mastery of the urban world. In some sports, bestowing points for good posture is an attempt to evaluate the magnificence of the spirit in what is visible in the physical; for example, posture points scored by the dressage rider for the harmony of the human spirit with the animal. That which is evaluated by the posture points in dressage is the somatic style of the rider.

So, I understand the style-creating 0/+consumption of "Yes to this, no to that!" as being coherent with its underlying spirit. In a simplified but not entirely false economic interpretation, the somatic style can be understood as a restriction on 0/+consumption. Where it is violated, a signalling failure occurs, which will be discussed in chapter 10. Where it is observed, the overall style retains the substance and authenticity that are prerequisite for both communication and identity. Emphasising individuality, QTC is a consumer theory of the Western world; in its accommodation of the somatic style it remains, however, amenable to Eastern philosophy.

---

22   Saisselin 1997.

The Material versus the Social

A question still lingers: what sets a person apart from their style? If the world of objects is viewed as the structured framework that allows society to exist, then the person is the creation of their style. The world of objects is then the subject, whose language-like communicative capacity existed before the people using it. Alternatively, the world of objects can be viewed as a medium into which people write their intentions and beliefs.[23] In this case, style is created by people, and a person is to be viewed as the subject that already existed before the world of objects it uses.

When you take into account couturiers, designers, creative directors, the trendsetters in the hotspots of hip cities, and charismatic leaders, you tend to take the second view: (human) commerce makes style. However, the problem with this view is that it implicitly assumes the world of objects to be soft – people write into it whatever they wish, as if into warm wax. In the first view, by contrast, the world of objects is hard – what can be read in it has always been there, people themselves do not cause anything. This view has a different problem though: social innovation is difficult to imagine.

If you wish to avoid these problems, you must find an analytical compromise between the human being and style – between subject and object. To do this, the hitherto strict separation of the material and the social world must be overridden – that is the necessary compromise. The Actor Network Theory (ANT), a theory popular in cultural anthropology, offers that potential.[24]

Central to ANT is the concept of agency as an autonomous, but not necessarily intentional source of *action*. In ANT, both humans *and* things have agency. The difference merely lies in humans acting intentionally, which things cannot. But like humans, things can act autonomously: fences, paths and gates, for example, do not pursue goals, but they do affect people by means of non-verbal communication. Congestion and panic can be the results of the 'actions' of fences, paths and gates in sports stadiums – just as human actions are sometimes dysfunctional. The digital revolution is a case in point: if the wheel of digitalisation can no longer be turned back, then this metaphor for the 'acting' world of things demonstrates exactly what ANT is about. It is this symmetry between humans and things that allows both to interact in a network of actors: things 'act' and humans act, the material world is autonomously manipulated by humans, and so is the social world by the material world.

---

23   Boast 1997.

24   Latour 2005.

But the crux of the ANT approach in its application to style is that stylistic innovations are syntactic innovations. For example, a recombination of the world of objects into a new subset (bricolage in fashion), the re-emergence of an accessory long forgotten (the hipster's moustache), a new way of behaving (parkour). However, syntactic innovation does not suffice for creating social distance and proximity. For this, semantic innovation (expression) is also needed: with the new syntax, new allusions need be made (expression) to another domain (the social).[25] That is to say, only with semantic innovation as expression can a new social reality be produced. It may be immediately obvious to you that fences, paths and gates exercise agency, and even how. But whether and how this agency could be so potent as to autonomously manipulate complex processes such as the production of social distance and proximity remains obscured. Convincing examples of this are lacking. Herein lies the crux I mentioned above.

Here, semiotic anthropology offers an alternative to ANT.[26] In semiotic anthropology the material plays only a passive role. Subsequently, the interrelationship between the material and the social, with all its degrees of freedom, emerges from an iterative process between culture and the social (semiosis). Consequently, it remains strictly in the human domain. In this iteration, it is culture that determines the mutability of the language-like communication capabilities that the world of objects affords. The current culture is the crystallisation of all these past mutations ('crystallised history').

However, here yet another problem arises: although semiotic anthropology reduces the degree of ambiguity between the material and the social, it doesn't eliminate it. A specific interrelationship between the material and the social can be established *post festum*, but it cannot be predicted. But since, epistemologically, the world must be *one* and cannot be two, this ambiguity is arbitrarily assigned by semiotic anthropology to the world of objects and not to the world of the social: (almost) arbitrary objects can signify a specific social feature. The Birmingham School's analysis of British lower class styles is a case in point: velvet (material) is not an object of interest as such, and the ambiguity of its symbolic potential is not worth analysing. Only as the cloth of the suit of the *mod*, whose place in the English social structure the school defines as fixed, is velvet of interest, because the mod's velvet suit – NB *post festum* – signifies the mod's place in the social structure. This attribution – the material as ambiguous, the social as unambiguous – is surprising.

---

25   Hellman 1977.

26   Parmentier 1997.

The *o/+consumption* approach to the production of social distance and proximity provides the following bridge between ANT and semiotic anthropology:

- As in ANT, the material is an object of interest ex ante, but unlike in ANT, it
  has no agency of its own.
- Only humans act (semiotic anthropology).
- The social is ex ante undetermined (ANT).
- Instead, the material is less ambiguous than semiotic anthropology
  admits.
- The material order is the structure, {∘, |, ᛘ}, of singletons, chains and trees in
  the world of objects.
- The subsets, {∘, |, ᛘ}, of the world of objects structure the social by means of
  their properties of incomparability and comparability.
- Human agency, via o/+consumption, produces social distance and proximity.

Overview

Establishing the order of singletons, chains and trees, culture determines the in-
comparability and comparability within and between subsets {∘, |, ᛘ}; that is, the
material, loaded with meaning, by which consumption produces social distance
and proximity. In the following, when I speak of the world of objects, I am referring to the world of things-cum-behaviours that has already been assigned by
culture.

This ordering power of culture is symbolised by □ and, for sake of simplicity,
I will (mostly) equate it with culture itself: culture is □. I define the world of objects as a thing-cum-behaviour world, ordered by culture into disjoint subsets of
X. A singleton is an incomparability, (∘, □), ordered by □. A chain is a totally
ordered subset of strict but comparable non-identities, (|, □), of X. And a tree is
a partially ordered subset, (ᛘ, □), of X with the ordering properties of chains, |,
in each of its branches. Hence, the subsets of singletons, chains, and trees of X,
{∘, |, ᛘ}, are also ordered by □. Thus, it is culture alone that creates the world of
objects, $(X, □)$, from the unordered material, X. Only through culture does the
social emerge – the distance between and proximity within social groups.

Piña is made into an object that expresses Filipino identity only by the shared
knowledge of its role in stripping American colonial rule (culture). The (art-historical) appraisal of Titian (culture) makes his oeuvre a coherent ensemble of
things representing an entire epoch. The examination of the Oriental carpet's

attributes (culture) turns carpets into objects that are more or less authentic. Traditional notions of gender roles (culture) let the cut of clothes be more or less macho or sissy. And it is culture that puts the poses of an Emma Hart and Beau Brummel into different subsets of the world of objects. The world of objects, $(X, \Box)$, is an order created by culture, $\Box$, out of the unordered thing-cum-behaviour world, X.

Table 1 presents the overall picture. Style is defined as $0/+consumption$ of $\{\circ, |, ⋔\}$ in a human agency network. Style is therefore not only that which consumers display with their "Yes to this, no to that!" decisions, but this communication is also loaded by culture with dissimilarity information, $\{\circ, |, ⋔\}$, that is to say with information about the comparability and incomparability of objects. Examples: brown versus black dress shoes communicates a different bilateral dissimilarity between two wearers than brown dress shoes versus bath slippers; piña as a fabric versus cotton communicates a different dissimilarity than thin versus thick cotton; a smartwatch on one wrist versus a vintage watch on another person's wrist communicates a different dissimilarity than a vintage *Omega* versus a vintage *Tissot*.

The consumption of quality is always to be understood in this sense. A given quality is one side of a dissimilarity *potential* of an object which is this quality; this quality/object is only consumable jointly with other qualities/objects, which provide other sides to that potential, thereby creating concrete dissimilarity relations between these qualities/objects and that with the initial dissimilarity potential. A given quality is thus consumable only in a pack of qualities, as a dissimilarity between them. The 'commodities' consumers consume are these dissimilarities. They are created by culture.

Table 1: Overview.

Sphere	Key Function	Key Process	Output	Discussed in
World of things-cum-behaviours	input X			Part 1
Culture □	organising authority	determination of dissimilarities in the world of things-cum-behaviours	ordered world of objects (X, □) with {∘,|,♪}	Part 1
Economy	human agency	*0/+consumption* of {∘,|,♪} in the agency-network =: collective production of styles	bilateral dissimilarities	Part 2
The Social	communication	elective affinity	social distance and proximity	Part 3

The world of things-cum-behaviours is the unordered input into culture, from which it receives its meaning as (bilateral) dissimilarities. Thereby, the world of things-cum-behaviours becomes an ordered world of objects. In the economy, the world of objects is used (instrumentally) by human agency in *0/+consumption* for the production of (bilateral) dissimilarities between individuals. In the social realm, elective affinities are formed from these bilateral dissimilarities and social distance and proximity are produced.

The Micro and Macro Composition of Style

In his art-theoretical treatise *Point and Line to Plane*, Wassily Kandinsky, founder of abstract expressionism in painting, identifies two key features of the human experience of the world of objects. We can experience a subset of the world of objects – in his case every instance of a painting – either as a whole (exterior) or by its constituent parts (interior). In this, Kandinsky broke with the practice prevalent in art theory at the time, of searching for the effect of a painting in its exterior only, i.e. in the subset as a whole – in his case, the whole plane of a canvas. He argues instead for searching for the effect of constituent parts – in his case, dots and lines – whose peculiarities would approach the viewer by coming out of the plane of the canvas like someone approaching us by stepping through a door.

Yet, Kandinsky continues, a particular element has no independent effect, but is effective as part of the composition of all the elements on the plane of the canvas. For him, composition is the internal, functional subordination of basic elements and their build-up within a specific painterly objective. Using different compositions of dots and lines on the plane, he demonstrates how subsets of basic elements are perceived by the viewer as compositions. Although arising from its elements, a composition functions separately. The implication of Kandinsky's conclusion for consumption theory is this: consumer utility is not directly derived from the properties of basic elements, but from a composition of constituent elements, which has become a new property separate from them.

I will operationalise this for style in the following way: Kandinsky's dots and lines are basic elements that correspond, for example, to buttons and cords on uniforms; they affect utility only in the form of a composition, a painting or a uniform. I define such a composition of basic elements as an object, x, from the world of objects (X, $\square$). As a composition of basic elements, the object possesses an independence lent by culture.[27] Objects, x, are the input into o/+consumption. Its output is style and its effect social distance and proximity. Kandinsky's compositions form the micro world of style.

For once, the orthodoxy is right in defining consumer goods as utility generators at the aggregate level of Kandinsky's composition, i.e. paintings, uniforms, etc., as a whole, each composed of basic elements. But not for good reason: in the orthodoxy, a consumer good is that which carries a price tag, something Kandinsky's dots and lines do not. Only the painting does. Object, x, and the orthodox consumer good only coincide by chance if the value chain spits out the consumer good exactly when it has attained the Kandinskyan composition property. That this only happens by chance is because the orthodoxy deems value to be exchange value, whereas QTC views it as the use value of social distance and proximity.

Kandinsky reveals the cultural ties of objects even further: according to him, the dot functions as sound, the line as colour. Since no dot is a sound and no line a colour, these functions are not contained in the physical painting, but in the mind of the viewer. That is to say, Kandinsky's world of objects begins to exist only in the viewer's perception – no object 'artwork' can exist without the viewer as the subject. Applying this understanding to consumption results in a radical conclusion: no object that a consumer can consume exists 'out there, in the world'. Instead, every

---

27 An object can therefore be understood as $x = (x, \square)$. However, since I take $(x, \square)$ as given, i.e. since I do not deal with the nano-issue, whereby, for example, a subset of gold buttons and field-grey cloth constitutes a particular composition (uniform) compared to a subset of pineapple fibre and horn buttons, I stick with the shortened notation x.

object, x, and thus every composition of objects, and hence every style, only begins to exist in the senses of the consumer – barong tagalog from piña, Titian's works, uniforms, costumes, art styles, living statues, dandyism, the Cosmati mosaics in Westminster, kogyaru, the gentleman, Klimt's *femmes fatales*, the emancipated female, hip hop, as well as Kandinsky's compositions of dots and lines. Not even in the micro world of style does the material exist without culture. Only the black in the paint box is still without culture.

The micro world of style is still unordered, consisting only of singletons, but these are already Kandinskyan compositions. The macro world of style begins with the ordering of objects, as at least | or ⋔. Orders, |, ⋔, or {∘, |, ⋔}, are macro compositions consisting of Kandinskyan micro compositions. Style, both individual and common, is thus a macro composition.

One such macro composition of objects is Titian's oeuvre, ⋔ (Figure 3), although his pieces are not gathered in one place. The collection of paintings by Gustav Klimt in Gilles Néret's book *Gustav Klimt* is, however, a macro composition that can be viewed together as a whole, ⋔. A collection of Louis Armstrong records, arranged in order of year of production, |, is a macro composition that can be viewed, heard and grasped. Regardless of the number of objects contained in a macro composition, it is an entity created by culture: each object it contains is arranged in a certain order in relation to other objects it contains, as a chain or tree. Some chains can be extended, for example, by adding a previously lost Louis Armstrong recording to the collection without disturbing its order. It is still a macro composition. In the same manner, some trees can be combined with some other trees to form even larger ones without disturbing their order. For example, if Klimt's oeuvre is combined with all the works (of other painters) in his style.

You also find singletons, chains and trees united in larger subsets, {∘, |, ⋔}. You can find the record collection, |, together with purple batik scarves, |, prints of Klimt's paintings, ⋔, and a vintage car, ∘. They are fragmented arrangements, which are still united in a subset of the world of objects by the simple fact that a consumer surrounds themself with them in *0/+consumption*.

Macro compositions, {∘, |, ⋔}, are typical of consumer styles. One outside observer may be bewildered by {∘, |, ⋔}, to another outside observer it may be familiar – as when the one but not the other comes to grips with the macro composition of Louis Armstrong records, purple batik scarves, Klimt prints and the vintage car. Sometimes consumers demonstrate less complex macro compositions, which may even shrink down to a {⋔} – for example, if in the above-mentioned composition Louis Armstrong's music is replaced by sitar music, the *femmes fatales* by photos of a guru, and a Dutch bicycle is stored in the garage instead of the vintage car. In any case, consumer styles are macro compositions, {∘, |, ⋔}. For simplicity's sake I define it in the result of the consumer's *o/+consumption* as {○, |, ⋔}: if style is the individual itself, then the individual is {○, |, ⋔}.

So, for further analysis, I view the consumer as being solidly fused with all they surround themself with, as well as with all they steer clear of. Critics of capitalism denounce that fusion as 'consumerism': consumption is seen as a collective fetish, corrupting and infantilising the human being. So, do I think of society as a decadent consumer temple? No! A consumer's individual style or the common style of their group can be precisely what consumerism critics decry, but it can just as easily be quite the opposite: an ascetic style, a minimally hedonistic style, an intellectual style, an artist's consumer style, etc. My approach does not narrow the scope of consumption down, it allows for both, the capitalism critic's hell as well as their heaven.

I define as *style system* the entirety of styles that exist side by side in society, which is the set of all $n \cdot m$ styles, $\{ \{○, |, ⋔\}_1, ..., \{○, |, ⋔\}_{n \cdot m} \}$.[28*] Thus it is clear that social distance and proximity cannot be individually produced, but only collectively. A consumer contributes only a small part to the whole system of *o/+consumption* in society, which produces social distance and proximity only as a whole. The household production of style is always society-wide collective production.

Where the number of members of society is greater than the number of common styles that exist in that society, several people have flocked together around a style that is constitutive for them as a group. There are the Nationalists and 'Americans' in the Philippines, there are the dandies and the rest of the Regency, the punks, nerds, hipsters, hippies, yuppies, emos, hip hoppers and mainstreamers in the present. Social distance between them and proximity within them are brought about by the cultural dissimilarities which inhere within the style system. That raises the question of what exactly cultural dissimilarity is.

28* With n as the number of social groups with m members each.

Chapter 3
Distant and Near Vision

> "There is a correct tree of life [...]. The same can-
> not be said for judgements of taste or of mu-
> seum convenience."
> *Richard Dawkins[1]*

> "[A]s if people were always looking down on oth-
> ers, and as if it were not part of our daily experi-
> ence that others can be strangers to us in ways
> that leave us with no say as to whether they are
> located 'above' or 'below' us."
> *Gerhard Schulze[2]*

In *The Ancestor's Tale – A Pilgrimage to the Dawn of Evolution*, evolutionary biologist
Richard Dawkins reports the state of knowledge about the 'true' tree of life – and
warns us *passim* against hoping to discover such a tree outside nature. His warning is preaching to the choir of cultural studies: the echo from there is that cultural order is always ambiguous. But exactly why a 'true' cultural order can't exist
is a matter of disagreement. So, in this chapter I will begin exploring what exactly
makes culture so ambivalent. To this end, I will first aim for the greatest imagi-
nable formal analogy between nature and culture. For this, I conduct a thought
experiment to define the cultural equivalent of that which, in biology, determines the dissimilarity of two species – the molecular order in the genome. It is
in the differences between the molecular order in nature and the 'molecular' order in culture that we discover the causes of the cultural ambiguity emphasised
in cultural studies.

---

1   Dawkins 2005, p. 178.
2   Schulze 2005, p. XXI.

We need to work with two key concepts: *dissimilarity* and *diversity*. Diversity is grounded in dissimilarity, which is why both come as a pair. But since there exist (at least) two concepts of dissimilarity, there are two corresponding concepts of diversity, making up two pairs of dissimilarity-cum-diversity, in which *0/+consumption* can be further explored. In this chapter, I will assign each pair to a different aspect of identity, the individual and the collective. So, finally, social distance and proximity as well as the common and individual style are all based on these two different pairs of dissimilarity-cum-diversity.

Excursion: from Nature to Culture

In *The Ancestor's Tale*, Richard Dawkins shows how kinship in a subset of species is coded in their genomes. Surprisingly, he is using an example from culture, where, as he claims, the same order of dissimilarity is found: in different versions of an original text, copied long before the invention of letterpress printing, when generations of copyists continuously made new mistakes and perpetuated existing ones. The analogy between nature and culture is extensive. The extinct common ancestor of a subset of species, for example today's gibbon monkeys, corresponds to the lost original of a literary work – in Dawkins' example, *The Canterbury Tales* by Geoffrey Chaucer from the 14th century. The copies of the *Tales* that exist today correspond to a subset of live species, for example the twelve species of gibbon monkeys. Differences in the coding of amino acids in the DNA (the molecular source of morphological differences between gibbon monkeys) correspond to differences in the spelling of words and phrasing of sentences in different versions of the *Tales*. The genome of a gibbon species corresponds to an entire text of the *Tales*. The genetic mutations of the DNA over time correspond to mutations due to copying errors in the *Tales* over time. Furthermore, evolutionary biologists and linguists share the same plausibility-based conviction: degrees of kinship of (natural or artificial) objects do not result from convergence from many different origins, but from divergence from a single origin, from a common biological ancestor or, in Dawkins' example, from Chaucer's original.

Following Dawkins – and in order to better grasp the common 'molecular' order of dissimilarity in nature and culture – let's take the first line of the Prologue of the *Tales* in four of the still existing versions, V1 to V4:

V_1: »Whan that Aprylle / wyth hys showres soote«
V_2: »Whan that Auerell w^t his shoures soote«
V_3: »Whan that Aprille with his showres soote«
V_4: »Whan that Aueryll w^t his shoures soote"

In biology and linguistics alike, dissimilarity is identified via commonalities and differences in sequences: in biology via sequences of DNA, in linguistics via sequences of letters and punctuation marks (which in biology encodes the building instructions of phenotypic expressions and in writing the expression of entire texts).

Table 2: 'Molecular' order of dissimilarity.

Line one in the prologue of four versions of the Canterbury Tales							
V_1:	Whan	that	Aprylle	/	wyth	hys	showres	soote
V_2:	Whan	that	Auerell		wᵗ	his	shoures	soote
V_3:	Whan	that	Aprille		with	his	showres	soote
V_4:	Whan	that	Aueryll		wᵗ	his	shoures	soote

Shown here is a cultural object (text), as an analogy for the molecular order of dissimilarity in DNA (according to Dawkins 2005).

In Table 2, the differences in the first line of the four versions are marked in italics and bold. The complete commonality in the first two words and the last one shows the close degree of kinship of all versions (the taxon of *The Canterbury Tales* – similar to the taxon of the gibbon monkeys). Differences in the spelling of the other words and in the use of a punctuation mark show, however, that they are not identical texts, but different versions. V_1 to V_4 are related, but to differing degrees. V_1 and V_3 are more closely related than either of them is related to V_2 or V_4, which in turn are more closely related than either of them is to V_1 or V_3. The analysis of about 80 versions of the *Tales* has revealed that V_1, the version kept in the British Library, and V_3, the so-called Egerton version, are closely related, as are V_2, the Christ-Church version, and V_4, the Hengwrt version, but both clusters are more distantly related to each other. Dawkins then discusses how biologists, following this pattern of analysis, determine the kinship of species – for example of the twelve gibbon species. This is how biologists determine trees in nature, ᛘ, like the taxon of the gibbons. And similarly, trees can be found in culture, cultural taxa, like the taxon of *The Canterbury Tales*, ᛘ.

Can this correspondence between the genome in nature and *The Canterbury Tales* be generalised within culture? In other words, how does this pattern of analysis have to be modified when you move from one cultural medium to another – from reading to hearing or seeing? Music too, is a sequence, one of notes, just as the *Tales* are sequences of letters. In music, too, the sequence matters, just as the sequence of letters matters when reading. (By the way, the exact position of a gene in the genome also matters for the formation of the phenotype; the same molecular structure at a different location in the genome causes something different, or often nothing at all.) Thus, the pattern suitable for determining dissimilarities in texts also has potential for determining trees in music. In contrast, the visual, for example painting, behaves quite differently from music in one respect. In music, time conveys information, but not in painting. For example, a song lasts 90 seconds, and it makes a difference when which note is heard in these 90 seconds. One can hardly think of a painting on a timeline. Yet we also find the 'molecular' order *mutatis mutandis* in painting.

Art historian Heinrich Wölfflin paved the way to this insight. Even before Kandinsky's *Point and Line to Plane*, Wölfflin introduced that very same analysis of paintings – syntax above semantics, interior above exterior, genotype above phenotype – to art history. He discovered the syntactic (inner, 'molecular') differences between Renaissance and Baroque painting and thus discovered two distinct styles (taxa) of painting. Four of their syntactic distinguishing features are the principles of focal point, line design, spatial composition and illumination. Together they form a feature space in which objects, in this case paintings, can be positioned.

The *focal point principle* is all about where the eye of the viewer is directed – at a single thing in the painting, behind which everything else recedes (one focal point), or at multiple (or no) focal points. High Renaissance painting features multiple focal points. Thus, in Leonardo's *The Last Supper* (1495-97), not one person stands out from the group, not one recedes behind the others. In contrast, in Rubens' triptych *Descent from the Cross* (1612-14) the viewer's gaze is directed not only at the central panel, but also away from the masses of live figures towards the one dead body.

According to the *line design principle*, lines create shapes (for example, bodies). Lines, and thus the boundaries of shapes, can be painted or drawn sharply or blurred. In *The Last Supper*, Leonardo's lines are sharp and the bodies stand out clearly from each other and from the background. In *Descent from the Cross*, Rubens' lines are blurred, and the bodies blend into each other and into the background.

The *spatial composition principle* involves painted depth versus painted flatness. *The Last Supper* is flat, not in the sense of Kandinsky's physical plane, but flat in the depth conveyed. There are only two pictorial planes – the bodies and the windows partially concealed by them – whose distinctiveness is not painted but can only be deduced by the viewer's experience. *Descent from of the Cross* depicts bodies set back in spatial depth to the left and right of, and above and below the centre (showing the lifeless body).

The *illumination principle* concerns the effect of painted or not particularly accented light. In *The Last Supper* not a single ray of light is directed at the bodies or the background, the whole scene is without shadow and does not come across as a painted transient moment. In *Descent from the Cross*, some bodies are illuminated and others are shaded, clouds darken the day, and when the lifeless body is retrieved at night, light falls from it on the faces turned towards it. *Descent from the Cross* is not only painted illumination, the illumination also tells a story.

From these syntactic features, i.e. in this feature space, Wölfflin discovered the inner, 'molecular' dissimilarity between Renaissance and Baroque painting styles. Renaissance painting is 'molecular' like Leonardo's *The Last Supper*, Baroque painting is 'molecular' like Rubens' *Descent from the Cross*. For many, this 'molecular' order in painting can not only be used to distinguish Renaissance and Baroque styles but can also be applied more generally. With surprising results. In a generalisation of Wölfflin's approach, cultural sociologist Albert Bergesen analyses *The Last Supper* by Leonardo (1495-97), *The Last Supper* by Tintoretto (1592-94), *Triumph of Galatea* by Raphael (1514), *Red Blue Green* by Ellsworth Kelly (1963), *Hôtel des Roches Noires, Trouville* by Monet (1870) and *Number 1* by Jackson Pollock (1948).[3] What is stylistically closer and what is only distantly related?

Art historians favour a diachronic analysis by searching for the chronological origins of artworks, following the principle that 'only what came before can influence what comes after'. *Number 1* is seen as being in the tradition of *Hôtel des Roches Noires, Trouville*, two paintings that they assign to the taxon of modern art, with the second painting positioned closer to their common origin than the first. Art critics, on the other hand, focus more on the phenotype, declaring that the two versions of *The Last Supper* belong together and are only very, very distantly related to *Red Blue Green* and *Number 1*. But how does the dissimilarity of these artworks appear in Wölfflin's feature space? Table 3 shows the findings.

---

3   Bergesen 2000.

Table 3: Wölfflin's 'molecular' order.

		Focus point principle	Line design principle	Spacial composition principle	Illumination principle	(Medium)	(Chromatics)
Dissimilarity in painting							
Object subset	Features Space						
The Last Supper (Leonardo)		multiple	sharp	flat	without	painting	polychrome
The Last Supper (Tintoretto)		single	blurred	deep	with	painting	polychrome
Galatea (Raffael)		multiple	sharp	flat	without	painting	polychrome
Red, Blue, Green (Kelly)		multiple	sharp	flat	without	painting	polychrome
L'hôtel ... (Monet)		single	blurred	deep	with	painting	polychrome
Number 1 (Pollock)		none	sharp	flat	without	painting	polychrome

Six paintings (after Bergesen 2000).

In spite of their phenotypical similarity, both versions of *The Last Supper* reveal 'molecular' differences: multiple focal points in Leonardo and only one in Tintoretto, sharp lines in Leonardo, blurred ones in Tintoretto, Leonardo's painting is flat and without painted illumination, Tintoretto's has depth and illumination. 'Molecularly', they only distantly resemble each other despite their common motif. In contrast, 'molecularly' similar are Leonardo's *The Last Supper* and Kelly's *Red Blue Green* – that is, High Renaissance painting and abstract minimalism have a close 'molecular' structure. And Pollock's *Number 1* 'molecularly' only distantly resembles Monet's *Hôtel*.

Even though, in contrast to Table 2, the sequence of features (in Table 3 from left to right) does not convey any information, in both, dissimilarity follows from the comparison of features in a feature space. And in both, the feature spaces considered are only part of a larger space. The feature space of the *Tales* could be enlarged by the second and third lines, and so on, which would improve the precision of the dissimilarities thus obtained. The feature space in Table 3 could also be enlarged, for example by those features Wölfflin additionally took into account, thus also improving the precision of the dissimilarities obtained. To be sure, dissimilarity in paintings has the same 'molecular' order as dissimilarity in literature, and dissimilarity in literature has the same order as dissimilarity in nature. An interim conclusion can be drawn: the concept of dissimilarity of cultural objects can, in principle, be further developed from the concept of dissimilarity in nature.

Yet, it is precisely here, at the 'molecular' level, that fundamental differences surface. Molecules are *in* the DNA and unfold their epigenetic effect *in* the species. Likewise, letters and words are in the *Tales*, and lines are in *The Last Supper*, but their cultural 'epigenetic' effect does not unfold there, but in the beholder. Art, for example, is constructed by the artist as representation or exemplification and is interpreted by the beholder, who exploits a degree of freedom in doing so. All the way through to the constructive interpretation of representation and exemplification: the artist's expressive intention clashes with the expressive interpretation of the beholder. This creates ambiguity in culture that is not found in nature. It may well be that Leonardo's *The Last Supper* and *Red Blue Green* are the same at the 'molecular' level, but that does not necessarily imply that both elicit the same effect. Semantics still remains contingent on context and thus open to interpretation.

Do not confuse this cultural ambiguity with chaos. Nature's unambiguity is replaced in culture by consensus. When two people agree that 'a' exists, then, between them, 'a' exists, regardless of whether 'a' is based on, say, 'A' or 'B'. Such consensus can embrace all of society, be limited to savants, or be temporary. But it always follows that those, for whom there is consensus in the interpretation of an object, use it amongst themselves in their o/+consumption to produce social distance and proximity. Cultural ambiguity is no barrier to the social. But it does fragment it. A shared culture, □, reaches its limits where this consensus ends, beyond it another culture with consensus among other people prevails. Cultural trees, chains and singletons, the whole world of objects, $(X, □)$, must be understood as existing and valid only for its consensus community. In all such cultures, the dissimilarities in their respectively ordered world of objects remain, however, the result of bilateral comparisons of objects in a feature space, such as the one in Table 3.

Yet another ambiguity comes into play: a group of people can be in complete agreement as to which features are to be included in a feature space. But they can still disagree on how to interpret the feature values, for example, as binary, cardinal or ordinal values. In Table 3, following Bergesen, a binary interpretation of the feature values has been applied: a painting has either a single focal point or else multiple/no focal points; its lines are either sharp or blurred; it has depth or is flat; it has painted light plus shadows or neither shadow nor light. A principle from nature has been applied: a gene, analogously, has either the feature value a_1 (flat) or a_2 (deep), but never a_1 (flat) plus a little a_2 (deep). Jason Gaiger, art historian and follower of Wölfflin, offers a graduated interpretation of feature values instead.[4] The line design principle, for example, merely marks the extremes on a continuum of gradations in possible line design. Each painting is positioned somewhere between these extremes. The same also applies to the principle of spatial composition. Every painting is positioned somewhere between the very flat and the very deep. With Gaiger, in the unchanged feature space, there are no binary differences between objects, but graduated ones. They are all varying degrees of flat, purple, illuminated, etc. In the 'molecular' order in the arts, therefore, there exists something that does not exist in nature: analogously, not only do the (instruction for) the whale fin and the hippo's toed-foot exist, but so do fin-toed feet as a melange of both. Here, culture is more complex than nature.

Again, it is culture itself that prevents cultural chaos. Not so much by explicit consensus of the viewers on whether the lines in Leonardo's *The Last Supper* are to be regarded as entirely sharply painted versus only fairly sharply painted (*sfumato*), but rather by a shared habit of observation. But even in a world of ordinal gradation of feature values it is still true that, with a shared habit of observing, dissimilarities remain the result of bilateral comparisons of objects in a feature space, such as the one in Table 3.

A subset of the world of objects that is ordered in a feature space can be a totally ordered chain. At one extreme of the chain, an ideal type is positioned as supremum, for example Leonardo's *The Last Supper*, and the chain shows how close an object comes to the ideal type, considering all the features. In Bergesen's binary approach (Table 3), Leonardo's painting receives 1 point for each feature, i.e. a total score of 4; but Raphael's, Kelly's and Pollock's paintings also each receive a total score of 4. On the chain, they are positioned together on the supremum as four specimens with identical feature values. The Tintoretto and the Monet each score zero in all their features and are positioned on the chain's infimum as two specimens with identical feature values. The chain shows the inferiority of these two paintings measured against the molecular ideal of High Renaissance painting.

In contrast, in Gaiger's graduated approach, each painting is assigned a value between zero and one in each feature and the sum of all its feature values marks its position in the chain. Instruction for cultural ordering, □, can also assign different weights to features, for example assigning a larger weight to the focal point principle than to the line design principle.

---

4   Gaiger 2002.

In this simplest case, 'graduated' means leading to marks on a cardinal scale. This interpretation of the feature space makes everything else simple. This is because the comparatively better performance of a painting in one feature can be offset against a worse score for another feature. (In constructing phylograms, evolutionary biologists also use a cardinal scale, like that shown in Figure 1 on the right).

But often, in culture, only ordinal comparisons make sense, for example, of sharpness, depth, shadow. With an ordinal scale, and maintaining the 'molecular' ideal type of the High Renaissance as supremum, you arrive at the same ranking as Gaiger would, with the Tintoretto and the Monet 'behind' the Leonardo, the Raphael, the Kelly and the Pollock. On ordinal scales, however, an advantage in one feature cannot be offset against a shortcoming in another feature.

For instance, to me, Ludwig Kirchner's *Scene at a Café* (ca. 1926), discovered in 2016 under his *Sleigh Ride* (1927-29), shows less depth and less shadowing than *Sleigh Ride* and is thereby closer to the assumed supremum of the High Renaissance. But *Scene* directs my gaze to the void in the middle of the painting, whereas it meanders over the whole landscape of *Sleigh Ride*, so that judged by the focal point principle, *Scene* is further away from the given ideal type than *Sleigh Ride* (note that the semantic commonalty of *Scene at a Café* with Leonardo's *The Last Supper* does not play a role in this syntactic assessment.) *Scene at a Café* and *Sleigh Ride* cannot be neatly ranked according to the 'molecular' ideal of the High Renaissance.

Nature is more starkly ordered. The chain of fossils that documents a live species' evolution is a chain reconstructed in a (morphological) feature space. If a fossil from this chain is also an element of another chain of fossils, at the end of which another live species stands, they are not separate chains, but form in the biologists' understanding a tree, ⋔. This fossil can only be a node or an even older common relic of at least two evolutionary lines. Firstly, because biologists are convinced that all life (including past life) originates from a common origin (the idea of the tree of life!), and, secondly, because the elements at two ends of a branch cannot by definition be ordinally ranked, i.e. the overall order cannot be a chain.

Segmented Order

Culture's complexity can be reduced by taking subsets from the world of objects that can be uniformly ordered, e.g., ordinally. In this example, each object in the subset is ranked in *each* feature against other objects in the subset: a painting that has more depth than another, showing fewer focal points and more blurred lines and shadowing, is therefore positioned further away from the supremum in the chain. An object of this subset is either superior or inferior to another object in all features (unless they are equal in all features). Such a *dominance order*, $\Box_d$, generates cultural chains, $|$.[5*] Table 3 is an example of such a complexity reduction by restriction to a suitable subset of objects, assuming culture dictates Wölfflin's feature space: all six paintings can be grouped into two sets that can be ordinally ranked.

In contrast, Lascaux's cave paintings and Picasso's *Les Demoiselles d'Avignon* cannot be unequivocally ranked in this feature space. But perhaps they can in a different one, archaic style. It is culture – 'crystallised history' – that defines the feature spaces and their corresponding scales. With it, human agency sorts the world of objects into corresponding subsets. This creates the symbolic structure of singletons, chains and trees, {∘, |, ⋔}, the segmented material, with which consumers produce social distance and proximity.

Consumers must come to grips with a multitude of such 'tiny' orderings, standing incomparably side by side. This sets limits as to how much complexity can be reduced. This reducibility of complexity is further limited because an object can simultaneously be an element in different orders. *Scene at a Café*, for example, can be in the dominance order of renaissance, $|_1$, and at the same time in the dominance order of – let's say – the Kirchner Museum Davos' memorabilia, $|_2$. Or *Les Demoiselles d'Avignon* can be in the dominance order of the archaic style, $|_3$, and at the same time with Lyonel Feininger's *Western Sea* (1932) in the dominance order of cubism, $|_4$.[6*] Which order applies to a given situation is determined by culture itself.

Summing up: culture is more ambivalent than nature – Dawkins is right. For example, a floor decoration can be an element of the 'authentic oriental carpets' chain or tree, and it can also be an element of other chains or trees, such as family heirlooms or status objects in the home. There is no cogent logic as to how exactly culture, $\Box$, glues the world of things and behaviours, X, into an ordered set

---

5*   Let K, $K = \{f_1, ..., f_M\}$, be a finite set of ordinal scales $f_i : X \to R$, and $i = 1, ..., M$. The dominance order $(X, \Box_d)$, created by K, is defined as follows: For each $x, y \in X, x \Box_d y$ if and only if $f_i(x) \leq f_i(y)$ for all $f_i \in K$. That is, x is dominated by y, if and only if x and y are distinguishable according to K and $f_i(x) \leq f_i(y)$ for all $f_i \in K$.

6*   Fuzzy logic makes various simplifying assumptions about dominance orders to alleviate clustering in 'fuzzy' tasks. Objects that do not meet the conditions for a dominance order in a given feature space are thereby assigned to different clusters to varying degrees, e.g. to Renaissance painting and archaic style to varying degrees. One and the same painting can thus belong to two styles at the same time, more or less (cf. Bothe 1995).

$(X, \square)$, segmented in $\{\circ, |, \text{ᵐ}\}$. Habits of observation, shared within society and being part of human agency, order the world of objects further. Yet, it remains nearly all the time a segmented one.

This segmentation of order is reflected in the dissimilarity of objects. However, the trivial idea of dissimilarity is not the issue here, that the same things (identical specimens) are nevertheless numerically dissimilar. The issue at hand is the non-trivial dissimilarity of strictly non-identical objects that display qualitative differences of some sort.[7*] These are exactly the objects found in the *0/+consumption* goods type basket.

Comparability

The phylograms of evolutionary biology are based on the following understanding of dissimilarity[8]:

Definition DIS_c: two objects are dissimilar if and only if they are distinguishable and comparable.[9*]

Comparability concerns two objects that are asymmetrically related to each other: object a is darker, older, livelier, smarter or more valuable than object b,

---

7* Every binary dissimilarity relation is irreflexive and symetrical: a and a cannot be dissimilar and if a is dissimilar to b, then b is dissimilar to a.

8   Basili and Vannucci 2013.

9* Definition of dissimilarity as comparability: $P_o(X)$ and $DIS(X)$ are the set of all partial orders and the set of all irreflexive symmetrical relations on X, respectively. A dissimilarity function D from $DIS(X), D: P_o(X) \rightarrow DIS(X)$, is a process for the extraction of dissimilarity relations from X. $\square^{-1}$ is the inverse of $\square$ so that $x\square^{-1}y$ if and only if $y\square x$. For each pair of partially ordered sets $(X, \square_1)$ and $(X, \square_2)$ from $P_o(X)$, $D(\square_1) \neq D(\square_2)$, if $\square_1 U \square_1^{-1} \neq \square_2 U \square_2^{-1}$. Let $\square_x = \{(x,x) : x \in X\}$, and for every binary relation $R \subseteq X \times X$, let $R^{-1} = \{(x,y) : (x,y) \in R\}$ and $R^c = \{(x,y) : (x,y) \in X$ and $(x,y) \notin R\}$. Then for every partial order $\square$ on X, $DIS_c(\square) = (\square U \square^{-1}) \cap (\square_x)^c$. Example: let $\square$ be the ordinal dominance order of purple shades, $\square_d$, with 'almost blue' as supremum, and let $\square^{-1}$ be the inverse ordinal dominance order with 'almost red' as supremum. Then $(\square U \square^{-1})$ are all dominance orders, which rank purple shades either by their red or blue portion. $(\square_x)^c$ excludes all identical pairs of shades, (x,x), one with 'almost blue' and the other with 'almost red' as supremum, from the set of all purple shades, and hence from the procedure DIS_c for the determination of dissimilarity. Comparability therefore only applies to non-identical objects and requires at least an ordinal scale for $\leq$ ordering.

which in turn is more punky or hip hoppy than a. At the very least, ordinal comparability is required. No more than that will be required in the cultural context for most of what follows.

The concept of dissimilarity as comparability will result in the search for dissimilarity in the vertical of the dissimilarity structures | and ⋔. With chains this is trivial, because there is only one dimension, a single association between objects in the subset. In Figure 1 (left side), for example, B and D are more distinctly dissimilar in their shades of purple than C and D; and this can be deduced from (and only from) the relative position of B, C and D in the vertical.

The case is more complicated with trees. In addition to the vertical, there is also the horizontal (Figure 1 right side). But in trees also, two objects can be compared vertically. This is because of the construction principle of trees, which consist of chains joined at (at least) one point. In the phylogram of Figure 1 with the cardinal scale in Myr, by vertical addition of the millions of years, it follows that species C and D are more akin than either of them to B; and these three are more akin than either of them to A. In the cladogram of Figure 2 with the ordinal scale, the vertical structure contains the information that species C and D are more akin with B than to A. And in Figure 3 (left side) it follows from the vertical that Titian's painterly phases B and C are semantically more akin than either of them to A or D, and these in turn are semantically more akin than either of them to B or C.

Obviously, 'vertical' and 'horizontal' only mean 'at right angles to each other', i.e. *orthogonal*. You can turn | and ⋔ on a side and extract the same dissimilarity-as-comparability information from it. Then 'vertical' is simply replaced by 'horizontal' and the fact remains that there is a second dimension in the subset ⋔. I will stick to the convention of the vertical as a source of information about dissimilarity as comparability, because it is the convention in biology to map trees that way.

However, from a subset consisting of singletons, {○,○,○}, no information about dissimilarities can be read, if dissimilarity is understood as comparability, DIS_c. This is because subsets of singletons do not possess a vertical structure, as they are positioned horizontally next to each other without connection. The same holds true for subsets of singletons, chains and/or unconnected trees, {○,○, |, |, ⋔, ⋔}. There, you find structures with verticals and hence comparable objects, but the subset as a whole also contains non-comparable objects.

Ornament

The following ornamental styles can be found in the classic pattern books *L'Orne-ment polychrome* and *L'Ornement des tissus*: primitive, Egyptian, Assyrian, Greek, Etruscan, Greco-Roman, late antiquity, Chinese, Japanese, Indian, Indo-Persian, Arabic, Moorish, Ottoman, Celtic, Byzantine, Russian, Armenian and also the European early medieval, medieval, Renaissance and those ornaments typical of the following centuries.[10] Elements of this subset of around 25 ornamental styles can be compared in various ways.

Objects in the same style show the typical characteristics of the style to a greater or lesser extent. Early medieval ornamentation still works with symbols of ancient Rome – lions fighting knights as the symbolic heritage from the time of the gladiators. Different objects in this style show more or less pronounced suggestions of antiquity. They are thus ordinally comparable in this feature. All these ornamental styles show typical characteristics like these.

Diachronic transitions are yet another point of comparability in ornamental styles. The lily emblem of France, for example, goes back to the 12th century, the time of Louis VII. Over time, however, the French lily changes its shape, so that a lily from the 18th century has no more than a structural similarity with one from the time of Louis VII. The longer and more lance-shaped the central petal is, and the less the two outer petals bend downwards, the older the lily is. More recent lilies show an increasingly pronounced curvature of the outer petals, and all three petals become more similar in length. France's lily can therefore be ordered into younger/older on the (vertical) timeline.

Another point of comparability are geographical transitions resulting from intercultural exchange, commerce or political influence. Along the Silk Roads, from east to west, there are Chinese, Indian, Indo-Persian, Persian, Armenian, Arabic, Byzantine, Venetian and Western European ornaments. You can distinguish them by their ideal type, but the geographical transitions are smooth. Features of Chinese ornamentation can therefore also be found further west, and features of Western styles can be found still further west – and vice versa. Two objects may be more or less Chinese, Indian, Armenian, Arabic or Western European. For example, the so-called *Hom* motif of Western European objects from the 12th–14th centuries shows spotted cats that resemble cheetahs, with collars on (dog) leashes attached to candelabras, evidence of the customs of Asian princes. Quite a few Venetian Renaissance inlays show Persian symbols, indicating intercultural exchange that went hand-in-hand with long-distance trade. And in

---

10   Racinet and Dupont-Auberville, undated (1869–1888 and 1877).

Spanish and southern Italian embroidery patterns dating from the same period you can find stylistic parallels owing to the Moorish political influence in both areas, so that the Spanish and southern Italian ornaments of the time are also a little Moorish.

Diversity Based on Comparability

Dissimilarity always refers to two and only two objects. For more than two objects, I follow the standard terminology in biology, where what is dissimilarity between two objects, for three or more objects is called *diversity*. From the two alternative ideas of dissimilarity – comparability and incomparability – we also arrive at something different for diversity, depending on which idea of dissimilarity you start from. Dissimilarity and diversity thus come in two pairs. The idea of diversity based on the idea of dissimilarity as comparability I call DIV_c. It extracts diversity information from the vertical structure of an ordered set.

Take, for example, a set of species with (extinct) common ancestors. Evolutionary biologists measure the diversity of the great apes (Figure 1, right side) by adding the lengths (representing millions of years) of the vertical branches in their phylogram. Thus $DIV_c = 41$ in Figure 1 (right side). The extinction of a species in the taxon reduces its diversity. For example, $DIV_c = 35$ would result in the taxon of the great apes if species C or D were to disappear.

Evolutionary biologists usually also add to this diversity the dissimilarity (in Myr) between the taxon at hand and its next superordinate taxon. In the example, this is the taxon of the Old World monkeys, from whose total of about 100 species the great apes separated 25 Myr ago. Then, 25 - 14 = 11 Myr is added to the diversity of 41, resulting in $DIV_c = 52$ for the 'rooted' phylogram of the great apes.[11] Step by step, such 'rooting' results in the tree of life. Since we cannot hope to discover the tree of culture, I will put little effort into 'rooting' cultural taxa in this sense, for example, 'rooting' the taxon of ornaments in the superordinate taxon of visual expressions. In culture, 'unrooted' diversity is a more practical concept.

An excursion into the economics of species protection helps sharpen the understanding of DIV_c. Economists, accustomed to tight budgets, base their analysis on diversity information DIV_c when they advise which species should be

---

11   Following evolutionary biology, 'rooted' is meant here, and only here, as the vertical link to the next higher taxon. Later, when addressing social proximity, I will use the term, without quotation marks, in a very different sense: rooted then refers to the commonalities of individual styles in the common style they share.

given priority protection in the interest of the largest possible diversity.[12] In Figure 1 (right side), A contributes more to diversity than C or D. If not all species have the same probability of becoming extinct, economists also take this into account. Suppose D is not endangered, and C and A are equally critically endangered. Economists then conclude that if there is not enough money to protect all, funds should be diverted away from C towards A. The reason is simple: D is a good safeguard for the preservation of diversity, because if C died out, a branch of only 6 Myr would be lost. C is therefore more dispensable than A, which, if lost, would eliminate a branch of 14 Myr. In protecting A and letting C disappear, ('unrooted') $DIV_c = 35$; otherwise it is 27. In the final step of priority setting – since C (presumably) has the same probability of survival as A if both are left to themselves – the economist abandons C and puts the money into the protection of A. This increases the probability of greater overall diversity.

Considering species D and sacrificing C, this calculation may seem perfidious. Nevertheless, there's a more general take-away: diversity DIV_c is based on the idea of an asymmetric contribution of single objects to diversity (of three or more objects). This is because dissimilarity DIS_c, on which it is based, is a symmetrical relationship between two objects *only*. Therefore, one object can make a greater or lesser contribution to diversity than another object in a subset of at least three.

Phylograms, like the one in Figure 1 (right side), are based on a metric scale, as is the chain in Figure 1 (left side).[13*] In culture, we mostly have to settle for noncardinal dissimilarities, as with the semantic variety in Titian's style (Figure 3, left side). It makes no sense to give the dissimilarity between A (the Paduan frescoes) and C (portraits), for example, a distance of 14, as between orangutan and chimpanzee/bonobo/human. Therefore, DIV_c conveys less information. But what diversity information is left? One possibility in Figure 3 is to count the number of nodes, which gives $DIV_c = 3$. Were all paintings of any one stylistic type of Titian's oeuvre to burn, then $DIV_c = 2$, no matter which one burns. The types, viewed in this way, are symmetric in terms of diversity, and thus, in contrast to what is otherwise characteristic of DIV_c, they do not make an asymmetrical contribution to diversity.

Quite rightly, a bad feeling arises. You may accept node-counting when only one stylistic type of Titian's oeuvre burns. But if two go, is it still diversity-neutral which two they are? A (the early Paduan work and all works in this style) and D

---

12   Weitzman 1993.

13*   In chapter 5, the length of a chain will be defined as the (simple) length above the supremum multiplied by the number of its objects.

(works with mythological subjects) are semantically more akin than either of them are to B (works resembling still lifes) and C (portraits). If A and D were to both burn, you might justifiably feel worse than if D and B were to burn. Because then you would still have remaining two rather different types within Titian's individual style, his Paduan frescoes (A) and his portraits (C), still documenting an impressive range of his oeuvre. In the first case, you would be left with only the still lifes (B) and portraits (C) and thus a smaller selection of his oeuvre. Somehow, by simply counting nodes, information (the degree of kinship), expressed in the length of branches, has vanished. The greater ambiguity in culture compared to nature also pertains to the choice of scale.

In culture, this ambiguity leads to cautious statements. *The Canterbury Tales* are the exception. Archaeologists, art historians, art critics and linguists, not to mention philosophers, feel the need for this caution because culture, $\square$, is more stingy than nature in its instructions for forming dominance orders, $\square_d$.[14] They fluctuate between apodictic rejection of what economists recommend based on the idea of asymmetric contributions to cultural diversity, and apodictic glorification of the elitist idea that not each and every piece contributes the same to cultural diversity (e.g. the high brow versus low brow divide). In this seesaw of contrasting positions, those taking the elitist position that there are more and less valuable cultural items, implicitly rely on the idea of diversity based on comparability, *DIV_c*.[15]

Consumers are in that mess too: Louis Armstrong records, purple batik, prints of Klimt paintings and a vintage car in the garage may find meaning in it as a whole or just in parts. But the meaning is firmly set by the dissimilarity of two objects, together with their twin, the diversity of overall *0/+consumption*. But consumers are not only confronted with a single twin-type of dissimilarity/diversity, namely dissimilarity as comparability and diversity based on comparability. Incomparability is an equally potent basis for dissimilarity/diversity considerations.

---

14   Here, it is worth noting the difference between culture, $\square$, and culture, $\square_d$. Culture, $\square_d$, is the (dominance) order-creating authority in the world of objects. It is culture, then, that decreases disorder. But to limit the whole of culture to this capacity would rightly meet with fierce opposition from cultural studies. Because culture is also a driver of disorder, of breaches of taboos and conventions, and only this makes development possible. For this reason, a distinction should be made here between the 'smaller' culture, $\square_d$, and the 'larger' culture, $\square$. The latter maintains the balance between order and disorder, as well as the continual fragmentation in all cultural order.

15   For example, Haselbach, Knüsel, Klein and Opitz 2012.

Incomparable Ornaments

In spite of graduated transitions, and thus partial (vertical) comparability, ornamental styles remain incomparable in a fundamental sense. Take, for example,
the Viennese art historian Alois Riegl, who decoded the arabesque in the late 19th
century. Riegl discovered the formal design pattern of the arabesque in the pro-
files of the lotus blossom and the palm frond protruding fan-like from a goblet-
shaped stem (semantics). As two complementary forms, they ornament ceram-
ics, textiles and the scrolls of column capitals. Riegl traced the ornamental evolution from the stem into the later design element of the line, which later unfolds
in wavy bands, which themselves can be combined into continuous ornamentation. Thus the arabesque is born, which has been stripped of its origin of representative elements derived from plant shapes (semantics) and now relies entirely
on the complex play of geometric patterns (syntax).[16] Riegl's decoding of the arabesque thus proceeds from the semantic to the syntactic; only there does he find
the specifics of the arabesque.

Alois Riegl had always rejected the two explanations for design that were
prevalent in his time – the dictate of the technical properties of the media being
worked on (materialism), and the dictate of natural forms (naturalism). Thus,
with Riegl, the arabesque (or any other ornamental style) is no longer caught in
an artistic corset that would allow for comparability across ornaments. Statements about what is special about an (ornamental) object cannot be made either
from the way the material is handled, nor by drawing analogies with nature.

Riegl instead credits the arabesque (and every other ornamental style) to a
universal impulse of the human spirit, its *kunstwollen* (art volition): the human
desire to use aesthetic forms to express something specific about the broader human context. *Kunstwollen* comes from the human need for expression. Riegl fell
into oblivion after his *kunstwollen* was criticised by other art historians, including
the founder of art history iconology, Erwin Panofsky. Interest in Riegl has since
been reawakened and the conceptual potential of his *kunstwollen* for art history is
now acknowledged. Also acknowledged is that members of the guild, such as
Ernst Gombrich and his London Warburg Institute, have always implicitly relied
on it. Riegl's *kunstwollen* was always quietly present.[17] *Style volition* of consumers,
in their striving for social distance and proximity, is as present in QTC as Riegl's
kunstwollen, as the quest for utility of *homo economicus* is always present in the orthodoxy.

---

16   Arnheim 1995.

17   Elsner 2010.

In *kunstwollen* we find one cause for the incomparability of objects. According to Riegl, what wishes to be expressed arises from a specific social and intellectual reality. Expression obeying *kunstwollen* serves to convey this reality. Because this reality is context-specific, so must be a style.

Take, for example, the post-revolutionary neo-classical American style. The Americans' *kunstwollen* was aimed at expressing the cultural values of a new era, cleansed of absolutism. Due to this specific historical ideology, it is fundamentally incomparable with the Rococo of the former British colonial masters, which aimed at allowing the splendour of the monarch shine everywhere. Take another example from Riegl himself: the late Roman style was an expression of growing social uncertainties specific to the times. In conclusion, *kunstwollen* creates context-specific styles, i.e. incomparable styles and incomparable objects belonging to different styles.

Riegl's *kunstwollen* reveals that the search for ornamental dissimilarity necessarily involves our acceptance of the existence of incomparability. It is only because of this incomparability that the concept of different (for example, ornamental) styles makes any sense at all. They are incomparable precisely because they are different forms of the otherwise universal human desire to create art – restricted by nothing other than their specific social and historical contexts. You find such fundamental incomparability not only in ornamentation, but in all forms of art and handcrafts, and not only there, but also in the most mundane things.

Incomparability

I refer to this idea of dissimilarity, widely implicit in cultural studies, as *DIS$_{ic}$* with the definition:

DIS_{ic}: two objects are dissimilar if and only if they are incomparable.[18*]

Incomparability presupposes that two objects are distinguishable and implies that they are not comparable (a tautology). However, this implies most importantly for all else that follows, that two objects that are incomparable stand in a *symmetric* relationship. They cannot be brought into a (vertical) hierarchical

---

[18*] Definition of dissimilarity as incomparability (see notation of footnote 9*, this chapter): $DIS_{ic} = \left(\Box \cup \Box^{-1} \right)^c$. In words: DIS_{ic} are all dissimilarity relations between two objects that are not a dominance order, i.e. do not produce an $\leq$ ordering.

relationship but remain (horizontally) side by side. With the idea of dissimilarity as incomparability, the banker style does not stand above that of punk. They remain side by side, as strangers in a way that does not allow classification of one being 'above' or 'below' the other. It is the same with the relationship between the arabesque and the Celtic styles, or between Rococo and the neoclassical American styles.

The notion of dissimilarity as incomparability, in dissimilarity structures {○, |, ⋔}, leads us to search for dissimilarity in the horizontal. For singletons this is by their definition imperative. Two singletons, (○,○), are incomparable because they are singletons. In a chain, |, elements are by definition comparable, so incomparability can only refer to a chain as a whole. Since elements of a chain are only comparable in this chain, you can take one of their elements, for example their supremum *pars pro toto* and place it (horizontally) next to the supremum of another chain. Two unconnected chains, (|, |), are incomparable, simply because one element from each chain, for example their suprema, placed side by side, are incomparable. That is, two unconnected chains are incomparable because they are not branches of the same tree. In a tree, ⋔, elements of two chains/branches above their connecting node are comparable, below this node they are incomparable in a fundamental respect.

Despite belonging together in the taxon depicted in the phylogram in Figure 1 and thus despite their (cardinal) comparability (in Myr), species A, B, C and D remain incomparable in a fundamental respect. Humans and chimpanzee/bonobo have become incomparable through their different development over the last 6 Myr in a way that is not discounted by their also being comparable. In this fundamental respect, the objects in phylograms and cladograms are incomparable. It follows for sets of singletons, chains and trees, (○,○, |, |, ⋔, ⋔) in general, that all singletons and the suprema of all unconnected chains and the suprema of all trees are incomparable.

Diversity Based on Incomparability

As has been shown, diversity based on comparability, DIV_c, is built extracting diversity information from the vertical structure of ordered sets. Diversity based on incomparability, DIV_{ic}, is based on the extraction of information from the horizontal structure of ordered sets, i.e. the structure that escapes dominance ordering. The basic structure for determining DIV_c is the chain/branch. In the ('unrooted') phylogram of Figure 1, $DIV_c= 41$ is therefore calculated by adding the lengths of the branches. The basic structure for the determination of DIV_{ic} is the opposite of the chain/branch in the horizontal, the *antichain*. I symbolise the antichain with $\sqsubset\!\sqsupset$.[19*] In Figure 1 (left side), the antichain consists of a single element, for example (D). In Figure 1 (right side) and figure 2 the antichain is (A, B, C, D), in figure 3 (left side) it is (A, D, B, C). An antichain is a totally dissimilar subset – no single element is (at least) ordinally related to another: the barong tagalog from piña, the shoe of Manitu, Duchamp's *Fontaine*, the lollipop, the Imperial Orb at Aachen, the Veil of Veronica.

Diversity based on incomparability, DIV_{ic}, can in principle be determined by numbering the objects in the antichain. Let this number be #. In Figure 1 (left side) the antichain (as in case of a singleton) consists of, for example, (D), i.e. #=1. In Figure 1 (right side) and Figure 2 the antichain is (A, B, C, D), i.e. #=4. In Figure 3 (left side) antichain (A, D, B, C) also numbers #=4. In principle, diversity based on incomparability of a set, (X, $\square$), is DIV_{ic}=#($\sqsubset\!\sqsupset$). Diversity is the cardinality of the antichain.

'In principle' warns of the necessity of choosing between alternative antichains beforehand, whose elements are then counted. Because, in (∘,∘, |, |, m̂, m̂) there is usually more than one antichain. Figure 4 is for illustration. There are 4 horizontal layers of objects. The shortest horizontal antichain (at the top) counts #=2, the next two below #=3, and the lowest #=4. Depending on the choice between these antichains, DIV_{ic} is therefore 2, 3, or 4. In addition, there are 'diagonal' antichains, such as those that include the topmost element in the tree and the second, third, or fourth object in the chain (from the top). However, none of them are longer than the lowest horizontal antichain, numbering #=4, and none are shorter than the top horizontal antichain, numbering #=2. If there were also singletons in the subset, their number would have to be included in the equation for #($\sqsubset\!\sqsupset$).

If more than one antichain exist, which one is to represent diversity? The simple answer is: it depends on the context. The maximum and the minimum (horizontal) antichains possess special appeal. For biodiversity protection, the longest (horizontal) antichain is of particular interest. In Figure 4, this would be the lowest horizontal antichain with #=4. The interest in biodiversity protection draws attention to the greatest diversity and thus the longest antichain. In the cultural

---

19*   Definition of the antichain: Let ‖ be the incomparability relation based on $\square$. From footnote 9*, this chapter, ‖= DIS_{ic}= ($\square \cup \square$-1)^c. The binary relation ‖⊆X ×X comprises the set of all pairs ordered as incomparable, given $\square$: For each x,y∈X, x‖y, if and only if x$\square$y and y$\square$x. An antichain $\sqsubset\!\sqsupset$ of (X,$\square$) is a set A⊆X, so that x‖y for each x,y∈X with x≠y.

context this also applies to historical monument protection.[20*] Nevertheless, the shortest antichain must not be ignored for the diversity count. For example, in a context where originality matters most, attention is drawn away from the highest possible number of originals to the lowest possible number.

Figure 4: Multiplicity of antichains.

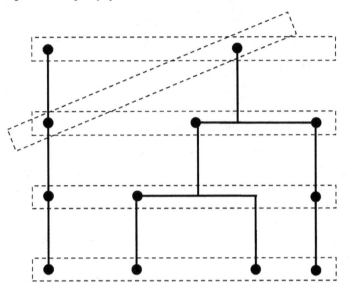

Example of a set consisting of a chain and a tree with a total of twelve objects (black dots). The objects in a perforated rectangle each form an antichain.

Take-away: Ontology of the World of Objects and the Social Realm

As Table 4 reiterates, dissimilarity as comparability and diversity based on comparability come as a pair, just as dissimilarity as incomparability and diversity based on incomparability do. The question now is whether these twin-pairs are simply two alternative perspectives of the ontology of the world of things, i.e. the

---

20* Basili and Vannucci (2010) show that there are at least two different methods for selecting the antichain for the diversity count: search for the longest antichain, or search for the antichain consisting of exclusively undominated elements. In Figure 4, both are identical (the lowest horizontal antichain), but in general they are not.

consumption space existing 'out there', or whether they are two fundamentally different ontologies of the world of objects. I advocate for the latter.

Table 4: Different perspectives or different ontologies of the world of objects?

		Diversity (multilateral)	
		upon incomparability	upon comparability
Dissimilarity (bilateral)	incomparability	(DIS_{ic}, DIV_{ic})	
	comparability		(DIS_c, DIV_c)

As an outside observer, you may choose to see the world of objects $(X, \square)$ through the lens (DIS_c, DIV_c) or through the lens (DIS_{ic}, DIV_{ic}).[21*] Evolutionary biologists have historically had their pick of these alternatives. Nothing stands in their way, because in biology the two twin-pairs are in fact different scientific perspectives on the one ontology of nature.

You could treat the consumer's world of objects in the same way. But that wouldn't help to better understand the production of social distance and proximity scientifically. Because it doesn't help knowing which lens is available to the outside observer for the analysis of the social, you must know which lens consumers actually use when o/+consuming. For when the outside observer uses the (DIS_c, DIV_c) lens of biologists, whereas consumers judge their o/+consumption by looking through the (DIS_{ic}, DIV_{ic}) lens, the outside observer will not understand them.

Consumers must have *already* seen the dissimilarities and diversity in the world of objects *beforehand*, so that they can make consumer decisions. That is, they must make their consumer decisions looking through one of the two lenses. This in turn implies that the lenses cannot offer the analyst *access to* the ontology of the world of objects $(X, \square)$ existing 'out there'. Instead, the lens is itself *part of* this ontology. Consumers' choices are not based on their knowledge of $(X, \square)$, but their knowledge of $[(X, \square), (DIS_i, DIV_i)]$, with $i = c$ or $i = ic$.

[21*]   Specification of the lens analogy using footnote 9*, this chapter: the lens is the dissimilarity function D from $DIS(X)$, $D: P_o(X) \rightarrow DIS(X)$, only through which surfaces dissimilarity-cum-diversity (DIS_c, DIV_c), or (DIS_{ic}, DIV_{ic}). The main text simplifies this analogy by equating lens D with its projection (DIS_j, DIV_j), $j = c$, ic on the wearer's retina.

Yes, in this I cross the line to constructivism in epistemological terms: the world of objects awaiting consumption is not simply there like nature, which the biologist sees. Dissimilarity and diversity of $(X, \square)$ are not predefined, but are constructed by consumers with (DIS_i, DIV_i). In other words, the world of objects $[(X, \square), (DIS_i, DIV_i)]$ would not exist without the consumer – it only exists through the consumer. However, this is not by deliberate choice of human agency: the consumer does not choose their lens (DIS_i, DIV_i), but has it firmly in place.

Contrary to this view, you could now proceed as orthodox Identity Economics does.[22] It first lets the consumer choose identity, assuming identity-specific (orthodox) consumer preferences. The consumer chooses their identity in such a way that their lifetime utility is maximised, anticipating the effect of the identity choice on their future preferences. *0/+consuming* can be thought of precisely this way, by replacing identity with (DIS_i, DIV_i).[23*]

This is not my way of proceeding, because *0/+consumption* (DIS_i, DIV_i) serves the communication of social distance and proximity. It therefore must be understood by third parties. Hence the consumer cannot simply choose a (DIS_i, DIV_i) lens, instead it is already firmly in place. But not once and for all. I argue that (DIS_i, DIV_i) is situationally fixed, just as there are lenses for distance vision and for near vision. In one situation the consumer has the (DIS_c, DIV_c) lens in place, and in another situation the (DIS_{ic}, DIV_{ic}) lens, because everyone else in the same situation also uses this lens. In this situation, it is only because of this that they can communicate with each other with their *0/+consumption*. (DIS_i, DIV_i) can therefore be understood as a situation-specific convention that everyone adheres to for the moment. Put this way, $[(X, \square), (DIS_i, DIV_i)]$, $i = c$ or $i = ic$, is the habitual way of looking at the world of objects following that convention in a given situation.

For the production of social distance and proximity, in-group situations (within one's own elective affinity) and out-group situations (*vis-à-vis* other elective affinities) are of key importance. The question is: is the social situation at hand an issue of social distance to other groups or of proximity in the in-group? I will focus on these two situations as the relevant contexts of consumption. Through which lens, i.e. following which convention of viewing, are groups confronting each other? And through which lens, i.e. following which convention,

---

22   Akerlof and Kranton 2010.

23* The consumer chooses (DIS_i, DIV_i), with $i = c$ or $i = ic$, knowing its effect on $[(X, \square), (DIS_i, DIV_i)]$ and chooses $i = c$ or $i = ic$, depending on which of the two lens alternatives maximises utility.

do members of one's own group face each other? I argue that social distance is created by way of the (DIS_{ic}, DIV_{ic}) lens convention and social proximity is created by way of the (DIS_c, DIV_c) lens convention.

Psychology of Distant and Near Vision

Gerhard Schulze's claim that we can be alienated from each other in a way that leaves us speechless can be stated more formally: the alienation stems from the (DIS_{ic}, DIV_{ic}) way we look at things, bringing the incomparable into the foreground and letting the comparable disappear. No other way of looking at things allows for a quicker and more reliable construction of social distance. Conversely, there is no better way to construct social proximity than letting the incomparable disappear and bringing the comparable to the fore. This basic pattern, of grasping a social situation by letting certain parts of what is there disappear, and moving other parts into the foreground, has been studied in social psychology.[24] The application of this basic pattern to the issues at hand is shown in Table 4.

In the first step, by *situation-classification*, the individual organises the perception of their environment, including the world of objects: is it a work, happy hour, vacation, or family situation? If the situation is interactive, i.e. a social one, the world of objects is classified in a way that also takes other individuals into account: what is this object in this interactive situation involving these people? Social classification is self-referential, i.e. the objects shown by other individuals are classified in terms of similarity and dissimilarity compared to objects the observer shows. Which implies that the individual is aware of the bilateral dissimilarities, DIS_i, between themself and the individual under scrutiny.

Step two is *meta-contrasting*. It consists of two psychological mechanisms. Both sharpen the distinctions between the in-group and out-group(s). The first mechanism lets group members appear more homogeneous to the observer than they actually are: the observer tends to see what everyone in a group is showing and to overlook what distinguishes them from one another. This results in the in-group member looking at what connects them with their in-group. Connectedness requires at least comparability. Without comparability there is no possibility of connection! The (DIS_c, DIV_c) lens, as per my assumption for QTC, is the lens for internal social relations within a group. It is always used by the individual, when it comes to checking their place in the in-group. [$(X, \square)$, (DIS_c, DIV_c)]

---

24   Bessis, Chaserant, Favereau and Thévenon 2006.

is the culturally ordered world of objects for the moderation of intra-group relations.

The second mechanism of meta-contrasting lets the in-group and out-group(s) appear more different than they actually are: the individual tends to see what lets groups differ and to overlook what they share. The individual looks at what separates their in-group from the out-groups. Their gaze is drawn to what is incomparable between the groups. The (DIS_{ic}, DIV_{ic}) lens, as per my assumption for QTC, is the lens for external social relations of each group. It is used by group members when observing what's special about their own group *vis-à-vis* other groups, affirming their distance from them. [$(X, \square)$, (DIS_{ic}, DIV_{ic})] is the culturally ordered world of objects for the moderation of the external relationship of a group.

This constructed perception of the social is not a purely cognitive phenomenon, but at least as much a self-evaluative one. The groups brought to the fore by the egocentrism of the (collective) perspective end up clearly separated from each other and internally cohesive. The individual thus finds their place in the social, i.e. their social identity, with which they can be content: on an equal footing but apart from other groups, by [$(X, \square)$, (DIS_{ic}, DIV_{ic})], and connected with other in-group members by [$(X, \square)$, (DIS_c, DIV_c)]. All that is moderated by the culturally ordered world of objects. Table 5 summarises this construction of the world of objects by situation classification and meta-contrasting.

Table 5: The situation-classified and meta-contrasted world of objects of individualistic society.

		Social Situation	
		out-group	in-group
Meta-contrasting Lens	for distance	[$(X,\square),(DIS_{ic},DIV_{ic})$]	
	for proximity		[$(X,\square),(DIS_c,DIV_c)$]

Proximity in the Collectivistic versus Individualistic Society

In Table 5, bilateral proximity is operationalised by DIS_c, i.e. by (a form of) *dissimilarity*. We could operationalise social proximity by *similarity* instead.[25*] Both concepts of proximity are operationalisations of the notion of non-identity (in the mathematical, not in the socio-psychological sense). In their formal denomination they differ only slightly, but in their social connotation they are fundamentally different.

Their formal difference becomes apparent when considering the gradual transition from (mathematical) non-identity to (mathematical) identity. If object a has become increasingly similar to object b to eventually almost be b, then with the operationalisation of proximity based on similarity you can rightly claim the statement "almost b and b are similar" to be true. Also the statement about identity, "b and b are similar", is true. Now, turning to the operationalisation of proximity based on dissimilarity, DIS_c, the statement "almost b and b are dissimilar" is formally just as true. But the statement about identity, "b and b are dissimilar", you cannot claim to be true. Therein lies the formal difference between similarity and dissimilarity. In the mathematical transition to the identity of two objects, similarity relations include identity whereas dissimilarity relations do not.

Reversing this thought experiment, however, you will end up with statements that are always formally true: If object a increasingly differs from object b until both have almost nothing in common, the statement that they are (still) similar is formally as correct as the statement that they are dissimilar. However, transferring the thought experiment to the social throws a spanner in the works.

Regarding the social, the statement that I (being a) and my in-group role model, (who is b and whom I almost mirror) are similar, is not only formally correct but also socially telling. But given the same situation, the statement that we are dissimilar is only formally correct. Socially it has no bearing whatsoever, it's just splitting hairs. The same holds true in the opposite direction: the statement that a and b – who have almost nothing in common anymore – are dissimilar, is not only formally correct but also socially telling. But the statement that they are (still) similar is only formally correct, communicatively it is splitting hairs without any social bearing.

This is only confusing at first. We simply have a degree of freedom in interpretation. If I consider one formally correct statement to be telling and the other to be splitting hairs, it is because (with the very best of intentions) I am projecting

---

25* Every binary similarity relation is reflexive and symmetric: a and a are similar and if a is similar to b, then b is similar to a.

ideas, paradigms, prejudices, etc., from my outside perspective into this open space of interpretations. This projection is exactly my definition of interpretation. Some projections are simply better than others.

I propose to make emic projections. That is, to model how the consumer perceives the world in which they live. As I have argued so far, consuming is a communicative action addressing the in-group and out-groups. To adequately model this action regarding the modelling alternatives of similarity versus dissimilarity, it is first necessary to answer the question: what does the consumer intend to achieve with in-group communication? Do they want to fuse with the in-group, to be one with it, or the role model within it? Or is the aim to sublimate their own individuality in the group while adhering to the restrictions imposed by group cohesion?

In a group-wise fragmented but collectivist society, the first motive is stronger: everyone wants to disappear into their in-group. This is where the statement that I (being a) and my imitated in-group role model (who is b) are similar, is not only formally correct but also in emic terms. In contrast, the equally formally correct statement, "we are (still) dissimilar", is not correct in emic terms in case of a collectivist society. Having approximately reached my goal of fusing with others there cannot be residual dissimilarity, similarity must be attained. Here, similarity is the emic concept of proximity within groups. Jewish communities in the diaspora are one example. They maintain distance from the outside and are collectivist inside. The Asian personality is another example.[26] This personality more actively seeks to fuse with its in-group than the Western one. For Asian societies, similarity is therefore the emic operationalisation of proximity.

The second motive is stronger in an individualistic society. Everyone is a member of an elective affinity, but none want to disappear into it and lose their individuality. "We are different" is communicated to the outside, "I am special" is communicated on the inside. Even when two members of a group (a and b) are by chance approximately matched, they do not see their similarity, but the remaining dissimilarity. And if the unthinkable were to occur and everyone were to become exactly the same, their individuality would completely vanish, and the concept of dissimilarity would no longer be conceivable. For an individualistic society, dissimilarity is the emic operationalisation of proximity within groups.

Nevertheless, the loner is not the ideal type in individualistic society. The ideal type is someone who accepts help, when working on their identity, from others in the chosen elective affinity, without surrendering individuality.

---

26 Heine and Buchtel 2009.

Internal cohesion is provided by the cement of their common style, within which all group members can cultivate both their individuality and commonality. Unsuitable for this purpose is dissimilarity defined as incomparability, DIS_{ic}, since it is needed for creating rifts between elective affinities. But dissimilarity as comparability DIS_c, is adequate for securing individuality in social groups. When looking at internal individual styles, attention is drawn to what is comparable but non-identical, to what binds together and at the same time makes individuality visible. Youth cultures, neo-tribes, *Bobos in Paradise*, the Creative Class and last but not least the remaining mainstream of Western society are examples of such groups in the individualistic society. In this society, the individualistic consumer produces proximity by means of preserving dissimilarity as comparability. For this reason, Table 5 cannot be transferred to collectivist societies; it applies (only) to individualistic ones.

This individualistic consumer receives undivided attention in the second part of the book. The analysis of the collectivist consumer will remain an unfinished task. Its exclusion is necessary, because in the field of culture there is no 'one size fits all'. Culture is not universal, though it is universally present. Therefore, consideration of culture requires acceptance of cultural differences. Therefore, in the following I will explore the consumptive production of social distance and proximity in Western, individualistic society.

Distant and Near Vision and Style

Heinrich Wölfflin's differentiation of individual and common artistic style can now be merged with dissimilarity/diversity. Remember: individual style is manifested in the works of a particular person (known by name or not); in which resides the artistic signature that makes that person unmistakable. Thus, Titian's individual style is manifested in his oeuvre. A style which, while in proximity with the individual styles of other High Renaissance painters, nevertheless retains its distinctiveness – its artistic non-identity with this group of painters. Contrary to the individual style, the common style fails to refer to a specific originator. It serves taxonomic purposes only – for example, classification as a picture in the High Renaissance style. Table 3 is another example of such a taxonomy; the artists' names only serve to uniquely identify the works; they bear no relevance in the attribution to their common style. The common style merely implicitly refers to a group of originators who may be unknown both in name and number, but who share commonalities in style. Someone is assigned to a common style, not because of who they are themselves, but because of these commonalities.

I apply this conceptual distinction, between common and individual artistic style, to style as mediator of social distance and proximity. The common style identifies an elective affinity, which manifests itself solely in its common style, expressing the proximity of all its members. It is through this style that an elective affinity as a whole distinguishes itself from other elective affinities. The set of common styles defines the set of elective affinities in society and vice versa. If there are n elective affinities, there are also n common styles.

The individual style shows the distinctiveness of the individual within their elective affinity. The member remains a distinct individual, no matter how close all members are. The individual style simultaneously creates both proximity within the elective affinity, as well as the individuality striven for within the individualistic society.

The common style thus moderates social distance outward, and the individual style social proximity within the elective affinities. Which is why everyone is viewed with specific meta-contrasting lenses (see Table 5) and everyone is building on the world of objects thus construed from the stylistic inventory: the common style building on $[(X, \square), (DIS_{ic}, DIV_{ic})]$ and the individual style building on $[(X, \square), (DIS_c, DIV_c)]$. Table 6 summarises this correspondence.

Table 6: Situation-specific styles.

		Social Situation	
		out-group (external demarcation)	in-group (internal differenciation)
Function of Style	moderation of social distance	common style building on $[(X, \square), (DIS_{ic}, DIV_{ic})]$	
	moderation of social proximity		individual style building on $[(X, \square), (DIS_c, DIV_c)]$

The individual artistic style refers to an individual originator, and shows their distinctiveness and the uniqueness of their oeuvre. The common artistic style refers to a group of works of multiple origins, and indicates artistic proximity therein. That is, the individual artistic style unmistakably shows something that is discernible as typical in the common style. In other words, the individual artistic style is nested in the common style, varying from it in sublimation or attenuation, but never beyond its boundaries. Applied to elective affinities, each individual is distinguished by two styles: their own individual style and the common style of their elective affinity. Here too, the individual style is nested in the common style, varying from it in sublimation or attenuation, but never beyond its boundaries.

The crucial point for everything that follows is that consumers cannot nurture their individual style with one subset of the world of objects, while contributing to the social distance of their elective affinity with another subset. They must accomplish both with one and the same subset of objects. The *one* subset they choose, together with the chosen subsets of all other in-group members, moderates social proximity within *and* social distance *vis-à-vis* the out-groups. Individual style and common style are therefore two different tools cast in the same mould. This is because, depending on the social situation, two meta-contrasting lenses create from *0/+consumption* either the common or the individual style (Table 6). The two tools from the same mould are interdependent though: manipulation of social proximity affects social distance, and vice versa. This trade-off turns *style volition* of consumers into an economic problem, and its result – human *stylisation* – into a cultural-economic phenomenon.

By explicitly acknowledging the interdependence of the individual and common styles (and thereby of social distance and proximity) I implicitly model a transparent social present. How someone lives today may not yet be completely transparent, but it is more transparent than it has ever been before. Stylistic Dr Jeckylls (common style) and Mr Hydes (individual style) become decreasingly sustainable in an increasingly transparent world. In the following I will discuss the transparent (individualistic) society, in which nobody has anything external that does not also exist on the inside, and inside nobody has anything that can be concealed from the outside.

Part 2: The Productive Consumer

Not only does the orthodoxy pretend that increasing quantities of goods are the source of happiness/utility. Implicitly, it also pretends that happiness/utility are sold to the consumer. Everything of economic impact on the consumer's happiness/utility must pass through the market first. For the orthodoxy, the market is the key process in the economy. From this premise, it is only logical to define the value of goods as exchange value and ignore the use value of things. The blinkered scientific view that this entails is evident by now. As is the very different understanding that results when, within the Quality Theory of Consumption (QTC), the curation of social identity becomes the focus instead of the exchange of goods.

Another consequence of the orthodoxy's market focus is its division of economic agents into two (ideal) types: producers and consumers. The one type supplies and sells what the other type demands and buys. Consequently, the orthodoxy also pretends that, *grosso modo*, people do not themselves produce what they consume. Here too, the orthodoxy is flying blind, now concerning the value chain of the consumer sector as a whole. Contrary to this, Part 2 is devoted to a radically different, cultural-economic understanding of this value chain.

If people consume social distance and proximity, they consume what they produce themselves in their capacity as consumers. Because, if you accept the idea of consumption of social distance and proximity, you can hardly reject the idea of self-production of that same social distance and proximity by the consumers themselves. QTC puts the production of social distance and proximity by consumers in the foreground and, consequently, the production (contribution) of industry in the background. If you accept the idea of self-production by consumers, you might also consider two follow-up theory-building paradigms of QTC.

Firstly, the individual effort to produce social distance and proximity is merely individual input into their collective production. What individuals produce, they always produce as an in-group, i.e. collectively, and in symbiosis with their out-groups, in which other individuals input individually into their respective in-groups. Social distance and proximity are produced collectively because they are produced by communicative acts. The first follow-up paradigm is this: self-production by consumers is collective production.

Secondly, the collective production of social distance and proximity is not a process separate from consumption, in the way that home-gardening precedes the eating of the harvest – first one and then the other. Not only does it happen simultaneously with consumption, but is inseparably fused with it. Consumers produce by consuming, and they cannot consume unless they produce. The second follow-up paradigm of QTC is this: social distance and proximity are produced by consumption in its communicative capacity.

Part 2 deals with this production process of social distance and proximity. In the combination of both paradigms, it is not the market that is the key process in economic activity, but culture instead. Culture turns consumption into a communicative act without which the social cannot be produced.

Chapter 4
Inside Culture's Sorting Plant

"When I saw the light of day and then the mid-
wife, I was stunned. I'd never seen this woman
before in my life."
Attributed to Karl Valentin

It happens all the time: one doesn't know exactly how to classify a thing, a behaviour, a person. When shopping, one comes across unfamiliar things. Is that textile part of an authentic traditional costume or a new retro designer piece? Or, one finds things that are familiar in and of themselves, but which are somehow not exactly the way one knows them: is it a corkscrew or a decorative toy for adults? The uncertainty is disturbing, and one draws on other sources of information: the merchandise on display next to it, the overall impression of the shop – luxury boutique or junk shop (too bad if one is surfing the web). Or when observing others: are they taking a lunch break or are they just hanging around? Or, is the guy in the biker outfit at the bar a real rocker or a businessman on a day off? Some uncertainty remains. One can't clearly assign the thing, the behaviour, the person to a style or a group, even when considering all available information. The consumer has to cope with that uncertainty, because only then can they make sense of what others want to tell them by their choices from the world of objects, and successfully communicate back.

The challenge is pattern recognition in things, behaviour and people, despite fuzzy information. One has to decide which objects, showing fuzzy patterns, belong to which style. Or decide to which social group a person should be assigned. What further complicates the issue is that the types and number of styles and social groups are not set in stone. A changing bouquet of styles makes a changing bouquet of social groups. These are the challenges that mark out the consumers' scope of action and the means they have at their disposal to cope with the situation.

Pattern Recognition

By way of illustration, take the example of Table 3: you have six objects, x_i, (paintings by Leonardo, Tintoretto, Raphael, Kelly, Monet and Pollock), or in general a subset $\underline{x_i}$, $\underline{x_i} = (x_1, \ldots, x_N)$, of N objects. You also have a feature vector, with four features differentiating these objects, m_j, (principles of focus, line design-, spatial composition, illumination), or generally a feature vector $\underline{m_j} = (m_1, \ldots, m_j, \ldots, m_M)$ with M features (an M-dimensional feature space). Each object, x_i, is therefore characterised in the feature vector $\underline{m_j}$ by the object-specific feature values $\underline{m_{ij}} = (m_{i1}, \ldots, m_{iM})$. Leonardo's *Last Supper* has the feature value $\underline{m_{ij}}$=(multiple, sharp, flat, without). More generally, every object, x_i, can be characterised by its feature value $\underline{m_{ij}} = (m_{i1}, \ldots, m_{iM})$. I denote this characterisation with $\underline{x_{ij}}$. In Table 3 there are six such characterisations, generally N, with $\underline{x_{ij}} = (\underline{m_{1j}}, \ldots, \underline{m_{Nj}})$.

The consumer's challenge now is to put each of these N objects, characterised in this way, into one of n object clusters whose components 'match up' in the feature space. Matching means that two objects from the same cluster demonstrate a better fit in their feature values, $\underline{m_{ij}}$, than each of them has with any object from another cluster. In Table 3, Leonardo, Raphael, Kelly and Pollock are a good fit and therefore belong in one cluster, while Tintoretto and Monet belong in another cluster.

Table 3 dealt with two given clusters, labelled Renaissance and Baroque, and the task was to determine which paintings belonged more to either of them. Let Q_k be a given cluster label and suppose there are L of them. The challenge for the consumer is to sort each element of a subset $\underline{x_i}$ – a googled list of slippers, a storefront display, an assortment of hats stacked in the store or a collection of pictures on a wall – into one of the clusters $Q_1, \ldots, Q_L$, according to their characteristics, $\underline{x_{ij}}$.

It goes without saying that one and the same feature vector, $\underline{m_j}$, is not equally apt for every conceivable subset of objects $\underline{x_i}$. Sorting six bottles of wine on the basis of Wölfflin's painting features would make as little sense as sorting six paintings using the features space of the Parker's Wine Guide. Suppose, for sorting the world of objects, X, into clusters, the consumer has K alternative feature vectors at their disposal, $\underline{m_1}, \ldots, \underline{m_j}, \ldots, \underline{m_K}$, which may include Wölfflin's and Parker's. But which of these feature vectors will the consumer apply to a concrete subset, $\underline{x_i}$? Two answers are possible, and both have their merits.

The first answer lets the applied feature vectors be exogenous – as if by an invisible hand. Conjured out of a hat by culture, $\square$, when ordering $(X, \square)$, which also includes the assignment of feature vectors, $\underline{m_j}$, to objects, $\underline{x_i}$: That is $\underline{x_i}$ from

X already presents itself to the consumer in fixed combination with situation and subset-specific feature vectors $\underline{m}_j$. Consumers perceive $\underline{x}_i$ and $\underline{m}_j$ inseparably merged as $\underline{x}_{ij}(\square)$, with $\underline{x}_{ij}(\square) = \left(x_1, \dots, x_N, \underline{m}_j(\square)\right)$. Be it internet recommendations, storefront displays, a wine cellar stock, that of a second-hand shop or a luxury boutique, the assortment in a gallery or a record store, the consumer perceives them in a situation and subset-specific way in an automatically activated feature space. Perception is subset-specific, because a medal shown on a carnival costume is appraised differently than one shown on a tailcoat. Also, perception is situation-specific, because the tailcoat at the carnival ball is different from the tailcoat at the Nobel Prize ceremony.

What does that imply? The consumer has no agency here! The manipulation of the feature vector, $\underline{m}_j(\square)$, remains outside their control. What is the impact of culture in this? I have introduced culture into my previous argumentation as 'crystallised history'. It is time to clarify this notion.

If culture pulls the feature vectors out of its hat, subset and situation-specific, then 'crystallised history' is the consumer's library of 'operating instructions' for the clustering of the world of objects. And just like the operating instructions for a technical device, those for the clustering of subsets within the world of objects are the same for all users: human agency is – handling mistakes aside – automated.

This psychological mechanism is known as the 'perspect manager'.[1] It lets people do the right thing, as if guided by an invisible hand. We don't throw a lighted matchstick into a petrol tank to see if there is still fuel in it. And we don't have to explicitly decide against it by considering all alternative light sources – it works automatically. We automatically do many things right, i.e. appropriate to the situation, because the perspect manager suppresses that part of our total knowledge (about the luminosity of the matchstick and about the total inventory of all feature vectors), which is redundant or even dangerous for the accomplishment of a given task. Thus, the eye scans a painting for focal points, searches the surface for depth and notices light and shadow. But when the eye scans a land map, completely different features move into the foreground. The perspect manager not only prevents people from doing stupid things when checking the fuel tank, it also provides consumers with the right $\underline{m}_j(\square)$ for the specific classification tasks, $\underline{x}_i$.

The second possible answer to this question of selecting feature vectors is this: the consumer experiments. Trying this and that, applying the feature vector $\underline{m}_h$ to that same subset, $\underline{x}_i$, whose elements all other consumers classify by the

---

1   Lengbeyer 2007.

feature vector $\underline{m}_j(\square)$. Resulting in a different classification. This is exactly how the supermarket of styles (chapter 2) was born: archaeologists, art historians, critics and philosophers are experimenting with new pairs of terms – signature versus expression, the how versus the what, etc. – and are thereby constantly creating new feature vectors for classifying artefacts.

In their own world of objects, consumers can do the very same. Men's long hair is classified in the feature space of individuality, say, instead of in that of hygiene (military); the tattoo is classified in the feature space of fashion, instead of in that of social marginalisation (sailors, prison inmates); and insects, instead of in the feature space of the disgusting, are classified as food by way of the feature space of environmental responsibility.

This experimentation clearly carries the risk of failure, that the experimenter will be the only one to apply this feature space. On the upside, however, there is a chance that others will follow, adopting the new feature space and beginning to see the world of objects with fresh eyes. The ultimate success is the change of culture, such that $\underline{x}_{ij}(\square)$ is now removed from the library of the perspect manager and replaced by $\underline{x}_{ih}(\square)$, and long hair on men is now seen as a feature of individuality, a tattoo as a feature of beauty, insects appreciated as a delicacy.

Experimenting with feature vectors, $\underline{m}_h$, is a source of style innovation and therefore not everyone's cup of tea. Its use is reserved for an elite, who are the nucleus of new styles and elective affinities, although they may not be fully aware of it. In this interpretation, the consumer has agency; not every consumer, but those turned into the avant-garde by a random name generator or their own destiny, who have the industry's trend scouts hot on their heels.

So, which is the right answer? Both are right! With the help of the avant-garde only, there could be no 'crystallised history', no widely practised way of seeing things, of classifying them. The world of objects would lose its function as a medium of communication, styles would die out and elective affinities became extinct along with them. But without an avant-garde, there could be no cultural development either. History would not just be crystallised for now, but remain the same for all time, and no one could explain how it came about.

Thus, we are bound to accept a special paradigm of human agency: $\underline{m}_j(\square)$ is fixed for the majority of consumers, only a few can (successfully) manipulate the feature space for classifying objects. I call them the *style leadership*.

Fuzziness

What is the source of the fuzziness that troubles the consumer, if the perspect manager selects the feature space for them in such a manner that doubt never crosses their mind? There are three causes of fuzziness in pattern recognition.

First, a particular feature can be either a crisp or a fuzzy idea. Natural features are usually crisp, such as the weight and size of a painting. The definition of a natural feature is usually beyond doubt. But the perspect manager does not only provide natural features – sometimes $\underline{m}_j$ ($\square$) contains not a single natural element. Unnatural features are fuzzy. The feature space of Table 3 is a case in point. Leonardo's *Last Supper* has multiple focal points, *Number 1* has none and Tintoretto's *Last Supper* has one. This is easily agreed upon. But does Kirchner's *Sleigh Ride* have one, two or three focal points, Günther Uecker's calligraphic *Kama Kura* paintings (1984) one or not even one? We can all agree that there are focal points, but where exactly the border is between focal point(s) and lack of focal point(s) remains unconfirmed. This uncertainty stems from the fact that 'focal point' is a semantic term whose meaning is under permanent negotiation or else remains un-negotiated. The same applies to the line design principle. What exactly is a line in the viewer's perception? Is a rectangle's outline a line? Is the rectangle itself a line when the ratio of unequal side lengths is less than 1/x? The same goes for the spatial composition principle. What precisely does space in a two-dimensional object mean? Is it the perspective perfected in the Renaissance, with two vanishing points? Do the well-known staircase drawings in the reversible-figures technique convey the impression of space or (by revealing an illusion) of physical flatness of the canvas surface? The same holds true for the illumination principle. What exactly is a shadow, and where does light commence? Tintoretto's *Last Supper* demonstrates what light and shadow are. But is there really nothing of this in Pollock's *Number 1*? All this fuzziness stems from the semantic nature of these features. Even 'painting' as a medium is a fuzzy concept. All six objects in Table 3 are the results of applying moist chemical substances to a surface. But are Niki de Saint Phalles' colour orgies paintings or sculptures? Or, is René Magritte's *Ceci est un morceau de fromage* (1936), the still life of a piece of cheese exhibited under a cheese dome on a miniature easel, a painting or is it object art? What is a railway carriage 'embellished' by graffiti sprayers? Polychromy and monochromy are natural physical features, like weight and size, but what about the terms 'coloured' and 'not coloured'? Does physics always trigger the same thing in us? Is *Number 1* 'coloured'? Or does it depend on which object it is compared to? Compared to *Red Blue Green*, no! Compared to *Kama Kura*, yes! If you look at it alone, well, maybe! The idea of the feature itself causes fuzziness, although the idea as such should be crisp. In culture, the perspect manager provides the consumer with semantic rather than natural feature spaces: coolness, elegance, luxury, asceticism, hip hop, etc. Fuzziness is part of the daily cultural routine.

Second, for almost all cultural features, the choice of scale is a fuzzy task. Differences in size and weight are measured on a metric scale. Take as an example the cardinal colour shades in Figure 1 (left side). In the field of culture, however, you often have to settle for ordinal scales. What exactly does 'more focused' mean, for example? Is it easy to spot focal points in a painting and is it straightforward to sum them up, meaning a cardinal scale could be used? Is this how the eye (and the brain behind it) functions? Or will it cease counting after five identified focal points, or after only two, assigning paintings with more focal points to the category of 'multiple' or 'no' focal points? The temperature of a mojito can be measured in Celsius, but how 'cool' is it as a drink? Still? Today? In this situation? Decisions cannot easily be made at the feature level. Not making a decision does not here mean that two people are arguing about it, but that the consumer as an individual cannot make sense of it. Sometimes we simply do not know how 'cool' an object is, not even in comparison with other objects. We're just convinced that it is somehow 'cool'. All that remains to do then is to take the object (because of this feature) out of the given subset of comparable objects and place it in another subset (singleton, other tree) that is incomparable to it.

Third, there is also the type of fuzziness that has already been exemplified in chapter 3. In cases where a subset of objects, $\underline{x_i}$, can be ranked ordinally, it is pure chance if the ranking in one feature is the same in all other features and the consumer is faced with a dominance order, $\underline{x_{ij}}(\square_d)$. Then each of the paintings considered has the same rank for all features. But too bad if there are conflicting rankings, for example in the line design principle and the illumination principle. In chapter 3, using ordinal scales, two such objects were simply left standing next to each other, unranked, because one cannot subtract opposing rankings, for example in the illumination and line design principles. Yet, this third cause of fuzziness does not categorically exclude the classification of such subsets, for example in paintings in the Renaissance or perhaps the Baroque style.

Assigning Objects to Styles

Fuzzy logic has a number of different classifiers – procedures with which a given object, x_i, can be allocated to one of L object clusters, Q_k, given a feature vector, $\underline{m}_j = (m_1, ..., m_M)$.[2] And for that purpose, a subset of N objects, which have been ranked in each of the M features, $\underline{x}_{ij}(\square)$, needs *not* be a dominance order, $\underline{x}_{ij}(\square_d)$. The question is, however, how the consumer is able to handle this task. Presumably they'll try out a simple procedure that doesn't produce counterintuitive results.

Consider the (ordinal) feature values $\underline{m}_{ij} = (m_{i1}, ..., m_{ij}, ..., m_{iM})$ of object x_i. The consumer could simply consider only the extremes of $\underline{m}_{ij}$ for classification. Take, for example, the classification of a painting as either Renaissance or Baroque. The one extreme value could be a third rank, in terms of the number of focal points – two ranks behind the one stylistic ideal, Leonardo's *The Last Supper*, and one rank behind Raphael's *Galatea*. And in terms of illumination intensity, suppose it ranks only second to the other stylistic ideal, Tintoretto's *The Last Supper*. Following fuzzy logic, the beholder would then classify the painting as Baroque. Stylistically, it also has something of the Renaissance (in terms of focal points), but in its extremes it is more baroque (i.e. in terms of illumination). The beholder may well be left with a twofold feeling of unease.

First, the consumer must classify N paintings (in a museum, on the internet, in a quiz) as either Renaissance or Baroque, but in the way just exemplified, their classification depends on the given subset of paintings as a whole, $\underline{x}_i$. With two more paintings with the Baroque (stylistic) intensity of a Tintoretto, the beholder would classify x_i as being Renaissance, because the highest rank in the Baroque features would now only be rank four. The beholder will have to live with that! Style cannot be defined in absolute but only in relative terms, relative to objects in different styles. Which is why a world with only one style has no style. Which in turn is why, in a world with two or more styles, everything remains and must remain relative. It is like a dictionary: if a new entry (i.e. a new object) is added to the subset, it can only be defined in words from the already existing entries, which, in turn, can change their meanings depending on the new entry.

Precisely this insurmountable relativity is what the founder of (European) semiotics, Ferdinand de Saussure, has postulated. The style of an object is its meaning, and nothing but meaning, and can therefore only be relative. The styles of ornamentation, even Alois Riegl's *kunstwollen*, design styles (such as aesthetic functionalism, technicism, demonstrative aestheticism, deconstructivism, post-

---

2   Bothe 1995.

modernism, Memphis, gadget design), as well as music and painting styles can only exist relative to each other. 'Existence' is not abstract existence here, but existence by comparison to concrete objects from different styles. Which is why, regardless of the style at hand, the conceptual structure of art books on a style, for example that of the Nabis or the Vienna Secession, is *grosso modo* always the same: positioning it in a style system *vis-à-vis* referential styles, followed by detailed art-historical and art-critical treatises, in which general conclusions are drawn referencing concrete works.

The second feeling of unease arises in the beholder when all features do not seem equally relevant to every style. The focus principle may be deemed less relevant for the Baroque – Rubens' *Three Graces* (1635) has three focal points – but the line design and illumination principles may be deemed all the more important. And the illumination principle may be less important to the beholder for the Renaissance than the focal point principle – after all, Raphael's *Miraculous Draught of Fishes* (1515) also shows a little light and shadow. Overall, it may seem to be too simplistic for the beholder to take the extremes of features simply as they are.

This unease is partly lifted if features are given the 'right' weighting. Let γ $(\underline{m}_j)$ be the 'sympathy vector', defining the degree of membership of the feature vector $\underline{m}_j = (m_1, \dots, m_M)$ to L style clusters Q_k: γ $(\underline{m}_j) = \left(\gamma_{Q_1}(\underline{m}_j), \dots, \gamma_{Q_L}(\underline{m}_j) \right)$. The sympathy vector, with values between zero and one for each feature, determines how important a feature is for the assignment of an object to style Q_k. For example, the top rank for the focal point principle (a single focal point) does not assign a painting to the Baroque if the weight for this principle, for assigning an object to this style, is zero, i.e. if this feature is irrelevant for classification into this style.

Let's call the largest feature value, weighted with the sympathy vector, the 'primary sympathy value'. Classification, then, is still not a trivial task for consumers, but it is perhaps manageable for them, consisting of assigning objects that have already been assigned feature values, $\underline{x}_{ij}(\Box)$, into a style according to their primary sympathy value. All they need for this task, in addition to the ranking in the feature space provided by the perspect manager, $\underline{x}_{ij}(\Box)$, is the 'right' sympathy vector for each style. But what is the 'right' sympathy vector that the consumer should apply?

Again, there are two good answers – as was the case with the question about where the feature vector came from in the first place. And they are the very same answers. The first one deprives the consumer of agency and assigns the choice of sympathy vector to the perspect manager. Assessing the relevance of features for a set of styles is, once again, not everyone's cup of tea. Here too, culture can be described as 'crystallised history': Just as culture provides consumers with the appropriate feature vector for each subset of objects, $\underline{m}_j(\square)$, it also provides them with the style-specific sympathy vector, $\underline{\gamma}\left(\underline{m}_j\right)$. In this interpretation, the sympathy vector is $\underline{\gamma}\left(\underline{m}_j\right) = \underline{\gamma}\left(\underline{m}_j, \square\right)$. This means the sorting of objects into styles, controlled by the perspect manager, is a habitual process for the consumer.

The second, equally good answer, reassigns agency to consumers. The avant-garde, and others striving for style leadership, experiment with $\underline{\gamma}\left(\underline{m}_h\right)$ hoping that others will follow their lead in the weighting of features. Only a few succeed. The industry trend scouts are hot on their heels here too.

Similarity of Objects

It was emphasised in chapter 3 that dissimilarity, not similarity, is the appropriate concept for the relationship between two objects in *consumption*. This still applies. But in the sorting plant of culture, in which consumers are *at work*, sorting precedes consumption. First, that which belongs together is brought together, and only then is that which remains divided consumed. Sorting follows similarity considerations. It is not what is dissimilar that is thrown together, but that which is similar. That is, consumer happiness/utility only results from the *production* of object clusters according to similarity criteria. This is the first step towards clarification of the term 'productive consumer', which untill now I have been rather vague about.

But what does 'sorting according to similarity criteria' actually mean? The consumer's sorting procedure described so far is already deeply imbued with style. This sorting procedure relies on style-*specific* criteria – the feature vector, $\underline{m}_j$, in combination with the style-specific sympathy vectors, $\underline{\gamma}\left(\underline{m}_j\right)$. This is simply due to the exogeneity of object clusters, Q_k, assumed so far. But a style itself is nothing more than such a cluster of objects. In other words, assuming preset clusters, the consumer is forced to sort every object into one of the given L clusters, without exception, even if some do not actually fit into any of them. Accordingly, an oriental carpet, say, shall be classified as belonging either to the design style of aesthetic minimalism (Walter Gropius) or to Memphis (Ettore Sottsass). In doing so, the consumer is prohibited from defining a new style, i.e. from sorting two similiar objects into a new cluster, which do not fit anywhere else in the given set of clusters. For example, to define the oriental style separately from the furnishing styles of aesthetic minimalism and Memphis. Nor is the consumer allowed to eliminate, for example, Memphis and assign the objects already sorted into it to aesthetic minimalism or the oriental style.

But the consumer is free to do this if necessary – sorting objects on the basis of their features alone, without restrictions on the drawers into which they can be put. For this, an idea of the similarity of two objects *per se* is needed, freed of predefined styles. Their use for utility generation only comes afterwards. This is why I call the individual, who sorts objects by similarity criteria, the *worker* in the sorting plant of culture. The worker becomes a *consumer* only once they perceive the world in terms of utility generating dissimilarity criteria.

A similarity measure developed in fuzzy logic is *rank distance*.[3] Applied to the worker in the sorting plant of culture, it concerns the ranking of a subset of N objects, $(x_1, ..., x_i, ..., x_N)$, on a feature vector, $\underline{m}_k = (m_1, ..., m_M)$, which is provided by the perspect manager, and is cluster-*independent*. Cluster independence here means the worker has no prior knowledge of the object clusters/styles, $Q_1, ..., Q_L$, into which these objects will be finally sorted. With this task, the clustering into styles is dependent on a given subset of objects, as opposed to the previous task, where the clustering of a single object was made dependent on a given (sub)set of clusters/styles. Feature values in the feature vector $\underline{m}_k$ are rank numbers, r_k, for each feature, m_k, such that every object, x_i, is represented by its rank vector $\underline{r}_i = (r_1, ..., r_k, ..., r_M)_i$. The rank distance d_{ij}^r between two objects x_i and x_j is then a weighted sum of all rank distances $|r_{ki} - r_{kj}|$, $k = 1, ..., M$, where r_{ki} and r_{kj} are the kth ranks in the rank vectors $\underline{r}_i$ and $\underline{r}_j$.

But what properties should the rank distance between any two objects satisfy? The worker in the sorting plant of culture might make the following plausible requirements, which are summarised in Table 7.

---

3   ibid.

Table 7: Relativity of rank distance between two objects.

Rank Distance Principles
1. **Minimum Principle:** Two objects with identical rank positions in all features (identical properties) have zero rank distance.
2. **Maximum Principle:** The greater the number of features considered, the greater the maximum rank distance.
3. **In-Between Principle:** The rank distance between two objects increases if an element is added to the subset of objects and this element is ranked between them in at least one feature and in no feature dominates both or is dominated by both.
4. **Outside Principle:** The rank distance between two objects decreases if an element is added to the subset of objects and this element dominates both objects or is dominated by both in at least one feature and is not ranked between them in any feature.

First, for any two objects, the minimal rank distance should be zero, which is always achieved when two objects occupy the same rank for each feature (minimum principle). In the binary version of Table 3, for example, Leonardo's *The Last Supper* and Raphael's *Galatea* have the same rank for all features and the rank distance is therefore zero.

Second, the maximal rank distance should increase as the number of features used for object comparison increases (maximum principle). Tintoretto's *The Last Supper* and Kelly's *Red Blue Green* have diametrically opposed values for each of the four differentiating features. Thus, the distance between them is maximal. If, however, the dichotomy between representation versus exemplification were to be included as an additional differentiating feature, Raphael's painting would have the characteristic 'representation' and Kelly's the characteristic 'exemplification'. The worker in the sorting plant of culture probably wants a measure for rank distance that also possesses the second characteristic. That is, in the example, increases the rank distance between Raphael and Kelly because they also differ in this additional feature.

Third, the rank distance between two objects should be sensitive to the presence of an additional object to be ranked. In Table 3 the two versions of the *Last Supper* have the maximal rank distance. If a new object, for example Magritte's

The Treachery of Images, moved between them in one or more features, then the rank distance between the two versions of the *Last Supper* should increase (in-between principle).

Fourth, if Duchamp's *Fontaine* is added to Table 3 as the seventh work of art, which is so different from the other six paintings in all features, then the rank distance between the two versions of the *Last Supper* should decrease. Because now, despite all the differences between them that persist, *vis-à-vis Fontaine* they can be regarded as more similar than before (outside principle).[4*]

Rank distances that have these four properties allow for a flexible sorting of subsets of objects into clusters that are not predefined right from the outset. Without the Duchamp, the worker in the sorting plant might want to form two clusters for the objects in Table 3. Whether he calls them Renaissance and Baroque or A and B is of no importance. With the Duchamp in the subset, things look different. The worker might want to stick with just two clusters but put all six paintings of Table 3 in one cluster and make the Duchamp the sole member of the second cluster, as a singleton. Or the worker might want to have three clusters – with the Kelly, Pollock and the Duchamp together in one of them – and call them Renaissance, Baroque and the postmodern. How this cluster formation is to be achieved will now be addressed.

Clustering in Nature

The procedure for clustering in evolutionary biology can be shown by the example of the phylogram of the great apes in Figure 5 (left side). Clustering at the great ape level is only one of many alternatives. It could instead be done at the superordinate taxonomic level of approximately 100 Old World monkeys. This would result in a lengthening of the phylogram in Figure 5 (left side) in the vertical and widening in the horizontal to a total of approximately 100 branches (not shown here). Or else New World monkeys could be added too, which would enlarge the tree again in both dimensions, length and width. And so forth, extended further and further to the phylogram of the fauna, which could even be extended to include the flora. With ever greater rank distances between them, up to the (imagined) tree of life, which vertically connects, i.e. makes comparable, the

---

[4*]   The rank distance according to Kendall, $d^r_{ij} = 1/(h-1)^2 \sum_{k=1,...,M} \left(r_{ki} - r_{kj}\right)^2$, with $d^r_{ij} \in [0, M]$, satisfies these four conditions, with h being the number of objects and M being the number of features.

human being and the bacterium, and thereby showing their similarity compared to non-living material.

In evolutionary biology, clusters are formed by capping an (imagined) tree (of life), albeit starting from its trunk. This divides a set X (for example, of all life forms) into two, then three or more subsets. The more clusters formed this way, the shorter the branches of the trees. Just as when a cauliflower turned upside down is separated from the main stalk with a knife. The further away from the stalk you cut, the more, smaller and shorter pieces you get. With this 'haircut in a headstand' method, increasingly smaller and more numerous clusters are formed from the (imagined) tree of life, on different taxonomic levels, for example, the clusters $Q_1, ..., Q_K$ at the level of fauna families. Eventually, such continued 'haircutting' leads back to the initial cluster of Figure 5 (left side) as one of $L, L > K$ clusters. However, the options for clustering are still not exhausted. For example, the *haircut* could be placed at the level of the horizontal line d_N in Figure 5 (left side). Then the cluster of the great apes falls apart into two new ones, with A (orangutan) as the only member in one cluster and the other great apes in the other cluster. Ultimately, the haircut will be so short that there is only one species left in each cluster. In Figure 5 (left side) there are then four clusters. In the general case of the (imagined) tree of life there are then as many clusters as there are living beings on the taxonomic species level, which is the basic set, X, on which the tree of life stands.

Figure 5: Clustering.

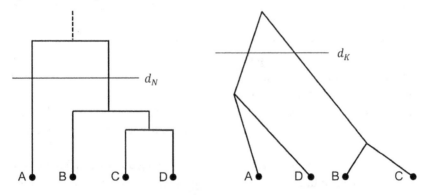

Left: in the phylogram of great apes. Right: in the cladogram of the semantic variety in Titian's style.

Clustering as a *method* of evolutionary biology aims at determining d_N in the tree of life, whereby the number of clusters and the distribution of species in the clusters are determined. The threshold value d_N determines the maximal height of the tree of each cluster. Nodes above lead to other clusters, nodes below connect species in the cluster.

The above procedure results in an important general cluster characteristic: all pairs of objects (species) in a cluster are more similar than any pair from different clusters. I will apply this basic idea of clustering in nature to culture. But I have to acknowledge a complication: in culture, there are generally no cardinal scales available for clustering as there are in nature. Mostly, only ordinal scales are available. In order to apply the method from evolutionary biology to the field of culture, the ordinal scale must first be converted into a cardinal scale. The concept of rank distance from Table 7 is useful for this purpose.

Clustering in Culture

Titian's semantic style cladogram in Figure 5 (right side), only contains ordinal information, for example that A and D are more similar than A or D and B or C (and vice versa). Rank distance, d_{ij}^r, is, however, defined on a cardinal scale. Cardinal scaling is problematic in culture, as has been already stressed a number of times. However, the concept of rank distance does not presuppose cardinality in culture. It merely deduces cardinality from the available ordinal information. This is because rank distances are derived solely from ordinal rankings of objects, $\underline{r}_i = (r_1, \dots, r_k, \dots, r_M)_i$, in the feature space, $\underline{m}_j$. Therefore, the core idea of the 'haircut in a headstand' method is solely based on such intuitive ideas as those summarised in Table 7. The similarity of two objects is lower the more other objects are ordinally ranked between them in a given feature, and the more features this applies to. Similarity is greater the more objects there are that have not moved ordinally in between them. And identical rankings are possible. These are modest demands on the world of objects, which are not generally unachievable in the field of culture.

The semantic variety in Titian's individual style is just one example. In a simple, initial approach, the feature vector, $\underline{m}_j = (m_1, \dots, m_M)$, only generates a two-dimensional space, i.e. $\underline{m}_j = (m_1, m_2)$. Feature m_1, say, shows itself in the work as the significate 'the human being as the most special in all of creation', and feature m_2 as the significate 'the human individual in its own particular highs and lows of being human'. Titian's Paduan early works (A) and his late mythological phase (D) are positioned next to each other (or on equal rank) in feature m_1, with his still lifes (B) and portraits (C) in third and fourth place respectively. Let's apply to this the rank principles of Table 7.

The existence of B and C lets A and D move closer together in terms of rank distance and vice versa. This is intuitive and is what people always do when ranking three (or more) objects by their features. While two of them may have already been ranked before, when a third is added, the previous two are seen in a different light. And looking at the first two objects, but taking an additional feature into account, they are again seen in a different light. Titian's early Paduan works (A) and his late mythological phase (D) rank in feature m_2 behind the still lifes (B) and portraits (C), which are at the top of this list in this feature, one immediately after the other. Once again, A and D move closer together, as do B and C, and thus both pairs move further apart.

Using the intuitive rank distance principles from Table 7, the variety in Titian's semantic style, obtained by ordinal comparisons only (Figure 3), has been replicated in Figure 5 (right side). Therefore, the use of the rank distance concept, with its cardinal scale, is not *per se* an impermissible analytical operation in the field of culture. The field of culture is not closed to cardinal scales, only they have to be chosen with care. The rank distance with its properties from Table 7 reflects ordinal aspects of comparison that connoisseurs of culture (such as art historians and art critics) deem important. When constructed from rank distances, length as a measure of diversity, based on comparability, can make sense in culture as well. The phylogram representation, in other words, is not necessarily incompatible with culture.

I claim that consumers too, are capable of making similarity assessments of objects as expressed in the rank distance principles. For this, as an inexperienced museum visitor, the consumer does not need to know what Renaissance is, nor know Titian's stylistic signature. It is sufficient when consumers understand their own similarity assessments as for the time being only, and are ready to revise them if new considerations arise in the form of additional reference objects or additional features. It is in this sense that I define the productive consumer as an economic agent that is *able to learn* in the world of objects.

In culture, the threshold value of the rank distance, d_{ij}^r, has the same function as the threshold d_N for clustering in nature. Rank distances, d_{ij}^r, above the threshold are those of objects in different clusters. Higher thresholds tend to result in fewer clusters with more objects in them. Lower thresholds tend to result in more clusters containing fewer objects. Distance d_K in the cladogram of Figure 5 (right side) *represents* (has the same effect as) the threshold for the rank distance: reduction of d_K tends to result in more clusters containing fewer objects and vice versa. However, d_K *is* not the threshold value of the rank distance, because in a cladogram, visualising ordinal relations only, it would be meaningless as a cardinal value.

Using the threshold for rank distance, the worker in the sorting plant of culture can perform clustering by shifting d_K up or down. This is also a purely ordinal procedure. If it is adjusted as shown in Figure 5 (right side), two clusters, Q_1, Q_2, follow, Q_1 containing objects A and D and Q_2 containing B and C. With this threshold, the beholder regards Titian's Paduan frescoes and his mythological paintings as being so different from the still lifes and portraits that the pairs are packed in different clusters. Until further notice, they belong to separate trees. For the beholder, the differences in the semantic features have been brought to the fore so much that similarities between objects belonging to different clusters seem to disappear. The perspect manager accomplishes this as well.

The perspect manager determines the level of abstraction at which clusters are formed in the 'haircut in headstand' method. Several options always exist. In art, clusters can, for example, be formed at the genus level (music, object art, performing arts) or at the geographical (Asian, American, African, European) or epochal level (antiquity, Medieval, Renaissance, etc.). Or, clustering can be done within an epoch, say within modernism, into abstract, figurative, naïve art, Surrealism, Pop Art, the modern classical, Cubism, Art Nouveau, etc. Different clusters are created by different levels of abstraction, defined by the perspect manager. The higher the level of abstraction, the greater the order of the output of culture's sorting plant, the lower the level of abstraction, the less ordered its output.

The question of human agency leads once again to the already familiar answers. For most of the individuals the perspect manager does the 'haircut'. Style leaders, on the other hand, manipulate the threshold value d_K. As the style leadership's following grows, the threshold set by the leadership is taken over by the perspect manager of the style followers. The ordering {∘, |, ⋔}, of the world of objects (X, □), is crafted by style leaders, and as 'crystallised history', it is their legacy. Be they political leaders like Peter the Great or Ramon Magsaysay, philosophers like Herder or Kant, artists like Bowie or Warhol, or nameless people, it is the style leadership that bequeaths the way in which the world is seen as ordered.

Style Leadership and Innovation

From what has been said so far, I can now define the scope of actions of the individual – human agency. Two types of agency exist, the style followers and the style leaders, which interact via the perspect manager. Style followers are controlled by the perspect manager, which in turn is (partly) controlled by style leaders. Table 8 lists the scope of action of individual agency.

Table 8: Individual agency.

Individual Agency in the World of Objects	
Style Leader/Experimenter	*Style Follower*
Manipulates the feature space $m_j(\square)$ and thereby the characterisation of objects $x_{ij}(\square)$	Adopts $m_j(\square)$ and hence $x_{ij}(\square)$
Manipulates the sympathy vector in case of cardinal feature values $y(\square, m_j)$	Adopts the sympathy vector $y(\square, m_j)$
Instructs on how to cluster, e.g. to reward extreme or moderate feature values	Follows the instructions
Sets the threshold value d_K for clustering	Performs clustering with the threshold value d_K
Enlarges the world of objects as inventor $(X, \square)$	Deploys inventions
Reactivates pre-existing objects for a style	Dares using reactivated objects
Both jointly determine the viscosity of the style by their *0/+consumption*	

The productive consumer is productive either as style leader or style follower. Depending on this, they have different options for action.

Style leaders/experimenters can manipulate a style by manipulating the work performed by style followers in the sorting plant of culture. They have various options for action. They can induce style followers to search the world of objects for new features or to disregard previously heeded ones. They can induce them to alter the weighting of features in the case of cardinal feature values they themselves may have set. They can induce their followers to cluster objects by giving priority to moderate or extreme feature values. And they can induce the clustering of the world of objects into more or less finely subdivided styles.

The above manipulations of their followers depend on communication. Style leaders may write or speak, but they communicate most effectively by showing. Setting an example, they show what they think is suitable for their followers. Or their followers take example from the leadership, which they did not intend to be followed.

Style leaders have yet another option for manipulation. They can be inventors by enlarging the world of objects, X. Works of art are such inventions, as are new DIY consumer goods, or amateur performances like parkour, or the music of the

Sex Pistols. Through the creation of inventions in the world of objects, new styles may even appear as if from nowhere. It is in this sense that Picasso's *Demoiselles d'Avignon* (1907) is regarded as the pioneering work of Cubism.

Alongside inventions for the world of objects, there are also (re-)activations of objects (formerly) used elsewhere, which now suddenly belong to a given style. Style leaders in hipsterism amply apply this innovation technique. The jute sack, the sleeveless, white, fine-ribbed undershirt worn visibly, the cheese cutter cap, horn-rimmed glasses and the moustache – all these things existed before. Hipster style leaders merely retrieved them all from consumerism's warehouse. And it is not a rare occurrence that the inconspicuous (the jute sack before reactivation in hipsterism) or something utterly alien to a style (the mohawk hairdo before activation in punk) turns into a paradigmatic object that stands almost on its own for the style as a whole.

Such style leadership manifests itself only superficially in the introduction of reactivated objects into a style. The crucial question is how style leaders can succeed in such a coup. After all, the perspect manager had previously manipulated the followers into giving object, x_j, the rank distance, d_{ij}^r, which is 'larger' than the threshold level, d_K. This is exactly why that object had initially been sorted out of this style. This makes it clear that the stylistic innovation technique of reactivating an object must be futile without the aid of one or more of the other manipulation options in Table 8. Reactivation will only be successful if style leaders are able to modify the way in which followers work in culture's sorting plant. The fine-ribbed undershirt, the mohawk hairdo, the tattoo or the petticoat must be legitimised into a style by the style leadership, by way of their manipulation of the work practices in culture's sorting plant. This legitimization process has been studied in detail in a number of cases. For instance, how the tattoo, previously classified as subcultural (sailors, criminals), has become fashionable in the mainstream.[5]

Human agency in the world of objects, as summarised in Table 8, is a differentiated concept. In particular, it is not limited to the purchasing act alone, as is assumed by the orthodoxy. There, it is essentially a stunted concept, limited to calculation, purchase and devouring, however much methodological individualism pretends to properly account for self-determination and autonomy of action. But this is not what actually happens in this scientific practice.

Human agency, as defined in QTC, is rich in the means by which people pursue their goals. Human agency is rich because it includes the shaping of culture, which is a non-issue in the orthodoxy. There, the individual acts *de facto* outside

---

5   Irwin 2001.

of culture, because, due to assumptions regarding its options for action, it has no way of influencing it. In QTC, culture is 'crystallised history' that has been written by the style leadership. It is the history of stylistic innovation. Style leaders and all those who dared to experiment with the world of objects wrote this history. And all those who experiment with it today continue to write it.

Style followers have more limited options for action. They are told by the perspect manager how to see the world of objects. For them, culture cannot be shaped. Culture remains 'crystallised history' as long as they do not dare to experiment with the world of objects. In spite of this, the theory of the style follower, as presented here, is still a richer theory of action than that contained within the orthodoxy. There preferences for alternative goods have fallen from the sky. In QTC the style follower also has exogenous (sorting) preferences, but these preferences are endogenously shaped by style leadership.

Repertoire and Structural Fluidification

The agency specified in Table 8 is an operationalisation of the repertoire theory of culture, which determines a set of evaluative criteria by which people justify their entitlement.[6] Within QTC this entitlement concerns social distance and proximity. Culture's instructions given to its sorting plant, form this set of evaluative criteria, by which style followers justify their entitlement. This set is in turn manipulated by the agency of style leadership. The order created by the sorting instruction, $(X, \square)$, is the communicative repertoire with which these entitlements are realised, for example by communicating one's own 'discriminating taste'. From the perspective of repertoire theory, culture is not a general way of living, but a 'toolbox', $\square$, of mental frames, schemata and categorisation modes, with which people make sense of the world.[7] In QTC, this world is the world of objects and with the repertoire of style leadership the world is changed.

The agency developed here shines a light into the black box of alternative sociological theories. Bourdieu's sociology of distinction is a structural theory in which pre-existing class structure determines class-specific preferences, which in turn stabilise that structure.[8] For him, culture is 'crystallised history'. The agency summarised in Table 8 (right side) coincides with Bourdieu's view if you assume that there are no style leaders/experimenters. Agency then is reduced to

---

6   Boltanski and Thevenot 2006.

7   Swindler 1986.

8   Bordieu 2010.

the execution of all that the perspect manager prescribes, which in turn dictates that which stabilises the social structure. Societal development is non-existent. That is typical of modernist sociology, from the viewpoint of which – according to the agency defined in Table 8 (right side) – societal development is somehow inhibited by (power) structure. In Table 8 (left side), however, is listed what exactly needs to be inhibited by the (power) structure to prevent cultural development. QTC identifies the prerequisites for structural theory – and postulates that they are not fulfilled: the repertoire of style leadership makes social structure fluid.

Postmodernist sociology, on the other hand, postulates that everything is determined by the free will of the individual.[9] However, *how* this can happen is also kept in a black box. Here, too, QTC takes it a step further. A stylistic structure that manifests itself in elective affinities is created by agency as defined in Table 8 (left side). It is created by inventing new or reactivating old objects, and above all by manipulating the way in which the style followers work in the sorting plant of culture.

Stylistic Viscosity

What is the contribution of consumption itself to stylistic innovation? Style leaders exemplify the new in their o/+consumption. And style followers then show individual variations of this in their own o/+consumption. So, if the style leadership innovates by means of its o/+consumption, then this shouldn't be categorically ruled out for its followers.

This is why I assume that every individual style, every individual o/+consumption, contributes to the stylistic innovation of the common style in which it is nested. Whoever is contributing to the colourfulness of the world is contributing to stylistic innovation. This is a trivial, almost tautological statement. It becomes more substantial though when it is coupled with a concrete idea of how individual styles affect the common style. The idea of the *viscosity of style* offers this substantiation.

I have defined the similarity of two objects by the rank distance, d_{ij}^r, having the properties listed in Table 7. Stylistic viscosity is then a result of the in-between and the outside principles. If a new object is added to the set and its feature values are positioned between object x_i and object x_j, their rank distance increases (in-between principle). It decreases if the feature values of the new object

---

9   Schulze 2005.

are completely different from those of x_i and x_j, that is, if an 'exotic' is included in the appraisal (outside principle). The uniforms of the general and of the lieutenant fall apart in their similarity if the uniform of the major (with more decoration than that of the lieutenant and less than that of the general) is included in the appraisal. And all three move closer together if the samurai's garb is also taken into consideration.

The similarity in any subset of objects is thus affected by every extra object added. But this is exactly what each individual style does with new objects that differ either slightly or markedly from those already contained in the subset of the common style. Each new object that is added to an elective affinity affects the similarity of two already existing objects in its common style. In that way, the individual style affects how viscous or thin the fluidity of a common style is, that is, how close or distant its objects are from one another. Thus, the viscosity of the common style of an elective affinity is affected by each and every *o/+consumption* therein, be it the individual style of a style leader or that of a style follower. Stylistic viscosity is the fruit of multiple agency. This is why in Table 8 the bottom row is merged into one, for both the style leadership and its followers.

But even here, the style leadership differs from its followers. The inventions and (re)activations of style leaders tend to make the common style more viscous. This is because they occupy the peripheries of the common style, introducing the 'exotic', such as the mohawk hairdo, which causes all other objects of the common style to become more similar, according to the outside principle. It is precisely because the mohawk hairdo is so completely different from piercings, safety pins in eyebrows, full-body tattoos and apocalyptic clothing that it causes these elements of the common punk style to become more similar. So, the coherence of a common style is paradoxically increased by rule-breaking inventions and the reactivations of misfits in elective affinities.

Style followers, with their hesitant experimentation in their *o/+consumption*, here and there applying a nuance differently from everyone else, position themselves with their new objects in the midst of their common style. They introduce similarity to a style, which, according to the in-between principle of rank distance, causes everything else to become less similar. It is precisely whenever the similar is so very similar to what has already been seen that it lets what has already seen become less similar. So, the coherence of the common style is *diminished* by rule-compliant *o/+consumption*. Which is why it is so difficult to describe the mainstream in terms of style. Due to their sheer number, the followers in the mainstream style drive it apart.

Here you are confronted with a stylistic innovation paradox: style leaders hold a common style together by violating its norm, style followers drive a style apart by adhering to its norm. Yet the mechanism behind the innovation paradox is simple: what falls outside of the norm directs the eye all the more to what is common to the normal, whilst what stays in the norm directs the eye all the more to what falls outside of it.

Classification of People

The workers in the sorting plant of culture cluster objects into styles, and by doing so create styles. They also have to sort people into groups, thus creating social groups. Elective affinities do not fall from the sky nor are they created by o/+consumption per se. Rather, they are created by sorting the observed o/+consumption into clusters, which only come into being through this process. Feature recognition and feature processing of objects must be transferred to the recognition and processing of the features of people, according to 'Le style c'est l'homme même'.

Consumer k establishes a subset of N objects, $(x_1, ..., x_i, ..., x_N)_k$, by their o/+consumption decision. They show this subset to the worker in the sorting plant of culture. The consumer shows, for example, all objects A to D from Figure 5 (right side), by talking about and praising them (behaviour) or by hanging them on the wall as prints. The worker only needs to see this subset as an ensemble. The worker achieves this by pushing the threshold value of the rank distance, d_{ij}^r, so far up that all rank distances in the subset $(x_1, ..., x_i, ..., x_N)_k$ come to lie below the threshold value. To 'see as an ensemble' is seeing the subset of objects shown by the consumer as a 'natural', exogenous cluster of objects, from which, for reasons of consumer sovereignty, an object can neither be removed nor added. Adjusting the length of the haircut, d_K, is the means by which the ensemble becomes visible as such. Le style c'est l'homme même is the very order of this 'natural' cluster of objects, revealed by the 'haircut in a headstand' procedure. If the worker is able to make sense of a consumer who has surrounded themself with Louis Armstrong records (A), batik scarves (B), Klimt pictures (C) and a vintage car (D), then the 'haircut in a headstand' procedure has revealed a level of abstraction at which the worker sees l'homme même in A to D.

This 'natural' cluster of objects belonging to consumer k is their individual style, s_k. It is an order, such as the one in Figure 5 (right or left). The worker can conceive of it as a single object, with specific features such as those from the phylogram or cladogram in Figure 5. Other consumers show themselves to the worker in this same way by their individual style, s_j. Thus z individual styles, $s_1, ..., s_j, ..., s_z$, appear before the worker in culture's sorting plant.

The worker's job now is to cluster the z individual styles in n common styles, S_i, $1 \leq n \leq z$. They could classify all consumers as singletons, as stylistically unique, by giving them a short enough haircut. Then $n = z$ and a society with no inner structure would be produced. Or they could gather all individuals into a single cluster, into society as a whole. In a clustering where $1 < n < z$, the worker groups consumers with similar individual styles into a common style of which there are several. This group formation is accomplished in the same way as in our earlier thought experiment of the construction of the tree of life, namely by constructing rank distances between individual styles on the basis of the features of their objects and then shifting the threshold value, d_K, up or down. The common style, S_j, is then a cluster of m individual styles, $s_1, ..., s_j, ..., s_m$, whereby an individual style cannot belong to more than one common style, and whereby $m \cdot n = z$.

Preferences and the Nucleus of the Social Space

This clustering of consumers with their individual styles, s_j, into groups that share a common style, S_i, is the nucleus of the social space. That nucleus now needs to be characterised.

In my postmodern approach, the social space is *constructed* from the world of objects. Workers in the sorting plant of culture sort people by sorting the objects that they show and do not show. Taking that approach, without the world of objects there is no social space. But it is the heuristics that culture conveys that make the job of sorting manageable. Without culture there would be no sortability, without sortability there would be no social space. Therefore, without culture there is no social space. Culture exerts its power indirectly. Culture does not implant sortability into the objects themselves, but rather determines the *sorting preferences* of individuals, according to which workers in the sorting plant perform their job: this or that feature vector, this or that weighting within it, this or that curvature of the ranking function, this or that threshold value for the 'haircut'. It is worth stressing that in QTC the preferences do not determine what the consumer likes to consume, as they do in the orthodoxy, but instead how the individual *wants to perform the job as worker in the sorting plant of culture*. Preferences here determine the *manner of working*, not the manner of consumption. Preferences of the productive consumer are *production preferences*. However, fully in line with the orthodox epistemic credo *de gustibus non est disputandum*, they are the very same for all individuals within a culture.

But while, in the orthodoxy, preferences are equated with a certain *desire for possession*, in QTC's view culture lets preferences be a certain *desire for understanding*. The difference is quite significant. In QTC, culture is a culture of understanding – of how people want to understand the world of objects. The desire to understand is not dependent on a desire to possess. People understand first and only afterwards do they realise what this implies for their happiness/utility. As a consequence, the social space does not arise from the (Veblenian) desire of those who are worse off to also possess, and the desire of those who are better off to show that they possess, but from a coherent way of *understanding* one another.

The idea of the social space went through a metamorphosis in the (mental) transition from modernism to postmodernism. In modernist sociology, the social space is essentially animalistic: hitting and stabbing (Veblen); or (Bourdieu) no hitting and stabbing because hitting and stabbing simply would not change a thing – the idea of economic efficiency entering sociology! In QTC, the social space is instead essentially humanistic: wanting to understand who the other is, how diverse and yet similar being human is. It is curiosity that drives the social, not hungriness and opulence.

It is this humanism that lets people find a home in an elective affinity. Home manifests itself in their common style. It allows room for the individual, which shows up in the individual styles of group members. Thus, the social space is revealed as social distance and proximity. Social distance reveals itself as the difference between the common styles of groups, proximity shows up under the roof of the common style – a proximity in which the individual thrives.

Identification and Identity

The orthodoxy's *Identity Economics* addresses how people manipulate their belonging to one or another social group by utilisation of their resources.[10] This is not a topic in QTC, because it concerns a social world – completely free of money – in which the resources of all individuals are (almost) identical. With this assumption, it is then possible to discover which factors other than resources allow the social to emerge. If, in the Identity Economics approach, all economic agents had the same resources, they would all be buying themselves into the very same social group and the social world would be desolately monotonous. In QTC, the social world would only be monotonous if there were only one consumer good. An ordered world of objects alone, $(X, \square)$, which does not consist of a lonely

---

10   Akerlof and Kranton 2000.

singleton, is in QTC sufficient to allow social diversity to emerge. Here, the diversity of the world of objects is not due to the need for a social world, but the diversity of the social world is due to the diversity of the world of objects. In QTC, the world of objects is causal for the social world and not vice versa.

Common to both approaches is that they shortcut the process leading to social identity. Both abstract from the process of initiation and (self) confirmation. This process is what allows an individual to become member of a group, after they have identified with the group. In *Identity Economics*, identity is simply paid for by the investment of personal resources – nothing else can prevent the realisation of sought after identity, only too tight a budget. Also, so far in QTC, identity comes about without social resonance.

In Table 1, this simplification is underscored by the perforated vertical arrow pointing from the economic to the social sphere. QTC, as enhanced by social resonance, will be dealt with in Part 3. There, *o/+consumption* will be interpreted as a signal that ellicits feedback from others – good or bad. Identity is thus made dependent on identification-cum-resonance and is the result of mutual understanding. Whereas in *Identity Economics*, identification-cum-identity is the result of simple calculation. There, the identification process is identical to individual optimisation, and to identifying the group, the choice of which maximises their utility. The subsequently attained identity is then given by the group-specific preferences over goods alternatives.

In QTC, the identification process is the work practised in the sorting plant of culture, and identity thus brought about reveals itself in the mutual understanding of the strong similarity of individual styles as the (sole) commonality in a group, jointly with a mutual understanding of the weaker similarity across groups. Together the individual styles constitute a common stylistic home with which the individual identifies. That is: individual i, with their individual style, identifies themself with an elective affinity, precisely because individual j, with their own individual style, also belongs to it; and j identifies with it precisely because i with their individual style also belongs to it. Through reciprocity alone, identification is transformed into identity.

Above-Average Type/Syndrome and Extreme Type/Syndrome

The clustering of objects into a style can be heavily governed by feature values that are a little above average, and weakly or not at all affected by extreme values. Styles that develop according to this principle differ only by degrees of 'neither fish nor fowl'. I refer to them as styles of the *above-average type*. On the other hand, clustering in a certain style may heavily depend on the existence of extreme feature values. A style that has been built upon this principle shows as a whole the extreme. I call it a style of the *extreme type*. Styles of the above-average type have in common not *what* they show, but *how* they show it, i.e. with what is simply a little above-average. The same applies to the extreme type of style: whatever it shows, it shows to an extreme.

Again, the issue of human agency arises. And again, the answer is that for most consumers, the perspect manager (of culture) dictates whether an object is to be clustered according to one or the other principle. What they habitually 'do the right way' is for style leaders a decision to be made. For them, the principle of *how* to 'make' a style is a variable.

Yet, the principle activated by the perspect manager is not the same for all styles. For example, if we assess an object by whether it is mainstream, we give less weight to some extreme feature values (such as how extremely inconspicuous the grey of the flannel trousers is, or how very English a jacket is). Instead, we give credit for the presence of sufficiently typical features: not impractical, not really colourful, not really extravagant, not really cheap, etc. Mainstream objects show enough of everything that makes them what they are, nothing more extreme is needed. The flower power and the esoteric styles also do not prize the extreme, although it's not completely ruled out in the details. The fabric must be sufficiently cheap, the cut sufficiently flowing, the material sufficiently natural.

The colours of the drag queen, on the other hand, should not just be colourful, they must be shrill. Due to its extremeness, a safety pin in the eyebrow as depreciation of bourgeois jewellery almost makes the punk on its own. Ellsworth Kelly's *Red Blue Green* is an object of the extreme type: red, blue and green are of the purest colours, the lines of greatest sharpness. Minimalist objects all belong to the extreme type: if it's canvas, it's without a frame. Dada rewards the extremely provocative. Marcel Duchamp's *Fontaine* (1917) provoked his contemporaries not only by insisting that even an everyday object, properly staged, can be art – no, it had to be exemplified by a urinal. Objects are attributed to punk, minimalism and Dada according to the extreme principle. Thus, they all belong to the extreme type.

The consistent adherence to one of these principles of classification produces complementarities between the world of things, patterns of behaviour and moral values, and generates a comprehensive style that embraces all areas of life. Why? Because the type-specific principle is a blueprint both for legitimation strategies (values) of individuals as well as for their role model (behaviour). Showing extreme feature values from the world of things is a non-verbal legitimation of their generalisation beyond the world of things. Whoever shows the extreme, can themselves be extreme (behaviour), and also demand it of themself and others (values). This is because the coherence demonstrated between things, behaviour and values is what makes a person authentic. Whoever shows only slightly above-average things, may be slightly above-average him or herself, and may also demand little from others. The concept of somatic style (see chapter 2) precisely addresses the coherence between the world of things, personal behaviour and internal values.[11] This all-embracing coherence of *how* a style is made accounts for the type of style.

How a style is made has consequences. The production principle unfolds effects beyond the style. That which is extreme provokes other elective affinities; that which is only above-average does not. What is extreme catches the eye, what is just above average does not. Instead, the above-average helps overcome conflict and bring about harmony, which the extreme cannot. Herein we find confirmation of the insight, discussed in chapter 2, that there cannot be a clear distinction between the *how* of a style and its *what*. The principle of production (how) also influences the effects of object and style.

It is worth reserving the terms 'above-average type' and 'extreme *type*' for the constitutive principles of production, and to use the term 'syndrome' for their effect on other elective affinities. Accordingly, I use the term 'above-average syndrome' when I refer to the effect of the making of the above-average type, and extreme syndrome when I refer to the effect of the style of the extreme type.

Table 9 classifies styles according to the above-average and extreme types and the above-average and extreme syndrome. Many of the cases discussed in chapter 1 are examples of either one or the other.

---

11   Shusterman 2011.

Table 9: Styles of the extreme and above-average type.

Extreme Type (Syndrome)	Above-Average Type (Syndrome)
Dandyism (19th century)	Gentleman (18th century)
Juvenile gangster style	Classicism in Naples (19th century)
Kogyaru	Vienna Secession
Hiphop	Hipster
Skinheads	Reggae/Rastafarians
Punk	

The types are distinguished by the way styles are 'produced', involving the use of objects with extreme versus above-average feature values. The associated syndrome is the overall effect of the alternative production principles on the style system as a whole.

The dandyism of Beau Brummel is of the extreme type, effecting the extreme syndrome. His wardrobe selection, heightened to the extreme, is combined with behaviour that elevates exclusivity to the point of aloofness, and values that make disdain for others a virtue. Unsurpassed superficiality is considered the pinnacle of excellence. By contrast, the gentleman of the English provincial town in the 18th century belongs to the above-average type, effecting the corresponding syndrome. Wealth is only displayed to the point of decent distinction, appreciation also granted to the less fortunate, liberal education emphasised. [12]

The juvenile gangster style is of the extreme type: clothing that is expensive for youth is combined with their constant readiness to punish for the slightest sign of disrespect, and with the glorification of the jail experience. In contrast, the better Neapolitan society in Emma Hart's time is of the above-average type. Unlike Beau Brummel, the admirers of the classical did not have to labour day and night to hone their stylistic clout and work their way to total victory or defeat. Their path to happiness/utility lay in quiet enjoyment and in sensible conversation, and was closed to no one. [13]

The Japanese *kogyaru* is of the extreme type. The complexion should not appear a little tanned, it must be deeply tanned. As if there were no black-haired Europeans, the hair must be dyed blonde or brown. The colour of the contact lenses must be exactly according to the supposed Western ideal, and the

---

12   Stobart 2011.

13   Rauser 2015.

behaviour must be far from the Japanese oneness with the whole.[14] The syndrome manifests itself in the irritation of the Japanese mainstream, which retaliates with the term *kogyaru* – infantilised girl. The Vienna Secession, in turn, is of the above-average type. It did not dictate exactly how society should be, but rather, in quite different artistic ways, merely exemplified what it was no longer supposed to be. Klimt's castrating *femme fatale* was a truth, because it showed the lie, it was not dogma about the way things had to be. Exclusion of the wrong instead of definition of the right allowed Klimt a well-off life (syndrome) between court (party) and bohemianism.[15]

The hyper-masculine hip hop is of the extreme type: macho values, macho behaviour and macho clothing as a celebration of the extreme. Only in baggy pants is there a real 'dick', what's contained in skin-tight pants is contemptible, in fact evil.[16] The hipster is of the above-average type. He stands out visibly from the average of the mainstream, but only to a certain degree – with single items that the mainstream has just dumped yesterday, with values that don't really provoke, with behaviour that allows for living in the midst of the mainstream (syndrome).[17]

Skinheads are of the extreme type. They reject everything contained in the prettiness of the bourgeois. Proletarianism is elevated to lumpenproletarianism. Living on the fringes of the mainstream is impossible, only outside of it is life possible.[18] And from the point of view of the mainstream observer (syndrome), that is where they indeed belong. Reggae, born from slavery, is once more of the above-average type. The musical escape 'back to Africa' by turning to the white Bible, which did not provoke the ruling classes, produced black identity through minimal differentiation.[19] Its modern offshoots, the Rasta dreadlocks, khaki pants and marijuana, are only of moderate conflict potential for the mainstream (syndrome). In turn, the punk, this super-alienated creature showing self-mutilation, full-body tattoos, apocalyptic clothing and a mohawk hairdo is, in its constant rejection of any form of conformity, of the extreme type.[20]

---

14   Black 2009.

15   Néret 2007.

16   Penney 2012.

17   Greif, Ross, Tortorici and Geiselberger 2012.

18   Hebdige 1988.

19   ibid.

20   Force 2009.

New Age and Performance Cult

The philosopher Mario Perniola distinguishes two fundamentally different life-styles: *New Age* and *Performance Cult*.[21] New Age is the aesthetic confluence of es-otericism, Eastern spirituality and alternative therapies. It features a flat intel-lectual profile and the lack of a rigid ethos. Experience of the self in harmony and reconciliation is the goal. The world is portrayed as if conflict and contradiction could be overcome by means of quietude and conciliation. For Perniola, the som-aesthetic experience of New Age is similar to that of weed (cannabis).

In contrast, Performance Cult conveys a somaesthetic experience similar to that of speed (amphetamines). It features emotional overinvestment, perfor-mance pushed to the limit, and constantly setting new records. The Performance Cult does not aim for enjoyment, but for the constant upkeep of excitement. For Perniola, New Age is a modern offshoot of the classic Kantian aesthetics, with the ideal of the detachment of the true art lover. The Performance Cult is for him a modern variant of Baudelaire's anti-aesthetics of excessive interest, with the dandy as its paragon.

Parallels exist between Perniola's lifestyle concept and the production type concept of styles that has been elaborated here. They both show themselves in an aesthetic union of things, behaviour and values. In both lifestyle and production type of style, what belongs together comes together. New Age and the above-av-erage type of style form a tandem. New Age's lack of rigid ethos and its low de-mands on intellectuality are selected with the stylistic production principle of the above-average type. Moreover, the low weighting of extreme feature values fa-cilitates the quest for harmony and the overcoming of conflict and contradic-tions. Performance Cult and the stylistic production principle of the extreme type also form a tandem. There is nothing more effective for exaggeration and constant excitement than systematically rewarding extreme feature values of things, behaviour and values with a bonus. New Age and the above-average pro-duction type of style, on the one hand, and Performance Cult and the extreme production type of style, on the other, are kindred.

However, because each concept – lifestyle and (production) type of style – has pros and cons over the other, depending on the question at hand, I will distin-guish them further. For an ongoing interest in the sorting plant of culture, the concept of the (production) type of styles has its advantages, because the lifestyle concept, be it weed or speed, is focused only on the output of the sorting plant. It doesn't tell us *how* (as if by an invisible hand) things, behaviour and values have

---

21   Perniola 2007.

become coherent. The distinction between the above-average and extreme type of styles discloses the sorting *procedure* that leads to a coherent style. However, this comes at a cost: the cultural wealth inherent in the idea of lifestyle, is partially lost in the idea of the production type of styles.

Another advantage of the concept of the (production) type of styles over that of lifestyle is that the term 'style' can be reserved for what is specific to the group and the individual in it. The term 'style' thereby covers something different from Perniola's lifestyle, which takes effect only at the (meta) stylistic macro level. In contrast, QTC is more micro-focused. It starts from the premise that striving for social distance and proximity manifests itself not only in a few lifestyles, but in many different variants of them. The world of objects offers potential for shaping social life that remains untapped by lifestyle alone. This will be the subject of the next chapter.

Chapter 5
Social Volition and Cultural Prowess

> "The budget constraint shows the various bundles of goods that the consumer can afford for a given income. Here the consumer buys bundles of Pepsi and pizza."
> *N. Gregory Mankiw und Mark P. Taylor*[1]

The orthodoxy positions agency somewhere between an objective function (volition) and restricted action (prowess). Wedged between these, agency is a purely computational activity. Agents (consumers) tend to use their scope of action such that their objective function (happiness/utility) is maximised. With this methodical individualism in its analytical toolbox, the orthodoxy predicts human behaviour. Little Max has £20 pocket money (prowess) and shrewdly divides it over the price of however many Pepsis and pizzas (volition). The number of Pepsis and pizzas Little Max buys with however much pocket money is a typical prediction of the orthodoxy.

In the orthodoxy, volition can, but need not be directed towards a social goal. Little Max may want to consume his Pepsis and pizzas himself and not share them with others, or he may (also) use them to win favour among his friends. In QTC, *0/+consumption* serves only one social goal: the manipulation of social distance and proximity. Here volition is exclusively oriented towards the social. The orthodox theory is therefore more general than QTC. The upside of this is the ability to analyse even Robinsonades. Its downside is the shallowness it imposes on the cultural and social realms. The downside of QTC is its insensitivity to quantities and prices, and the upside is the depth to which it allows us to dive into the cultural and social realms.

---

1   Mankiw and Taylor 2008.

Another difference between the orthodoxy and QTC is epistemological interest itself. For the orthodoxy, volition (in the form of an objective function) is an input into the analysis. Its output is the prediction of consumer behaviour, based on this input which has fallen out of the sky. No reflection on the objective function and its motivation occurs, nor is it needed. In the orthodoxy, volition is simply anything that can be sought, as long as it can be pursued by an agency that can be thought of as calculation. Since volition can be anything, there is indeed no need for motivation. And since you don't need to motivate it, you can immediately accept it as a given: once there, always there!

In contrast, my considerations so far – and those in this chapter to be discussed in more detail – are primarily aimed at finding social volition in a *specific* objective function. This specific social volition is an output of the analysis and not its input. Like the orthodoxy, however, I also started with an input that fell out of the sky: humans strive for a place in the social, this place is determined by the specific social distance and proximity, which they can manipulate. At the beginning of the analytical journey, this social volition was as general a meta-preference as the volition for utility assumed by the orthodoxy. However, it then took on more specific forms from chapter to chapter. The current status of this specification of social volition is summarised in Table 6.

In the orthodoxy, prowess is defined by possession: Little Max has his weekly pocket money, later on he has his fortune, experience and a network. He also has what the orthodoxy calls cultural capital, i.e. his schooling, and the ability to move around in the social sphere like a fish in water or a bull in a china shop. Everything the agent possesses is used for volition, and the finitude of possessions limits their prowess. In the orthodoxy, different actions are solely due to different possessions and identical possessions always lead to identical actions.

In QTC, the consumer does not possess anything of their own that would allow them to act differently from others. All they have is what everyone else has: the world of objects, which, according to my assumption, is even available for free. All consumers use it to achieve their goals. Prowess is owed solely to culture. The prowess of the productive consumer is that summarised in Table 8. It depicts style leaders as Supermen and Supergirls who organise the world of objects according to their own interests, by providing their followers with instructions for its use. This is a win-win situation, a bigger win for the style leadership and a smaller one for their followers. So far, there are free lunches everywhere and no restrictions anywhere, just as if Little Max had overflowing pockets, or if Pepsi and pizza were available for free. But without any restrictions on capabilities, everyone would always revel in infinite happiness/utility. Individual agency would lose its analytical power altogether, and socially effective actions would lead all to Paradise. Without restrictions there is no economic problem – and this is also true of QTC.

What are the restrictions in *o/+consumption*? Prowess is limited by culture. Within the world of objects, cultural trade-offs have to be respected, which prevent infinite bliss. Social volition collides with the limitations of cultural prowess. It is only through this collision that agency is relevant as a creative force for the social. These are the topics addressed in this chapter.

Proximity Clarified

As summarised in Table 6, the individual style moderates social proximity within the in-group. It is what distinguishes the individual from other members of their elective affinity despite all similarities, and what unites the individual with them despite all differences. Proximity, in other words, is the measure of individuality within the group to which the individual voluntarily belongs. All that makes an individual incomparable with their elective affinity alienates them from it. Everything that makes them comparable with their elective affinity, and is not identical, cultivates their individuality in it. Social proximity thus feeds on comparisons along the lines of 'more or less authentic, modern, original', etc., or more generally 'more or less pronounced in features of the common style of the elective affinity'. Social proximity thus develops from the gaze of all members of the in-group through the meta-contrasting lens that hides the incomparable within the group and shows the comparable (Table 5). Individual styles establish social proximity in the ordered world of objects, $(X, \square)$, by using the meta-contrasting lens to filter out dissimilarity as comparability, DIS_c, and/or diversity based on comparability, DIV_c. 'And/or' needs to be clarified. To that end, I first distinguish the common style, S, of the elective affinity from the individual styles, s_j, of the m members that constitute it. I then determine the *bilateral stylistic root*, R_{ji}, between an individual style, s_j, and any other individual style, s_i. Figure 6 serves to illustrate.

Let the elective affinity be composed of two members only, i and j. Their common style, S, consists of the subset of objects (A, B, C, D, E). The individual styles are nested in the common style as two subsets $(B, C, E)_i$ and $(A, D, E)_j$. Diversity based on comparability of the common style, DIV_c^c, is the sum of the vertical lengths in Figure 6. The bilateral root of the individual styles s_i and s_j has two components. The first component (a) consists of all vertical parts in the tree of the common style above the objects shown in *both* individual styles. The second component (b) consists of all *joint* vertical parts of each pair of objects shown in *different* individual styles. In Figure 6, E is shown in both (all) individual styles of the in-group. The vertical part above E thus belongs to the bilateral stylistic root of individual styles s_i and s_j (a). C belongs to individual style i and D to individual style j. Hence, the dashed vertical parts in the common style tree above the node connecting C and D, both individual styles have in common (b). The dashed vertical parts (a) and (b) in the common style tree are the bilateral stylistic root, R_{ji}, of the two individual styles.

This stylistic root must be clearly distinguished from that of evolutionary biology (see footnote 11, chapter 3). There, the root is the single vertical connection of a phylogram to the next higher taxon (for example in Figure 1, right, the dashed vertical connection of length 11 MJ of the phylogram of great apes with Old World apes). The stylistic roots, by contrast, are the commonalities of individual styles within the cultural taxon 'common style', which can be derived from comparability and which manifest in length.

Figure 6: Individuality and proximity in common style.

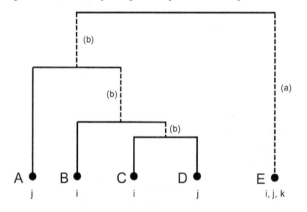

Obviously, the bilateral root of their individual styles contributes nothing to the bilateral individuality of two consumers. C and D are different, but C and D also *jointly* differ from B and A. For consumer j object C from style s_i is too much like object D from s_j, that D could underpin the individuality of j *vis-a-vis* i with the whole dissimilarity of D and B. Conversely, the same applies to consumer i: C and B are too much like D, for the individuality of i to be underpinned by the whole dissimilarity, *jointly* of C and B *vis-a-vis* A.

Therefore, for determining the individuality of an elective affinity member, j, *vis-a-vis* another one, i, the bilateral stylistic root of their individual styles must be omitted from consideration. This holds true for all other bilateral stylistic roots consumer j shares with any of the other members of their in-group, and hence for the entire stylistic rooting of the consumer's individual style, s_j, in the common style, S, of their in-group.

I am now able to specify social proximity between a member and their in-group. Let R_j^c be the *rooting of the individual style, s_j, in the common style, S,* with $R_j^c = \sum_{i=1}^m R_{ji}$, where $R_{jj} \equiv 0$. Let the consumer's individuality, I_j, which determines their proximity to their in-group, be

$$I_j \equiv (m - 1) \cdot DIV_c^c - R_j^c, \quad j = 1, \dots, m \qquad (1)$$

This definition of individuality is intuitive. Individuality of a member in their in-group as a whole depends on three factors.

First, it depends on the diversity (based on comparability) of all objects in the common style, DIV_c^c. It is the common component of all members' individuality. The more diversity within the common style, DIV_c^c, the greater the individuality of the members of the elective affinity. The less the diversity (based on comparability) of the common style, the less the individuality of members. All the way to the borderline case of zero individuality when diversity within the common style is zero. This borderline case has two variants. Either the common style consists only of a single object, in which case both diversity and the rooting of the individual in the common style, R_j^c, are zero. Or, more generally, the *o/+consumption* of all elective affinities is identical, in which case both terms in (1) have equal values.

Second, individuality depends on the rooting of the individual in the common style, R_j^c. The more the individual style is rooted in the common style (i.e. the greater the anchoring in it, shared with other individual styles), the less individual the individual style is. The less the individual style is rooted in the common style, the more individuality there is.

Third, individuality also depends on the size, m, of the in-group. In the borderline case, $m = 1$, individual j is a loner not belonging to any group. The loner's individuality *vis-a-vis* themselves (as being their own in-group) should therefore be zero. For $m = 1$, $I_j = -R_j^c$. But for $m = 1$ the rooting of the individual in the common style is zero. Hence for $m = 1$, $I_j = 0$. A loner shows no individuality towards their in-group. A group of at least two makes individuality possible. In a group of two, however, both members possess the same individuality, $I_j = I_i$, because they share identical rooting in their common style, $R_j^c = R_i^c = R_{ji} = R_{ij}$. For $m = 2$, $DIV_c^c \geq I_j = I_i \geq 0$. Individuality of the two sole members of a group is equal to the diversity of the common style they share, if their individual styles possess no bilateral root. For example, this is the case in Figure 6 if the common style, S, is composed of the subset (C, D) and the two individual styles are the subsets $(C)_i$

and $(D)_j$, respectively. Then $R_j^g = R_i^g = 0$. However, their individuality is zero if both show exactly the same objects in their individual style, because then $(m-1) \cdot DIV_c^c = R_j^c = R_i^c$. For $m \geq 2$, $(m-1) \cdot DIV_c^c \geq R_j^c$, and hence $(m-1) \cdot DIV_c^c \geq I_j \geq 0$. Generally, individuality in the in-group takes values between zero and $(m-1)$ times the diversity (based on comparability) of the common style. This is intuitive, too: the consumer, whose individual style does not share any bilateral roots with the other individual styles, gains the $(m-1)$-fold individuality by the $(m-1)$ stylistic contributions of all the other $(m-1)$ in-group members to the common style. In general, the individuality of the consumer grows with each new individual style that is added to the common style. There are two reasons for this: first, the greater number of the other members in the elective affinity, even if they look almost alike. Second, the individuality of all members serves to make the consumer's own individuality all the more visible.

In-group members differ in their individuality, though, if their individual styles have an unequal rooting in the common one. Figure 6 shows that the rooting of individual styles can indeed be different. Suppose that, besides members i and j, the group also includes consumer k, whose individual style consists only of object E – the ascetic variant among the individual styles. Further suppose E is shown by all individual styles in the group. The vertical part (a) is the whole of k's rooting in the common style, whereas i and j share in addition (b) as part of their rooting in the common style. Therefore $R_j^c = R_i^c > R_k^c$, and hence $I_j = I_i < I_k$. An unequal rooting of individual styles in the common style is the source of differences in individuality within an elective affinity. The more different the individual rootings, the more different the individualities within a group; the larger (smaller) the rooting in the common style, the smaller (larger) the individuality. The most extraordinary person within the elective affinity, who stylistically shares the least with the rest, but still just belongs to it, enjoys the greatest individuality.

I can now define social proximity in terms of individuality. Social proximity within an elective affinity is the inverse of a consumer's individuality within it. Let P_j be the social proximity of individual j and its in-group:

$$P_j \equiv I_j^{-1} \qquad\qquad (2)$$

The smaller (larger) the individuality of the consumer within the in-group, the larger (smaller) their proximity to it. This relation represents a schizoid practice in individualised societies: while no one can be without a home in a social group, once in it, the main concern is not disappearing in it.

Dominance Order in Proximity

Orderings such as those in Figure 7 contain objects that relate to one another through the dominance order, $\square_d$. In each feature of the vector, $\underline{m}_j = (m_1, \ldots, m_M)$, an object dominates another object from the same chain or is dominated by it.[2*] If a common style contains a dominance order, this must be taken into account when determining diversity, DIV_c^c, and the rooting of the individual style, s_j, in the common style, R_j^c.

Figure 7: Dominance orders in the common style.

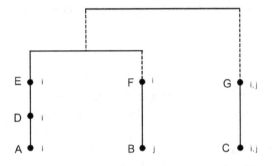

Here consisting of two individual styles of two in-group members, i and j.

According to convention, let the supremum of the objects ordered in a chain be positioned at the lower end. The suprema in the common style shown in Figure 7 are objects A, B and C. Object A dominates objects D and E in each feature of the feature vector $\underline{m}_j$, und D dominates E. For example, let A, D and E be three art prints from Gustav Klimt's *femmes fatales* with the strongest expression of 'fatality' in A (for example, Klimt's Judith, 1901) and the weakest in E (for example, Klimt's portrait of Emilie Flöge, 1902). And let B and F be two collections of Louis Armstrong records, with B being more comprehensive than F, and let C and G both be a Borgward Isabella Coupé vintage car from 1955 with C in a more original condition than G.

The diversity, DIV_c^c of a common style, S_1, containing subset (A, B, C) is smaller than the diversity of style S_2, containing (A, B, C, D, E, F, G). For example, if S_1 is enlarged by D to become the subset (A, B, C, D), DIV_c^c increases by the sum of all vertical lengths above A: by the length between A and D (the dissimilarity

---

2*   See footnote 5*, chapter 3, with K as the set of ordinal scales, f_i, of features, m_i, $i = 1, \ldots, M$, of the feature vector, $\underline{m}_j = (m_1, \ldots, m_M)$.

between D and A) plus the length above D up to their joint node with the vertical branch above B (the dissimilarity between D and B). Adding an additional dominated object, D, to a style increases its diversity, DIV_c^c, by the same value as the supremum, A, by which it is dominated. In general, DIV_c^c of a style, containing dominance orders, $\square_d$, like (A, D, E), (B, F) and (C, G) in Figure 7, can be calculated by multiplying the lengths above each supremum by the number of objects ordered in this dominance order.[3*] This accounts for all bilateral dissimilarities within each dominance order and for the diversity between all dominance orders.

Let $\partial(X, \square_d)$ be the increase in the number of objects of the common style, by addition of one object to the subset X of dominated objects in the dominance order $\square_d$, (for example by showing the additional object D in the common style (A, B, C) in Figure 7). Then we arrive at:

$$\partial DIV_c^c / \partial(X, \square_d) > 0 \qquad\qquad (3)$$

The diversity (based on comparability) of the common style increases with each additional dominated object shown in it. This can be intuited quite simply: the more varied the individual styles in an in-group through the use of dominated objects – for example, the use of batik scarves in different shades of purple – the greater the diversity of the common style. Obviously, this also holds true if a chain is lengthened by a new supremum, i.e. if the new object now dominates a former supremum.

All that remains is to determine the effect of dominance orders on the rooting of the individual in the common style, R_j^c. In Figure 7 there are two individual styles, s_i showing the objects (A, C, D, E, F, G), and s_j, with the objects (B, C, G). Style s_i exhibits the dominance orders (A, D, E) and (C, G) and s_j exhibits the dominance order (C, G). Expanding two styles that already share one object, for example C in Figure 7, by adding another object, for example G, which is dominated by the first object, has no effect on the bilateral root of these individual styles. But suppose G had been a supremum in both individual styles, which are now augmented by the shared object C. Then their bilateral root R_{ji} and both rootings of their respective individual styles in their common styles, R_i^c and R_j^c, increase by the length between C and G.

The rooting of styles is also affected by dominance orders such as those of (B, F): B belongs to s_j and F to s_i and the one object in one style dominates the other object in the other style. In such cases, the lengths above the dominated

---

3* Let x_i^{sup} be the supremum of the dominance order $\square_i$, $i = 1, ..., h$, in which $\#_i^c$ objects are ordered. For $\#_i = 1$ let $x_i^{sup} \equiv x_i$. Let L_i be the total length above x_i^{sup}. Then $DIV_c^c = \sum_{i=1}^h \#_i^c \cdot L_i$.

object belong to the bilateral root, R_{ji}, of the two individual styles. For $R_j^c = \sum_{i=1}^{m} R_{ji}$ it follows that, in the presence of dominance orders in the common style, the rootings of the individual styles, s_j, $j = 1, ..., m$, in the common style of an in-group cannot be smaller than the rootings in the absence of dominated objects. That is:

$$\partial R_j^c / \partial(X, \square_d) \geq 0 \qquad (4)$$

The rooting of the individual style, s_j, in the common style does not decrease with the enlargement of a dominance order as a subset of the common style.

For (1) it follows that, given (3) and (4), the individuality of in-group member j, I_j, is influenced by two opposite effects when adding an object to a chain. The diversity of the common style increases, which enhances the individuality of all in the elective affinity. But, on the other hand, the rooting of the individual style, s_j, in the common style also increases (or stays constant), which is detrimental to the individuality of j (or lets it remain constant). However:

$$\partial DIV_c^c / \partial(X, \square_d) \geq \partial R_j^c / \partial(X, \square_d) \geq 0 \qquad (5)$$

The enlargement of a chain in an individual style with an additional object never increases the diversity of the common style by less than it increases the rooting of the individual style it contains. This is because the addition of an object to a chain always increases the diversity (based on comparability) of the common style by the full length above the supremum, whereas the rooting increases by that length at most.

There is now an important relationship to be noted between a dominance order, $(X, \square_d)$, and individuality within a common style, I_j. From (5) it follows that:

$$\partial I_j / \partial(X, \square_d) \geq 0, \; j = 1, ..., m \qquad (6)$$

The enrichment of the common style with additional objects from a dominance order, by showing them in any individual style, either increases the individuality of the members of the elective affinity or it remains constant. Conversely, for proximity within an elective affinity, it follows from (2) that:

$$\partial P_j / \partial(X, \square_d) \leq 0, \; j = 1, ..., m \qquad (7)$$

The social proximity within an elective affinity decreases or remains constant when chains are augmented with additional objects.

Distance Clarified

As summarised in Table 6, the common styles of in-groups moderate the social distance between them, i.e. between an in-group and its out-group(s). Distance is what distinguishes different groups despite their similarities. In other words, distance is a measure of what distinguishes the members of one elective affinity as a whole from the members of all other elective affinities.

Everything that makes them comparable clouds the perception of what separates them. Social distance results from the gaze of all in-group members through the meta-contrasting lens, which lets the comparable between the groups disappear and the incomparable appear (Table 5). In the common styles of elective affinities, social distance is extracted from the ordered world of objects, $(X, \square)$, in the form of dissimilarity as incomparability and the diversity based on it, (DIS_{ic}, DIV_{ic}). This also needs to be clarified. Figure 8 serves to illustrate.

Figure 8 is a system of two common styles, S_1 and S_2. Each consists of a subset of chains, branches (of a tree) and singletons, $\{\circ, |, \text{♏}\}$. As elaborated in chapter 3, dissimilarity as incomparability and diversity based on incomparability are not based on the vertical structure of ordered subsets, but on their *horizontal structure*. From this horizontal structure, antichains, $\sqsubset\sqsupset$, can be extracted that only contain information on incomparabilities because they are totally dissimilar subsets (see footnote 19*, chapter 3). There are different ways of forming antichains. In the following, the subset of suprema, i.e. of the undominated objects, is defined as the antichain, $\sqsubset\sqsupset_h$, of the common style S_h.[4] In Figure 8, the antichains of the undominated objects of the two common styles, $\sqsubset\sqsupset_1$ and $\sqsubset\sqsupset_2$, are marked by the two perforated boxes. Obviously, all singletons of a common style are elements of this antichain, as are, by convention, the lowermost elements (suprema) in its chains. Conversely, no object dominated in a dominance order, $\square_d$, belongs to it.

---

4   Basili and Vannucci 2013.

Figure 8: Nucleus and periphery of two common styles S_1 and S_2.

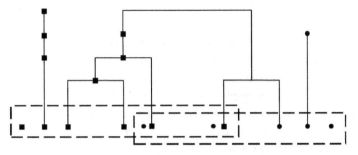

S_1 shows ■ objects and S_2 shows • objects. The two perforated boxes contain the antichains of the suprema of the styles S_1 (left) und S_2 (right). The intersection of the two antichains is the shared periphery of the two common styles. The nucleus of a common style is its antichain less its periphery.

Diversity based on incomparability of the common style S_h, DIV_{ic}^h, is the cardinality, $\#_h$, of the antichain $\sqsubset\sqsupset_h$, $DIV_{ic}^h = \#(\sqsubset\sqsupset_h)$. It is obtained by counting the elements in the antichain. For example, in Figure 8 $DIV_{ic}^1 = 6$ und $DIV_{ic}^2 = 5$. The first style has a greater number of incomparable objects than the second and is therefore more diverse in this sense.

However, social distance is not the result of incomparability within a common style, but of incomparability between styles. Here we have a complication to consider because, in practice, different common styles are not disjunct sets. They can contain objects that are also displayed in one or more other common styles. For example, the banker style, the 'smart casual' style of the venture capitalist and the professional creative style can all display the *blucher* as a shoe. In Figure 8, the elements within the intersection of the two perforated boxes belong to both styles. Needless to say, shared elements of two common styles cannot contribute to their incomparability, even if they are incomparable within the respective styles.

This leads to the distinction between *style periphery* and *style nucleus*, from which a simple definition of dissimilarity as incomparability can be derived. Let P_{hk} be the style periphery of two common styles, S_h and S_k, with $P_{hk} \equiv \sqsubset\sqsupset_h \cap \sqsubset\sqsupset_k$, defined as the intersection of the antichains of both styles. The style nucleus, N_{hk}, of style S_h is the subset of its antichain that does not also belong to the antichain of the other style. Then $N_{hk} \equiv \sqsubset\sqsupset_h \backslash \sqsubset\sqsupset_h \cap \sqsubset\sqsupset_k$ and $N_{kh} \equiv \sqsubset\sqsupset_k \backslash \sqsubset\sqsupset_k \cap \sqsubset\sqsupset_h$.

Let the dissimilarity as incomparability of two common styles be the sum of the cardinalities of both their nuclei, that is $DIS_{ic}^{hk} \equiv \#(N_{hk} \cup N_{kh})$, that is, the sum of the union of the disjunct sets N_{hk} and N_{kh}. Also, $DIS_{ic}^{hh} = \# (N_{hh} \cup N_{hh}) = 0$. The dissimilarity as incomparability of a common style with itself is zero, because the nucleus of the common style compared to itself is an empty set. For example, in Figure 8, $DIS_{ic}^{1,2} = 7$. The dissimilarity as incomparability of two common styles is simply the sum of the elements of their two style nuclei, that is, of those elements of their antichains that are not also shown by the other style.

The social distance between elective affinity h and all other $n - 1$ elective affinities (that is, the distance to the social whole), can now be defined as the sum of the bilateral dissimilarities of style S_h with every other style $S_k, k = 1, \dots n, k \neq h$. Let D_h be the social distance between the elective affinity h and all other elective affinities:

$$D_h \equiv \sum_{k=1}^{n} DIS_{ic}^{hk} = \sum_{k=1}^{n} \# (N_{hk} \cup N_{kh}) \qquad (8)$$

The social distance between elective affinity h and all other $(n - 1)$ elective affinities is the sum of the objects in the n stylistic nuclei of the style system, containing n common styles, in *each* case related to the common style S_h. That is, in a style system with n common styles there exist $n \times n$ style nuclei (with the principal diagonal consisting of empty sets), because the style nucleus is defined relative to another common style.

This is not the only possible definition of social distance. An alternative would be to interpret the nucleus of a style *vis-à-vis* the *union* of all other antichains, $\sqsubset\sqsupset_{-h}$, with $\sqsubset\sqsupset_{-h} = \sqsubset\sqsupset_1 \cup \dots \cup \sqsubset\sqsupset_{h-1} \cup \sqsubset\sqsupset_{h+1} \dots \cup \sqsubset\sqsupset_n$, and define the nucleus of a style by $N_h \equiv \sqsubset\sqsupset_h \setminus \sqsubset\sqsupset_{-h}$. Then the number of nuclei in the style system is equal to the number of common styles and the distance, D_h^*, between the elective affinity h and the social whole is:

$$D_h^* \equiv \sum_{k=1}^{n} \# N_k$$

Then $D_h^* = D_k^*$ for all h and k, that is, all elective affinities are always at an equal distance from each other.

In the D_h^* interpretation of social distance, the mohawk hairdo of punk is part of the style nucleus of punk if and only if it is not shown in any other common style of the whole style system of society. But if a single goth follower shows up with this hairdo, the mohawk hairdo is banned from the style nucleus of punk and contributes nothing to its social distance to any other elective affinity. Only those objects from the antichain of a common style moderate social distance D_h^*, that are not found in any other style.

In the following, social distance is defined as in formula (8), because D_h has two advantages compared to D_h^*. The first is that the social distance to the social whole can vary from elective affinity to elective affinity, whereas in the D_h^* interpretation, all elective affinities are always equally distanced from the whole. The second advantage is that, in the D_h^* interpretation, the social distance disappears altogether if all objects from all antichains exist in at least one other antichain. This is because, in the D_h^* interpretation, there always exist, implicitly, only two relevant groups: we (the in-group) and the rest! Conversely, the D_h interpretation allows for a richer social structure, because the social distance that a group maintains *vis-à-vis* the social whole is made up of the (different) bilateral distances that it maintains *vis-à-vis* the different groups of the social whole.

A special case from (8) is worth noting. In a style system free of bilateral peripheries, i.e. where P_{hk}=0, $h \neq k$ for all antichains:

$$D_h \equiv \textstyle\sum_{k=1}^{n} \# \left(\sqsubset \sqsupset_k \right) \qquad (8')$$

With no bilateral stylistic peripheries, the distance maintained by an elective affinity to the social whole is equal to the number of objects in all the antichains of the style system. But without stylistic peripheries, it is also true that $N_{hk} = \sqsubset \sqsupset_h$, $h, k = 1, ..., m$, and therefore $D_h = D_h^*$. This means the social distance is the same for all groups, just as when individuals only distinguish between the in-group and the rest. Hence, it is not the style nucleus but the style periphery that causes differences in social distance between elective affinities. In other words, it is precisely what two common styles share, not what separates them, that creates the difference.

The reason is this: if bilateral differences account for the sharing of distance, only bilateral sharing can create differences. However, since shared distance is at a minimum always something bilateral, bilateral sharing can only bring about differences *vis-à-vis* third parties. The shared periphery of S_h and S_k shortens the bilateral distance of their elective affinities, but it can contain more or less objects than the common periphery of styles S_h and S_i. However, via its antichain, each style contributes the same number of objects to every bilateral distance it is a party to. Therefore, only differences in the peripheries in the entirety of all bilateral stylistic relationships can cause differences in the social distance between single groups and the social whole. This is why what is shared bilaterally creates group-specific differences *vis-à-vis* the social whole.

This also explains why, in a style system that consists of only two elective affinities, it is always true (i.e. with or without a stylistic periphery) that $D_h = D_h^*$

from (8) and (8'). For $n = 2$, by definition, the shared periphery of the two styles is the periphery of each of them with all others.

Style Nucleus and Periphery in the Social Whole

Addressing an issue in game theory in a meaningful way, you have to assume a minimum of two economic agents – game theory's minimum society consists of two members. In *style theory* there is a minimum of six: two individuals, each with their individual styles, to deal with issues of social proximity/individuality, in a total of three common styles, to deal with issues of social distance. In this sense, the 'style society' is more complex than the 'game society' that is so highly developed in economics.

Let $\partial \# N_{hk}$ be the increase in the number of objects of the common style S_h by enlarging its nucleus by one more object. Let $\partial \# N_{kh}$ be defined as such an increase in style S_k. From (8) it follows that:

$$\partial D_h / \partial \# N_{hk} = \partial D_h / \partial \# N_{kh} > 0 \qquad (9)$$

The distance between elective affinity h and the social whole increases when adding another object to any style nucleus of the style system.

Let $\partial \# P_{hk}$ be the increase in the number of objects of common style S_h by enlarging the periphery, which it shares with style S_k, by another object. Then $\partial DIS_{ic}^{hk} / \partial \# P_{hk} = 0$. That is, the dissimilarity between styles S_h and S_k is not changed by the newly shared object. Let this additional object not be an element of the other $(n - 2)$ antichains in the style system. Then from (8) it follows for $n \geq 3$ that:

$$\partial D_h / \partial \# P_{hk} = \partial D_k / \partial \# P_{hk} > 0 \text{ and } \partial D_i / \partial \# P_{hk} > 0 \text{ for all } i \neq h, k \qquad (10)$$

A new object in a style periphery that was not previously part of *any* antichain of the style system increases the social distance between *every* elective affinity and the social whole, which consists of at least three elective affinities. Here, our intuition tells us that, vis-à-vis all *other* elective affinities, the new object augments the style nucleus of S_h and S_k and hence the social distance between each of them and every other elective affinity i.

Let $\partial \#\sqsubset\sqsupset_h$ be defined as the increase in the number of objects of the common style S_h by augmenting its antichain by one more object, and let it not be an element of the other $(n - 1)$ antichains in the style system. Then it follows from (9) and (10) for $n \geq 2$ that:

$$\partial D_i / \partial \; \#\sqsubset\sqsupset_h > 0, i = 1, ..., n \qquad (11)$$

The distance of any elective affinity to the social whole increases when a new object, that did not previously belong to any antichain of the style system, is added to an antichain. This can also be easily intuited, based on what has been said so far.

The distance to the social whole of *existing* elective affinities is not affected by an increase in the number of common styles in the style system, if the total number of objects in the style nuclei remains constant. From the example in Figure 8, it follows that $D_1 = D_2 = 7$. Now, if a new style S_3 is produced by splitting off the singleton and the single chain on the left side from style S_1, such that only S_3 shows this singleton and chain, the number of objects in the style nuclei of the style system remains constant and therefore $D_1 = D_2 = 7$. This form of stylistic diversification has no effect on the social distance between the former elective affinities and the (now larger) social whole. But the social distance between the newly added style and the social whole is no larger than that of the former elective affinities, only if, in the case of (8'), there are no peripheries shared between the former styles. If there is at least one style periphery in the former style system with n styles, then the social distance between the new style, S_{n+1}, and the social whole, D_{n+1}, is larger than that of the former styles. In the example in Figure 8 containing a shared periphery of S_1 and S_2, it follows, for example, that $D_{n+1} \equiv D_3 = 11 > D_1 = D_2 = 7$. This form of stylistic diversification results in a distance between the new elective affinity and the social whole that is larger than that of the former elective affinities, because the new style is not burdened with a style periphery. As a result, the antichains of all former styles contribute fully to the formation of social distance for the new elective affinity.

These observations highlight the fact that an object from the antichain of a style makes no universal contribution to social distance in the style system; that is to say, no contribution independent of the internal structure of the style system. This is the case even though the distance to the social whole is based on the simple counting of elements found in the antichains of common styles. The principle of 'one object one count' does not apply. The contribution of each and every object from the antichains of common styles to the social distance within society is dependent on whether the object is shown in several styles or only in one. If it is shown in several styles, a shared periphery of otherwise different styles is born or augmented. Peripheries, however, diminish the distancing potential of the antichains and, in this sense, are cultural wastefulness. Only objects from the style nuclei develop the maximum distancing potential of incomparable objects.

Let $\emptyset D$ be the average distance between styles and the social whole. From (8), we arrive at $\emptyset D = \sum_{h=1}^{n}(\sum_{k=1}^{n} \# (N_{hk} \cup N_{kh}))/n$, and from (8'), for a style system without peripheries, it holds true that $\emptyset D \equiv \emptyset D' = \sum_{k=1}^{n} \# (\sqsubset\sqsupset_k)$. For a fixed total number of objects in the antichains of the style system, $\#'$, $\#' \equiv \sum_{k=1}^{n} \# (\sqsubset\sqsupset_k)$, we arrive at:

$$D'(\#') \geq \emptyset D(\#') \qquad\qquad (12)$$

with strict inequality if, in (8), $N_{hk} \subset \sqsubset\sqsupset_h$ holds true for at least one pair of common styles. For a given total number of objects in the antichains, the average distance *vis-à-vis* the social whole is smaller in the presence of stylistic peripheries than their absence. But then, given a total number of objects in the antichains of the style system, stylistic peripheries are culturally inefficient if one is pursuing the goal of maximum average distance *vis-à-vis* the social whole. In this sense, only the objects in the style nuclei are efficiently allocated in the style system.

However, as already mentioned in the previous section, this does not imply that stylistic peripheries are ineffective. They are the sole source of differences between styles in terms of their distance *vis-à-vis* the social whole. It is now possible to formulate the objective function of the *o/+consumer*.

Objective Function in the Social

In the orthodoxy, consumer utility, U_i, is a function of the *quantities*, q, of v goods that consumer i buys:

$$U_i = V(q_1, ..., q_v)$$

Apart from pathologies/anomalies, the orthodox motto is 'the more of everything, the better!' Style as a property of ensembles of goods can be accounted for in this orthodox *quantity* theory of consumption with reference to the concept of complementarity between goods of one common style, and substitutability between goods of different common styles. However, this is true in principle only! Because for as long as they are lacking in cultural substance, the ideas of (economic) complementarity and (economic) substitutability will remain a shell devoid of content. Only the crudest predictions can be made – not to mention Max

Weber's insistence that social phenomena must not only be predicted but also understood. That is where QTC steps in and sets itself apart from the orthodoxy.

Just as the orthodoxy abstracts from qualities, so I have abstracted from quantities when expanding on the idea of *o/+consumption*. This idea compels a radical departure from the orthodoxy. Because in the *o/+consumption* approach, even those goods that consumers never buy provide utility. It is only consequential then to abstract entirely from the controlling function of prices and the household budget, which are so central to the orthodoxy. This allows the effects of the quality of goods to be isolated in their purest form. QTC is therefore an economic theory devoid of money.

In the second step of my argumentation I have specified exactly what can be consumed in *o/+consumption* with the things and behaviours that are shown and not shown: it is differences that can be consumed; differences between people and between groups of people. These differences are entirely due to *o/+consumption* – with no money involved. This makes *o/+consumption* the constitutive foundation of the social realm, as the aggregate of individual differences – with no money involved. In this way, QTC also becomes an economic theory of sociological postmodernism, of a society in which the social structure is neither stratified nor predetermined by the differences in human endowment. Rather, it is an economic theory of the horizontal structure of elective affinities that is produced by *o/+consumption* – with no money involved.

A simple formulation of the effect of this social embeddedness on happiness/utility of an individual is:

$$U_i = U(Distance, Proximity) \equiv U(D_h, P_i^{-1}) = U(D_h, I_i)$$

That is, happiness/utility is a function of collective existence as part of an elective affinity within the system of all elective affinities (distance *vis-à-vis* other groups) and of one's individual existence within this elective affinity (individuality as the inverse of proximity to the other members of the elective affinity).

In the penultimate step towards identifying the relationship between *o/+ consumption* and the happiness/utility of the individual, social distance and proximity were operationalised. The starting point for this operationalisation was the assumption that suitable specifications of social distance and proximity must be based on the basic idea of individual dissimilarities between any two people. But there are (at least) two fundamentally different basic ideas for this purpose: dissimilarity as comparability, DIS_c, and dissimilarity as incomparability, DIS_{ic}, and, building on this, two corresponding ideas of diversity for groups with more than two members, DIV_c and DIV_{ic}. An assignment of these alternative ideas to the different social contexts – in-groups and out-groups (Table 6) – leads to the following clarification of the objective function:

$$U_i = U[D_h(DIS_{ic}, DIV_{ic}), I_i(DIS_c, DIV_c)]$$

Up to this point, human happiness/utility is a function of precise but abstract dissimilarities and/or diversities. What they refer to is still completely up in the air. Happiness/utility still needs to be grounded in the world of objects, as it shows up in the observable individual and common styles, through which (word-less) communication takes place. For this final step we can look to the results of the present chapter.

Let individual i with its individual style, s_i, be a member of the elective affinity h, showing the common style, S_h. From (1) and (8) it follows that:

$$U_i = U(D_h, I_i) = U[\sum_{k=1}^{n} \# (N_{hk} \cup N_{kh}), (m-1) \cdot DIV_c^c - R_i^c] \tag{13}$$

The consumer's happiness/utility is a function of properties of their individual style and the common style of their elective affinity, in which their individual style is nested, as well as of the entire style system of all elective affinities in society.

Specifying the utility function as in (13) allows for the following traditional assumptions of the orthodoxy to be maintained *mutatis mutandis*:

$$\partial U_i/\partial D_h > 0, \partial U_i/\partial I_i > 0, \partial^2 U_i/\partial D_h^2 < 0 \text{ und } \partial^2 U_i/\partial I_i^2 < 0 \tag{14}$$

That is, positive but decreasing marginal utility of the distance between the elective affinity and the social whole, and positive but decreasing marginal utility of the individuality of the consumer in their elective affinity.

The concrete specification of the determinants of happiness/utility, is at all times influenced by culture as 'crystallised history', $\square$, which forms out of the world of objects that ordered set, $(X, \square)$, that allows the *o/+consumption* of all individuals to become collectively effective. In other words, with their *o/+consumption*, the consumer can manipulate but not control the determinants of their individual happiness/utility.

Psychology of the Objective Function

It is time to position QTC within the psychology of the self. QTC addresses the collective production of the self through o/+consumption. Consumption results in a multiple social identity: collective identity in an elective affinity (brought about by the common style), and individual identity within the elective affinity (brought about by the individual style). They are interdependent. The common style is composed of individual styles and the individual style allows for greater individuality the more diverse the common style is. QTC is thus also a theory of human identity.

As a theory of identity, there are three touchpoints with social psychology: *identity theory*, *social identity theory*, and *self-categorisation theory*. Social identity theory and self-categorisation theory are more closely related and are sometimes treated as one (social-identity-cum-self-categorisation theory). Whether the commonalities between identity theory and social-identity-cum-self-categorisation theory outweigh their differences remains an open question.[5] The question of whether QTC belongs to one of these theories is therefore a matter of degree. However, social identity theory and self-categorisation theory are themselves dissimilar enough to distinguish in them two separate strands of research.[6]

Identity theory has little in common with QTC, as its origins lie not in psychology but in modernist sociology. Its main concern is identity born out of role-playing in a given social structure. It asks what identity emerges when people slip into the role assigned to them by society.[7] It is concerned with *what one does* in order to fulfil these expectations, which is why freedom of choice is negligible here.

Both social identity theory (SIT) and self-categorisation theory (SCT) have their roots in psychology. Their main concern is the identity that results from membership in (social) groups. Accordingly, they are concerned with *who a person is* when they join a social group (SCT) or when they happen to find themself in it (SIT). Choice is a prominent issue in both approaches. There are commonalities between them and QTC, but there are also differences that need to be clarified now.

The origin of SIT is the *minimal group paradigm* from a famous experiment. Subjects who believe themselves to belong to an in-group, which is in fact completely meaningless, start to prefer individuals (over an out-group) who they also

---

5   Hogg, Terry and White 1995; Stets and Burke 2000.

6   Hornsey 2008.

7   Hogg, Terry and White 1995.

believe to belong to this in-group. The minimal group that has social impact is thus the one that individuals simply believe they belong to.[8] This led to the socio-psychological theory of intergroup behaviour, the demarcation of and preference for one's own group over others. The 'distance' argument in the objective function (13) represents this basic hypothesis of SIT. For a member of an in-group, it turns separation from out-groups into a value in itself. SIT leaves the question mostly open, however, as to how this separation is achieved. QTC steps in here, proposing operationalisation of this separation by means of diversity theory's concept of width. It stresses the incomparability of common styles as that which is significant for separation.

SCT is an outflow from SIT.[9] It distinguishes three levels of belonging: the uppermost level of *human identity*, the middle level of belonging to an in-group (*collective identity*) and the bottom level of self-categorisation based on interpersonal comparisons (*personal identity*). Individuality, then, is the result of these interpersonal comparisons. The 'individuality' argument in the objective function (13), defined as the inverse of the individual's 'proximity' to the in-group, represents this basic hypothesis of the SCT. It allows individuality as interpersonal differentiation to become a value in itself for the individual. SCT leaves open the question of who the object of this interpersonal differentiation is. QTC defines the members of the in-group as the reference group for that comparison. Alternatively, it could be the out-groups, or both. Plausibility considerations favour the in-group: the potential for physical proximity, the significance of the in-group compared to other social groups and thereby the significance of its members *vis-à-vis* society as a whole, the frequency of resonance. Furthermore, SCT also leaves open the question as to what the aspirational personal identity consists of. Operationalisation as (part of) the (diversity theoretical) length of the common style is QTC's proposal for precisely what individuality could consist of. It emphasises what is different but comparable between the individual styles of the in-group – as that which constitutes individuality. The *personal* identity of SCT corresponds to the *individual* identity in QTC, although, in the latter, it is more precisely specified.

Early on, SIT and SCT regarded collective and personal identity as antagonistic. SIT distanced itself from the more individualistic approach of the SCT, arguing that collective identity is the primary basis for the definition of identity, and that group behaviour could not be derived from individual behaviour. From that viewpoint, SCT, with its openness to individual choice, is a more natural

---

8   Tajfel, Billig, Bundy and Flament 1971.

9   Turner, Hogg, Oakes, Reicher and Wetherell 1987.

touchpoint for economics than SIT. However, the orthodoxy with its *Identity Economics* remains ambivalent towards both theories.[10] On the one hand, in *Identity Economics*, group membership is generally understood to be the resource-dependent result of individual decisions (cf. SCT). On the other hand, its assumption of group-specific exogenous preferences leads to exogenous collective behaviour (cf. SIT). By contrast, the objective function (13) has been developed out of a special model of social circumstances (postmodernism), as a goal that is appropriate to these circumstances and to emic meaning. Thus, the objective function is generally a societal variable and not a function exogenous to it. It is fed by the social whole (modernism, postmodernism, etc.) and, thereby, determines the social realm in its smaller spheres (within and between groups).

Over time, SIT and SCT have moved closer together in their efforts to respond in a more nuanced way to the human desire for individuality and, at the same time, for group belonging (multi-identity motivation).[11] Today, psychologists do not even shy away from postulating an optimal internal balance between the separate subgoals of collective belonging – the *we!* – and individuality – the *me!*.[12] Experimental consumer research has shown, for example, that consumers indeed simultaneously demonstrate multi-identity motives through their choice of an object, such as the motive of belonging through their choice of *brand* and the motive of individuality through their choice of *colour*.[13] A business model based on this psychology is the 'singularity mass production' of brands such as Nike, where customers can design their 'one-offs' in Nike's internet configurator. Another business model based on multi-identity psychology aims at balancing experimentation (striving for individuality) and risk avoidance (avoiding social exclusion).[14] In QTC, too, the simultaneous striving for individuality and group belonging is no contradiction. The objective function (13) is an operationalisation of this simultaneous striving.

The self-categorisation of SCT includes as one of several dimensions the perceived 'goodness of fit'.[15] It is operationalised in the objective function (13) in its 'proximity' argument as diversity based on comparability. QTC thus abstracts from SCT's other dimensions of personal identity, such as emotional involvement, social embeddedness in daily interaction, ideology and narration.

10   Akerlof and Kranton 2000.

11   Hornsey 2008, p. 216.

12   Brewer 1991.

13   Chan, Berger and Van Boven 2012.

14   Holzer 2013.

15   Ashmore, Deaux and McLaughlin-Volpe 2004.

In QTC, 'fit' also determines collective identity. But not as 'goodness of fit', but as 'badness of fit' – operationalised as dissimilarity-as-incomparability. In this respect, QTC differs from SIT, which operationalises the relationships between groups in behavioural dimensions such as out-group discrimination and in-group favouritism. Thus, in QTC, 'fit' as the result of clustering in the sorting plant of culture determines, in different definitions, both the individual and the collective identity. These different definitions are given by the meta-contrasting lens through which individuals see themselves within their in-group and, respectively, their in-group versus out-groups (see Table 5). This is also part of the tradition of SIT and SCT, where the salience of the personal from the collective identity is understood as being contextually activated.[16]

The basic premise of QTC is symbolic interaction, which allows identity to emerge collectively. The means of symbolic interaction is *0/+consumption* as an individual and collective subset within the world of objects. The mutually understood 'language' of the world of objects is the crux of this interaction. QTC thus is also aligned with the tradition of Russel Belk's influential concept of the *extended self*, according to which identity, both in terms of self-image and outside perception, is also inherent in material things.[17] From this viewpoint, people interact with objects not in terms of their material functionalities, but the meaning they convey.[18] The world of objects is not limited to the purely material, behaviour also creates identity. Here, the arguments of QTC's objective function (13) align with the multidimensionality tradition of SCT's self-categorisation.[19]

It is well worth comparing QTC with a formal SIT/SCT model.[20] Moses Shayo's model of identification and identity can be described in his chosen application as follows. Individuals differ in their exogenous endowments, including income and wealth (1). Three exogenous groups are given: the poor and the rich (class), and the nation (2). In their self-categorisation, individuals can assign themselves either to one of the two classes or to the nation (3). The utility resulting from this identity depends on two factors. The first is the utility of the identity, which the group, chosen via self-categorisation, provides; among classes, the class of the rich provides greater utility than that of the poor (4). The second is the proximity to the prototype of the chosen group (5). The smaller the differences between the individual and the prototype (for example in terms of income),

16   Hornsey 2008, p. 208; Howard 2000, p. 369; Stets and Burke 2000, p. 224.

17   Belk 1988.

18   Howard 2000, p. 371.

19   Ashmore, Deaux and McLaughlin-Volpe 2004, p. 83.

20   Shayo 2009.

the greater the utility (6). In their self-categorisation, individuals choose the group that offers the greatest utility – for the poor, this can be the nation and not their class. Individuals take part in political elections only after their self-categorisation (7). In these elections, those poor individuals who have chosen their class show limited altruism (8) by voting for redistribution, which those poor individuals who see themselves as belonging to the nation do to a lesser degree. Thus, the model predicts that redistribution is lower in countries where the nation is held high than in countries whose citizens feel more strongly attached to their class than to their nation.

Whereas in Shayo's model exogenous endowment determines which group an individual will join (1), in QTC the endowment has no influence on group membership. Only the 0/+consumption of individuals determines group membership. Self-categorisation is thus not based on a comparison of exogenous endowments, as in the Shayo model, but on a comparison of endogenous consumer behaviour.

The most important difference between the two models is the exogeneity of social groups in Shayo (2) and their endogeneity in QTC. In Shayo's model, groups *exist* (as categories) before people categorise themselves. In QTC, groups *become* by virtue of people joining them in the sorting plant of culture.

With Shayo, self-categorisation is unconditional (3), it is a purely mental act. Since, in QTC, 0/+consumption determines assignment to a group, groups are only formed by consuming. Self-categorisation is thus not a mental but an economic act. This implies that consumption does not directly contribute to happiness/utility but does so by allowing for self-categorisation.

Both models operate with the happiness/utility provided by the selected in-group (4). In QTC, it is created by the distance of the in-group to the social whole, which is operationalised as width (diversity based on incomparability). Width is collectively created by all groups acting together, and therefore the groups are interdependent in terms of the happiness/utility they jointly create. What's good for one group is good for all. In Shayo's model, however, there is no systematic relationship between the utilities that membership in different social groups confers on their respective members.

In both models, proximity within the in-group also brings about happiness/utility (5). In Shayo's model it is the proximity to the prototype and thus to a (constructed) individual at the centre of the in-group. Proximity results from comparing the exogenous endowment of the individual with the exogenous endowment of the prototype. In contrast, in QTC, proximity to the in-group results from the comparison with all other group members, operationalised as diversity theory's concept of length (diversity based on comparability). And whilst proximity is defined by way of example of the prototype in Shayo's model, this does not apply to QTC, where differences to all are what counts.

In Shayo's model, utility increases with increasing proximity to the prototype (6). This implicitly models a collectivist society – the individual wishes to merge with it, to be absorbed into it. In contrast, QTC models the individualist. They, too, want social belonging but seek individuality within it. This is why happiness/utility decreases when the proximity of the individual to its in-group increases. All group members strive for the greatest possible individuality within the group, yet without losing their membership.

The two models also differ in terms of the timing of action (7). In QTC, action is the starting point for finding identity; in Shayo's model, action (e.g. at the ballot box) is the result of the chosen identity. Thus, in QTC, action in the form of *0/+consumption* constitutes identity. In Shayo's model, action is the opportunistic outflow of a pre-determined identity.

Shayo's model allows for parochial altruism in favour of the in-group, not as a goal *per se* but as a result of self-interest (8). The class-conscious poor vote for redistribution, because rising class income (not just personal income) raises class status. QTC accommodates unlimited altruism, likewise not as a goal but as the result of individual action. This aspect of QTC needs to be further clarified.

Egoism/Altruism Obsolescence

The objective function (13) brings two present-day phenomena to the fore: egoism of the individual combined with indifference towards others on the one hand, and on the other hand a society in which the gain of the individual, their happiness/utility, is a gift from the social whole. Here is a paradox of QTC: individuals work at the social (solely) for themselves, and yet they receive everything of value to them as a gift from the social whole.

Objective function (13) is fully contained in the orthodoxy's tradition of methodical individualism. All striving has its origin in the individual, everything of value is expressed as the individual's advantage. There is not a spark of public welfare motivation in the objective function (13). Individual striving is not even aimed at the fulfilment of the volition of other individuals (altruism), not even at that of one's own elective affinity (parochial altruism). The individual works on the social for themself alone. Nevertheless, alone, the individual achieves (almost) nothing. Its happiness/utility is (almost) entirely produced collectively. The *0/+consumption* as the single control variable of the individual is not an argument of objective function (13). Not even the individual style that emerged from it appears in the concept of objective function (13) as a determinant of happiness/utility. The individual style of the egoist influences their goal attainment only indirectly, through their contribution to the common style of the elective affinity and to the style system consisting of all elective affinities in society.

Consider the contribution of the individual style to the happiness/utility of the average egoist in Table 10. Its contribution to the common style of its elective affinity of m egoists is $1/m$. The common style is the 'club good' of the elective affinity. Given the minimum group size of $m = 2$, the maximum possible contribution of the individual style to the club good is 1/2 and the contribution of the $(m - 1)$ other club members is at least 1/2. The larger the elective affinity, the smaller the individual contribution.

Suppose there are n elective affinities in the style system. Then the contribution of the individual style of the average egoist to the contribution of the average elective affinity to the style system of society is $1/m \cdot n$. The style system is the 'collective good' of society. Suppose society consists of z (style-capable) individuals. Then $m \cdot n = z$, and the average contribution of the egoist to the whole style system is $1/z$. The larger the number of style-capable members in society, the smaller their individual contribution to the style system.

Table 10: *Average individual contribution ($\emptyset$) of the egoist to the determinants of their happiness.*

Determinants of the Objective Function			
Term in the objective function (13)	*Characterisation*	*Source*	*Agency level*
$\sum_{k=1}^{m} \# \, (N_{hk} \cup N_{kh})$	stylistic nuclei of all common styles	style system (collective good with $\emptyset = 1/z$)	society
(ditto)	(indirectly: the bilateral stylistic peripheries of the common styles)	style system (collective good with $\emptyset = 1/z$)	society
m	In-group size	style system (collective good with $\emptyset = 1/z$), and common style (club goods with $\emptyset = 1/m$)	society/ elective affinity
DIV_c^c	diversity based on comparability of the common style of one's own elective affinity	common style (club goods with $\emptyset = 1/m$)	elective affinity
R_i^c	rooting of the individual in the common style	common style (club goods with $\emptyset = 1/m$)	elective affinity

m: number of members of an elective affinity; z: number of style-capable members in society.

Table 10 shows the social scaling expressed in formula (13). Although the egoist is doing everything just for themself, they only contribute a minor part to their own advantage. They owe the majority of it to a grander collective, to the elective affinity as a whole and to society as a whole. The bigger the collective, the smaller their own contribution to their individual advantage. Consumption is a collective activity and the individual advantage is a gift from the social whole.

The objective function (13) not only expresses altruism-free egoism, but also extreme individualism. The individual not only attempts to distinguish themself as part of a group from other groups, but also to distinguish themself as an individual within the group from other group members. If the pursuit of individuality were missing, the objective function could be simplified to

$$U_i = U(DIV) \qquad (15)$$

with *DIV* as a measure of the diversity of the entire style system. Objective function (15) expresses pure joy in the diversity in society and thus an appreciation of each other, including everyone's individual contribution to the joy of all. In the objective function (13) a different approach comes into play: indifference towards third parties instead of appreciation.

The paradox inherent in the objective function (13) lies in the fact that even the consumer who disrespects all other members of society and pursues only their self-interest receives (almost) everything they value as a gift from the social whole; and (almost) everything they do purely for themself is actually their gift to all the rest. Pure egoism and total altruism lead to the same happiness/utility for all. With the objective function (13), the concepts of egoism and altruism lose their predictive power.

Poststructuralism of the Objective Function

Poststructuralist Jean Baudrillard begins his early work *La société de consommation* with the following words:

> "There is all around us today a kind of fantastic conspicuousness of consumption and abundance, constituted by the multiplication of objects, services and material goods, and this represents something of a fundamental mutation in the ecology of the human species. Strictly speaking, the humans of the age of affluence are surrounded not so much by other human beings, as they were in all previous ages, but by *objects*. Their daily dealings are now not so much with their fellow men but rather, on a rising statistical curve, with the reception and manipulation of goods and messages." [21]

In his introduction to the English translation of *La société*, George Ritzer describes the essence of this work with words that recall QTC. [22]

> "The world of consumption is treated like a mode of discourse, a language [...]. As a language, consumption is a way in which we converse and communicate with one another."

QTC interprets, or rather defines *0/+consumption* as the language with which people speak to each other.

---

21   Baudrillard 2009 (1970) (emphasis in original).

22   ibid., p. 6–9, 15.

"[C]onsumables become sign-values."

In QTC, individual consumer goods do not become signs, each performing for its own sake, but as goods type baskets, individual styles (from 0/+consumption) become the syntax of their communication. The value of 0/+consumption is its language-equivalent capacity.

"When looked at from the structural perspective, what we consume are signs (messages, images) rather than commodities."

QTC is precise about whose signs the individual consumes. It is both the signs that it sets itself and, without qualification, the signs that are set by everybody else. The individual thus consumes the entire communication from the style system.

"This means that consumers need to be able to 'read' the system of consumption in order to know what to consume."

In QTC, it is a prerequisite that everyone comprehends culture's instructions for its sorting plant, that is, that everyone belongs to the same culture. Only then can they recognise the effect of an additional concrete object on social distance and proximity and make their own choice.

"Commodities are no longer defined by their use, but rather by what they signify. And what they signify is defined not by what they do, but by the relationship to the entire system of commodities and signs."

This emphasises what leads to the obsolescence of egoism/altruism in QTC. The individual does not consume what is provided by the single object it shows, but what it provides in conjunction with all other objects in the style system; the benefit to the individual, its happiness/utility, is a gift from the social whole.

"There is an infinite range of difference available in this system and people therefore are never able to satisfy their need for commodities, for difference."

Here, Baudrillard's concept of the fundamental mutation of the human species is further clarified – it is no longer goods that are consumed, but differences between people, which manifest themselves in differences in consumption. This is the fundamental paradigm of QTC.

"Baudrillard urges the abandonment of the 'individual logic of satisfaction' (need and so on) and a central focus on the 'social logic of differentiation'."

QTC responds to Baudrillard's urge for a new logic by specifying the social logic of differentiation – it is collective social distance and individual proximity that are consumed, which shows up in 0/+consumption.

"What people seek in consumption is not so much a particular object as difference and the search for the latter is unending."

Neither poststructuralist consumption nor 0/+consumption leads to saturation. In both, there are no differences between people that could not be replaced by even greater differences, thus further increasing happiness/utility. For Baudrillard, this leads to the "fantastic conspicuousness of consumption and abundance". In QTC it leads to the ever-increasing world of objects, as will be shown in the following chapter.

"[I]n Baudrillard's view, it is the code, or the system of differences, that causes us to be similar to, as well as different from, one another."

This is the poststructuralist simultaneity of social distance and proximity. In QTC, it is operationalised by the psychological lens that, depending on the situation, either makes the incomparable (width) visible in 0/+consumption and the comparable (length) invisible, or vice versa.

"Baudrillard concludes that the sociological study of consumption (and everything else) must shift from the superficial level of conscious social dynamics to the unconscious social logic of signs and the code. In other words, the key to understanding lies at the level of deep structures."

In the sorting plant of culture, this logic of signs and the code is at work. In chapter 6, QTC will be augmented by the cultural dynamics that consumers themselves produce in the sorting plant at the level of deep material structures. And in chapter 7, the social impact that results from these material dynamics is addressed.

"[B]ecause of their training, the upper classes are seen as having some degree of mastery over the code. It is the middle and lower classes who are the true consumers because they lack such mastery."

QTC abstracts from stratifying parameters and thus from the sociological category of class. But it distinguishes style leadership from style followers. Style leadership evinces a limited mastery of the code (see Table 11), which their followers are denied. In QTC, style leadership is the 'upper class' and its followers are the 'middle and lower class'.

> "In his view, 'anything can become a consumer object'. As a result, 'consumption is laying hold of the whole of life'."

Baudrillard's poststructuralism and QTC share an all-encompassing interpretation of consumption. All that produces differences is consuming, and consumption is all that has ever produced differences.

QTC is a poststructuralist theory. It abstracts from modernism's social structure of consumption and has its theoretical roots in semiotics. The objective function (13) captures this poststructuralism in a concise form. In QTC, as in poststructuralism, social volition takes place in the depths of culture. However, the formalisation of poststructuralism in the objective function (13) allows for a sharpness of analysis that is closed to the original.

Club Goods and Public Collective Goods Production

The private provision of public goods is a well-covered topic in economics. The orthodox concern is the conditions under which public goods can be provided efficiently, not only by the state but also by the private sector. This question, however, only makes sense if the good in question can be provided both by the state and by private entities. In the orthodoxy, this is assured by the premise that the production technology used to manufacture the good (e.g. public security) is the same whether it is utilised by the state or by private entities. This assumption simplifies the question of the efficiency of (alternative) private provision of public goods into a question of financing: under what conditions do private entities provide sufficient funding for the production of efficient quantities of public goods?

In this respect, too, QTC differs from the orthodoxy. Yet there is common ground in the private production of public goods. In QTC it is the common styles as club goods and the style system as the public good that are produced by private entities; in the orthodoxy it is, for example, public security. However, by assumption, the funding question does not arise in QTC – the world of objects is available for free. This shifts the issue of private versus public provision back to the production technology issue. Here it is evident that the orthodox theory of the private provision of public goods and QTC are dealing with disjunct topics. Not only would the assumption of identical production technologies for the state and the consumer be absurd. It is difficult to imagine how the state might be able to produce social distance and proximity for individuals. The consumptive production of social distance and proximity is the domain of the consumers themselves.

Restrictions for Style Followers

Which restrictions are consumers subject to? In the orthodoxy it is the budget restriction dictated by income and the goods price vector: don't spend more than you have. The budget can be divided into alternative consumption bundles, defined as quantity vectors of goods. Little Max can afford to buy so and so many Pepsi and pizzas with his pocket money. In the consumerism modelled by the orthodoxy, money is the limiting factor.

In QTC, the financial budget is irrelevant. The world offers its objects free of charge. By the definition of *0/+consumption*, of each element, x_j, from the world of objects, X, either one unit (or more) or no unit is consumed. The *0/+consumer decision* sets the individual style, s_i – that subset from the world of objects that the individual shows. The individual style either shows the quality x_j, or not. Let r be the number of style followers in the style system. The only restriction for style follower i, or more precisely, its stylistic composition restriction is:

$$s_i \subseteq X, \qquad i = 1, ..., r \qquad\qquad (16)$$

All style followers are subject to the same restriction. Each individual style is a subset of the given world of objects, the finite set X. This is due to 'non-rivalry' in the consumption of qualities. If consumer i shows object x_j in their individual style, $x_j \in s_i$, then this object can also be shown in any other of the r individual styles. The composition restriction (16) can also be interpreted as an individual communication restriction in the style system. That is: everyone can say the same thing, $s_i = s_j, i, j = 1, ..., r$, but do not have to; everyone can say all that can be said, $s_i = X, i = 1, ..., r$, but no one has to. The only restriction is the availability of objects, the finite set of what can be nonverbally used to communicate.

The composition restriction (16) is the essence of the egalitarian postmodern antithesis to capitalist consumerism: everyone is an equal forger of their own happiness/utility! The sociologist Gerhard Schulze pinpoints this egalitarian property of (16) with his diagnosis of the postmodern losers in terms of happiness/utility: "In the members of the former lower classes one could see the exploited, the deceived, the powerless, people who had to be helped to realise their rights. The new distinction sees subjects where previously there was talk of objects, it sees actors instead of victims. It irreverently denies respect to all those who waste their day with nonsense and eat till they are fat and sick."[23] Condescension in postmodernism is thus directed at those who could make something good out of their lives, like everyone else, but fail to do so. Compared to the budget restrictions of orthodox consumerism, composition restriction (16) shifts the self-responsibility of the individual into the foreground. Where endowment differences no longer play a major role, meritorious concerns, such as those of a caring sociology, lose their legitimacy.

Restriction (16) not only represents the egalitarian side of postmodernism. In conjunction with the objective function (13), it directs the individual's decision-making interests away from accumulation towards lifestyle. Happiness/utility no longer depend on what one has, but on what one does.

Restrictions for Style Leadership

Table 8 from chapter 4 shows the increased agency of style leaders compared to their followers. But where are their restrictions? One of them is the counterpart to composition restriction (16). Let s_j be the individual style of style leader j, and let X' be the finite set of objects that can be loaded into it. X' contains not only that part of the world of objects usable by style followers, but also the subset of all stylistically usable objects that the style leader can invent. The style leader's counterpart to the stylistic design restriction of the style follower is:

$$s_j \subseteq X' \supset X \qquad\qquad (17)$$

The world of objects that the style leader can use is larger than that of its following. It can utilise qualities – the proverbial object that no one expected – that followers are not yet able to communicate with. Here, however, a temporal structure not shown in Table 8 must be taken into account. Restriction (17) applies in the short term, while in the long term, style followers are able to learn from their style leaders. Successful style leadership can be defined as accomplished learning of style followers, i.e. for successful style leadership the following applies in the long term:

---

23   Schulze 2005, p. XXI (my translation).

$$\lim_{t \to \infty} X = X' \qquad\qquad (18)$$

The set of objects that can be utilised by style followers in the long term converges towards the usable set of objects of their style leaders.

(17) is not the only restriction for the successful style leader. Style leaders must also observe restrictions on the part of their potential followers: not everything that style leaders are able to produce, are followers able or willing to reproduce. The exogenous culture for style followers, $\square$, the set of instructions for the sorting plant of culture, however, is only to a certain extent 'crystallised history' for style leaders. Let $\square'$ be the subset of culture that even style leaders cannot manipulate. Let $\square' \subset \square$, that is, culture harbours taboos, conventions and norms for the creation of order in the world of objects, which the successful style leader cannot ignore. For that part of culture that can be manipulated by the style leadership, $\square''$, $\square'' = \square \setminus \square'$. Table 11 summarises the restrictions for the style leadership, described in Table 8, and gives examples.

Table 11: Agency and individual restrictions for the representative style leader.

Options and Restrictions to Successful Style Leadership			
Agency		Restrictions	
Option for action	Example	Type of restriction	Example
Manipulation of the feature space $\underline{m}_j(\square'')$	Transformation of objects into a different object category (e.g. positioning of insects as food)	Culture as crystallised history $\square'$ even for style leaders	Tabu as avoidance commandment (e.g. food tabu) or tabu as cognition interdiction (e.g. Dumpsterdiving)
Manipulation of the sympathy vector $\underline{v}(\square', \underline{m}_j)$	Weighting of stylistic oppositions (see Chapter 2)		Tradition/habit/ideology (e.g. traditional higher weighting of museum art over popular art)
Choice of type of make (above-average vs. extreme type)	Performance cult (e.g. Beau Brummel)		Conventions, e.g. in the segregation of private from non-private life
Determination of the threshold value, d_R, for clustering	Separation (e.g. of rock 'n' roll from rhythm 'n' blues)		Tradition/habit/ideology, e.g. the traditional distinction between black and white music
Expansion of the world of objects, X, as inventor	DIY (e.g. base-jumping)	$s_j \subseteq X' \supset X$	Avoidance commandments, e.g. of danger, habit
Reactivation of pre-existing objects for a style	Bricolage (e.g. the jute sack in hipster style)		Ideology, e.g. avoiding what is old
0/+consumption			

$\square'$ is the non-manipulable subset of culture, $\square$, remaining even for style leaders, and $\square''$ the manipulable part. The non-manipulable part of culture resists its manipulation by being taboo, mass habit, beloved tradition, defended ideology or stubborn (social) norm.

Culture as Dynamic Institution

The options for action and their restrictions shown in Table 11, turn $\square$, the set of instructions for the sorting plant of culture, into a dynamic economic institution. It contains taboos, habits, traditions, conventions and norms. With it, the unordered set of objects, X, is converted through consumptive production into the ordered set $(X, \square)$. It is exogenous to most people in society, the style followers – they can only use it as it is. For a few, the style leaders, part $\square''$ of these instructions is a variable. Through exemplary presentation, through wordless communication through their own *0/+consumption*, style leaders can give style followers new instructions for the sorting plant of culture.

Style followers ensure institutional constancy, style leaders effect institutional change. Style followers maintain taboos, cultivate habits, respect traditions, adhere to conventions, indulge in ideologies and heed norms. Style leaders breach taboos and break from habits, they are disrespectful of traditions and ideologies and do not adhere to conventions, nor follow norms. With their agency, style leaders influence style followers by changing what they adhere to in the sorting plant of culture. This is how they change the order $(X, \square)$ in part $(X, \square'')$: taboos drop or are replaced by others, habits change, traditions are superseded, conventions are replaced by others and norms are adapted.

It is too simple to assume that the non-manipulable part of culture would remain unchanged over time, $\square'_t = \square'_{t+1}$. Then there would be an immutable institutional core of culture that would survive for all time. This institutional core exists in the form of a few commandments and interdictions such as the taboo of incest or prohibition of killing. However, it is so small that it can be neglected here. Instead I assume:

$$\lim_{t \to \infty} \square'_t = \varnothing \tag{19}$$

In the long run, the subset of instructions for culture's sorting plant, which cannot be manipulated by the style leadership, is the empty set.

Lingua franca as Restriction

Culture changes in the social realm. You can distinguish two types of social interaction. First, the interaction between style leaders – in the correspondence between Goethe and Schiller, in the liaison between Marianne von Werefkin and Alexei Jawlensky, or in the polemics of the architectural reformer Adolf Loos against the *Wiener Werkstätte* around Josef Hoffmann. Secondly, the interaction between style leaders and followers. A conceivable specification of the second type of interaction, to start from, is: followers only follow the style leadership of their own common style, i.e. style leaders have no influence on style followers in other elective affinities; and there is only one style leader in each elective affinity.

This specification has two consequences. First, the culture of society would eventually crumble into n subcultures, one for each elective affinity, because the sole style leader of an elective affinity is its cultural monopolist. Each elective affinity, i, will develop its own culture, $\Box_i = \Box_i''$, combined with their elective affinity-specific order of the world of objects, $(X, \Box_i)$. It will no longer have anything in common with the order given to the world of objects in other elective affinities. The world of objects will lose its capacity for communication across social groups, it will lose its capacity as a *lingua franca*, understood and 'spoken' by everyone. Sectarianism, but also the mantra of parallel societies in urban centres could thereby be embedded in QTC.

The second consequence of this specification of leader-follower interaction, is that you implicitly assume a total loss of cultural and also social dynamics, above the level of the elective affinity. Because the emergence of new elective affinities, and with it the further differentiation of postmodern society, cannot be imagined when abstracting from the existence of (anonymous) individuals, who experimentally move out of existing elective affinities, but recruit their new followers from that reservoir. The capability of the style system as a whole to undergo change presupposes the existence of style leaders, whose manipulative agency transcends the boundaries of elective affinities. This in turn necessitates the ability to communicate on both sides.

But then you have an interaction between style leaders that culminates in their collective agency. It is the collective agency of style leadership which develops a social and cultural impact. The social impact is the allocation of followers between elective affinities, and the cultural impact is the transformation of the non-verbal *lingua franca* while maintaining its society-wide unity. It is only by this collective agency of style leadership that social distance and proximity can be produced by consumption.

This is the analytical pathway I will be following. Postmodernism thereby is understood as a society capable of permanent differentiation, in which the ability of non-verbal communication among all its members is preserved by the collective agency of style leadership.

The Cultural Trade-off

Collective agency of style leadership negotiates instructions, $\square$, for the sorting plant of culture, which are uniform for all elective affinities. Hence not only the punk himself, but also the banker assigns him to punk. A trivial social trade-off and a non-trivial cultural one result from this. In the social sphere, an individual cannot be a member of all elective affinities at the same time. In the simplest case, each individual belongs to only one elective affinity. If you allow for situation-specific elective affinities, each individual is allocated an individual alter ego portfolio, whose elements are activated by the perspect manager according to specific situations. So, the punk is a punk in the evenings and a blue collar worker during the day. In this social triage, the trade-off is by definition trivial, just as in the orthodoxy the trade-off imposed by the budget constraint is a trivial one. But in QTC the social trade-off is one of affiliation – belonging to an elective affinity excludes some others: a banker can perhaps pass for a gentleman, but hardly for a punk, and a punk can pass for a worker, but hardly for a banker. These social trade-offs are collectively negotiated.

In the sphere of culture, however, a non-trivial trade-off is effective. It is inherent in the distinction made in chapter 3, between dissimilarity as comparability and dissimilarity as incomparability. There, social proximity/individuality within the elective affinity was operationalised by (DIS_c, DIV_c) and social distance between affinities by (DIS_{ic}, DIV_{ic}). Both operationalisations are included in the objective function (13). Social volition of the individual, in terms of its objective function (13) and its properties (14), aims to achieve more of both: more dissimilarity/diversity as (or based on) comparability/incomparability. The collective cultural prowess of style leaders is subject to a non-trivial trade-off between these subgoals.

This is because social proximity results from (vertical) lengths of objects shown in a common style (Figure 6). Social distance, in contrast, results from the (horizontal) width of the common styles, defined by their antichains (Figure 8). Social distance and proximity are thus in an orthogonal relationship, as width (horizontal) and length (vertical). The cultural trade-off is this: for a given unordered set of objects, X, if its subset $(X, \square_d)$, ordered by a dominance order, $\square_d$, is enlarged, then the cardinality of all n antichains in the style system, $\#'$, $\#' \equiv \#$ ($\sqsubset\sqsupset_1 \cup \ldots \cup \sqsubset\sqsupset_m$), declines. Figure 9 shows this dependence.

The cultural trade-off can be exemplified in Figure 8. For example, if a new sorting instruction, $\square''$, requires that one of the singletons becomes an object in one of the existing dominance orders, then the subset $(X, \square_d)$ is enlarged by one and $\#'$ decreases by one. The order of the world of objects that shows itself in length grows richer and the order that shows itself in width gets sparser. This new sorting instruction increases the capacity of the world of objects for moderating social proximity, and its capacity for moderating social distance decreases. Hence, for a given set of objects, the potential for moderating social distance is minimal if all objects were arranged in a single chain. It is maximal if all objects were singletons; the potential of the world of objects for moderating social proximity then is nil. [24*]

Figure 9: The cultural trade-off.

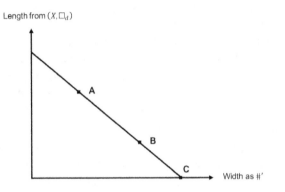

Length from $(X, \square_d)$

A

B

C

Width as $\#'$

The more objects from the finite set, X, that are dominated, the larger the length of the dominance order, $(X, \square_d)$, and the smaller the largest cardinality, $\#'$, of all antichains in the style system. At point B of the trade-off line, more width and less dominance order-induced length is possible than at point A and vice versa.

Cultural (In)efficiency

The dominance order and the order of a set of singletons are polar special cases. The first orders a set as a chain, $|$, the other as an antichain, $\square$. In a chain, one object dominates another object in each element of the feature vector, $\underline{m}_j = (m_1, ..., m_M)$, or vice versa. Both objects therefore contribute exclusively to length. Two singletons, in contrast, are incomparable in the feature vector. An equivalent formulation is that in each feature, m_i, of the feature vector a singleton dominates the other singleton and at the same time is dominated by it. A rank

---

24* For a general characterisation of the trade-off between length and width see Basili and Vannucci

    2013.

distance between these non-identical objects cannot be established and therefore both contribute exclusively to width. A third formulation is that a singleton does not possess feature values but is a feature itself.

In the general case, however, one object dominates another object in one feature, m_i, and it is dominated by the other object in another feature, m_j. Both then relate to each other as two objects in a phylogram. They contribute to both length and width. Of course, such a partial order of objects has special properties for the achievement of objective (13). It moderates social distance *and* proximity. But a phylogram is a special case in itself. It is a tree, ⋔, free of dominated elements, i.e. free of chains. Let this special case be symbolised by ⋔'. The general case, ⋔, is a tree which also contains chains, |, (Figure 7).

From this I now derive the idea of *cultural (in)efficiency*. From an economic perspective, culture produces the output of a segmented order from a given input of non-ordered objects. This output has properties that have already been defined as length and width. Length and width moderate social distance and proximity/individuality. These are the determinants of objective function (13). From an economic perspective, the issue now is whether there exist *order types* that are more efficient in moderating social distance and proximity than other types. Four such order types have to be compared: the chain, |, the antichain of singletons, ⊏⊐, the tree containing dominated objects, ⋔, and the phylogram, ⋔'.

Cultural inefficiency of one order type compared to another exists when, for a given non-ordered set of objects, a second order type is better able to moderate distance (proximity), without moderating social proximity (distance) to a lesser extent than the first order type. According to this definition, order type B is culturally more efficient than order type A (that is, A is inefficient), if – for a given set of objects – A does not moderate greater width than B and B moderates greater length than A.

Let $A \prec B$ imply that order type B is culturally more efficient than type A. Let X be a non-ordered set of h objects. Let $(X, ⋔')$ be a phylogram containing all elements of X. Let $(X, ⋔)$ be a tree, containing all elements of X, which contains at least one chain. Let $(X, ⊏⊐)$ be the set X, ordered as singletons only, and let $(X, |)$ be a chain containing all elements of X. The length of $(X, ⊏⊐)$ is zero and its width, #⊏⊐, is h. The width, #⋔', of each phylogram, containing all elements of X, is #⋔'= #⊏⊐= h. This property of each non-ordered set, X, is seen for example in Figure 6: There $X = (A, B, C, D, E)$ and $h = 5$; and irrespective of whether (A, B, C, D, E) is ordered as an antichain of singletons or as a phylogram, width is $h = 5$. However, the length of $(X, ⋔')$ is positive and hence greater than the length of $(X, ⊏⊐)$. Order type $(X, ⋔')$ is able to moderate the same social distance than order type $(X, ⊏⊐)$, but greater social proximity/individuality than

$(X, \sqsubset\sqsupset)$. Hence, for any non-ordered set X, order type $(X, ⋔')$ is culturally more efficient than order type $(X, \sqsubset\sqsupset)$. That is, $(X, ⋔') \succ (X, \sqsubset\sqsupset)$.

Now, turn to the (in)efficiency of the chain in comparison to the phylogram. According to (13), the chain positively affects goal achievement only by diversity DIV_c^c. If we find a phylogram with DIV_c^c at least as great as that of any chain, given X, then there exists an order of type $(X, ⋔')$, which is more efficient than all chains, because it is also able to moderate greater social distance than chains.

Phylograms derived from rank distances have this potential. This can be shown in an example with two objects. This is the minimal number of objects, h, on which the order types $(X, ⋔')$ and $(X, |)$ can be applied. The existence of a chain also presupposes at least the existence of a single feature in the feature vector $\underline{m}_j = (m_1, ..., m_M)$, that is, $M \geq 1$. For $h = 2$ and $M = 1$ the rank distance of the chain is $d_{ij}^r = 1$ (see footnote 4*, chapter 4). In contrast, the existence of a phylogram requires at least two features in the feature vector, that is, $M \geq 2$. Because with only one feature, only the order types $(X, \sqsubset\sqsupset)$ and/or $(X, |)$ are applicable on X, that is, with only one feature any two objects are either positioned one above the other in a dominance order, $\square_d$, or as singletons side-by-side in an antichain, $\sqsubset\sqsupset$. For $h = M = 2$, $d_{ij}^r = 2$, regardless of whether X is ordered as a chain or phylogram (see footnote 4*, chapter 4). The width of the chain is $\#\sqsubset\sqsupset = 1$, from the one dominant object. Every chain with $h = 2$ and $M = 1$, and hence $d_{ij}^r = 1$ can be transformed, however, into a phylogram with $d_{ij}^r = 2$, by a simple cultural manipulation: replace the feature vector $\underline{m}_j = (m_1)$ with the vector $\underline{m}_j = (m_1, m_2)$, with the properties that in feature m_2, that object dominates the other object, which is dominated by that object in feature m_1. By this cultural manipulation, a set of two objects ordered as a chain with $d_{ij}^r = 1$ and $\# \sqsubset\sqsupset = 1$ is sorted into a phylogram with $d_{ij}^r = 2$ and $\#\sqsubset\sqsupset = 2$. This phylogram is more efficient than the chain from which it was derived by enlarging the feature space.

This cultural manipulation can be generally applied to any (finite) number of objects greater than one in the non-ordered set, X, as well as any (finite) number of features in the feature vector. The length, DIV_c, of any chain, built from a finite number of objects, h, and a finite number of features, M, is finite, and its width remains $\#\sqsubset\sqsupset = 1$. Every enlargement of the feature vector by one more feature, which causes a reversal of dominance in this feature of at least two objects compared to the chain, does not decrease DIV_c of the phylogram compared to the chain, and the width is at least two.

Let C be the set of chains that can be built from the non-ordered set X by order type $(X, |)$, and let P be the set of phylograms that can be built from that same set by order type $(X, ⋔')$. From the preceding considerations, for each chain, built with a finite number of features from a non-ordered finite set of objects, there exists at least one phylogram that is more efficient than the chain, that is, $\forall \, | \in C \; \exists \; ⋔' \in P$, such that $⋔' \succ |$.

There remains the case of the (in)efficiency of trees containing chains, $⋔$. On chains in trees the same cultural manipulation of feature vector expansion can be applied, as has already been used for showing the inefficiency of the chain compared to the phylogram. For as long as at least one object exists in a tree that is dominated by another object, and culture activates an additional feature so that the object is no longer dominated, length will not decrease and width of the tree will increase. This potential is only exhausted when the tree has become a phylogram. Let T be the set of all trees of order type $(X, ⋔)$ that can be built from X. Then for each tree, $⋔$, there exists a phylogram from this non-ordered set, which is more efficient than this tree, that is, $\forall \, ⋔ \in T \; \exists \; ⋔' \in P$, such that $⋔' \succ ⋔$.

It is now possible to make a general statement on the cultural (in)efficiency of the four order types $(X, ⋔')$, $(X, ⋔)$, $(X, ⊏⊐)$ und $(X, |)$. Let $\underline{m}_j^*$ be a feature vector with a greater number of features than $\underline{m}_j$, such that the number of dominated objects is smaller when $\underline{m}_j^*$ is applied than when $\underline{m}_j$ is applied. Then the efficiency properties of the order types of culture are:

$$(X, ⋔') \succ \left\{ \begin{array}{l} (X, ⊏⊐) \\ (X, |) \text{ if } \exists \; \underline{m}_j^* \\ (X, ⋔) \text{ if } \exists \; \underline{m}_j^* \end{array} \right\} \qquad (20)$$

The efficiency of culture in the consumptive production of social distance and proximity is greater when it orders a non-ordered set, X, as a phylogram, compared to when it orders it as an antichain of singletons, or as a chain (i.e. with a single undominated object), or as a tree with chains. The first efficiency statement (on the antichain) is without reservation. The other two efficiency statements (on the chain and on the tree in general) are subject to potentiality. They are valid under the condition of a sufficient capability of culture, to reduce the number of dominated objects to zero by activating additional features of objects. In the following chapter I will argue that this capability is almost unlimited.

From objective function (13) and the cultural restrictions and trade-offs discussed in this chapter, we are now able to derive predictions for individual and collective behaviour.

Chapter 6
Cultural Selection

"Time ensures that we live in a dynamic flux. It was for this reason that Marshall believed that 'the Mecca of the economist lies in economic biology'."
Richard Bronk[1]

"There is no such thing as the [sic] culture; there are cultural processes."
Wolfgang Lipp[2]

What place does the individual occupy in the social whole, in the postmodern space of social distance and proximity, of width and length of diversity? Which social structure results from this, which style system? These are the issues discussed below.

The orthodoxy predicts by simulating human optimisation. That is, it would address these issues by determining the simultaneous effect of $m \cdot n$ individual optima for the $m \cdot n$ objective functions (13), for given decision options and restrictions (Table 8 and 11) and given the cultural trade-off (Figure 9). The social-cum-style equilibrium thus found would be a static one. No individual style in the common style and no common style in the style system could be repositioned in the plane spanned open by width and length without the happiness/utility of the initiator of the change being adversely affected. The follow-up question about the relevance of this equilibrium, the orthodoxy would answer by determining its stability properties. If the interaction of $m \cdot n$-fold optimisation led to this equilibrium, the orthodox predictions would also include statements about

---

1   Bronk 2009, p. 69.
2   Lipp 2014, p. 121 (my translation).

the trajectory (into the equilibrium) and the parameter constellation, which would make it stable. Culture and the social would have a mechanical relationship, driven by economic optimisation, and social change would be as predictable as the course of the stars.

Neuropsychology continually refutes the idea that the human brain is an organ for optimisation. Fast, habitual, unconscious thought is the default. Slow, conscious thought is the exception, yet it can be activated at any time by the experience of an inconsistency between what is habitually expected and what actually happens.[3] At first, we act unconsciously and spontaneously without calculation. Until the unexpected happens, then we act slowly, deliberately, with calculation. This has consequences for many traditional concepts of the orthodoxy. For its optimisation paradigm it follows that it is empirically only of limited productivity. To the extent that habitual action does not lead empirically to surprising results, the paradigm remains unproductive.[4] That is, conscious action, including optimisation, remains conditional – dependent on the experience of failure of habitual thought and action. Optimisation is therefore only an occasional corrective in human thinking.

This must be taken into account in QTC. By my assumption, individuals choose their o/+consumption habitually. It is not always the result of optimisation. New objects (from industry) and new object combinations (bricolage) initially find habitual entry into o/+consumption. Investments in nudging[5] thus pay off for the industry (and perhaps also its customers). In the sorting plant of culture, innovations are spontaneously assigned a place as a singleton, an element of a chain, in a tree. Fashion is thus initially the fruit of habitual individual and collective experimentation, and new objects have (initially and repeatedly) some positive or negative effect on the efficiency of culture, on individuality and the social distance from the social whole. The style system is in (orthodox) disequilibrium at all times.

But only part of the perceived effect of o/+consumption is in line with consumer expectations. Some expectations are more than met, for example, a tried and tested object strengthens individuality more than expected: Emma Hart made the surprising experience that as a living statue she could move the Neapolitan society even to tears; Beau Brummel that his snide remarks were of no small service to him. And some expectations will be dashed: Ramon Magsaysay had good experiences with piña, but he might have been disappointed by another

---

3   Kahneman 2011.

4   Duhigg 2013.

5   Thaler and Sunstein 2008.

experiment that didn't produce the anticipated effect. Such experience brings slow, deliberate thinking into play: what worked for piña, what didn't work for the other attempt, and what do I learn from it with regard to the objective function (13), and the options and restrictions for taking action (Tables 9 and 11)? Thus, fast and slow thinking gives rise to tension in the style system: between habitual and deliberate action, between success and failure, sub-optimality and striving for improvement.

Style followers think and act fast with regard to showing and not showing objects; if they think slowly, for example by reflecting on new instructions for action in the sorting plant of the culture, they do so only with regard to showing and not showing (Table 8). Their slow and fast thinking revolves solely around o/+consumption. When thinking slowly, they never question the operating instructions for the sorting plant, and if they do, they become style leaders. When style leaders think slowly, they act (like their followers) in their own interest (13). But not exclusively by showing and not showing. Their slow thinking is also directed towards the instructions for the sorting plant of the culture – primarily in their elective affinity, but also in the entire style system. Their slow thinking aims at manipulating the manipulable part, $\Box''$, of culture, $\Box$, (Table 11). It's their slow thinking that lets culture, as 'crystallised history', liquefy at its melting edge, $\Box''$.

I assume that the slow thinking and acting of the style leadership, repeatedly thrown back by the fast thinking and acting of everyone, nevertheless has a tendency to show effects. This is to say that the agency of style leadership pushes the style system towards cultural efficiency, thereby tending to enhance the happiness/utility of all – through increasingly better instructions for the sorting plant of culture. So, the slow thinking and acting of style leadership results in cultural selection. It is the subject of this chapter. QTC is therefore also a theory of cultural evolution.

The theory of cultural evolution, which has been thriving for a few decades, does not shy away from drawing parallels between the evolution of genetically coded information and the proliferation of socially transferred information, encoded in beliefs, skills, norms, traditions and conventions.[6] Such information, according to QTC, are the instructions of the style leadership for the sorting plant of culture. Consequently, cultural evolution is not a random cultural drift or mutation. It is systematic cultural selection due to human agency.

---

6   Mesoudi 2017.

Feature Inflation

The efficiency properties of culture, relations (20), direct analytical attention to the feature vector as a variable that can be manipulated by style leadership (see also Table 11). The question is whether a feature vector, $\underline{m}_j^*(\square'')$, exists in that part of culture, $\square''$, that can be manipulated by style leadership, instructing workers in culture's sorting plant to order the set of objects X into a phylogram. If so, the objective function (13) sets the collective incentive for the style leadership to instruct its followers to replace $\underline{m}_j(\square'')$ by $\underline{m}_j^*(\square'')$. For a given set X, an expansion of the feature vector by additional features tends to reduce the number of dominated objects. This is because the more features taken into account, the greater the probability that an object is not dominated by another object in all features. Encouraging workers in the sorting plant to take more and more features into consideration will therefore help improve efficiency.

A licence from the style leadership to its followers, to order the world of objects according to any and as many features as they like, would be an indication that style leadership acts in the interest of cultural efficiency. Such conduct would spark a long-term stylistic evolution towards cultural efficiency and, over time, lessen the inefficiencies caused by habitual experimentation.

In practice, we actually find such manipulations by the style leadership – and nowhere more so than in art, the most widely observed subset of the world of objects. Thomas Girst's and Magnus Resch's collection *100 Secrets of the Art World*, of artists, museum directors, gallery owners, auction house insiders, and art critics, is full of invitations not to interpret the feature space for ordering art objects too narrowly.[7] Some examples are:

- "[A]rt is an object in space ..."
- "Everyone is an artist."
- "Turn art into a real and singular experience by approaching it through anecdotes."
- "Art is a place without borders. It is [...] in a space that is infinite. Art has the power to disorient; like being in a cloud, or caught in an avalanche, not distinguishing up from down. [...] Art breaks down borders and overcomes restrictions with the goal of stimulating both conscious processes and conscious thoughts. [...] These dots, lines, strokes lead beyond the canvas, the page, the concert hall, into the unknown where again your best friend is the imagination."

---

7   Girst and Resch 2016.

- "Walking around the National Gallery with Cecily Brown beat all of the art history lessons I had at school."
- "The question then is what makes art become something."
- "Artists' secrets can only remain secret."
- "The biggest secret in the art world is that no one knows what's contemporary art!"
- "Whatever reason brings people into the art world, it is for a good reason."
- "If you want to break an artist's heart, pay him/her a compliment that starts with 'Your work reminds me of...'"
- "Visit museums on a slow day, wear comfortable shoes."
- "Art is long, life short, judgement difficult, opportunity transient."
- "The secret of art is seeing. [...] Go in deeper."
- "My grandmother was a conceptual artist. Wherever she spent her holidays, for many years, she always sent me a postcard with the same line: 'Alles Scheiße, Deine Emma' [...]. And Emma wasn't even her name!"
- "There is no such thing as a secret to success in the art world, just hard work."
- "We should remember that the artist Marcel Duchamp [...] was fighting a system that rewards some and ignores others."
- "Gone are the days when a small coterie of informed insiders [...] sustained an ongoing conversation [...] enveloping art in what Arthur Danto called 'an atmosphere of theory'."
- "Art is just a moment, a moment of sublimity."
- "The first thing about art is that it does what it's not supposed to do."
- "Look with an open and thoughtful mind."
- "Great pictures, like close friends, always have something new to teach us. There's no end to them."

Such statements invite the almost limitless expansion of the feature space and thus the tendency to rearrange objects, previously dominated in all features, into objects which are not dominated in at least one feature, whereby chains are thinned out. Style leadership in the art business produces a cultural selection in the direction of cultural efficiency.

I can now formulate the first hypothesis:

Inflation Law (H_1): the feature space, $\underline{m}_j$, for the establishment of partial order in the world of objects, X, grows larger and larger.

Hypothesis 1 states that even with a stable non-ordered world of objects, X, culture becomes ever more complex, in that sorting rules are employed which over time take more and more features into account. The familiar 'But you also have to take this and that into account' is not a curiosity of our time, but systematically laid out in the incentive system of postmodernism.

The Rise of Anti-Aesthetics

The aforementioned manipulation by the style leadership increases the likelihood that previously dominated objects will become suprema, simply by the *unspecified* expansion of the feature space. However, the style leadership in the art sector also provides *specific* guidance for the transformation of dominated objects into suprema. Consider the following 'secret' from the collection of Thomas Girsch and Magnus Resch:

> "Nothing will be conceptually or visually interesting if there are no oppositions, if there are no contradictions, if there are no parallels, if there are no extremities. I believe that everything co-exists in this world but I would like to keep or see polarity/ambivalence/opposition /contradictions/parallels/extremities next to each other/facing each other."

This is an invitation to abandon the simple truths of dominance orders and acknowledge the world of objects in its inconsistencies, contradictions and incompatibilities. As a consequence, dominated objects are not transformed into suprema solely by the 'law of the great number of features', but by deliberately observing what distinguishes them from other objects and why they chafe each other.

Anti-aesthetics is a movement that propagates exactly that. The isolationism of the art world, which comes hand-in-hand with the Kantian ideal of the purposeless nature of art, is a thorn in its side: how can one be involved with art without searching for and finding in it the turmoil of the world? It is an approach that discovers dissolution of order in the smaller art world that exists in the greater world. Chains, |, are subsequently dissolved because they conceal the true contradictions of their objects. The apocalyptic aesthetics of punk is anti-aesthetic as an approach and exemplary for all marginalised elective affinities, in eternal opposition to the mainstream with their common styles.[8] The subordinate rank assigned to them by the mainstream, by virtue of beauty considerations, they ridicule with irony and sarcasm. Features are introduced which, in

---

8   Mohr 2016.

opposition to those of the mainstream, turn this ranking upside down. The well-ordered world of chains, |, and trees with chains, ⋔, is replaced by phylograms, ⋔', which take better account of the inherent conflicts, oppositions and contradictions.

Objective function (13) in conjunction with the efficiency properties of the order types (20), and the agency of style leadership summarised in Table 11, deliver the economic explanation for these empirical findings. It can be expressed in the following hypothesis:

Anti-aesthetics Law (H_2): the proportion of anti-aesthetic features in the feature space, which operationalise social contradictions in the world of objects, is becoming increasingly large.

Hypothesis 2 predicts the triumph of anti-aesthetics over (classical) Kantian aesthetics. This is due to the latter's postulate of a purpose-free art, which compared to anti-aesthetics, constrains the opportunities for bringing objects into (societal) opposition to each other. However, in QTC the hypothesis is neither socio-politically, structurally nor dialectically motivated, but purely micro-economically. Individual happiness/utility of style leaders establishes a collective interest in manipulating culture, in such a way that social contradictions, dilemmas and oppositions are also reflected in instructions for the sorting plant of culture. With this economic perspective, anti-aesthetes such as Marx, Nietzsche, Heidegger, Freud, Wittgenstein, Bourdieu, Poe, De Quincey, Stendhal, Heine and the founder of anti-aesthetics, Baudelaire, have merely made their (selfish) contribution to the improvement of cultural efficiency. In this economic interpretation, the politicisation of art and culture is not causal for the dynamics of the style system, but vice versa: cultural selection is politicising.

Singletons adieu

Relation (20) identifies the antichain of singletons as a culturally inefficient order type. Style leaders have therefore the collective incentive to accommodate singletons in phylograms, by giving conductive instructions to the sorting plant of culture:

Singleton Law (H_3): singletons disappear.

Singletons are endowed with the aura of uniqueness, which already makes them unsuitable candidates for a place among the dominated objects. For establishing a place in a phylogram, only new features are needed that establish comparability with other objects. This way even former singletons can be made comparable. For example, as unique as the *piña* sewn to the barong tagalog and the Veil of Veronica may be, they can still be compared by their textile features (weight and fineness of fabric) and their symbolic features (more or less iconographic coding). Which features are considered relevant is decided by the style leadership.

Thus, over time, the singleton piña becomes one of many signs of Philippine identity, Marcel Duchamp's *Fontaine* one of many comparable works of Dada, and the ancient Egyptian *Letters of Heqanakht* an early example of commercial thinking. In cultural selection, the archaeological principle reigns over singletons: you find something that you've never seen before, but you don't give up until you can locate it somewhere in what's already familiar.

The antichain $(X, \sqsubseteq)$ is nothing but the non-ordered set, X, itself. Our sense for orderliness that shows itself in upbringing, education and guidance turns the antichain into something disturbing. In QTC, love of orderliness is owing to the interest in improving cultural efficiency. Self-set rules are a case in point. The card game *Quartet* demonstrates the principle. In grammar there are no words that do not belong to some category. In literature there are no works that do not belong to some genre. Art history as a science is a singleton extinction machine. As is archaeology. As long as it falls under an overarching motto, people can collect whatever they want without ridiculing themselves. Only the proverbial vendor's tray is taboo. In this way, we learn to extinguish singletons that we increasingly experience as something disturbing. Only after we have somehow made them comparable with other objects will we be content.

Phylomania

From hypotheses H_1, H_2, H_3 and relation (20) the following hypothesis is:

> Ordering Law (H_4): in the long term, every object is ordered in a phylogram, ff'.

Hypothesis 4 states that workers in the sorting plant of culture increasingly apply the efficient order type. Their upbringing, schooling, further education, and the constant manipulations of their style leadership allow them to position objects in the efficient order type, the phylogram, ff'. Under the guidance of the style leadership, the work in the sorting plant of culture tends to allow consumers to fully exploit the potential of the non-ordered world of objects, X, for the joint production of social distance *and* proximity.

H_4 predicts the postmodernist mania of discovering in everything and everyone the unique, the incomparable, as well as the comparable, the kindred. The phylogram is the order type that maps this mania for 'both this and that' and 'this on the one hand and that on the other'. Phylomania is the passion of postmodernism. Nothing is so completely different that it does not fit in somewhere. And nothing is so similar to something else that it has lost all of its uniqueness. Everything is simultaneously known and unknown, familiar and unfamiliar, ordinary and special. The pinnacle of arty zeal is the ability to fit each work of art in somewhere and at the same time to underline its uniqueness. Everyday life becomes more and more devoid of clear-cut verdicts. Gone are the times when something could clearly be better than something else, but also gone are the times when a comparison was completely out of the question. Leonardo becomes comparable with Warhol, Bach with Madonna, but there is also something special in every dilettantism. Phylomania in the world of objects is transferred to the human being. Nobody ever belongs nowhere and there is always a jewel slumbering in every stick-in-the-mud.

It is only on the individual level that phylomania does not manifest itself. The meta-contrasting lenses (Table 5) provide situational clarity for the moment. At the level of the style system as a whole, however, phylomania is a synchronous cacophony of contradictions that makes an object both incomparable and comparable. In light of QTC, the much-commented loss of certainties in postmodernism is due to cultural selection in the direction of efficiency.

In Figure 9, for a given set of objects, X, cultural selection shifts the current position on the trade-off line from, for example, point A or B, towards its intersection with the horizontal axis, C. Length from $(X, \Box_d)$ decreases and width increases over time. *Ceteris paribus*, this cultural selection would lead to a complete disappearance of length from $(X, \Box_d)$ and lead to the maximum width at point C, which is attained when X is fully ordered as a phylogram. However, this *ceteris paribus* condition is violated intrinsically in the model, as shown below. Efficiency remains a property of culture never fully achieved by cultural selection.

Quality Inflation

Cultural selection with the vectors of feature inflation, rise of anti-aesthetics, extinction of singletons and phylomania is due to the agency of style leadership. But style followers also affect cultural selection through their *o/+consumption*.

Another vector component of cultural selection, to be credited to their agency, is the long-term increase in available qualities:

Quality Law (H_5): the number of objects in the style system is growing.

However, this also increases the number of dissimilarities and the consumable quality differences in the world of objects. H_5 postulates a Saysian law of quality. The classical Say's law of economics maintains that every supply will create its own demand. Of course, this refers to quantities, so that every quantity offered is also sold. In QTC this condition-rich law finds a counterpart in the Quality Law (H_5). Because the objective function (13) sets an incentive to admit all objects available in the world of objects to the style system. Every new object created by industry tends to make its way to the consumer. For industry, the simplest (and most economical) expansion of the world of objects, X, is by offering ever more objects that fit into a dominance order. Skirts are getting shorter, trousers tighter, hair longer, hotels more family-friendly, clubs trendier, yachts more exclusive, cars more environmentally friendly.

The enrichment of chains with further elements (dominated elements or new suprema) leaves the cardinality of the n chains constant, built from their suprema, $\sqsubseteq \sqsupset_h$. Therefore, the social distance (8) of the common style, in which the new object is included, remains constant to the social whole. The effect on objective (13) thus depends only on the effect on individuality. From (6) it follows that the addition of an additional object to an individual style, *ceteris paribus*, increases individuality, I_j, in the elective affinity or leaves it constant. The enrichment of the individual style with a new object that has not been used in the style system so far is, *ceteris paribus*, not to the detriment of the consumer.

Happiness/utility of consumer j remains constant only if this new object increases the rooting in the common style by the *entire* length of the chain in which it is inserted. But this is only the case if the new object of the individual style, s_j, is approximately identical to the supremum of the chain in which it has been put, *and* if that supremum is also an element of the other individual styles in the common style they share. So, only if the new object has almost the same quality as a supremum that is already also shown by all of the other members of the elective affinity, will the happiness/utility of consumer j remain constant. An example is the supremum E in Figure 6, if individual j does not actually show E but adds an almost identical object E' to s_j. For a new object that is in this sense not almost identical, utility increases if the consumer incorporates it into their individual style. This is always the case when industry offers new objects, discretely different from their previous supremum. That is why such newly offered objects always attract demand in the style system.

What remains to be examined is the effect of new elements of a phylogram and of new singletons on the objective function (13). A new element of a phylogram is by definition a (trivial) new supremum. Its use in an individual style enhances individuality (formula 1), because diversity, DIV_c^c, increases more than the rooting R_j^c. Therefore, relation (6) applies as strict inequality. In contrast to a new element of a chain, the width in the style system increases *ceteris paribus*, the common periphery remains constant and social distance (8) increases. A new object expanding the phylogram in a style system enhances the happiness/utility of the consumer who incorporates it into their individual style. New objects on offer and thus new qualities will therefore meet with demand.

Singletons are neither determinants of diversity of the common style, DIV_c^c, nor of the rooting of the individual style, R_j^c. Hence, according to (1), singletons in an individual style, s_j, have no effect on the individuality of the consumer in the present version of QTC. For example, if Ramon Magsaysay had actually introduced the barong tagalog made of piña into the Philippine style system, this would have not increased his individuality within his elective affinity of Filipino nationalists. But the adoption of a singleton that is new for the style system into an individual style, s_j, increases social distance to the social whole, D_h, of the common style to which it belongs. Therefore, the extent of goal accomplishment (13) of consumer j increases and, to the same extent, so does the goal accomplishment of all other members of their elective affinity. If the barong tagalog made of piña did not already belong to the Philippine style system, it would have therefore been to Ramon Magsaysay's personal benefit to introduce it, simply because it would have increased the social distance of the nationalists from the Philippine 'Americanists', and for this very reason also benefitted his Filipino followers.

New singletons gain entrance to the style system via at least one individual style. No new object, however incomparable, will ever be invented by a creative mind that will not find its place in the style system. Nothing will ever be so weird to us that it will not become a means to enhance social distance. Every object, no matter how repulsive, bizarre, or fantastic it may be, will be seized upon by some elective affinity. There will always be an individual who will mould even the most outlandish idea into an individual style. The first mohawk hairdo of punk displays the agenda.

This establishes the (Saysian) Quality Law (H_5): the supply of consumable *qualities* will always find its demand. No matter whether a new object appears in chains or phylograms or as a new singleton, it is always to the advantage of some consumer to show it in their individual style.

Up-to-Date Forever

Just as it is to the benefit of at least one consumer to show a newly-offered quality in their individual style, it is to the benefit of at least one consumer that an object does not vanish from the style system. An object may be less and less on show, but there will always be someone to display it in their individual style, no matter its age. Every quality always remains up-to-date for at least someone.

Up-to-Dateness Law (H_6): objects will not vanish from the style system.

As a consequence of H_5 and H_6, in the long term there will be more and more 'old' objects in the style system. This is because new objects are always being added and even if they get old, they are not discarded. This distinguishes cultural from biological evolution. In evolutionary biology, fossils, physically tangible as they may still be today, have no place in the tree of life. This reproductive logic does not exist in culture. Cultural 'fossils' also belong to the world of objects, X. Put another way, the old junk in our collections will never fossilise – everything that has ever existed as a quality will remain up-to-date forever.

'Up-to-date forever' is accounted for in the objective function (13). Cultural chains and trees do not have to be ultra-metric (like phylograms of evolutionary biology), i.e. the vertical 'extension' of chains/branches do not have to be of equal length. In Figure 8, the chain in S_2 is shorter than the vertical extension of the tree. It illustrates, for example, the evolution of a traditional costume that had already come to an end. Take, for example, the Appenzell women's traditional costume, which today is only worn in variations from the chain, on traditional occasions, for example, Corpus Christi. It contributes little to individuality within the group of Appenzell women, but all the more to social distance (from the tourists).[9]

---

9   Not surprisingly, archaeology employs special concepts for systematising artefacts whose cultural evolution has come to an end (Lyman and O'Brien 2000). Archaeological trees have the vertical dimension time. It begins with the time of origin (soil layer) of the oldest specimen found (thought to be the joint ancestor of all subtypes in the feature space). It ends at each branching of the tree where a lineage ends in the archaeological records, i.e. where no more specimens of this type are found in the younger soil layers. Accordingly, in contrast to the evolutionary phylogram, the branches of the archaeological tree have different lengths back to their joint origin. This possibility, of a historical end to a development, has been accounted for in Figure 8 with a shorter chain. Nor is archaeological diversity measured in terms of length to the present day, as in evolutionary biology with its exclusive focus on existing fauna and flora. For example, the

The Up-to-Dateness Law (H_6) predicts our passion for collecting, and the popularity of TV series such as *Antiques Roadshow*. Hipsters conformed to it when they salvaged accessories like the cheese cutter cap, the jute sack and the moustache from near oblivion. The portable radio, hip in the 1950s, now a relic of an outdated technology in the age of smartphone miniaturisation, is back too.

More and More Savants

The Quality and Up-to-Dateness Laws thwart cultural efficiency, in a way. With their demonstrated predilection for any kind of quality, style followers dilute their leadership's selective striving for specific quality. Followers are constantly stuffing the style system full of new and exhumed objects for the chains. The set $(X, \square)$ loses its phylogram properties because of the agency of style followers, which is why the style leadership is constantly busy removing these introduced inefficiencies from the style system.

Of the means available to style leaders (Table 11), their own *o/+ consumption* is not particularly suitable for this purpose because it is non-verbal communication, which can only be used to show. However, the style leadership must demonstrate the comparability of objects that are regarded as incomparable by style followers, just as it must demonstrate the incomparability of objects in chains. To that end, telling leads them more reliably to their goal than showing. Style followers act by sorting and showing, while style leaders also act by telling.

---

length of the archaeological tree of a museum collection up to the present day would only give information about, for example, its importance for the culture of remembrance, or for research or funding. Instead, archaeological diversity is based on the idea of width in the historical dimension. It serves the interest of diversity of culture in the course of history. A measure of archaeological diversity is therefore the number of types/lineages (not specimens) from the same period (soil layer), as an indicator of the cultural diversity of the times. In Figure 4, the idea of archaeological diversity is represented by the *horizontal* perforated boxes that mark the antichains, with the timeline running from top to bottom. Archaeological diversity is the number of vertical branches/lineages at a given time. In Figure 4, initially diversity is therefore two up to the time of the first branching of the tree, then it is three up to the time of the second branching of the tree, and from there on to the present it is four. Typically, however, archaeological diversity increases over time and then decreases again. Arrowheads can be found in a series of soil layers, specimens as well as types, and they disappear again in younger layers. Insofar as the current width alone determines the present-day social distance of the productive consumer, only this width is relevant for QTC.

Intermediation Law (H$_7$): an intermediation industry proliferates in the style system.

Reacting to the flooding of the style system with objects, the style leadership theorises, intellectualises and idealises the world of objects. Style intermediation, supporting the style leadership in this endeavour, is a growth industry. Curators, advisors and critics tell style followers in magazines, books, TV and social media what they need to do to improve in their work in the sorting plant of culture. Efficiency-driven phylomania feeds an entire industry of savants who, backed by superior knowledge, instruct the workers in the sorting plant of culture. The 100 Secrets (of the Art World) exist for everything. De gustibus non est disputandum remains an empty phrase that the intermediation industry constantly violates. In QTC, their obsession with teaching others is owing to their selfishness contained in the objective function (13), in combination with the options for action listed in Table 11. From the point of view of QTC, savants in literary quartets, cooking shows, feuilletons, etc. produce social distance and proximity for everyone, including themselves. They are listened to and followed because they have options for action that remain closed to most.

Phasing-Out of the Uniform

For objective function (13) and for a given diversity of a common style, DIV_c^c, the rooting, R_i^c, of an individual style in the common style is cultural waste that results in an individual's desire to eliminate it. Style followers contribute to this elimination by avoiding duplication. In Figure 6, for example, consumers i and j can reduce their rooting in the common style, R_i^c, without diminishing its diversity, if they no longer show E in their individual styles, leaving it for exclusive use to the individual style s_k. Whenever an object is shown in at least two individual styles of a common style, is it advantageous to abandon this object in all but one.

De-Uniformisation Law (H$_8$): every quality shown in a common style will eventually be shown in only one of its individual styles.

Hypothesis 8 predicts the proliferation of nuances in the world of objects. The tie belongs to the common style of bankers, but there are a thousand different variations of it. The black leather dress shoe belongs to it, but it is available in a thousand nuances. The long-sleeved, collared shirt belongs to it, but there are a thousand variations to choose from. The dark suit belongs to it, but it comes in a thousand variations. The gold watch belongs to it, but it comes in a thousand versions. Their combination and recombination leaves billions of variations for individual bankers' styles, which together make up the appearance of a coherent common style. This wealth of variety finds its consumers. Where modernism had its stylistic beginnings in the uniformisation even of civilians, postmodernism takes its course in the rigorous de-uniformisation of the individual.

Jacques Tati, a film maker who cinematically satirised the times in which he lived, depicts this de-uniformisation in a scene in *Les Vacances de Monsieur Hulot* (1953). Two female members of a temporary elective affinity step out of neighbouring hotel rooms right at the same moment for a joint outing, but in identical summer dresses, eyeballing each other, only to disappear into their rooms again without saying a word.

Polytomisation

For reasons of mere plausibility, phylograms in evolutionary biology always branch out in twos. When part of a reproductive community develops into a new species, for example through geographical separation, then what was one before becomes two (evolutionary dichotomy). This is because it is extremely implausible that three or more new species will emerge at the same time from a single reproductive community. In this implausible case a polytomy would have resulted – an evolutionary node with three or more branches leading further down. However, in cultural evolution this plausibility reasoning lacks justification. Polytomies are not only a possibility in culture, they are even likely. Style leadership ensures this.

Each length above a node can be part of a rooting of an individual style, because at least two objects are placed below it, which can therefore belong to different individual styles. Therefore, for a given non-ordered set of objects, X, the potential for rooting is reduced as the number of nodes in the vertical structure of the order decreases. Polytomies reduce the number of nodes compared to a phylogram. For a given non-ordered set, X, that vertical structure possesses the minimum number of nodes in which all elements of X originate from a single polytomy. This case is illustrated in Figure 10.

Based on objective function (13), style leadership has, *ceteris paribus*, an interest in ordering objects into polytomies. This reduces the number of nodes in the vertical structure of the world of objects and thus reduces possibilities for the rooting of individual styles in their common style.

Figure 10: Polytomisation.

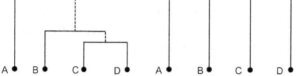

The phylogram of four objects, with its dashed lengths, offers two possibilities for rooting (if C and D belong to two different individual styles and/or if B belongs to a different individual style from C or D). The same objects arranged as a polytomy (right) offer no possibility for rooting.

Polytomisation is coupled with a simplification of dissimilarity (as comparability). In Figure 10 on the right, in contrast to the left, all pairs of objects are equally dissimilar in their bilateral lengths. Differences between pairs of objects, defined as lengths, converge by means of polytomisation. In the borderline case where the order of a given set X is a polytomy (Figure 10, right side), all pairwise quality differences are the same. A set of objects X ordered in a polytomy can therefore also be thought of as 'minutes' ordered on a clock face: with the number of 'minutes' equal to the number of objects in set X and with identical distances between all adjacent 'minutes'.[10]

The incentive of the style leadership to reduce the complexity of the vertical structure by means of polytomisation substantiates the following hypothesis:

> Polytomisation Law (H_9): dissimilarities (as comparability) converge in the world of objects.

This is why the history of elective affinities is exponentially disappearing from the curricula of the style followers. The idea of the sanguine phylogram of European nobility lists does not echo in postmodernism. While the elective affinity of start-up capitalism reveres Steve Jobs as its founding father, each member is regarded as equally related to him with the individual style of their venture. Elective affinities increasingly become identically kindred 'bee colonies'.

---

10   In chapter 9, I will return to the clock face analogy regarding the orthodox modelling of product differentiation.

Nucleation

According to (10), shared peripheries, P_{hk}, of two common styles, S_h and S_k, increase, *ceteris paribus*, social distance in a style system with three or more elective affinities, if they arise from new objects not previously found in the style system. A style leadership will therefore not seek to prevent its followers from incorporating new objects into the common style simultaneously with another elective affinity, i.e. the Saysian Quality Law does not spare style peripheries. This way, peripheries arise of jointly displayed objects in different common styles, which interweave with each other in this sense. Figure 8 is an example of such an interweaving. Formula (10) predicts the occasional mass proliferation of new objects in the style system. Fads thus develop into style-crossing trends – hair gets longer, skirts shorter, pants tighter, not just in a single common style. But there is always at least one common style that resists this style-crossing trend.

As soon as new objects have entered the style system, the style leadership has a limited incentive to eliminate peripheries by transferring their objects into a style nucleus. In Figure 8, for example, the periphery is eliminated when both common styles abandon the respective other object in their shared periphery. Each of these disentanglements has the same effect on social distances in the style system as the introduction of a new object into just one common style, and thus into its style nucleus. Therefore, according to (9), the social distance of a common style towards the social whole is increased. However, the abandonment of an object from a periphery of a common style must be brought about by the abandonment of that object in all of its individual styles, that showed it so far. Consequently, this unbundling also reduces individuality in the elective affinity. When unbundling the common styles, style leaders must therefore observe a trade-off: social distance between elective affinities increases, but individuality in at least one common style decreases. The general effect of unbundling on happiness/utility (13) is therefore indeterminate. Given a sufficient concavity (14) of objective function (13), with a minimum number of objects in the shared periphery of two common styles, such a disentanglement is also in the overall interest of that elective affinity, which completely abandons an object. However, if the number of common style objects is sufficiently small, unbundling is unfavourable for at least one member of the elective affinity, as lost happiness/utility from loss of individuality exceeds the utility gain from increase in social distance. For example, according to (1), if there are only two objects in a common style, the abandonment of one would result in the complete loss of individuality in the common style. This motivates the following hypothesis.

Nucleation Law (H_{10}): if the number of objects in a common style exceeds a critical number, it also contains a nucleus.

In conjunction with H_5 (Quality Law), H_{10} predicts the proliferation of common styles in the style system, which show objects not shown anywhere else. Increasingly more common styles, so the prediction goes, have such a stylistic fingerprint. This prediction does not contradict H_8 (De-uniformisation Law). In the long run, so the prediction from H_8 and H_{10} goes, only the banker (and his peers) will always show some variation of the suit and tie (originally from Savile Row), and the rest will never do so again.

It should be noted that until now, from the QTC perspective, nucleation is not a means for eliminating information asymmetries. It is therefore not signalling. The loss of individuality from nucleation therefore is not a signalling cost. From the point of view of information economics, work in the sorting plant of culture is always perfect. Nucleation is owed solely to the interest in broadening social distance, while taking into account its effect on social proximity. [11]

Charisma of Style Leadership

At all times, a 'crystallised history' exists as the valid operating manual, □, for the work in the sorting plant of culture. Experimentation in the do-it-yourself (DIY) technique by style followers, together with industrial innovation, modifies the non-ordered world of objects, X. This leads to constantly new inefficiencies: at any given time, there is pressure to offset cultural efficiency out of the interplay of a changing world of objects and culture as 'crystallised history'. The style leadership counteracts this pressure. Culture as a dynamic institution, as 'crystallised history with a melting edge', receives its evolutionary impulses, $H_1 - H_{10}$, from human agency.

Cultural selection is based on a potency of the style leadership that has not yet been addressed. Style leadership must be able to successfully counteract the pressure of randomness, of the opportunism of style followers and industry, and the cultural inefficiency that results from it. This capacity of style leadership is the only reason a consumer would want to follow it in the first place. Only leadership that gives its followers the benefit of leadership is worth following. Style leadership offers this benefit in the currency of efficiency of work done in the sorting plant of culture. This is the charisma of style leadership. That's the only

---

11   In chapter 10 QTC is further developed with regard to information economics.

reason it has any followers. What this charisma achieves for society is the topic of the next chapter.

Chapter 7
Social Evolution

"Consumption [...] actually does crucial social work, not only sustaining human lives and social institutions but also shaping interpersonal relations."
Viviane Zelizer[1]

"For us historians, a structure [...] is a reality which time uses and abuses over long periods."
Fernand Braudel[2]

"How do we begin coveting, Clarice? [...] We begin by coveting what we see every day."
Dr. Hannibal Lecter addressing Clarice Starling in The Silence of the Lambs

The consumers' objective in the social sphere is a driving force of cultural order. From its specification (13) and the agency of style leadership and their followers (Tables 8 and 11), hypotheses H_1 - H_{10} were derived as vector components of cultural selection. With culture, understood as a selection process that changes the consumers' choice space, consumption itself becomes a process that changes the social. This evolution of the social, driven by cultural selection, is the topic of this chapter.

---

1   Zelizer 2005, p. 348.

2   Braudel 2011 (1980), p. 368.

Opening of the Closed Society

Given objective function (13) and given the allocation of the world of objects to a given number n of elective affinities, according to formula (1), the individuality in an elective affinity grows along with the number of its members, m. At the same time, for a given allocation of objects to the common styles, the distance of each elective affinity to the social whole remains the same. It is therefore in the interest of all elective affinities to recruit new members at the expense of other elective affinities, and to dress them up with a subset of their own common style. Competition for members is part of postmodernist 'business'. This motivates the following hypothesis.

Competition (H_{11}): elective affinities compete for members.

A follow-up prediction of H_{11} is the disappearance of the closed society. As a relic of resource-driven modernism, it may have found its way into postmodernism in the form of exclusive yacht and polo clubs. But the logic of postmodernism's interests, condensed in the objective function (13), is making it disappear. The desire for individuality within the club fosters the interest in new members and thus in opening up the club. It is not operating costs that force them to open up, but the members' interest in sublimating their individuality lets them open up. In the 1960s, the tennis club was exclusive, today it is an ordinary club, just as golf has become an ordinary sport. Polo is still exclusive today.

Equalisation of Individuality and Happiness

A follow-up hypothesis from H_9 (Polytomisation Law) is:

Equalisation (H_{12}): within elective affinities, members' individuality and happiness converge.

H_{12} does not predict the vanishing of individuality. Members become more and more individual by phasing out the uniform (H_8). However, through polytomisation the rooting of individual styles in the common style, R_j^c, fades out. Hence, according to formula (1), individuality of all members of the elective affinity converges towards $(m - 1) \cdot DIV_c^c$. Because social distance of all members of the elective affinity to the social whole, D_h, is the same, happiness/utility of all members converge at a high level.

H_{12} is an irony in the transition from modernism to postmodernism: To the extent that (resource) endowment as a determinant of the social structure loses clout, and volition (to join an elective affinity) wins clout, happiness/utility converges in the elective affinity. Although there, egoism in the form of the drive for individuality has found its most extreme form. The egoism/altruism obsolescence elaborated in Chapter 5 manifests itself in equality of happiness/utility.

Passion for collecting is an example of this. The leadership of the contemporary art collectors' community portrays contemporary art less and less as a complicated tree with ramification upon ramification, or as being comparable to, say, the Renaissance. The styles of art history and of contemporary art are conveyed less and less as interconnected in layers (H_9). This is a symptom of the general equalisation brought about by the manipulations of social proximity by the style leadership. There is a tendency for all individual (collecting) styles to be understood as equally nested in their common style, making a differentiated search for (art-historic) traces by followers redundant. The collector of media art is indistinguishably united with the collector of punk art and that of Dutch still lifes, within the elective affinity of art collectors.

Through polytomisation, elective affinities become egalitarian affirmation communities: everyone tends to confirm everyone else the same (but not the identical) embedding in their joint elective affinity. From QTC's point of view, equalisation within elective affinities is not due to the game-theoretical exit option of its members (whoever can walk away must be treated well!), but to the agency of style leadership. Equalisation removes rootings in the common style that are detrimental to achieving goals.

Destabilisation of Elective Affinities

Why do new elective affinities emerge? Where does the variety in common styles come from? According to formula (8), the distance of an elective affinity to the social whole stays constant, as long as the total number of objects in the nuclei of the style system stays constant. A reallocation of these objects into more nuclei, i.e. more elective affinities, leaves the distance to the social whole constant. This is shown in the example of Figure 8. Out of an interest in social distance alone, an incumbent elective affinity would thus be indifferent to such a reallocation by the founding of new elective affinities. However, social start-ups are dependent on members and these can only be recruited from incumbent elective affinities. Only those incumbents are indifferent to start-ups whose members do not run away to a new elective affinity. Because the loss of members is at the expense of individuality within the elective affinity. Competition (H_{11}) therefore includes competition between incumbent and start-up elective affinities. Given consumer sovereignty (entry and exit option), a member will switch affinities if this increases their happiness/utility (13). The style leadership of incumbent elective affinities will therefore seek to shape the style system, in such a way that there is no individual incentive to switch to new social start-ups.

What are the individual incentives to join a new elective affinity? The smaller it is in the beginning the less individuality can be found in it. The sheer size of incumbent elective affinities thus offers protection against new competition. The mainstream is stable because it is large. However, this only applies, *ceteris paribus*, to the individual exit option: isolated disloyalty in the style system is rare, but mass exodus is not. This leads to:

Destabilisation (H_{13}): incumbent elective affinities are threatened by mass exodus.

H_{13} resembles bank run logic: the banking system becomes non-liquid when everyone believes it will become non-liquid, and therefore everyone wants to withdraw their money at once. In the style system, members resign from their elective affinity when everyone believes in the resignation of many others. The protective interest in their own individuality is the motivation for this. H_{13} opens the style system to elective affinities that rise like a phoenix from the ashes, only to descend there again sooner or later: for rehashed fashions that find a mass following and are again quickly forgotten, for trends that disappear as quickly as they appeared, for an industry whose business model is based on trend scouting and speed.

QTC thereby provides an alternative interpretation of the snob effect in fashion, jumping from a crowded stylistic train, and of the bandwagon effect, jumping onto a new, yet near-empty stylistic train. The orthodoxy offers theories of fashion in which both effects alternate deterministically in a wave-like manner. The fate of every fashion trend is thus already predetermined *ex ante*, and it takes arbitrary assumptions about consumer myopia or the market power of the industry, to conjure up demand for a fashion that is already doomed. QTC contrasts this orthodox view with a probabilistic model in which common styles are more or less exposed to the risk of mass exodus (snob effect), depending on their qualitative properties. New common styles are then more or less likely to receive mass influx (bandwagon effect) from the incumbent styles, depending on the very same properties of those styles.

Social Cellular Division

But what is the incentive for innovators to build a new elective affinity? It is the chance of increasing social distance in the style system. The presence of peripheries offers this opportunity. The example of Figure 8 showed that removing elements from the nucleus of a style with a periphery and combining them as the nucleus of a new common style, produces new distance to the social whole, greater than the (unchanged) distance to the social whole of the incumbent style. The reason for this is that a shared periphery shortens the bilateral social distance between two styles. With this legacy the new style is not burdened in the style system of constant width. Common styles with no periphery, in contrast to those with a periphery, make use of the entire width of the world of objects, opened up by culture. Exiting an elective affinity which has a style periphery thus offers a distancing benefit which runs contrary to a (perhaps initial) loss of individuality. In that trade-off of objective function (13), a social start-up may therefore be to the overall benefit of innovators. This leads to:

> Cellular Division (H_{14}): common styles with (large) peripheries are breeding grounds for new elective affinities.

Social cellular division is dependent on a cultural condition. The agency of innovators as style leaders must be so potent that it can prescribe a shortened 'haircut', in such a way that a new common style is created.[3] Technically, this requires a suitable reduction of the maximum rank distance for the *entire* style system (which in Figure 5 corresponds to a shortening of distance d_K towards the base of the cladogram).

This underlines two things. First, culturally, social cellular division is no triviality. It requires innovators to be able to manipulate the entire style system. By this demanding requirement, culture protects the social sphere from excessive cellular division. And secondly, a smaller maximum rank distance results in a more filigree structure of the entire clustering. However, social cellular division tends to reduce individuality in the style system, because the average number of members of elective affinities decreases. The social sphere thus also protects itself from excessive cellular division. The cultural and the social spheres work here hand-in-hand.

---

3   Social cellular division thus corresponds to speciation in evolutionary biology, the emergence of a new reproductive community.

Societal Structuring

Cellular division in the whole of the style system provokes two opposing effects: if peripheries exist, it heightens social distance in the system; and for a given number of members of society, it lowers individuality in the system. The agency of style leadership tends to balance out the two effects in the overall interest of objective function (13). Where this balance lies depends on the slope properties (14) of the objective function and thus on a fundamental property of the society. It can be more or less individualistic. The more individualistic a society is, the slower marginal utility of individuality declines and the more important social proximity is for happiness/utility. This leads to:

> Societal Structuring (H_{15}): more individualistic societies have fewer, but bigger elective affinities; less individualistic ones have more, but smaller elective affinities.

H_{15} is quite intuitive. The greater the marginal contribution of one's own individuality to happiness/utility, the greater the marginal contribution of other comparable individuals to it, and greater the incentive to join a big elective affinity. Conversely, the greater the marginal contribution of social distance to happiness/utility, the smaller the incentive to join a large elective affinity. Less individualistic societies thus show a postmodern social structure with many small, strongly separated social groups with little individuality inside. More individualistic societies show a social structure with few large groups possessing a high level of internal diversity. The mainstream thus turns out to be the programmatic group of Western individualistic society.

The Old with the Old – The New with the New

What can the style leadership of incumbent elective affinities do against the risks of H_{13} and H_{14}? To prevent innovators from exiting and taking objects from the nucleus of the common style with them, there is a simple countermeasure: just keep showing these objects in the incumbent style. They are then moved to a newly-formed periphery, which the incumbent common style now shares with the start-up style. Individuality in the incumbent style only decreases as the number of members decreases, m, but not also by the decrease in diversity, DIV_c^c. This is successful only to a certain extent at limiting the damage the incumbent style has incurred. But it damages the happiness/utility of the start-up founders, in that they suffer a loss in terms of the elusive new distance to the social whole. Because, instead of a new common style devoid of a periphery, they now get one with a periphery shared by their former elective affinity. Whether their distance to the social whole increases or decreases, depends on whether the new style periphery contains more or less elements than all pre-existing peripheries of the incumbent elective affinity. If it contains less, the distance to the social whole still increases. If it contains more, it is not worthwhile initiating the start-up.

Smart innovators will anticipate this. They can improve the chance for a positive distancing effect of their start-up by keeping their new common style sparse in terms of qualities shown. The Bauhaus made its mark with such aesthetic austerity vis-à-vis the styles it sought to overcome. Adolf Loos' polemic *Ornament und Verbrechen* against the Viennese style of his time also aimed at precisely that.[4] However, this austerity comes at the expense of individuality, and innovators must counter this by adopting only moderate stylistic austerity in their start-up. This is the downside of founding a new elective affinity by taking and recombining objects from already established styles (bricolage). Start-ups using *new* objects do not carry this risk, which is why DIY in the world of things is typical for new elective affinities. That is why craftsmanship and the new things thus created were so formative for the Bauhaus and Adolf Loos. This leads to:

Openness to the New (H_{16}): new elective affinities are more open to new objects than old ones.

With the new style made of new objects, the incumbent elective affinities also gain social distance. This inhibits their incentive to also include the new objects in their common style. Because if this were to happen, the additional distance the new style offers would again be compromised by increasing the shared periphery. Start-ups of elective affinities showing newly-invented objects are therefore particularly promising, with the incumbent elective affinities tending to give these new things the cold shoulder.

In this sense, new elective affinities are 'more modern' than old ones. Not because they are new *per se*, but because they show more new objects than the incumbent styles, and are therefore a better bet for greater distance in the social whole. The bet is that incumbent elective affinities will stick to their old objects but will also stay away from the new ones. The nuclei in the style system thus tend to wear vintage markers. People who gathered in the 1950s around rock 'n' roll

---

4   Stuiber 2012.

tend to keep its stylistic fingerprint and grow old with it. People who invent a new style today do not remain innovative but stay true to it.

Vintage thus becomes the trademark of social groups. This also has impact on the functioning of industry. The worst advice that trend scouts can follow is to look for the new in the very people in whom they have already made a find. Trend scouting is more of a localised business than personalised business; the emphasis is more on hotspots of style innovation than the persons of style innovation.

End of History

Addressing start-ups, H_{16} dynamically complements the incentive of incumbent elective affinities in nucleation (H_{10}). However, the downside risk of H_{13} and H_{14} also motivates incumbents to downsize their periphery *prophylactically*, by way of their own austerity. This is because cleaning up one's own peripheries by dispensing with their objects reduces the members' incentive to resign, and start or join a new group. Style peripheries begin to disappear in the whole style system. Common styles are becoming more and more distinct from each other. But in a style system devoid of any peripheries, (8') applies and the distance to the social whole is the same for all elective affinities. Social differentiation by means of new elective affinities then has completely lost its distancing capacity, and only its individuality-reducing effect remains. New elective affinities cease to form. This leads to:

> Slackening (H_{17}): the fewer objects shared in the style system by elective affinities, the weaker the further group-wise branching of society.

H_{17} predicts the end of the history of postmodernism. When the world of objects, X, has been completely absorbed by the nuclei of the style system, there no longer exists any incentive for the further horizontal differentiation of society. While style leadership continues to improve the efficiency of culture, in the end all groups are equally distanced (8'). It is precisely this beneficial contribution of style leadership that brings the history of postmodernism to its own natural end. The Saysian Quality Law (H_5) still holds, but new objects simply enrich particular, already established common styles. From then onwards, postmodernism has lost its organic dynamics (and romantic fascination). Style leadership brings social evolution to a standstill by the very means with which it fires it up.

At the end of postmodernism, people differ only as individuals within otherwise equivalent elective affinities. That is why everyone strives for that elective affinity that offers the most individuality. This is, *ceteris paribus*, the one with the largest number of members, m, and, *ceteris paribus*, the one with the weakest rooting, R_i^c, of the individual style. The risk of mass exodus (H_{13}) grows. For no one will stay in an elective affinity because of the social distance it confers. The size of the elective affinities, m, has converged, the phylogram of the world of objects has become a polytomy, and rootings have disappeared. Only by following this path does an elective affinity have any chance of surviving. As a follow-up hypothesis, H_{17} also predicts, for a style system with z consumers, size $m = z/n$ of *all* elective affinities. Together with vanished rootings and peripheries, this lets everyone have the same degree of individuality, the same distance to the social whole and the same happiness/utility. The economy (human agency) has then not only brought about full efficiency of culture, but also the perfect equality of people in all their self-created diversity – in a social sphere full of social distance and proximity.

Towards the end of postmodern history, culture also ceases to be a process. Cultural selection is slackening. New operating instructions for the sorting plant of culture are no longer needed. Style leadership is without a purpose and has lost its charisma. There's only one last directive to follow: to arrange each new object somewhere in the polytomy. A dice roll, assigning each new object to an elective affinity, can do this job. Differences in happiness/utility are only coincidental and temporary. Such is the convergent future of the productive consumer in the long run. It remains utopian.

Utopia and Disruption

But in the long run a lot will be different. Or, according to historian Fernand Braudel, by then the structure, in our case that of the style system, will have been used and abused time and again. Analytically, QTC is therefore most productive in the interim, after unpredictable disruptions and before the next ones, which are just as unpredictable. This is a time period in which the cultural order types (singleton, chain, phylogram, polytomy) are still in competition, where the rooting of individual styles in the common styles is not yet the exception, and where shared peripheries are still commonplace. The investigation of the style system in that state and in the light of cultural selection, i.e. by taking culture still as a process, is the topic of what follows later on. Beforehand, however, it is worthwhile identifying points of entry for distortions in the long-term model outlined above. What disruptions can there be in QTC? What causes the failure of the so-cial project of the end of postmodernist history?

Charisma: one point of entry for disruptions is the charisma of style leader-ship. QTC abstracts from charisma costs: manipulation of culture is costless for style leaders, just as their followers have no costs to bear when working in the sorting plant. But it is an open question how the convergence towards the end of postmodern history will affect the ratio of charisma/sorting costs. Sorting costs are lower the simpler the operating instructions for the sorting plant are. And these become ever simpler towards the end of history, just as access to the plant becomes increasingly easy: everyone's opinions are more and more sought after. At the same time, the de-intellectualisation of the world of objects that goes hand in hand with polytomisation also reduces the charisma costs. The phylogram is already easier to convey than a convolution of singletons, chains and trees; the polytomy easier than the phylogram, individual styles are diminishingly rooted and peripheries become rarer and smaller. The costs for the establishment of style leadership are therefore decreasing. This is why new style leaders are be-coming increasingly involved. The market for style leadership is booming with falling charisma costs. The human capital of curators, museum directors, pro-fessors, editors, columnists, collectors and conductors – accumulated at high costs in terms of time or money – is increasingly supplemented by the human capital of bloggers, vloggers, whistle-blowers and gurus. This is the breeding ground for charismatic disruption. Unconventional people push themselves into style leadership offering different ideas about the ordering of the world of ob-jects: Baudelaire, Kandinsky, Duchamp, Hayek, Jobs, Musk. On both large and small scales: Hayek's *Swatch* and Musk's *Tesla*; Baudelaire's *anti-aesthetics* and Du-champ's *Readymades*.

Objects: written language, the letterpress, the pill, the smartphone and social media have all disrupted the existing order to the extent that they have broken up the formerly closed coterie of style leadership. Written language allowed for asynchronous communication and thus reduced costs for style leadership. Just as the letterpress has facilitated mass followings, and allowed the dissemination of taboo-breaking operating instructions for the sorting plant more quickly and comprehensively. The pill and other emancipatory devices helped women attain style leadership, and thus provided the sorting plant with instructions that had previously been withheld. The smartphone and social media lowered communi-cation costs, and brought new competition to the established style leadership that was still working with expensive analogue media. The battle between the au-tomotive and IT industries for supremacy over the driving experience is a battle for the proper operating instructions for the sorting plant of culture. Which feature vector for ranking the driving experience will win out?

Politics: emancipation from the ruling powers, their retreat, loss of ideological orientation, political taboo breaking and migration create cultural distortions inasmuch as they destroy the trust of followers in the familiar operating manuals of culture. The fall of the Iron Curtain, the Arab Spring, Brexit, terrorism, 'America first!', turn the ordered world of objects upside-down – the good and the bad, the progressive and the backward, the beautiful and the ugly. The headscarf loses its Western meaning of female industriousness, the backpack becomes a potential weapon, the male hair parting a joke, and the monthly ticket for public transport becomes a migrant pass. The style system no longer develops smoothly, and instead entire elective affinity constellations become unstable.

As exogenous shocks, such disruptions, which are often complementary, prevent the end of the history of postmodernism. They ensure that cultural order types remain manifold and the order of the world of objects stays segmented and complex. They ensure that culture as a process is ongoing. Disruption preserves QTC as a bio-economic and medium-term theory of style.

A Variegated World and the Silence of the Orthodoxy

Inspired by classical mechanics and astronomy, the orthodoxy fails to predict the colourfulness of the world. It does not even notice it. Instead, it presents grey on grey as its prediction of what the world will be like. In the orthodoxy, when variegation is the result of analysis, it is only because it has already been introduced by assumptions or entirely by chance. By contrast, in QTC, the starting conditions for all consumers are the same and they all resemble each other at the beginning like peas in a pod. You can think of the starting conditions of postmodernism, as modelled in QTC, as a perfectly aligned North Korea. Everyone is identically endowed and everyone wants exactly the same things – and still the world becomes colourful, without everyone wanting variegation *per se*.

Lancaster's orthodox *product differentiation*[5], using the clock face of qualities, is an example of the exogenous preferences of consumer society: each individual is assumed to prefer a different quality right from the start. The remainder of the prediction (the number of minutes, i.e. objects, on the clock face and their uniform distribution on it) is solely based on the cost and market structure of industry. With polytomisation (Figure 10) QTC also predicts this uniform distribution

---

5   Lancaster 1975.

of qualities on the product circle. But not by packing consumer preferences for different qualities into the model by assumption. In QTC variegation is endogenous.

Gary Becker's orthodox modelling of *habits* and *addiction*[6] allows for people to have different experiences by chance, which influence their later consumer behaviour in different ways, making them become smokers and non-smokers, drinkers and teetotallers, phlegmatics and adrenaline junkies. What comes out in the end as variegation in the world is the result of pure coincidence at the start (with systematic subsequent effects). George Akerlof's and Rachel Kranton's equally orthodox *Identity Economics*[7] allows people with different resource endowments to choose between different identities. Here variegation is assumed in the model twice: first, as exogenous differences in resource endowment, and second, as an exogenously available set of different identities that can be freely picked, much like shampoo from the supermarket shelve. In QTC, the collective identity (social distance) granted by elective affinities is endogenous, as are the individual identities (proximity) in it and the number of alternative elective affinities. An initial assumption of differences between consumers is not needed.

In this respect QTC is fundamentally different from the orthodoxy. It predicts the variegation of the world instead of simply assuming it. This establishes as the most fundamental prediction of QTC:

Variegation of the World (H_{18}): otherwise identical individuals differ in their 0/+consumption.

Why does the orthodoxy remain blindfolded to the endogeneity of the variegation of the world? Its paradigmatic fixation, on upbringing, on quantities, prices, and endowments with quantities allows the orthodoxy to favour analytically what it already sees, *a priori*, day by day: quantities, prices and endowments. The othodoxy remains trapped in its paradigms. *A posteriori*, however, the variegation of the world calls for a paradigm shift. 0/+consumption and the *productive consumer* are just such a paradigm shift, which allows the variegation of the world to be predicted, and what is economically special about postmodernism to be understood.

---

6   Becker 1992.

7   Akerlof and Kranton 2010.

Variegation in Nature and Culture

Up to here, several similarities and differences in the variegation of nature and culture have been identified. *Grosso modo* they nourished the hope that biodiversity might be a good starting point for understanding the variegation of the world of objects. However, the biological model could not be adopted one-to-one, but had to be adapted to the particulars of culture. This adaptation has modified the phylogram – the diagram of diversity from the point of view of evolutionary biology – step-by-step. The intuited differences between nature and culture could thus be refined in terms of dissimilarity and diversity theory. In the resulting QTC, however, these differences have not proved so great that further endeavours within cultural studies to learn from biology would be a futile effort. The following considerations are further cases in point.

It would be wrong to assume that cultural diversity can be or even has to be thought of in ways different from biology *merely* because of the anthropocentricism of cultural studies, whereas biodiversity is what it is, and therefore in biology one is always measuring the same thing (albeit with different methods). Indeed, there exist also different concepts of biodiversity.[8] They are: *species richness* – in the survey area the number of species is determined; the greater the number, the greater the diversity. *Endemism* – in the survey area only those species that do not exist elsewhere are counted; the greater the number, the greater the endemism. *Disparity* – biodiversity is mapped in phylograms or cladograms; the concept from which I started the analysis. *Functional diversity* – species differ in their contribution to an ecosystem function, or they do not; the more ecosystem functions species assume in the survey area, the greater the diversity. *Ecosystem diversity* – identical/similar ecosystems are grouped together; the greater the number of different ecosystems in the survey area, the greater the diversity. *Intraspecies diversity* – the greater the number of different alleles in the DNA of a species, the more diverse it is.

Cultural studies thus do not stand alone against the challenge of multiple, competing diversity concepts. Against this background, the choice of a diversity concept in QTC must not be judged as right or wrong, but rather by the extent to which it serves an epistemological interest. As it is with biodiversity: a diversity concept "must be considered as telling the [...] story that best fits the diversity *observed*, but not necessarily as telling the 'true' story."[9] In QTC the *observed* diversity is that observed by the productive consumer. An empirical assessment of

---

8   Gaston 1994.

9   D'Arnoldi, Foulley and Ollivier 1998, p. 159. (my emphasis).

cultural diversity cannot therefore be carried out *ex cathedra*, but must assess diversity as consumers see it. But if you accept the productive consumer as the defining authority for cultural diversity, you can expect the number of alternative concepts to be greater than in biodiversity. For example, if even in a given style the *picture* is something quite different depending on the media used, such as in painting and literature,[10] there are only far-flung limits (if any) to the conceptualisation of cultural diversity.

Nor would it be of much help distinguishing biological and cultural diversity along anthropocentric lines, i.e. suggesting that cultural diversity always serves human interests, but biodiversity does not. In fact, there is always a human interest also in biodiversity concepts.[11] Respect for creation is itself one.[12] Depending on your interests, different concepts of diversity force themselves upon you, and biological as well as cultural diversity are subject to some anthropocentric bias or another. In this sense both are normative theories: how should diversity be seen in terms of a given human interest and in what respect should it change or remain the same? One is the interest in social distance and proximity. Here QTC remains firmly anchored in neoclassical economics, saying that the relevant diversity is that which gives the individual its social distance and proximity. Emic fit is the criterion for the conceptualisation of cultural diversity.

Biodiversity concepts are often based on indirect interests, i.e. those beyond the conservation interest *per se*: for example, genetic disparity in the indirect interest of ecosystem resilience or of genetic engineering, or intraspecies diversity in the indirect interest of survival probability of a species or of breeding success. In much the same way, the interest in cultural diversity is indirect: vernacular diversity in the indirect interest of regional identity; literature and film diversity in the indirect interest of national identity; media diversity in the indirect interest of democracy. QTC also postulates consumers' indirect interest in diversity. They strive for stylistic diversity only to satisfy their preference for social distance and proximity. But indirect interests open the door to different definitions of diversity. "There is no unique measure of diversity, and unless we know how and why diversity gives rise to *inherent* value it is not at all clear how we should operationalise the concept."[13] The operationalisation proposed in QTC has been developed from consumption activity and the basic idea of the object as a thing/behaviour with a culturally determined meaning.

---

10   Dundas 1979.

11   Sarr, Goeschl and Swanson 2008.

12   Perry 2010.

13   Mainwaring 2001, p. 85 (my emphasis).

Even if biologists agreed on a concept of biodiversity or accepted it as a convention, for example the cladogram, there would still be a degree of freedom in modelling in as much as there are always different possible ways to order a given set of species in it. The same degree of freedom also exists in the ordering of cultural objects. The two cladograms of Titian's oeuvre in Figure 3 are a case in point. This degree of freedom is a problem for biology, because cladograms cannot be scientifically falsified; a preference for one of several theoretically possible cladograms cannot be scientifically justified.[14] In contrast, the scientifically relevant order of the world of objects is that of the productive consumer, regardless of which of *their* options they choose. Whether they adopt it in the sorting plant of culture by habit, or as a result of their own slow, 'analytical' thinking makes no difference.

Biodiversity theory and QTC face related analytical challenges. In particular, the shared problem of where exactly value resides: "Thus, after selecting for an appropriate currency (characters) and a particular evolutionary model that will predict the distribution of characters over cladograms and trees, the remaining consideration is to decide whether the greatest value resides within individual characters or in combinations of characters."[15] In QTC, the feature value of the object is the 'currency', and the model is neither the phylogram nor the cladogram, but rather different yet similar geometric structures appropriate to the culture. The question of where value resides is answered exactly the same way as in biodiversity theory. Value resides in combinations of different feature values, not in the feature value itself. This basic premise makes *0/+consumption* the central focus.

In QTC, the value of the single object, of the individual style and of the common style can, in principle, be calculated. The value is its specific contribution to objective function (13), or else its contribution to the mapping of all individual goal achievements into a measure of collective welfare. Students of culture will exclaim at this point that diversity is not the only valid measure of the value of culture and that even that has various dimensions. They are in good company with biologists, who claim that biodiversity is not nature's sole gift; all of nature's services, including biodiversity, should ideally be weighted and then incorporated into a comprehensive measure of nature's gifts.[16] QTC is to be understood in exactly the same way: as the specification of a particular diversity value of culture, which, weighted and combined with other diversity values and with non-

---

14   Vogt 2008.

15   Humphries, Williams and Vane-Wright 1995, p. 101.

16   Banzhaf and Boyd 2005.

diversity values, can be included, in principle, in an overall measure of culture's gifts.

Biodiversity as a scientific concept as well as QTC operate with both basic ideas of diversity: measured as length and as width. Biodiversity's *species richness, endemism, functional diversity* and *ecosystem diversity* are measured by counting. All these concepts operate on the idea of width as the fundamental rationale of diversity. In contrast, the biological concept of *species disparity* is based on the idea of length. The special characteristic of QTC is its combination of both basic ideas in a single model.

The lack of integration of interspecies diversity and intraspecies diversity has been criticised as an open question in biodiversity theory. [17] Interspecies diversity compares between species what is shared by the specimens of a species, while intraspecies diversity illustrates what distinguishes the specimens of a species. Here again we have the analogy to the style system that was mentioned in chapter 2. Interspecies versus intraspecies diversity distinguishes between genes and alleles, QTC distinguishes between the common and the individual style. The common style results from the totality of individual styles in an elective affinity – just as the human species results from the totality of all specimens in its reproductive community. The lower level of individual styles corresponds to the lower level of specimens of the human being with different alleles, and the higher level of the common style corresponds to the higher level of the species. The common style is like a species, for example, the human being; the individual styles are like the specimen of a species, for example, an individual human being. And the style system with the variegation of its elective affinities is like the ecosystem with its richness of species.

Despite this analogy, there is a fundamental difference in the approaches to biodiversity and cultural diversity: reproductive communities are assessed by biologists (qua model assumption) for comparability, elective affinities of productive consumers (qua model assumption) for incomparability. In other words, interspecies diversity is measured as length, while in QTC the diversity of common styles is measured as width. In QTC, individual styles within an elective affinity are in a complementary relationship to each other. They promote diversity in the common style and thus elective affinity-wide individuality. The diversity-related complementarity of individual styles is, however, impaired by rooting. Substituting an individual style for another less rooted one is in the interests of diversity in the common style. It is precisely this effect that has also been postulated for biodiversity: intraspecies diversity will increase when a rooted subpopulation

---

is replaced by a less rooted one.[18] The rooting of individual styles in the common style corresponds, by a further analogy, to the 'within-subpopulation coancestry' of intraspecies diversity theory.

QTC models a non-spatial society: the geography of elective affinities and the position of individuals in physical space do not matter. As a matter of fact, the striving for and attainment of identity does not only take place in the social but also in geographical space, in the milieus of cities, and in the countryside. Elective affinities flock together not only in spirit, but also in physical places. QTC abstracts from this potentially effectual side of diversity. The study of spatial aspects of biodiversity could therefore provide further impetus for the analysis of cultural diversity. Size (number of specimens of a species and geographical area of occurrence)[19] and isolation/insularity[20] affect biodiversity. The size of elective affinities, their spatial distribution, and insularity/ghettoisation have already been dealt with in sociological and cultural studies, but their impact on and interaction with cultural and social diversity remains to be explored.

Keeping in mind these reservations from cultural studies towards the present model, but also the previously mentioned biological analogies, Part 3 will concern itself with clarifying to what extent contemporary phenomena can be predicted *and* understood with the help of QTC. To this end, I will abandon the formal analysis in favour of a more broadly reflective approach.

Gene(tics), Meme(tics), (Bio)semiotics, Human Being

Richard Dawkins, whose analogous comparison of DNA in nature and Chaucer's *Canterbury Tales* helped motivate QTC, answers in his book *The Selfish Gene* the question of whether nature and culture might essentially be the same – with an unequivocal yes![21] According to Dawkins, genes do not serve the survival of the phenotype they produce (e.g. the human species), they merely use it as a host in the interest of their own replication, by jumping from body to body (e.g. via egg and sperm cells). It is not the species that is the unit of biological selection, but rather the gene! And what is the gene in nature, Dawkins continues, is the *meme* in culture. Dawkins' neologism 'meme' refers to the smallest unit in culture that exists solely for the sake of its own replication and not that of its host (e.g. a body

---

18   Caballero and Toro 2002.

19   Whittaker, Willis and Field 2001.

20   Kadmon and Allouche 2007.

21   Dawkins 1989 (1976).

with a human mind). And accordingly, just as natural selection selects genes only, cultural selection selects memes and not their carriers. And just as genes 'want' to survive in a gene pool, memes 'want' to survive in a meme pool. Both genes and memes are found in a host organism and utilise it parasitically. A meme can be almost anything, according to Dawkins: a sound, melody, catchword, idea, garment, fashion, etc. For instance, a fashion 'seeks' to spread from body to body and an idea from brain/mind to brain/mind. The replication mechanism is imitation; a body imitates a fashion from another body and a brain imitates an idea from another brain. From these considerations, a veritable scientific school of thought has developed: memetics. In memetics, culture functions (almost exactly) like nature. Not surprisingly, memetics receives fierce criticism from scholars of culture, for example from semiotics, which I will address here, because it helps shed more light on QTC.

Semiotician Erkki Kilpinen claims the meme in memetics corresponds to the sign concept in semiotics and therefore is old (semiotic) wine in new (memetic) wineskins.[22] Kilpinen argues that in its broader, dynamic variant, which can be traced back to Charles Saunders Peirce (and not to Ferdinand de Saussure), semiotics has always understood culture as an evolutionary pool of signs, in which signs produce signs and signs can only evolve from signs. Accordingly, the memes of memetics are nothing more than the signs of semiotics, albeit scientifically poorly founded. Kilpinen goes on to say that, unlike genetics and semiotics, memetics is a theory devoid of empirical substance. A gene is physical, it can be separated and cloned, but a meme is little more than the term invented by Dawkins for a model of culture that can only be spoken of as if it existed. In this model, memes convey information as genes and signs do, but in contrast to genes and signs one does not know what the information is about, nor to whom or what it is addressed. In short, memetics is removed from the real world. By contrast, semiotics, with its concept of the *productive object*, is considered to be grounded in a real-world environment. It deals precisely with how concrete objects 'produce' the signs that they themselves represent. Thus, according to semiotics, from the outside world of the human being a corresponding inside world emerges.

In memetics and semiotics two competing scientific currents clash – the naturalism of memetics and the culturalism of semiotics. Culturalism regards the human being as living not only in a physical world but also in a symbolic one, created and changed by symbolic expression. Whereas naturalism regards

---

22   Kilpinen 2008.

culture as being formed by natural (or at least nature-equivalent, for example memetic) forces and laws.

Naturalism and culturalism are united, however, on the question of what the human species has in common with other species and what is different from them, for example in the archaeological findings of tool usage. The difference between humans and chimpanzees or ravens is, in this shared view, not the presence or absence of culture (e.g. tool usage), but the complexity of species-specific culture.[23] Culture and nature are not the same in this view but are interwoven and even partially interdependent.

Biosemiotics, a cross-disciplinary bridge between traditional biology and traditional humanities, attempts to systematise this view. It builds on two premises. First, that all life forms (from unicellular organisms to humans) rely on both the ability to process signs from the environment relevant for survival into information, and the ability as part of that environment to produce such signs for other life forms. The second premise is that human sign production and processing (anthroposemiosis) is only a small and, in evolutionary terms, young part of the semiotic potential of all life. Biosemiotics thus closes the gap between biology and traditional semiotics, from whose standpoint semiotics is the "oxygen of biosemiotics".[24]

QTC is positioned within the cultural tradition of semiotics. The material, X, from which social distance and proximity are produced, consists of different but concrete things and behaviours from the real outside world. They are the 'productive' objects of semiotics. The values of feature vectors generated in the sorting plant of culture from the world of objects are themselves vectors of signs that 'produce' other signs in the form of individual and common styles. As signs, they then 'produce' signs of social distance and proximity in the inner world, which in turn 'produce' elective affinities as a model of the outside world and thus correspond to it. In QTC it is not the subsets of the world of objects belonging to the outside world, X, that are consumed. Instead, it is the model of the outside world that is consumed, which exists in the inner world and consists of signs of the segmented order, $(X, \square)$. From a semiotics perspective, the arguments of the objective function (13) are the final links in the chain of signs 'produced' by the world of objects, X.

The central difference between QTC on the one hand and genetics, memetics and semiotics on the other is the site of agency. Genetics and memetics are

23   For example Haidle, Bolus, Collard, Conard, Garofili, Lombard, Nowell, Tennie and Whiten 2015.

24   Favareau, Kull, Ostdiek, Maran, Westling, Cobley, Stjernfelt, Anderson, Tonnessen and Wheeler 2017, p. 16.

positioned within the tradition of Actor Network Theory (ANT), in which genes and memes possess agency by virtue of their interest in replication. In genetics only genes have agency and in memetics only memes. The human being as the site of genes and memes (body cells, brain/mind) is in genetics and memetics merely a container devoid of agency. In contrast, QTC positions itself at the other analytical extreme by assuming only the human being, specified as style leaders and followers, possesses agency. The title of Part Two – *The Productive Consumer* – represents this idea of the site of agency, in which QTC fully subscribes to the economic orthodoxy.

In this respect QTC also differs from semiotics, which, by abstraction of signs/information from the sender/receiver, grants no agency to the human being. The human being as a species merely defines the scope of validity of the sign system studied (anthroposemiotics). Only objects and signs possess agency in their ability to 'produce' (other) signs (anthroposemiosis). For this reason, QTC is no sub-theory of (anthropo)semiotics in the sense of an economic theory of semiotics. But its reliance on semiotics while maintaining human agency makes it a 'semiotic economics' theory.

In semiotic economics, the site of agency shifts the source of style innovation from gene/meme/sign to the human being. In this view, the increasing variegation of the world is attributed to the fast and slow thinking and acting of style leaders and their followers, rather than to the self-replication urge of genes or memes or to the stylistic 'productivity' of objects and signs.

How the innovation process is conceived is another difference between genetics, memetics and semiotics on the one hand and QTC on the other. Semiotics remains silent on exactly how signs innovate – except arbitrarily *ex ante*. Signs 'produce' other signs, but not much more is said, except about how the new signs differ from the old ones and how they are built upon them. Semiotics is a nonpredictive *ex post* science.[25]

---

25   The beard in Russia, interpreted in semiotic terms by Lotman and Uspensky (1978), is an example of the simultaneous strength of comprehension and weakness of prediction in semiotics. Early on, according to them, the bushy beard was the sign of the Russian (old sign). Peter the Great's elegant French moustache (new sign) subsequently stood for the New Russia and made the bushy beard a sign of the Old Russia. Yet the new sign had become comprehensible only through the old sign. Without the old bushy beard, the new moustache could not have stood for modern Russia. The proposition of semiotics that (old) signs 'produce' (new) signs must be understood in the sense of this example. Semiotics thus comprehends the emergence of new signs ex post but cannot predict their emergence based on its knowledge of old signs. It comprehends that the new came from the old in such and such a way, but not that it will come from the old in such and

This is where memetics proves to be a more productive theory than semiotics. Yet, its premise that the dissemination of memes happens by imitation also remains a concurrent conceptual obstacle to understanding cultural innovation. However, on the upside, memetics examines nature's evolutionary processes and transfers them to culture as testable hypotheses. Memetics scholar Alex Mesoudi has outlined the following evolutionary-memetic processes.[26]

Variation (modelled after genetic mutation and recombination in sexual reproduction): examples of cultural mutation are the copying errors in the *Canterbury Tales*, which produced about 80 still-existing versions of the text. An example for recombination in style is the bricolage process in clothing fashion, for example in the hipster style.

Inheritance (modelled after Mendelian inheritance): an example is the emergence of the present-day book from continuous revisions of the manuscript. As in nature, a distinction is made between vertical inheritance (passed from parents to children) and horizontal inheritance (via parasitic invasion). The art and design styles preserved over time in academies such as the Bauhaus or in places like Florence during the Renaissance are memes replicated via vertical inheritance. An abstract memetic example in QTC of horizontal inheritance is the expansion of the periphery of a common style by incorporating an object from another common style into a member's individual style. The trivialisation of art in kitsch is a practical example of horizontal inheritance. The archaic style in painting and sculpture that emerged during the Upper Palaeolithic revolution and is still practised today is a meme that has been inherited not only vertically but also horizontally, for example by Picasso, inspired by the photographs of the Lascaux find. In contrast, the early medieval knight fighting a lion is a meme vertically inherited from ancient Rome (gladiator fights).

Selection (modelled after Darwinian selection): the cultural selection laws H_1– H_{10} in chapter 6, derived from the objective function (13), all belong to this category. In QTC, cultural efficiency is the counterpart to Darwinian fitness. It selects in favour of this efficiency: the hypotheses on social evolution, H_{11} - H_{17}, result from the selective effect of the objective function (13). Historical examples of cultural selection are diachronic yet systematic changes in a style, for example

---

such a way! For example, if Peter the Great had opted for a clean-shaven face instead of the elegant moustache, the old sign would have 'produced' a completely different new sign with the same meaning. This systematic arbitrariness of signs, already ascertained by Ferdinand de Saussure, brings human agency back into the semiotic game, and not only in the case of Peter the Great.

26   Mesoudi 2017.

the emergence of the arabesque from the geometry of lotus blossom and palm leaf, or the modification of the lily ornament in France between the 12th and 18th centuries.

Drift (modelled after natural drift in small populations as a random generator of the frequency of alleles): a memetic example would be the random disappearance of an ethnic group from an urban milieu. In QTC, the random retirement of a member from a (small) elective affinity with a corresponding decline in the individuality of the remaining members would be a case of cultural drift. Crafts threatened with extinction are memes affected by cultural drift.

Migration (modelled after gene flow): migratory flight, bringing with it cultural attributes, but also travel and tourism are memetic examples. The cheetah-like predatory cat in the Western European medieval *Hom* motif is a meme that came from Asia via intercontinental contact. Historical Sicily owes its Roman, Byzantine, Moorish, Frankish, Norman and Spanish inspired style to such a flow of memes, as does Western Europe's contemporary pyjama style. Holiday souvenirs and the influx of international cuisine are probably the most common cases of meme flow. Beau Brummel's appearance in elite London society during the Regency period was a meme flow across social boundaries. The gentleman meme, on the other hand, is likely to have also spread as a result of physical mobility in 18th century England.

As shown by these examples from Part One, memetic processes are accommodated in QTC. They can be divided into two groups: the disruptive processes that repeatedly throw evolution off-track towards cultural efficiency (variation, drift, migration), and the pressure towards cultural efficiency. In this sense, QTC can be interpreted as memetic economics that combines the complementary analytical potentials of semiotics and memetics. From semiotics it adopts the idea that signs in a system are connected, from memetics the analysis of how cultural evolution can happen. But it also imports the orthodoxy's model of agency and develops from it a new mechanism of cultural selection.

Many objections to the anthropocentricity of QTC can be raised. For example, artificial intelligence blurs the boundaries between the human being and things. Taking this into account in a more generalised QTC, agency would no longer be exclusively limited to humans. This would make the theory richer, but only as long as there is still human agency in it.

The example of art shows this impressively enough. A purely semiotic view of art casts the brightest light on its language of signs and on the way in which artworks differ in this language. But why the innovation of a new artwork occurs, is only known in retrospect (in the case of a work by René Magritte, for example, in order to denounce *The Treachery of Images*). It is only the artists' agency, their *kunstwollen*, that opens the perspective of art as an innovation process. Much like semiotics, sociology tends to deny artists any innovation-generating agency; it sees them as trapped in their field (and style). Sociology is thus more suitable for explaining the lack of innovation in art, especially since it does not even allow for the effects of chance. Although memetics introduces chance (variation, drift), its paradigm for memes, replicating by imitation, makes memetics equally inadequate for explaining artistic innovation. This is because, according to the choir of experts, art is about nothing *but* innovation: what is not innovation is not art, what is imitation is kitsch. But chance is only a good enough theory for innovation as long as there is no better one (as is the case in biology). In art, however, compared to chance, the artists' agency is a better model of innovation. Only in the arts?

In Part Three I will address, from the perspective of QTC, the stylistic-evolutionary processes in the present day. The site of the agency of innovation is the human being. Its objective function (13), expressing the human pursuit not of imitation but of social distance and proximity, is what allows it to be a stylistic innovator.

Part 3: The Stylish Present Day

The Quality Theory of Consumption (QTC) developed so far is the result of a thought experiment: apart from the distinction between style leaders and followers, what would happen if in all other respects people were identical and had the same metapreference? What would happen if this universal metapreference manifested itself in two motivations; the preference for individuality within a group, and the preference for social distance from other groups? What would happen if people were able to jointly decide on belonging to a group by way of binary decisions about their goods type basket – "Yes to this, no to that!" – and thereby also could jointly form new groups? And in doing so, what would happen if consumption did not burden the household budget?

This thought experiment reflects – as I have argued – what is economically special about the postmodern present. With this perspective of the present, the thought experiment brings to the fore a cultural selection process with concomitant social evolution. From initial equality and uniformity, cultural selection and social evolution lead to the variegation of the world – into a visible diversity of individualities and elective affinities.

As a sublimation of the present, QTC pretends that only postmodernism remains in it, as if all remnants of modernism had already disappeared. Instead of defining the present as postmodern, as was done in the first two parts, the aim is now to follow the trail of postmodernism in a more complex present.

Chapter 8
Cultural Juxtaposition
and Stylistic Fertilisation

> "Culture does not merely transmit but interprets
> and transforms that which it communicates."
> *Gerard Delanty[1]*

> "Prod any happy person and you will find a project."
> *Richard Layard[2]*

Grounding QTC in a model of the present requires a departure from the assumption of universally identical metapreferences. Proceeding from this reference case, people differ in the weighting of the two determinants in objective function (13). While some have a strong preference for individuality within the elective affinity (formula [1]), others have a strong preference for social distance of their elective affinity to the social whole (formula [8]). Individuals with a strong preference for social distance will then gather in elective affinities, where the distance from the social whole is broad, and individuality is correspondingly narrow. Individuals with a strong preference for individuality gather in elective affinities where individuality is broad, and distance from the social whole is correspondingly narrow.

There will be more than just one common style, in which individuals with similar such weightings flock together. Every common style belongs to one of two style types: the *distance type*, which is shown in the set of all common styles that sublimate distance, for people with a strong preference for social distance. Or, the *individuality type*, which is shown in the set of all common styles that

---

1   Delanty 2011, p. 640.

2   Layard 2005, p. 73.

sublimate individuality, for people with a strong preference for individuality. The shared desire of all for dissimilarity, in combination with varying strong preferences for social distance or proximity, is a contribution of postmodernism to the complex present.

People differ not only in their postmodern preferences for social distance and proximity, but also in other preconditions, such as the resources they command. This is the heritage of modernism in the complex present and the object of interest of the orthodoxy. This heritage includes preferences for vertical distinction, status, or its hamster wheel variant of 'keeping up with the Joneses', mediated via accumulation. With variety in the preconditions combined with a shared desire for dissimilarity, a style system of different, also precondition-driven styles is born. The present is therefore not a juxtaposition of a postmodern style system and a separated style-free modernism. Instead, the complexity of the modern-cum-postmodern present is reflected in the overall style system. The QTC to be further developed here is therefore not a thought experiment for a postmodern fiction, but provides *mutatis mutandis* insights into a more complex present.

The interrelationship between modernism and postmodernism is a dynamic one. It would not even be static if the individual preconditions of all people remained constant, that is if members of a society replicated themselves identically. This is because culture not only conveys the social, but simultaneously transforms it. This is how the connection between modernism and postmodernism is also transformed by culture. The cultural selection worked out in chapter 6 is the transforming force. It is itself owed to human striving in the social sphere. This is the complex reality of the present.

Distance Type and Syndrome – Individuality Type and Syndrome

For the sake of simplicity, I first assume that in postmodernism there are only preferences for either social distance or for individuality, that is, either formula (1) or alternatively (8) determine individual happiness/utility. A style of the distance type is shown by people in whose objective function (13) distance receives weight one and individuality receives weight zero. A style of the individuality type is shown by people when weights are distributed in reverse. Later on, this strict division is loosened again.

We can now assign these postmodern style types causally to the hypotheses derived in chapters 6 and 7. Each style type is causal for a different set of vector components of cultural selection and social evolution. Table 12 shows this assignment: on the left is the set of the causal effects of styles of the distance type, on the right of the individuality type, at the top is the effect on cultural selection, at the bottom on social evolution.

The dichotomy – left and right – is based on the assumption that elective affinities of the distance type ensure that their distance to the social whole increases, and those of the individuality type ensure the individual style is sublimated in their common style. Each style type is therefore causal for the set of vector components that promotes the goal pursued by people of that style type. Style followers use their *0/+consumption* for this purpose, style leaders also manipulate the operating manual for culture's sorting plant (selection). In this way culture transforms the social (evolution) in the combination of style types. New, width-increasing manuals for the distance-type styles transform social distance, and new length-increasing manuals for the individuality-type styles transform proximity in the social realm.

The vector components of cultural and social dynamics, caused by the two style types, are type-specific symptoms of their dynamic impact. I define the totality of this dynamic impact as the *distance* and *individuality* syndrome. 'Syndrome' in the sense used here does not refer to a symptomatic overall state of culture and society, but to a symptomatic overall direction of change. In the following, where I focus more on the state of the style system, I will use the terms distance and individuality *type*, and where I focus more on its overall direction of change, I will use the terms distance and individuality *syndrome*.

Table 12: Distance- and individuality syndrome (type).

	Cultural Selection		
Distance Syndrome (Type)	• H_1, H_4: Thinning of chains by feature inflation • H_2: Insistence on incomparability (anti-aesthetics) • H_5: Adding singletons to a style • H_{10}: Austerity and material fingerprint	• H, H_3: Elimination of singletons by feature inflation • H_5: Fashions • H_6: Retro, Collections • H_8: De-uniformation in nuances • H_9: Egalisation of material differences	**Individuality Syndrome (Type)**
	• H_{11}: Low competition for members • H_{13}: Stable membership numbers • H_{14}: Incubation sites for new elective affinities • H_{16}: Emergence of many small elective affinities • H_{16}: Vintage marking over time	• H_{11}: Membership competition • H_{12}: Egalisation of individuality • H_{13}: Instability of the size of elective affinities • H_{15}: Fewer, but larger elective affinities	
	Social Evolution		

The left side lists the symptoms of the distance syndrome. It is defined as the total effect of all styles of the distance type on cultural selection (top) and social evolution (bottom). The right side lists the symptoms of the individuality syndrome, defined as the total effect of all styles of the individuality type on cultural selection and social evolution.

Distance type and syndrome: dominance orders are combated, the incomparable is brought forth – what is previously unseen is discovered, shown and cultivated, however irritating it may seem. Savants are shamans of the extraordinary. Individual styles and the common style have a tendency for austerity in what they show. There is little competition for members. Elective affinities are stable. There are always new common styles emerging without the old ones disappearing. They can be chronologised. Boundaries to other common styles are sharpened. Many small elective affinities are formed.

Individuality type and syndrome: the unique is combated and the comparable is brought forth. Collecting is a widespread passion. Retro is cultivated. Savants are shamans of the fine distinctions. Increasingly more nuances are brought into previously uniform-like ensembles. There is a tendency towards egalitarianism. Elective affinities compete for members. They are unstable. They succumb to fashions. Boundaries between common styles become blurred. A few large elective affinities are formed.

We can now again abandon the assumption that in postmodernism, individuals exclusively seek either social distance or individuality. Instead Table 12 can be interpreted so that in the distance type, all common styles are united with a stronger preference for social distance than individuality. And in the individuality type are all those with a stronger preference for individuality than for social distance. The scripts for the syndromes of Table 12 should therefore be interpreted in relative terms – in the sense of more or less. In styles with distance as the stronger (weaker) motive, the script for the distance syndrome merely has a stronger (weaker) effect than the script for the individuality syndrome. Thus, a style of the distance type does not necessarily lack all of the syndromic characteristics that are powerfully evident in the individuality type, and vice versa.

Style Groupings

In chapter 4, I have divided styles into two metagroups, *above-average type/syndrome* and *extreme type/syndrome* (Table 9). In the present chapter I have defined two more metagroups, *distance type/syndrome* and *individuality type/syndrome* (Table 12). The first two distinguish styles according to their above average or extreme design. This distinction is in the style-theoretical tradition of the (art historical/archaeological) signature model from chapter 2. The other two metagroups distinguish according to the dominant motive for stylisation, the motive of seeking distance versus individuality in the social realm. This distinction is in the style-theoretical tradition of the (art-critical) expression model from chapter

2. The four metagroups form a pair-wise operationalisation of the style-theoretical distinction between the *how* and *what* of style. In style theory, however, a strict separation between the *how* and *what* of a style is problematic; the *how* can in particular influence the *what*.[3] That is why I have made a distinction between *type* and *syndrome* in the four metagroups. Type denotes the constitutive part of a metagroup, syndrome denotes the totality of the specific impact of its styles on the overall style system's direction of change.

From this style-theoretical division into metagroups, style groupings emerge. A stylistic grouping is composed of a set of styles that are of the same design (the *how* of style), and also share the dominant motive for stylisation (the *what* of style). Thus, four style groupings can be formed from the four metagroups. They are shown in Figure 11. The *what* of the distance and individuality types, and the *how* of the extreme and above-average types, span the two axes of the postmodern stylistic field as polar opposites. Common styles (and their elective affinities) are located in it.

As a fusion of the distance type with the extreme type, we find in quadrant I the variety of youth styles (juvenile gangster style, skateboarders etc.). In their opposition to the parochialism of the adult world, distance is the dominant motive. They produce distance with the extreme: the *juvenile gangster style* is extreme in its vulnerability of pride, *skateboarders* and *parkour* in their acrobatic stunts. *Bike couriers* do likewise in city traffic. Hyper-masculine *hip hop* distances itself from the white mainstream, just as *skinhead*, *punk*, *teddy boy* and *mod* seek distance from it – with different extreme forms. The mohawk hairdo of the punk is a synonym for everything never before shown in the style system, incomparabilities with which social distance can be gained with a few stylistic 'tricks'. Dick Hebdige brings many ghetto-like styles into a chronological order; new ones are added with old ones never disappearing completely.[4] Vintage replaces vogue. These common styles show sharp contours through stylistic austerity (the o/+consumption gets by with few + and many o), which sharpens the boundaries to other styles. In this style grouping we can find a multitude of styles, each for fairly small elective affinities.

---

3   Robinson 1981.

4   Hebdige 1988.

Figure 11: Postmodernist groupings.

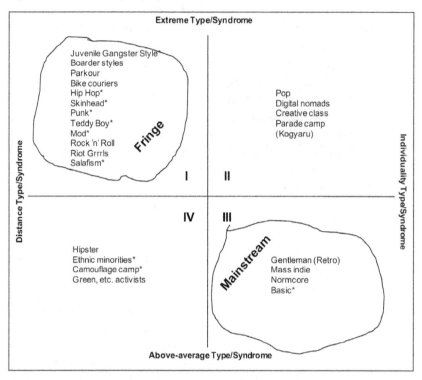

Many small elective affinities with sharp contours are of the distance and extreme type. A few large elective affinities without sharp contours are of the individuality and above-average type. The distinction made in modernist sociology between the mainstream and the subcultural fringes of society, is reflected in these two postmodern large-scale group-ings. The styles marked with * are, from the point of view of modernist sociology, subcultures constituted by their exogenous resource endowment (and whose style therefore has no constitutive function for and effect on them).

Exemplary of the fusion of the distance type with the extreme type is the style of *riot grrrls*.[5] Originating in the 1990s, another wave of feminism is evident in these girl bands. As with punk rock from which it arose, do-it-yourself dilettantism is a formative element of the style. Hence, electric guitar and drums, which girls did not typically learn in the context of traditional gender roles, are their preferred choices. The rock band, formerly a male domain, is another stylistic

---

5   Aragon 2008.

vehicle for opposing traditional gender roles. The exaggerated gestures of male rock musicians escalating to a wild dance, and the male ritual of disrobing is imitated provocatively. Not a purely musical style, it also presents itself in extreme bricolage of attire: combat boots with floral dresses, dissolving the traditional gender role. Macho language, contemptuous of women, is reappropriated ironically as part of their vernacular. All in all, the riot grrrls style pushes feminism to the extreme, in irreconcilable opposition and distance from the male-dominated world. The Russian band *Pussy Riot*, which has come into conflict with the Russian judiciary, exemplifies the style.

Another large-scale style grouping is the fusion between the individuality type and the above-average type in quadrant III of Figure 11. A few styles of large elective affinities can be found here. The dominant motivation is individuality. It is primarily achieved by the individual standing out just a little, in as many features as possible, from the average of their group. This is why this grouping does not belong in Asian societies, in which unity with a larger whole is the dominant motivation. In this grouping the number of objects of common styles is inflationary. Boundaries between common styles are blurred. Individuals can almost be assigned to two or more common styles simultaneously, they merely offer different perspectives on almost the same thing. Individuality is egalitarian individuality, no one really stands out, everyone is slightly different from everyone else and therefore everyone is somehow almost the same.

In this large-scale grouping we find the *gentleman* as an example of a retro style. Not showing his full financial potency, refraining from showing-off, he thus stays in touch with less well-off members of other social groups. Clothing, habitus and education only stand out a little, emphasising nuances. Therein we also find *mass indie*, the large clientele of brand labels with an irresistible tendency towards exclusivity, which is then lost because everyone displays it. And we find *normcore*: instead of being a burden,[6] the multi-option society is seen as an opportunity. The opportunities are seized, not by fusing with the larger whole, but by submerging oneself in it, in order to keep all options open – so as to be able to try out any interesting new combination in a stylistically unencumbered way at any time.

---

6   Gross 1994.

A New Home for Modernism

Modernist sociology is *stylistically* divided into the mainstream and the fringes of society. The fringes are made up of people with little material (money), social (network) and cultural (education) resources. They have never been able to break away from these basic preconditions and their styles mirror[7] or even stabilise[8] them. They remain trapped in communities they did not join voluntarily, unable to flourish in a postmodern elective affinity. Yet they too find their place in the groupings of Figure 11.

There the mainstream finds its place in quadrant III in the fusion of the individuality type with the above-average type: in particular, in the *basic* style, showing a multitude of only minor peculiarities meant to preserve one's individuality in the great current in which one is carried along. The fringes of society are contained in quadrant I. Their dominant motive is distance from the mainstream, which they produce with the extreme in the world of objects and with which they draw sharp boundaries. The dominant motive of the mainstream is individuality within its elective affinities, which leads to a blurring between its common styles and to the equalisation of individuality.

This stylistic nesting of modernism in postmodernism (Table 12 and Figure 11) throws new light upon an old discussion in sociology. Modernist sociology focuses on the different preconditions by which people are grouped into a hierarchy, in the belief that this hierarchy represents the present. Postmodernist sociology focuses on what is left in terms of individual freedom of choice, given the preconditions the individual must heed, which spans out the space of non-hierarchical differentiation, in the belief that this represents the present.

QTC provides a framework for continuing this discussion under new auspices. Because as Figure 11 shows, modernism presents itself in the stylistic dress of would-be postmodernism. The fringes and the mainstream find their homes in different postmodern stylistic groupings: as if the preconditions for all were the same; as if fringes and mainstream differed only in their respective dominant motives and preferred stylistic instruments – the fringes with the motive of social distance and the instrument of the extreme, and the mainstream with the motive of individuality and the instrument of the above-average. Group membership may be called elective or compulsory, depending on one's point of view. Stylistically, however, this makes little or no difference. This is the *a priori*

---

7   Veblen 1970.

8   Bourdieu 1982.

conclusion from QTC, a conclusion which, on the basis of the cursory empirical account presented here, also promises *a posteriori* validity.

Sociology should carry on its debate about precondition-rich versus precondition-poor society completely independently of style. Or, sociology should at least bid farewell to two of its conflicting paradigms: modernist sociologists should abandon the idea that endowment differences are causal for style differences, and postmodernist sociologists should abandon the idea that style differences do not correlate with endowment differences. The discussion should be steered away from the issue of causality or correlation, and towards the issue of the emic dimension of stylisation. What do people feel more driven by in their stylisation – their (alleged) preconditions or their (alleged) freedom of choice? Here, consumer anthropology offers support that is still untapped by sociology.

The transition from modernism to postmodernism need not be understood as the disappearance of endowment differences in terms of money, networks and education. Instead, it can be understood as an exhaustion of its effects on the style system. In postmodernism then, the style is decoupled from differences in people's preconditions. Style no longer shows what a person possesses, but who one is, no matter what one has. In a postmodernist democracy of taste *"Le style c'est l'homme même."* This precondition-free interpretation of society will be relaxed again in the final chapter, when the effects of different preconditions on the agency of style leadership and the agency of its followers will be addressed.

Special Groupings

The fringe and mainstream groupings in society are not the only ones in the style system. There are also the styles in quadrants II and IV. Together they blur the boundary between the mainstream and the fringes of society. The grouping in quadrant IV shares the dominant motive of social distance with the fringes and the preferred instrument of the above-average with the mainstream. The grouping in quadrant II shares with the mainstream the dominant motive of individuality and with the fringes the preferred instrument of the extreme.

Thomas Hecken, pop expert, sets *pop* apart from popular or mass culture.[9] For him, pop is typified by the seven features of: superficiality, functionalism, consumerism, showiness, immanence, artificiality and 'stylistic blend' (meaning the complementarity of things and behaviour, such as in the extreme type). The majority of these features are also a mark of popular culture – from tabloid

---

9   Hecken 2012.

journalism to hit songs, to TV series and advertising. Only showiness, pop-typical immanence, and openly displayed artificiality, he claims, are excluded from popular culture. Showiness is evident in pop's strict disinterest in human immanence, only the purely sensual is what counts. For example, the eye shows merely a sparkle and not the soul that popular culture sees in it. Immanence is always cited ironically. The car is a showpiece alone and not a conveyor of freedom and adventure as it is for popular culture. Artificiality is not unfamiliar to popular culture though, but only pop presents it openly: for example, not as the natural artificiality in the aesthetic functionalism design style, but as an exaggerated combination of artificiality (design) and technicality (functionality). According to Hecken's description, the *gadget* design style, which includes the beeping 'Detlef' egg, is therefore pop.

To which postmodernist groupings does pop belong? To answer this, let the popular or mass culture be located in quadrant III in Figure 11, which is the fusion of individualism as a motive with the above-average as instrument. According to Hecken, pop must not be confused with popular culture, but it is also not that easy to clearly distinguish the two. Pop therefore does not belong in quadrant I, where styles are sharply distinct from the mainstream. It belongs in quadrant II or IV, which blur the boundaries with grouping III. I suggest that pop be placed in quadrant II, as a style born out of the fusion of the individuality type and the extreme type. Individuality as the dominant motive, which it shares with popular culture, is, however, pursued with the instrument of the extreme. Rigorous showiness, a rigorously ironic approach to the immanent, and the artificial heightening of artificiality are stylistic means that make use of extremes. *Pop* shares with the mainstream the excessive use of the world of objects and the blurred boundaries towards other common styles. This is what makes it so hard to define. With the fringe styles it shares the penchant for the extreme in terms of showiness and artificiality wherever the contrast with popular culture is most pronounced. Media scientist Jörg Metelmann has coined the term 'mass original' for that which is typical of pop.[10] An originality that in mass production can only be preserved with a penchant for the extreme.

Digital nomadism hardly differs from normcore in terms of *o/+consumption*, except in the manner in which people work and live: with a computer, making ideal use of new media, with no permanent workplace but always travelling, with stopovers in places with good IT infrastructure. Software development is an occupation that can be performed in this way. Being completely independent of a fixed place of work, and thereby gathering as many new experiences as possible,

---

10   Metelmann 2016.

sublimates individuality compared to all those whose individuality disappears in traditional work and family life. Increasingly exceptional destinations and working conditions, collected like trophies, are the means for success. The fusion of the individuality and extreme types (quadrant II) is the grouping this style belongs to.

Digital nomadism is a stylistic variant of the *creative class*, the historical stylistic fusion of Protestant work ethos (mainstream) and hippiedom (fringe).[11] Its archetype is the creative mind in the IT industry: without a dress code or regular work hours, but still hard-working, and always seeking new experiences in work and leisure. This raises standing within the 'class'. The motive of individuality is pursued with the instrument of enhanced performance. The creative class therefore belongs in the same style grouping as pop. But both differ in what exactly is taken to the extreme. In pop it is showiness and the negation of immanence, in the creative class it is the opposite – immanence and the negation of showiness. Andy Warhol (pop) and Steve Jobs (creative class) are incarnations of this missing versus existing immanence and this existing versus missing showiness.

Quadrant IV is a grouping with very different common styles. They share the fusion of social distance as the dominant motive and the above-average as the preferred stylistic instrument. *Hipsters* dig up objects from the junk room of the world of objects which the mainstream has recently discarded. With these, they distance themselves from the mainstream, which they accuse of destroying the urban environment. And they stress their own competence in leading a good urban life.[12] With the fringes of society, they share the dominant motive of setting themselves apart from the mainstream, but they do not share their preference for pursuing this goal with the extreme. Stylistically, hipsters tend to be above average only, because one cannot shock the mainstream with objects that it has only recently abandoned. Unlike pop, hipsters do not use the world of objects excessively, but rather pick bits out of it selectively. They always know which bricolage is needed at any given time, until the mainstream discovers it as cool, at which point a new bricolage is needed.[13] Through these substitutions of a few objects at a time, hipsterism draws its boundaries with the mainstream. That's why it belongs in grouping IV.

The *ethnic minority* typically also belongs there. In order not to be absorbed into the ethnicity of the majority, it maintains its distance to it. Its choice of means is rarely extreme; its goal is achieved when the dissimilarity between the

---

11   Florida 2002.

12   Greif, Ross, Tortorici and Geiselberger 2012.

13   Mohr 2016.

ethnic minority and majority remains visible. Assimilation yes, but within clear limits. That's all it takes. *Activist* styles also belong in grouping IV, unless they use the extreme like the politically autonomous. Eco-activists are one example. They distance themselves from the ecological footprint of the mainstream but are not fundamentally opposed to the mainstream. With its smaller ecological footprint, its style stands out in a variety of features, but rarely dramatically so.

The homosexual style *camp* is a special one.[14] Instead of orienting finished identities like all other styles, in particular those belonging to grouping I and III, camp depicts the fluidity of its identities (for example, gender). It exposes the goals of the fringes (distance) and the mainstream (individuality) as an illusion. Individuality and distance are disillusioned by the stylistic proof of their artificiality. In this respect camp stands in contrast to both the fringes and the mainstream. However, it freely makes use of both groupings and, depending on its subtype, it shows the extreme or the above-average.

The *drag queen* with her make-up, glitter, feather boa and camp behaviour is the parade role of camp in grouping II. The Christopher Street parades show the variety of this subtype. Presenting a fake individuality, it is the lie that tells the truth about individuality. And, typical of the individuality type as a whole, boundaries blur, here especially the boundary to pop: Andy Warhol can be assigned to both camp and pop. The second, older subtype of camp avoids the extreme and uses the just-above-average with utmost caution. It belongs to grouping IV and is the camp bequest of modernism. Because of the social stigmatisation of homosexuality, there was a need to not attract attention and to communicate non-verbally with secret signs. Oscar Wilde's green carnation in the buttonhole is a classic example. In a subtle way that can only be understood by insiders, thus avoiding sanctions, distance to the heterosexual mainstream is established and proximity among themselves is found.

Camp belongs in two different postmodern style groupings (quadrant II and IV), because stylistically they are two distinct common styles. One is offensive like *riot grrrls* by means of the extreme. Deliberate irony, however, detracts from the aggression (grouping II). The other style of camp, like *normcore*, is defensive due to the very careful use of stylistic means. But the carefully chosen distinguishing features show all those who need to know their joint distance from the rest. If one wanted to label these camp styles, they could be *parade camp* (grouping II) and *camouflage camp* (grouping IV). However, the convention is simply to leave both styles combined under the label of camp. The widely-held belief in a

---

14   Bergman 1993.

homogenous group prevails here over phenotypic evidence and style-theoretic substance.

Refinement and Limitations

Style groupings could be further refined. The dominant motive, for example, need not be equally pronounced in all styles of a grouping. Hipsters may give more weight to their individuality than an ethnic minority, and would thus be positioned closer to the mainstream in grouping IV. The minority, in turn, could be more inclined to go to the extreme than hipsters, which would bring them closer to the fringes of society. Thus, boundaries between groupings become blurred. An ethnic minority, for example, can get close to *Salafism* in terms of style. Or a weaker preference for the extreme than parade camp would bring pop closer to popular culture.

Such a refinement of the style groupings would have to be empirically established. A further refinement would be the identification of trajectories in stylistic space. Do the common styles converge in a grouping or do they diverge over time? In the long run, do styles move in and out of groupings? Is there a trend in the style system as a whole in the weighting of the two motives and in the use of the basic means, i.e. in the stylistic *what* and *how*? All these questions must remain unanswered for now.

QTC, on which Figure 11 is based, cannot be applied to the whole of the present. It remains a theory of the West, cultures in which individuality in the group (formula [1]) – the more, the better – is an argument of the objective function. Therefore, dissimilarity and not similarity is the appropriate analytical concept. Similarity would be the appropriate concept for Eastern cultures, in which being one with the group would be the goal and proximity (formula [2]) the argument in the objective function – the more of it, the better. For these reasons it would be problematic to assign the Japanese youth style *kogyaru* from chapter 1 to any of the groupings in Figure 11.

Stylistic Encounters

For Gerard Delanty, cultural encounters are relationships between culturally different social actors, in processes by which some of these relationships shape long-term cultural regularities. He distinguishes six types of cultural encounters. First, *clash of cultures*, which leads to a persistent enmity between cultures, such as between political or religious fundamentalisms. Second, *cultural divergence*, where the cultural encounter leads to mutual differentiation and autonomisation, such as the Reformation and Counter-Reformation in Christianity. Third, *cultural assimilation*, in which a weaker culture absorbs elements of a stronger one, such as in colonialism. Fourth, *peaceful coexistence*, as expressed in the economic idea of international trade. Fifth, *cultural diffusion and adaptation*, which leads to a blurring of cultural boundaries and the merging of cultures, as in the case of Brazilian 'tropicalisation'. Sixth, *cultural fusion*, by which something completely new emerges from the fused, such as the US-American culture. [15] Although intended by Delanty for cultural encounters on a large scale – between ethnicities, religions, in colonialism, etc. – I use the approach to analyse encounters in the style system. Figure 12 summarises the result.

Stylistic fusion is typical for grouping I. Because the combination of objects previously thought to be uncombinable is a way of showing the extreme. It catches the eye, provokes and promotes social distance. The classic punk combination of tartan kilt and mohawk hairdo, and the riot grrrls' combination of military and girlish outfits exemplify this. Rock 'n' roll provoked the American mainstream with its fusion of black gospel with white country and western music. Dick Hebdige's *Subculture - The Meaning of Style* presents a whole collection of subcultural style innovations from the fusion of black and white styles. It also describes the origins of those black styles in the reggae of slavery. In such fusions, whites, mostly the youth from the lower end of the social ladder of modernism, could also gain autonomy. Grouping I is the pole position that leads to divergence and autonomy. The clash of cultures looms over its relationship with the mainstream. Grouping I is a hotbed of style innovation, of divergence and a breeding ground for 'brawling'.

---

15   Delanty 2011.

Figure 12: Syndromic encounters.

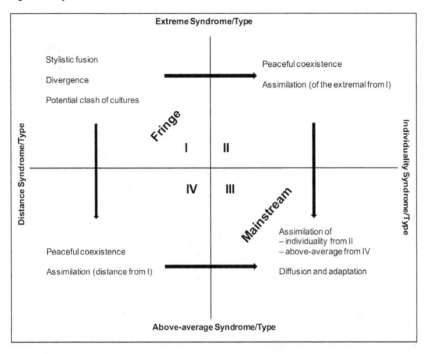

The mainstream and the fringes of society share no stylistic interface. The innovation impetus emanating from the fringes is paving its way into the mainstream via groupings II and IV. These have an intermediary function, because each of them has a different commonality with the mainstream and the fringes, a preferred means and a dominant motive. Grouping IV absorbs the stylistic potential of grouping I via the commonality of the dominant motive, and grouping II does it via the commonality of the preferred means. The mainstream absorbs the impetus from the fringes only from groupings II and IV, where it has already been weakened – from grouping II via the commonality of the dominant motive and from grouping IV via the commonality of the preferred means.

The mainstream and the fringes of society can only encounter each other directly in the (potential) clash of cultures. This is because they have no stylistic commonality, neither in the *how* nor in the *what* of style. Fringe styles are too alien to the mainstream, too scary for it to accept direct stylistic impulses from there. But groupings II and IV belong respectively to the other of the two style types combined in the fringes. By virtue of this commonality, they can partake in the fringes' stylistic productivity. At the same time, they belong respectively to the other style types combined in the mainstream. Through this complementary commonality, they pass on to the mainstream the impetus received from the fringes.

From grouping I, which pushes the social distance to other styles to the extreme, grouping II receives the impetus to push individuality to the extreme. Pop icons like Karl Lagerfeld were inspired by this. He assimilated manifestations of the extreme from grouping I and integrated them into his phylograms and polytomies, thereby adding length. Lagerfeld's personal clothing style was as extremely stylised as the velvet Edwardian suit of the *teddy boy*, but it did not, like the latter, fall completely outside the scope of the bourgeois business suit. It only exaggerated it, for example, with Lagerfeld's typical oversized shirt collar.

Sharing the dominant motive with the fringes, grouping IV also receives its impetus from there. For the purpose of clandestine communication, camouflage camp receives impetus in the form of new objects from the fringes. The earring worn on the correct side of the male head is an example (meaningless today). Living in geographical proximity to marginalised members of the dominant ethnic group, ethnic minorities experience social distance as normal in society. This also applies within the dominant ethnic group. In their distancing from the mainstream, hipsters receive impetus from the fringes and together they enliven urban milieus. The cultural encounter with grouping I results in assimilation in groupings II and IV. Grouping II assimilates what is extreme (the *how*) and grouping IV what is distancing (the *what*).

Encounters of groupings II and IV with other groupings are peacefully coexistent. The critique of the mainstream by pop, camp, hipster, the creative class or eco activists is moderate in comparison to the fringes, because they have already blunted the impetus they received themselves. It is only this process that makes what is received from the fringes palatable to the mainstream. The syndromes shared with the mainstream allow the attenuated to be diffused within it. The mainstream indirectly assimilates from the fringes what it would reject in direct contact. Contrary to popular belief, it is not the mainstream that is culturally strong, but the fringes. Not through their own effort alone, but because the fringes are supported by groupings II and IV.

The metamorphosis of the fringe tattoo of sailors and criminals into a mainstream fashion tattoo is a case in point. Distance-marking tattoos became fashion attributes that now convey individuality. Not by uncensored adoption of the fringe formats (e.g. full-body tattoo) and its symbolism (of belonging to a subculture), but rather in the form of smaller motifs on discreetly concealable body parts and with a symbolism that now signifies the values of the mainstream.[16]

---

16   Kjeldgaard and Bengtsson 2005, Irwin 2001, Landfester 2012.

Tattoos first entered the mainstream via youth styles, from where they were diffused into other styles in the grouping. It is difficult to imagine that young people, in the bosom of bourgeois families and exposed to their sanctions, carried out this creative metamorphosis in an autonomous act. They were dependent on intermediaries: on the pop idol (grouping II), not completely unknown to the parents, or on the next-door hipster (grouping IV), who had already taken the repulsiveness out of the tattoo. Thus, what was formerly distance-marking in the extreme became that what produces above-average individuality.

The career of the male earring is another example. Originally also fringe, for example in the style of travelling craftsmen, it was adopted by camouflage camp (grouping IV) as a secret sign not understood by the mainstream, only to be absorbed by the mainstream in sheer ignorance of its secret meaning. Its widespread distribution forced camouflage camp to find a replacement. Today the knowledge of which ear was the 'gay' one is lost, and the ring in the man's ear, no matter on which side, is part of popular culture.

The mainstream also absorbs from ethnic minorities (groupings IV). The success story of attenuated international cuisine is a case in point. Knowing the best deli, or where to get an 'authentic' kebab lifts the mainstream eater above the average. The hotness of the curry has long since been adapted to his/her palate. Traditional middle-class eating habits and meal times in traditional surroundings (family, circle of friends, at noon) are supplemented by time and location-independent food selection that was previously subcultural.

'Dumpster diving' – rummaging through rubbish bins for food – is stigmatised in the mainstream. Eco activists (grouping IV), who dissociate themselves from the food waste of the mainstream, tried to fight wastage with dumpster diving, which failed as a movement due to its stigmatisation. Only in the more moderate, dialectical form of 'foodsharing' did it become acceptable to the mainstream. Foodsharing is the organised rescue of food (almost) past its expiry date shortly before its disposal by supermarkets.[17] A taboo was thus broken by attenuation.

Syndromic diffusion from the fringes into the mainstream can be understood as a path-dependent step-by-step exchange of the *what* and the *how*. The *what* (distance) and the *how* (the extreme) leave grouping I and arrive in grouping II as the *how* (the extreme) and in grouping IV as the *what* (distance). From grouping II they are passed on to the mainstream as the *what* (individuality) and from grouping IV as the *how* (the above-average). Thus, at the end of the diffusion process, the *what* (individuality) is reunited with the *how* (above-average). This

---

17   Gollnhofer 2017.

postmodern diffusion process across the style system illustrates the impossibility of separating the *how* from the *what* as postulated in style theory.

Spiral into the Extreme

The fringes, and hence their extreme innovations, fuel the centrifugal forces of society. But there is also a counteracting force in the syndromic transformation of these innovations into the merely above-average in the mainstream: the constant striving to exceed the mainstream average lifts it up over time. It is a constant movement towards more extreme feature values, which in turn must be surpassed by ever-increasing extreme feature values of what was previously already above average. Small tattoos are getting bigger and bigger, shown more and more visibly. The now completely tattooed arm of the fashion-conscious professional soccer player shows this development.

This affects the whole style system. If the average of the mainstream shows individuality via increasingly extreme feature values, then individuality must be addressed with a corresponding escalation of the extreme in grouping II. What was considered extreme is no longer so, previous suprema in the phylograms and polytomies are constantly being replaced by new suprema producing increasing length. The superficiality displayed by pop is becoming increasingly superficial, artificiality increasingly artificial. Parade camp is becoming increasingly bizarre in the unmasking of 'finished' identities. The fringes must come up with an answer to this, or they themselves risk their distance. Thus, increasingly extreme stylistic fusions and innovations occur. The maintenance of distance using the extreme becomes increasingly extreme. The impetus sent out from the fringes becomes more and more radical: tattoos are trumped by self-mutilation, mainstream values are negated, elective affinities are politicised. The assimilation in grouping IV of these increasingly extreme stimuli from grouping I produces above-average results with increasingly large feature values. Thus, the above-average things that the mainstream assimilates from grouping IV reach increasing heights. This reinforces the inherent increase in the average. This in turn makes the spiral to the extreme steeper and steeper with each new round of innovation transformation.

That is why people mourn the past as a time when everything was more orderly, more normal, healthier, more reasonable, more moderate. The past is the old operating manuals for the sorting plant of culture, which have become obsolete due to the spiral into the extreme. What once stood out is no longer worth looking at today. What is normal today was once extraordinary.

The spiral into the extreme is a driver of behaviour independent of any increase in material wealth. In QTC, the spiral replaces the hamster wheel of accumulation in the orthodoxy (Veblen world, signalling of possession, 'keep[ing] up with the Joneses'). The consumer pursues their happiness/utility with increasingly extreme objects, both at the level of the extreme and at the level of the above-average. If they didn't do it, they'd fall behind, since there are plenty of others doing it. Whether they operate with the means of the extreme or with the means of the above-average, whether distance or individuality is their dominant motive, it does not matter, they are condemned to perpetual enhancement. Enhancement is a process that transforms the entire style system. Not one style grouping, and not one common or individual style in it, can resist this. All stylistic encounters flow into this spiral. The extreme, the peak of any quality, is the future and destiny of us all. This compulsion to constantly enhance quality is the price paid for the integrative power of the style system of Western society.

The Innovation Cycle

Figure 12, supplemented by the spiral into the extreme, is based on QTC in its transformative details, but not in the assumed direction of transformation. This direction is, however, based on a broadly accepted empirical finding: it is the mainstream that picks up stylistic elements from the fringes of society and not vice versa. Which is what forces the fringes to constantly come up with new stylistic innovations. Empirically, the fringes are the hotbed of stylistic innovation in society.[18] I have investigated elsewhere why this cycle does not collapse.[19] QTC complements this analysis with the precise diffusion path through the style system, as well as with the precise cultural transformation that stylistic innovation undergoes along this path. QTC also adds the 'fuel' that keeps the cycle going.

The diffusion of innovation takes two detours to the mainstream: via grouping II, which shares a penchant for individuality with the mainstream, and a penchant for the extreme with the fringes; and via grouping IV, which, like the mainstream, masters the craft of the above-average, and like the fringes has a stronger preference for social distance.

Digestibility of the heavy fare from the fringes does not spring up in the mainstream alone. It is also not obtained ready-made from the neighbouring groupings but is produced with them by division of labour. Grouping II supplies

---

18   Peterson and Anand 2004.

19   Mohr 2016.

what is already individual, but which is still too extreme. Grouping IV supplies what is already only above-average, but which is still too distant. The superficiality of pop from grouping II must be roughened up in the mainstream itself, and more authenticity must be brought into its artificiality. The foodsharing from grouping IV still needs to shake off the whiff of social criticism, through dialectical assimilation as economically efficient, ecologically effective and socially beneficial behaviour. The transformative capacity of the mainstream corresponds to the combined capacity of both neighbouring groupings. It must still transform the *how* in the transformed innovations from grouping II, and the *what* in those from grouping IV. In the neighbouring groupings stylistic transformation specialists are at work in either the *what* or the *how*. In the mainstream transformation generalists are at work in both the stylistic *how* and *what*.

The innovation cycle is fuelled by qualitative enhancement: the average and the above-average shift towards more extreme feature values, and old extremes are replaced by new ones. The innovation cycle would only dry up if no further enhancement were possible. The average and above-average would continue to rise for a while, moving ever closer to the extreme. The style system of Figure 11 would be compressed in the vertical. At the end of this stylistic tale there would only be the syndromic poles of social distance and individuality left. But is an end to qualitative enhancement, not as a slackening of volition but of ability, possible at all?

Groupings II and IV have an enzymatic function in the innovation cycle. The 'bad' taste of the fringes, as seen from the mainstream, is partially fermented there. Its fare now stimulates in the mainstream a good experience alongside the bad one. Thus, it acquires the charm of the unusual. What initially came from the fringes is now *cool* and attracts the interest of the more daring among the mainstream.

Cool

The stylish present offers a bonus for special performance: *coolness*. Cool is who stands out from the crowd, but still belongs to it, testing the style boundary of an elective affinity without overstepping it. Coolness is a concept of outside perspective: you cannot be cool without others finding you cool. Coolness is effective within elective affinities: you are cool if your elective affinity thinks you are cool. Coolness is relational: when others find you cool your self-esteem increases. Coolness is object-driven: without displaying something, be it a thing or a behaviour, nobody is considered cool. Thus, coolness is to be found in *0/+consumption*, but not in just any form of it. Coolness triggers an association: autonomy.[20] Not any kind of autonomy, but that which shows itself in norm-breaking behaviour. Not any norm-breaking, but the type that raises one's prestige.[21] Coolness is a manifestation of the somatic style, the fusion of the outside and the inside (chapter 2). The associative connection is between the observable exterior and the personal as perceived by the observer:[22] The outfit or behaviour itself isn't cool, but one is cool in how one exhibits the outfit or behaviour. It must fulfil three conditions: the conduct must be seen as intentional, the actor must be understood to be an expert in the situation at hand, and there must be a clear violation of a norm.[23]

The association of autonomy thus conveyed is *stand-out coolness*.[24] It conveys a trait of detachment from and indifference towards one's own elective affinity.[25] The egoism assumed in objective function (13) is the breeding ground of this indifference. The autonomy of those who are stand-out cool lets them try out the new and discard what everyone is displaying.[26] Whoever is stand-out cool is a style leader. Tables 8 and 11 summarise their agency.

Fit-in coolness is the non-authentic form of coolness.[27] Whereas stand-out coolness is counter-culturally cool, fit-in coolness is commercially cool: with trendy labels one stands out from the average. Fit-in coolness cannot trigger the association of autonomy. Stylistically, the fit-in cool consumer is merely an *early bird*, following a trend sooner than others and also jumping off sooner. The fit-in cool person is the early-acting agent in the fashion cycle and is a style follower. They differ from the uncool ones by acting faster in their style volition. Figure 13 positions the various forms of coolness within the mainstream as a desired characteristic of mainstream identity.

---

20   Warren and Campbell 2014.

21   Bellezza, Gino and Keinan 2014.

22   Pountain and Robbins 2000.

23   Budzanowski 2017.

24   Wooten and Mourey 2012.

25   Pountain and Robbins 2000.

26   Berger and Heath 2007.

27   Wooten and Mourey 2012.

Figure 13: Coolness.

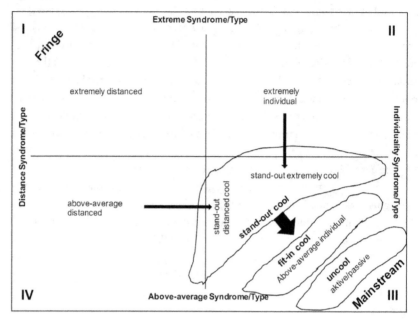

The style leadership of the mainstream is stand-out cool. As a boundary crosser, it is oriented towards the neighbouring style groupings. Stand-out coolness has two dimensions. A stronger penchant for the extreme, imported from grouping II, than is typical for the mainstream. And a tendency, imported from grouping IV, to also maintain some distance from the mainstream when showing one's individuality. The fit-in cool ones are style followers of the stand-out cool style leadership. Their coolness only shows itself as above-average individuality. The uncool members of the mainstream either show stylistic failure (actively uncool) or successful disregard for striving for the above-average (passively uncool).

The sizes of the spaces framed in Figure 13 do not reflect the relative share of the subgroups in the total number of mainstream consumers. Rather, they reflect the stylistic 'territory' they occupy in the style system. In the stylish present day, the number of uncool people is greatest, the number of fit-in cool people is lower, and the number of stand-out cool people is lowest. The large number of the uncool occupy the smallest stylistic territory, and their cultural penetration of the whole is the lowest. The smaller subgroup of the fit-in cool occupies a larger stylistic territory, and the smallest subgroup of the stand-out cool style leaders occupies the largest.

The stand-out cool ones edit the boundaries the mainstream shares with the neighbouring groupings. They are not afraid of stylistic poaching beyond these boundaries. Their coolness, associated with autonomy, is owing to this work. In the style system we can distinguish two kinds of stand-out coolness. The one, *extreme stand-out coolness*, draws its association of autonomy from the boundary to style grouping II. The other, *distanced stand-out coolness*, draws its association of autonomy from the boundary to grouping IV. The style leadership of the mainstream works by division of labour.

Extreme stand-out cool: not typical for the mainstream on the whole, extreme elements from grouping II are absorbed but also defused. These include pop superficiality, which does not completely negate immanence; exciting weekend-experiences of the creative class, which are not completely outlandish; the digital nomad's escapes from traditional workplace settings, which are not entirely irregular; a penchant for bold colours in parade camp. Autonomy is shown in more extreme feature values that are atypical of the mainstream. Extreme stand-out cool style leaders violate the norm of the stylistic *how* of their grouping, and thus give the impression of condescending superiority.

Distanced stand-out cool: a distance to the social whole, atypical of the mainstream, is adopted from grouping IV but also defused. Examples are: frequenting hipster hangouts; consumption of international cuisine that has not yet made it onto the mainstream menu; selective adoption of the positions of political activists or the practices of ecological activists; the import of a secret sign from camouflage camp, whose meaning is (as yet) unknown in the mainstream. Autonomy is shown in features that are not typically distancing for the mainstream. Distanced stand-out cool style leaders violate the norm of the stylistic *what* of their cluster, and thus give the impression of criticising the mainstream.

The extreme stand-out cool are rather apolitical and uncritical of society, or fit politically and socio-critically into the ranks of the mainstream. Their coolness is not proselytising. Criticism of the mainstream resonates in the style of the distanced stand-out cool. Their coolness is of a missionary sort.

The stand-out cool are the role models of the fit-in cool. Early imitation but no autonomy is associated with fit-in coolness. The fit-in cool are merely more stylising than the average of their grouping, but possess all its stylistic features: critique of the mainstream remains a platitude without consequences, material labels replace material substance. Only their faster pace of stylistic adaptation lifts the fit-in cool out of the legions of the uncool. The stand-out cool are the transformation experts of the mainstream for the stylistic *how* and *what*. The fit-in cool lack this transformative power. They are merely radiators of the diffusion of innovations from the fringes of society into the mainstream masses.

Coolness and Viscosity of the Mainstream Style

In my analysis so far, the coolness bonus granted by the stylish present day is the addition of a model-exogenous third argument in the objective function of the productive consumer:

$$U_i = U[Distance, Individuality, Coolness]$$

This bonus is larger for the stand-out cool than for the fit-in cool. But the closer these can move towards the stand-out cool, the larger their bonus too. As laid out in the previous section, coolness can be characterised in QTC. This characterisation can be further sharpened by the concept of viscosity of style introduced in chapter 4.

The fit-in cool person is driven by the desire to be seen as a stand-out cool style leader. They lag behind the role model, but at the same time stand out from the uncool masses. They are positioned in the feature space of the mainstream between the uncool and the stand-out cool. Stand-out coolness increases the viscosity of the mainstream style via the *outside principle* (see Table 7). Fit-in coolness reduces the viscosity of the mainstream via the *in-between principle* (Table 7). This is intuitive. Positioned at the boundary of their own style grouping, the stand-out cool person shows something more extreme or more distant than the fit-in cool and the uncool. With the stand-out cool as the most salient in the grouping, the fit-in cool and the uncool move stylistically closer together (outside principle). Thereby the stand-out cool strengthen the stylistic coherence in the mainstream masses. Fit-in coolness, on the other hand, shows stronger feature values than uncoolness and weaker values than stand-out coolness. With the fit-in cool in the grouping, stylistically sandwiched between the stand-out cool and uncool, these move stylistically further apart (in-between principle). The fit-in-cool thereby strengthen stylistic divergence in the mainstream. The uncool masses, on the other hand, bring the stand-out cool and the fit-in cool – as their most immediate followers – stylistically closer together again. Together, the stand-out cool, the fit-in cool and the uncool determine the viscosity of the mainstream style. What is the net effect?

Viscosity does not (solely) depend on the existence of the different forms of (un)coolness *vis-à-vis* each other, but also on the frequency of their occurrence in the mainstream (see footnote 4*, chapter 4, with h as the total number of mainstream members). The uncool lot make up the bulk, there are fewer fit-in cool members and even fewer stand-out cool ones. Let the (hypothetical) reference case be the viscosity with an equal distribution of mainstream members in these three subgroups. By comparison, the uncool masses allow the stand-out and fit-in cool to move closer together in terms of their rank distance. In contrast, the few stand-out cool members are only barely capable of reducing the rank distance between the groups of the uncool and fit-in cool. Compared to the reference case, the net effect allows the fit-in cool to move stylistically further away from the uncool masses and closer to their stand-out cool style leadership. It is therefore difficult for the uncool *and* fit-in cool to differentiate between the stand-out and fit-in cool. This unequal distribution thus increases the contribution of fit-in coolness to the happiness/utility of the fit-in cool members compared to the reference case.

Is this distribution stable with many uncool, less fit-in cool and even less stand-out cool ones? More specifically, why do the uncool not change sides when the coolness bonus beckons? Viscosity in the mainstream would decrease due to the decreasing number of uncool (outside principle) and the inversely increasing number of fit-in cool (in-between principle). The perceived differences between the subgroups would increase. The bonus on fit-in coolness would decrease. This is an endogenous stabiliser that counteracts the emergence of a uniform distribution and helps stabilise viscosity.

A further stabilising factor is modernism nested in postmodernism. In the final chapter I will introduce exogenous preconditions for fit-in coolness – *sensitivity to cultural selection* $(H_1 - H_{10})$ – which the masses do not possess. The lower number of those capable of cultural sensitivity then forms the upper limit of the number of fit-in cool. The scalability of the business model of exclusive consumer brands is limited by this cultural restriction.

Unequal distribution of wealth and income gives those who are better off the opportunity to buy into the smaller fit-in cool circle by displaying luxury labels. They thereby move closer to the even smaller circle of the stand-out cool. But there is a risk involved. Trying to buy into this group ends in social disaster to the extent that sensitivity to cultural selection is a necessary condition for achieving fit-in coolness. If this cultural capital is missing, luxury consumption merely shows cultural insensitivity and unmasks the pretender. The social bonus for pretence is negative.

Whether and to what extent this cultural capital itself is dependent on financial wealth or upbringing needs to be explored elsewhere. However, QTC does offer a precise definition of what exactly the cultural capital is that is so important in Bourdieu's tradition and whose origin must be traced: *the sensitivity to cultural selection (H_1 - H_{10})*. This cultural capital is *prima facie* quite different from what formal educational qualifications *grosso modo* imply and quite different from what the biographical career in a single class or milieu conveys. It seems more easily accumulated via postmodern wanderings through the style system than via stratified inheritance. To conclude, the internal stylistic structure of the mainstream can no longer be captured by concepts of modernist sociology.

The style innovation paradox from chapter 4 shows up in the mainstream as follows. The stand-out cool style leadership's crossing of boundaries brings innovations into the style grouping. In their wake, the leadership's stylistic autonomy compared to its followers is increased by the associated norm violation (distanced/extreme stand-out coolness). But what is new, deviant from the norm, does not drive the mainstream stylistically apart but closer together: stand-out coolness shines a light on what the majority has in common in the otherwise so heterogeneous ordinariness. The stylistic conglomerate of the gentleman (retro), mass indie, normcore and basic styles move closer together as a whole. Each new norm-breaking assimilation from the neighbouring style groupings II and IV makes the mainstream appear somewhat more coherent.

The innovation paradox throws new light on the situational prerequisites of the mainstream's style leadership (intention, expertise and violation of norms). It is the expert, deliberate and blatant violation of the norms of the mainstream that binds it together stylistically. The stand-out cool shamans of the mainstream lead their followers by deliberately violating their own operating instructions for the sorting plant of culture. Through this situational manipulation, the options for style leadership listed in Table 11 are made a success.

The irony is that style leadership does not manifest itself in the exemplary *0/+consumption execution* of their own manual, but rather by setting *0/+consumption exemplifications* of what its violation can consist of. The followers in the mainstream are thereby constantly being told that they have not (yet) understood the true operating manual. The followers are therefore constantly confronted with new stylistic challenges that need to be worked out anew. The followers do not respond to this constant disturbance with renunciation, but instead with admiration and gratitude. The question is why.

Aesthetic Liking and Interest

Fast, habitual thinking is the default of the human brain. We think in fast mode as long as our own expectations are met. These expectations include those about the individual style of other people, for example in our own elective affinity. If we notice the individual style of a punk or a work colleague in the way we expected, our fast, habitual thinking will continue. But if we see our own stylistic expectations violated, we switch into a mode of slow, deliberate thinking. The style that speaks up against our expectations is the stimulus that determines the mode of our thinking (chapter 6). If both match (approximately), then we possess (large) stimulus fluency: we can quickly make sense of the stimulating style and therefore remain in the mode of fast thinking. If both (strongly) diverge, we find ourselves in a situation of low stimulus fluency. We cannot (yet) make sense of the stimulating style and shift into the mode of slow, deliberate thinking. We use it to try to categorise the guy in the punk bar who doesn't seem to fit in at all. Stimulus (non-)fluency moderates not only the timing of the human response to the stimulus, but also the type of aesthetic response. Stimulus fluency triggers aesthetic liking/disliking by thinking fast, and stimulus non-fluency triggers aesthetic interest/disinterest by thinking slowly.[28] We constantly experience it ourselves in our consumption practice. We listen to a short sequence of sounds on the radio and know immediately if we like the song (stimulus fluency); we stand thoughtfully in front of an artwork in a museum and only find out after a while whether we are interested in it or not (stimulus non-fluency).

Stimulus (non-)fluency is also known in psychology as undercoding and overcoding.[29] An undercoded object is met with stimulus non-fluency, an overcoded object with stimulus fluency. Semiotics stresses the subjectivity of over/undercoding. What is familiar to one person may be unfamiliar to another.[30] In the following, I use the concept of under/overcoding for two reasons. First, because it is rooted in both the psychological and semiotic traditions. Second, because it refers to properties of objects, even though these properties only begin to exist in the brain; stimulus (non-)fluency, on the other hand, refers to a neuronal secondary process triggered by encoding (which in turn triggers the neuronal triage of liking and interest). The notions of under/overcoding therefore fit better with the (material) cultural-economic approach of QTC.

Whether and how strongly an individual positively reacts to an object (stimulus), be it a liking or interest, depends on the degree of its over/undercoding. The relation has the functional form of an ∩. On the vertical axis the dependent variable is liking/interest and on the horizontal axis the independent variable is over/undercoding. To the right of the peak there is overcoding, to the left there

28   Graf and Landwehr 2017.

29   Berlyne 1971.

30   Eco 1979.

is undercoding. A strongly overcoded stimulus bores you and you react with (quickly assumed) dislike. Art enthusiasts, for example, often disqualify a work that bores them with the label kitsch. With decreasing overcoding (from the right towards the middle), liking increases. The other extreme, a strongly undercoded stimulus, overstrains even slow thinking and one turns away with disinterest. Those unfamiliar with performance art, for example, are unlikely to develop a lasting interest in it. With decreasing undercoding (from the left towards the middle) interest increases. Moving from these two poles towards the middle, liking/interest reaches a maximum at the peak of ∩ at a subjectively felt moderate under/overcoding of the stimulus. In the mid-range of under/overcoding, the individual will approach a specific object or a whole style with the greatest liking or interest.

The mystery of why style followers in the mainstream react positively to the sly norm-breaking by the stand-out cool style leadership has now been solved: stand-out cool individual styles are relatively undercoded through their adoption from neighbouring style groupings, deploying stylistic elements in an original, surprising and stimulating way. They therefore reduce the overall overcoding of the common mainstream style, triggering interest in the slow-thinking mode. In turn, the stand-out cool style leadership is rewarded with a bonus from its followers for its contribution to the reduction of their boredom.

This psychological mechanism runs recursively through the whole style system. The original source of undercoding is the fringes of society in grouping I. The mainstream is so unfamiliar with these styles that it turns away from them disinterestedly. But the elective affinities from grouping II and IV are familiar enough with the fringes to be interested in them and to adopt elements from them. In turn, their styles are familiar enough to the boundary-crossing stand-out cool style leadership of the mainstream for them to find them interesting and adopt from them. In the end, even the mainstream finds interesting what was fringe to start with. The whole style system thus contributes to the reduction of boredom in the mainstream. The prerequisite for this, however, is the capacity and capability for cultural encounters.

In his book *The Joyless Economy*, economist Tibor Scitovsky analysed everyday American life in the 1970s, describing the very boredom left behind by a style system devoid of cultural encounters.[31] He described the lifestyles of the white American suburbs and countryside as bare of surprises. There are no ups and downs, everything is totally overcoded, no stimulus is unfamiliar enough to be inspiring. Joylessness prevails in spite of material prosperity. It emerges in a

---

31   Scitovsky 1976.

style system in which the mainstream completely recedes into itself, devoid of the ability to process stylistic impulses from other groupings. Different metatypes of styles existed in this America, showing their specific *how* and *what* (white suburbs, black ghettos), but the syndromic potency had run dry.

Honecker's Legacy

The egoism/altruism obsolescence (chapter 5) in the objective function (13) is manifested in a society that accommodates both social coldness and warmth. Coldness even to the extent that the style system accommodates extreme egoisms, to the point of disdain for those belonging to the same elective affinity. And warmth that does not depend on altruism of the individual or state care, but is fuelled by a comprehensive symmetrical integration of the individual into the social whole: you and me and our individual styles always contribute symmetrically to the social whole, no matter how poor I am and how rich you are!

Which social coldness and warmth the objective function (13) is able to accommodate and which not, becomes clear with the example of German reunification and the then emerging *ostalgia* (east nostalgia). Ostalgia is a longing for lost social warmth that glorifies the GDR past, due to the former belonging of the individual to a consumer collective, which (in the perception of the ostalgics) has been destroyed by FRG consumerism. In Honecker's GDR economy of scarcity, consumer happiness/utility was owed to the performance of the procurement collective to which one belonged: one member organised hotel rooms for a Black Sea vacation for the consumer collective, another organised washing machines. Warmth was thereby found in this consumer collective. The FRG consumerism that set in after the fall of the Berlin Wall was instead regarded as a reward system for individual success, and the life associated with it was felt as cold.[32] What the former GDR life and objective function (13) have in common is that individual happiness/utility is owed to a collective. But egoism, as assumed in (13), was not alien to GDR citizens: the promise "If the D-Mark does not come to us, we will go to it!" shows the immanent egoism at the time. It was therefore not the experience of egoism *per se* that triggered the perception of a new FRG coldness, but the experience of a new individuality of consumer success that was detached from a greater social whole. However, the individual as the source of success is absent in objective function (13), since the inherent striving for horizontal differentiation inescapably ties consumerism back into the social whole. Hence, despite the

32   Veenis 1999.

egoism/altruism obsolescence identified in chapter 5, the objective function (13) brings back into economics a mixture of cold-mannered egoism and warm-hearted collectivism.

To Have or to Be

Erich Fromm criticises Western consumerism as an incorporation fetish: "I am what I possess and what I consume!"[33] He contrasts this "being by having and accumulating" with the secular-religious vision of the *city of being*, in which human aspiration is towards *being* and not towards hoarding and incorporating.

What Fromm criticises is judged as grossly positive in the orthodoxy's argumentation: firstly, all consequences including individual benefit are driven by individual action (methodological individualism); secondly, individual action is focused on accumulation (to reduce restrictions); and thirdly, action serves personal benefit (teleological rationality) – what a person accumulates serves to their benefit. From this, normative orthodoxy concludes that individual accumulation is good: what is good for the individual is good for the whole (utilitarianism). Accumulation thus becomes the principal goal of normative orthodoxy. The goal, though, is relativised again under the heading of externality: what is good for one is not necessarily good for others, for example showing off is not necessarily good for the social whole. Yet, externalities are implicitly treated as exceptions to the rule, so that individual accumulation remains, in principle, good for the greater whole. Per capita GNP thus becomes the criterion, *grosso modo*, for the normative assessment of the greater whole. The average is the critical variable out of the belief that everything that is individually accumulated, is in principle available for the compensation of the losers of individual action (Pareto principle). Under these conditions, individual accumulation retains its basically favourable characteristics.

Fromm's *Having or Being* breaks with this orthodox credo by denying that accumulation is the only option for human action. Consequently, the success of both the individual and the whole does not depend solely on accumulation. Moreover, he adds, accumulation has a negative effect not only on third parties (externality) but damages the soul of the accumulating person itself. According to Fromm, everyone and thus the whole is better off without accumulation.

QTC, with its objective function (13) and the options for action, goes halfway down the road of Fromm: although it stays entirely in the tradition of

---

33   Fromm 2005 (1976), p. 43.

methodological individualism, accumulation is not an argument. Hoarding and incorporating more and more of the same is neutral in terms of happiness/utility. Social distance and proximity are independent of quantities. Objective function (13) does not reward individual accumulation of objects. Because it is of no use at all to show a new object in one's individual style if everyone else does so too. A 'gross quality product' (GQP) as a welfare-theoretical counterpart to GNP makes no sense. Individual qualitative austerity is conductive to the objective as is individual qualitative opulence. However, QTC lags behind Fromm in one respect: accumulation of quantities is not harmful to the soul but simply irrelevant for the achievement of the objectives, which is why QTC abstracts completely from quantities and prices.

As a *city of style*, QTC remained a vision like Fromm's *city of being*, if it left no traces in the present day. To the extent that postmodernism has become part of the present day, QTC is turning into a positive theory of *being* in its three experiential dimensions: individuality, in-group and out-groups. In these three dimensions, the two social identities – individual identity and collective identity – are formed. Three dimensions of experience result in just two identities, because identity does not arise from occupying a certain position in stylistic space, but from differences in these positions. Of these, there are only two: the difference of the individual to the in-group and that of the in-group to out-groups. The three-dimensional experience thus enters into objective function (13) with only two arguments.

This multiple identity is not one of *having*, but of *being*. One does not have one's individual style as something one carries along, but one is one's style – "Le style c'est l'homme même". One' s own group does not have a common style, but the group is that style. The style system does not have common styles, but it is they who make it up. The individual has nothing to show or not to show, but shows themselves, and experiences not what others have, but who they are. There is no *having* of basic conditions, which could be revealed by showing (possession signalling). Social identity is *being* in the style system.

Individual consumption can only collectively produce individual being. Not only is everyone always tied back to the social, but 'you are working on my being as I am on yours; I am through you as you are through me; only together we succeed; your project is my project and mine is yours!' It is in this spirit that everyone is unified.

Happy in Style

Up to this point, I have referred to the result of human striving as happiness/util-ity. They were not meant to be synonyms. It is now time to clarify what the hu-man being strives for in terms of the objective function (13): happiness or utility? It is happiness!

Of course, happiness and utility can be defined as the same. But the new re-search on happiness distances itself in its findings from the orthodoxy, in which utility is the familiar term.[34] As empirical science of what is actually good for the human being, happiness research sides with Fromm: accumulation is not the only source of human well-being. It is only one of seven factors (Big Seven): fam-ily, finances (accumulation), work, community and friends, health, freedom, and personal values. An intact family, orderly finances, a secure job, integration into a community, good health, personal freedom and something to believe in – all these things together promote human well-being. What the Big Seven bring together, happiness science calls happiness. Obviously, the single factors of hap-piness interact and there are trade-offs between them: if one only strives for ac-cumulation then family, friends, residential integration and health suffer. And in the end, one even sacrifices one's values for it. As a normative theory, happi-ness science thus opposes the *grosso modo* beneficial connotation of accumula-tion. Happiness is the result of a good mix of the Big Seven and thus between external (state) and internal (individual) factors.

However, the most fundamental difference to the orthodoxy is not this ex-tended scope for action, but the recognition that externalities are the rule with-out exception: whatever one does to promote one's own happiness in the family, in the neighbourhood or at work, influences happiness of others – family mem-bers, neighbours or work colleagues. Happiness research reduces this to a simple bottom line: there is no human action without externality. With that it negates the practicability of the analytical core of the orthodox approach: its formulation 'The whole unfolds from the particular' (methodological individualism and utili-tarianism) now no longer works. It must be replaced by the formulation 'The par-ticular can only be grasped from the whole'. The (new) happiness and the (old) utility are therefore not synonyms for human well-being, but placeholders for fundamentally different social science doctrines: the old utility (of the individual) flows out of the individual, but its new happiness only flows out of the whole.

QTC is happiness theory. The objective function (13) defines human well-be-ing as the result of a stylistic whole: individuality results from integration into a

---

smaller whole (elective affinity) and social distance from embeddedness in a larger whole (style system). Social distance and proximity thus arise from a collective externality. The individual receives what is good for them from the whole, and their own stylisation is their gift back to the whole. The objective U_i in function (13) is the happiness of the individual.

"Prod any happy person," says happiness science, "and you'll find a project! "[35] In QTC this project is the individual style. It is a social project because it brings the individual style into the stylistic whole as a contribution to the variegation of the world. The Romanticist Joseph von Eichendorff describes this project in the novel *Aus dem Leben eines Taugenichts* (From the Life of a Good-for-Nothing): one who has learned nothing (basic conditions), achieves nothing useful (accumulation), but whose pleasant manners and poetry (project) makes him, the useless, popular even with the nobility and the bourgeoisie (mainstream).

To the extent that postmodernism has entered the present day, QTC is also a contribution to so-called romantic economics.[36] It reflects the call of the economist Edmund Phelps for imagination and creativity to replace accumulation as the main object of scientific interest.[37] Imagination and creativity are the only conditions in the agency of QTC. They are the only input into the project of happiness. I will come back to this in the final chapter.

---

35   ibid., p. 73.

36   Bronk 2009.

37   Phelps 2015.

Chapter 9
Identity Industry

"A style is constant until further notice."
Rudolf Arnheim[1]

"A work can become modern only if it is first postmodern. Postmodernism thus understood is not modernism at its end but in the nascent state, and this state is constant."
Jean-François Lyotard[2]

"In order to be irreplaceable one must be different."
Attributed to Coco Chanel

The current structure of the style system is only temporary. Because the style system does not consist of a sequence of self-restrained styles, but is rather the plaything of syndromic forces that affect cultural selection in the field laid out in Figures 12 and 13.

The media scientist Rudolf Arnheim calls the play of forces in a field *gestalt*. His approach can be applied to style as well. The question is: which forces are changing the current structure of the style system? The *gestalt* of the style system includes style leadership and its followers. But it also includes industry. It is a service provider for the DIY identity of consumers and provides them with inputs in line with the DIY-store principle. This chapter addresses the value chains of fashion, design, lifestyle, music, hospitality, event and media firms, advertising

1   Arnheim 1981, p. 282.
2   Lyotard 2011, p. 361.

agencies, galleries, museums and the commercial part of the education system, all of which are defined here as belonging to the identity industry.

Stylistic *gestalt* differs from conventional approaches. Orthodox economics allows the role of industry to wither to nothing more than an executive hand: it only supplies what autonomous consumers demand. Traditional marketing theory, in contrast, sees industry as a moulding hand: with the right marketing, everything will be purchased, and the new 'nudging' techniques make this moulding hand even stronger. The anti-consumerist stance takes this a step further: industry systematically dumbs down the consumer! In contrast to all this, stylistic *gestalt* in QTC is the combined forces of the productive consumer and industry.

Industrial Revolution

The French Revolution is considered the incubator of the luxury goods industry. Before, the luxury cartel of the nobility stood in its way: in feudalism luxury goods were reserved for the nobility on pain of punishment. Merchants and bankers could be as rich as they wished but were still not allowed to show off with the feathers of the nobility. Social distance between the nobility and commoners was thus cemented. With the French Revolution the luxury cartel fell, and the Paris fashion and pleasure industry could develop, with new consumer goods for everyone who could afford them. This is a popular explanation for the emergence of the luxury goods industry, whose long absence is attributed to the luxury cartel.

I regard the reverse causality as the more plausible one: the absence of a strong consumer goods industry was the cause for the luxury cartel. Where limited choices from the world of things meet an unmatched demand for distinction, the 0/+consumption forced upon the lower classes remained the most effective way to sustain aristocratic distinction. Had there already been a strong consumer goods industry in feudalism, the nobility could have displayed distinction in the same way that the rich still do today: with expensive things that are out of reach for most. The luxury cartel would have been obsolete. The beginnings of the luxury industry are therefore to be found more in the beginnings of the industrial rather than the French revolution, concomitant as they have been.

This thesis can be substantiated with Norbert Elias' work on European civilisation. Elias brings to the fore the central role of industry in the production of social distance and proximity, despite the fact that it did not yet exist during Elias' period of investigation, ranging from the High Middle Ages to the end of feudalism.[3] Mannerism – here the constant refinement of behaviour – which Elias identified as the core of European civilisation (seen as a process), had in the pre-industrial era been the social equivalent of today's consumption of things. Because, in the absence of a lavish world of things, little remained in the world of objects for forging the social except patterns of behaviour.

It is therefore no coincidence that Elias ends his investigation with the very beginning of industrialisation (coinciding with the end of feudalism). Because the industrial revolution is the decisive rupture point in European civilisation: in *o/+consumption* moving away from showing and not showing behaviour patterns to showing and not showing things – that is, moving away from mannerism to the material consumerism that only became possible through industrialisation.

This glimpse back into pre-industrial times reveals today's industry's contribution to the DIY of the productive consumer: the provision of the world of things for the sorting plant of culture. The world of objects is large because of industry. Without it, a completely different game would be played revolving around objective function (13): perhaps still with 'object cartels', but certainly with a much stronger display of differing behaviour. It is only due to industry that the world of things is as varied as it is, and it is only thanks to it that social distance and proximity can be produced by DIY in so many different ways.

This is because behavioural patterns cannot be refined at will. The Rococo was not only chronologically the last feudal European style, but it pushed fine manners to a point never reached again. Today, people are once again dining more informally, thanks to the world of things that comes into use elsewhere. Even though postmodernism is conceivable without industry, with the limited stylistic possibilities of mannerism there would be fewer elective affinities. With the many new things of an expanding industry, new elective affinities with new common styles came into being and, within them, more non-rooted individual styles have become possible. Social distance and individuality increased as a result of industrialisation – and so did happiness.

On the demand side, the *Quality Law* (H$_5$) of cultural selection is based on the objective function (13), while on the supply side it is based primarily on industry, and only to a minor extent on the material DIY of the productive consumer. Almost every new quality is adopted by the market. Industrialisation was thus given a steady boost. But not all new qualities serve the business objective equally well. Entrepreneurship in B2C has become entrepreneurship in the style system, and the identity industry went this way.

---

3   Elias 1997.

The *Polytomisation Law* (H$_9$) of cultural selection predicts qualitative differences between objects, that tend to result in uniform lengths of objects in a tree with only one node (Figure 10, right side). However, uniform lengths up to a common node is a dissimilarity-theoretical operationalisation of uniform distances between variants on Lancaster's clock face of product differentiation. QTC thereby offers a different explanation for product differentiation. The orthodoxy must assume for the demand side, heterogeneous preferences with uniform distribution on the clock face. Uniform distances between qualities are then the result of economic competition for market shares in a perfect goods market. In QTC, on the other hand, uniform distances between qualities follow from uniform preferences (13) and endogenous cultural selection (H$_9$). QTC, unlike the orthodoxy, does therefore not need the auxiliary hypothesis of market perfection. *Culture as a process replaces the market as a process.* The rise of the identity industry was culture-driven, and the market as an institution for the exchange of quantities played a minor role.

In the style system, industry always comes second behind the productive consumer. It is a service provider for cultural selection (H$_1$ - H$_{10}$). Which business models will succeed in the style system?

Singularity Mass Production

A longstanding business model of the identity industry is the creation of singletons and their subsequent transformation into extremes in trees. Thereby, first the width (social distance) and then the length (individuality) increases in the style system. Therefore, singletons, as something incomparable in every respect, do not simply disappear (Singleton Law, H$_3$), but are systematically transformed after their deliberate creation into something comparable. This service is not an abstract idea of QTC. You find it in practice.

The art world provides the blueprint for it: a singleton, say, the first *Ready-made* by Marcel Duchamp, is supplemented by more and more objects of a *comparable* kind, so that over time a subset of objects emerges for which the collective term *Dada* will soon be found. The umbrella term standing for the tree of these objects is then placed by intermediary savants (gallerists, curators, critics), in the larger context of a superordinate artistic taxon (*Ordering Law* H$_4$). *Dada* now becomes collectible in the taxa of Surrealism, and contributes to the individuality of the collector in the elective affinity of Surrealism aficionados.

Haute Couture, the systematic subordination (of the needs) of the body under an artistic concept, came closest to the commercial production of singletons without ever actually doing so. The carefully cultivated name of the house (*Pierre Balmain*, *Coco Chanel*) made up a tree in which all creations, as unique as they might be, found their place. While Haute Couture is a business model of the identity industry, it is not a successful one, as its industrial insignificance shows today. It lacks scalability in the style system.

Another traditional business model also eliminates singletons, but without having created them in the first place. Wine guidebooks (*Parker*) and restaurant guides (*Michelin*, *Gault-Millau*) offer classification systems by means of which previously unique items can be compared with something else. They are pure service providers in the identity DIY and position themselves as intermediary savants, who know (and reveal) coherencies that were previously unknown to the rest. They offer instructions for the sorting plant of culture on how to integrate singletons into trees in a happiness-enhancing way. The downside of this business model is the dependence on third-party producers of ever more new singletons. The upside of this restraint is the nimbus of independence as a guide. Their capital is their reputation as savants.

There are firms integrating vertically by following this blueprint of the art world. The first *Swatch* was a singleton, the first fashion item with a watch function, incomparable with anything seen before in either the jewellery or functional watch traditions. *Swatch* gradually added similar new objects, amounting to a vast number of them today. This business model is based not only on a steady expansion of the world of objects, but also includes instructions for the sorting plant of culture, with the help of which the set of *Swatch* items from the world of objects is to be sorted into smaller but coherent subsets: vintage and special editions with specific motifs. This paves the way for collectors' affinities and provides them with fresh supplies. Collecting *Swatches* thereby becomes an identity-creating cult. *Illycafé* and *Rosenthal*, with their collector's cups editions, are further examples of this business model. *Absolut Vodka* markets the same product in a periodically changing bottle and label design. All of them, from the postage stamp businesses of the Vatican and Liechtenstein to contemporary art, apply the same business model: industrially created singletons (narrowly speaking) are joined together into comparable subsets of the world of objects by chronological sequences of salvos of similar objects. In this way, collectors' affinities emerge whose members show their individuality through their collections.

The sale of qualities that are difficult to reproduce, for example antique art, antique porcelain, historical stamps, etc., also serves the needs of collectors, but it is not as scalable as the industrial production of continuously new objects. However, their positioning initially as (mass-produced) incomparable singletons exposes them to the risk of oblivion. Yet, the subsequent positioning as a historical quality of a subset of comparable objects (editions) reduces this risk and opens up the potential as a collector's item, the supply of which is controlled by the firm itself. This business model further avoids the cultural inefficiency of chains. This is because editions create comparability, but carefully avoid dominance by other objects. The most reliable remedy to avoid being dominated is the involvement of different artists in the design of editions, as practiced by *Swatch*, *Illycafé*, *Rosenthal* and *Absolut Vodka*. Andy Warhol's label as the first artist commissioned by *Absolut Vodka* is programmatic.

There are three reasons circulating in science as to why artistic elements should be an integral part of a business model: to onboard cultural trends early on, to create a brand community, or to legitimise one's own activities as part of cultural production.[4] QTC offers affirmation: cultural trends are the vector components H_1 - H_{10} of cultural selection, in particular the trend towards the integration of singletons into trees, H_4; a brand community is a monopoly on a specific elective affinity; and the art industry produces unique works of art which it reliably places in a context of comparability (as in Table 3 in chapter 3) and to which it thereby confers collectability. Perceived as a part of the art scene, a consumer goods firm can throw new things onto the market without devaluing the old. This industrial, limited-edition business promises the buyer double bliss: first from the one-off piece and then as an element of a subset of comparable qualities. The criterion for success in this business model is that each 'collector's cup' has a fair chance of becoming a supremum in a tree with branches of equal length. The perfect 'singularity mass production' is equally fair to every produced quality in terms of its chance of becoming a supremum (and therefore to every collector). The selection, development and cultivation of the artist/designer network is therefore the most important HR task in this industrial business model.

Mathematically, this success criterion can be operationalised with an ultrametric scale of feature values. Ultrametric scales always provide phylograms or polytomies with branches of equal length. The business model of *Swatch*, *Illycafé*, *Rosenthal* and *Absolut Vodka* is therefore aimed at producing a large number of suprema in phylograms or polytomies.[5]

---

4   Dell'Era 2010, p. 86.

5   NB, ultrametric scales are used to generate evolutionary trees to express the belief that all live reproductive communities are always equally fit in evolutionary terms (for example, in Figure 1, right side). It may come as a surprise, but collectors' cups are the closest possible approximation of material culture to nature, and the underlying business model is the closest possible approximation of commerce to the biological idea of genetic disparity.

This *production of a history of the unique* by means of industrial editions is a vertically integrated business model in the value chain of the DIY identity. It promises greater profit than the production of the unique alone (artist profession), greater profit than the mere cultivation of history (museums, vintage car workshops etc.), greater profit than the service of intermediate savants and the mass production of copies of a single quality (Henry Ford's *Model T* business model). The *production of a history of the unique* imparts to cultural selection the industrial impulse of mass-produced and – as a result – comparable singularities.

Mass customisation such as of sports shoes and t-shirts by internet configuration is the current best-practice variant of this business model. Here, for sake of simplicity, the *production of history* is dispensed with altogether. Instead, automation minimises the risk of showing copies that reduce happiness. Internet configuration, the scalable accommodation of customers' needs for individualisation, and the mass production of one-offs results in products of almost identical quality. In comparison to the assembly line production of the *Ford Model T* business model, a minimal dissimilarity between qualities is produced *en masse*. Thus, industrial mass singularities find their explication in QTC.

Length Extension

Because length fosters individuality there is a business model that provides the DIY identity with increasingly longer lengths. This is how fashion is accommodated in QTC.

Prêt-à-porter, the greatest possible concession of *Haute Couture* to commerce and the greatest approximation of commerce to *Haute Couture*, delivers the most current fashions twice a year, thus pushing what was previously fashionable into the past. Existing suprema are replaced by new suprema, so that a supremum is now dominated by a new object. In this way, under the guise of up-to-dateness, chronological length is extended further and further. Those for whom the updating costs are low enough will stock up on new suprema twice a year. Luxury brands are in this business (*Akris, Armani, Gucci, Prada*). This DIY is individually scalable if there is a second-hand market for what is no longer current. Suppliers of durable luxury articles take advantage of this with constant new (pattern or colour) variations of basically the same merchandise (*Hermès* ties, *Louis Vuitton* bags). That is how this business model works its way through the available money. Secondary brands of *prêt-à-porter* brands (*Armani Collezioni, Miu, DieselStyleLab*) all the way down to the mass market are all in the length extension business. The 66 week long sheep-to-shop pipeline has now been replaced by vertically integrated fast fashion (*Benetton, Zara, Massimo Dutti, H&M*). QTC offers a simple explanation for vertical integration in the fashion industry: vertically integrated, length can be extended faster.

Accordingly, retro finds its explanation in QTC in that it is not the ostentatious consumption of the old-fashioned, but rather the postulation of the previously old-fashioned as the new supremum. A dominated object is taken as a blueprint out of its chain and placed at the current end of the same chain, extending its total length. However, industry does not achieve this by duplicating the 'original' old-fashioned item, but rather by modifying stylistic elements, making visible what is new (retro) and what is old (historical precedent). This makes someone who wants to surf a retro wave with dad's original an uncool dilettante. In orthodox logic, the underlying motive for the modification of the original is industry's interest in selling large numbers of specimens. By contrast, in the logic of QTC, modification is necessary to attain the position of the new supremum. That way the original remains where it was and is dominated by retro. Here the two logics complement each other.

Simplification of Thought

A standard claim of critics of consumerism is that it would infantilise consumers. Benjamin Barber provides the following explanation: influenced by consumerism, the fast is favoured over the slow and the easy/simple over the difficult/complex.[6] In other words, consumerism infantilises because preferences shift away from the slow/difficult/complex to the fast/easy/simple. We also find this tendency in QTC. But therein, it has nothing whatsoever to do with a change of preferences (through a manipulating industry) but is the consequence of the invariable objective function (13). Infantilisation – in QTC the term *simplification of thought* seems more appropriate – is demanded by the productive consumer for their DIY identity. Here's the rationale.

Whether the fast/easy/simple is preferred to the slow/difficult/complex depends, as was argued in chapter 8, on the over/undercoding of the objects providing the stimulus. The faster and the easier you can decode their meaning, the more stimulus fluent you are. The longer it takes you for decoding, the less fluent you are. Semiotically, stimulus fluency is a response to overcoded objects and stimulus non-fluency to undercoded ones. Translated into QTC, Barber's statement is therefore this: consumerism creates an overcoded world of objects whose

---

6   Barber 2008.

stimuli become increasingly familiar to consumers. The world of things and their operating manuals evolve together towards the quickly understood, easily mastered, simply handled. The simpler a thing is, the less complicated the instructions for sorting it need be, and the simpler the instructions the less complicated the initially complicated thing. Consumerism as an instruction manual never confronts consumers with tricky DIY decisions. Over time, it offers increasingly simple instructions for DIY identity and a simpler world of things to choose from.

The issue remains whether and where Barber's thesis manifests itself in cultural selection. You can find it in the *Polytomisation Law* (H_9). The phylogram on the left in Figure 10 is intellectually more demanding than the polytomy on the right. In this sense, the polytomy is fast/easy/simple, the phylogram slow/difficult/complex. The *Polytomisation Law* thus predicts a cultural selection towards a less and less intellectually demanding ordering of the world of objects, towards the undemanding polytomy. In other words, QTC offers the view that productive consumers demand a simplification of thought for their DIY identity, rather than having it foisted upon them by a manipulative industry. In QTC the simplification of thought is a sought-after service. It is yet another business model of the identity industry.

In practice, this thought-simplification business model can be found in mass markets. From the orthodox point of view, this business model rests on scalability and cost reduction. From the point of view of QTC, however, mass products are those with which you have become fluent. As difficult as they were to understand at first and as complex as they appeared, the more often they are shown, the more overcoded they will become. Slow, deliberative thinking, initially triggered by undercoding, is gradually replaced by fast, habitual thinking. Over time, an object, formerly situated in a complex order, finds its new place in an increasingly simple dissimilarity structure. Finally, it ends up in a polytomy alongside many other objects, all of which have become similarly quickly/easily/simply comprehensible.

For example, traditional costumes with their complex historical roots (chapter 1) are no longer maintained and carefully updated in their identity-giving tradition. The traditional costume has disappeared, except in a few rural areas. It has become a history-free fashion item, the fashion *tracht*, that can be shown situationally by anyone. Fashion *tracht* cannot be positioned in the tree of traditional costumes. Features such as colour, pattern or cut stand for nothing but themselves; the different apron knots of the traditional alpine costumes of the widow, married and unmarried woman are, in the fashion *tracht*, three knots devoid of meaning. Different costumes worn at the Oktoberfest are objects in a polytomy. The fashion *tracht* is mass-market thought simplification, pure and simple.

Intermediary savants prosper with the thought simplification business model. Mass media presents dissimilarity in a trivialising way. Whereas on other topics, for example nature, consumers are required to dig to some intellectual depth, this is (almost) completely absent when it comes to style issues. Fashion and lifestyle magazines, tabloids and celebrity shows on early evening television, dominate opinion on style. Savants, with the possible exceptions in art and literature, encourage fast thinking. For this purpose, up-to-dateness is glorified, the sheer postulation of the new and the hip overrides the argumentative rooting in the old. Star endorsement replaces semiotic reflection. But it still holds true: consumers are not stupefied against their will. Given objective function (13), consumers demand it.

Mass Market and Criticism of Consumerism

In the mass market, mass *quantity* production and mass *quality* production coincide. A trade-off between the two affects happiness. As already discussed, mass quality production (of singularities) improves individuality by reducing the potential for rooting the individual in the common style. But mass quantity production also increases the rooting, because many consumers show only specimens of one and the same object. The mass market thus affects individuality via two opposing effects: the negative effect of large quantities and the positive quality effect of singularity mass production.

Because of this trade-off, criticism of the industry for pushing consumerism demands more differentiated arguments than those given so far. True, it justifiably blames industry for the effect of its mass quantity production on individuality. However, you can only blame mass quality production for its simplification of thought. To this end, however, you must take the meritorious position that slow/difficult/complex is always preferable to fast/easy/simple, and consumers must be forced into happiness with the former.[7] Because the simplification of thought through polytomisation helps strengthen individuality. Whoever accepts individuality as an argument for happiness cannot blame industry for simplifying thought, in the very interest of happiness itself.

Criticism of thought simplification is therefore in need of an explicit affirmation of a third argument in the objective function (13) – aesthetic appeal:

---

7   It is the very argument with which school classes, rightly or wrongly, are hauled into museums.

$$U_i = U[distance, individuality, aesthetic\ appeal]$$

Aesthetic appeal is itself a function of the over/undercoding of the world of objects with the functional form of a ∩, as explained in chapter 8. Beyond the peak of ∩, in an overcoded world of objects, the aesthetic appeal wanes, and one becomes increasingly bored. The fast/easy/simple, as conveyed by polytomies, still promotes individuality, but due to the third argument of the objective function, it does not necessarily advance happiness. It is QTC, extended to include aesthetic appeal, that lends more clout to the criticism of industry for its promotion of simplification of thought. Simplification of thought only makes people happy within limits, too much of it makes them unhappy.

With this extension, Tibor Scitovsky's *Joyless Economy* can be understood as an anti-consumerist critique grounded in QTC. It is a critique of that vector component of cultural selection that brings monotony and boredom into society.[8] However, QTC also predicts that because of its singularity mass production, the identity industry will not let monotony and boredom rise boundlessly. Thus, the extended QTC offers a more differentiated view of industry than the orthodoxy: as a producer not only of quantities but also of qualities, its effect on monotony and boredom is ambivalent. It contributes to it, but not in an excessive way. Even if it is not a service provider of aesthetic appeal as the art industry is, and only offers inputs to manipulate social distance and proximity, its singularity mass production limits boredom in the mass market.

Fashion

Where the orthodoxy must rely on a number of special assumptions,[9] QTC offers a simpler explanation for fashion: the current fashion is defined by the length of a tree and the next one by the new, longer length of it. Consequently, on the demand side, fashions are not dependent on quantity: You don't have to assume that a trend that is currently followed by only a few will motivate people to jump on (bandwagon effect), and one that has already been followed by many will motivate them to drop out (snob effect), whereby the periodicity of fashion is implicitly seen as dependent on the exogenous reaction time of consumers. In the logic of length extension, you do not have to assume any consumer reaction time.

---

8   Scitovsky 1976.

9   E.g. Pesendorfer 1995.

Its periodicity depends solely on the speed at which the industry can profitably produce length. And that is solely dependent on vertical integration.

As was argued in chapter 7, the vector component *Destabilisation* (H_{13}) offers a probabilistic explanation for the bandwagon and snob effects at the level of whole elective affinities. From that point of view, mass exodus from an existing elective affinity and mass influx to a new one, are macrodynamic phenomena in the style system; they are due to the striving for social distance (width). Industry is redundant for this. In contrast, in the present perspective, the bandwagon and snob effects are triggered by the length extension business model of industry. Here the effects are microdynamic phenomena at the level of individual styles within the elective affinity of fashionistas. They are due to the striving for individuality (length).

Groupings I and IV in Figure 11 are less receptive to the fashion made by industry than groupings II and III, both of which are therefore the main targets of the fashion industry. Not only because it is big (orthodox argument) is the mainstream the Eldorado of the fashion industry. It is it also because of its stronger preference for individuality, and therefore receptiveness to the business model of the fashion industry (length extension). By contrast, the bandwagon and snob effects are less frequent on the fringes of society (grouping I) and the likewise distance-keeping grouping IV, and only occur there in a weakened form.

Dialectics of Postmodern Business Models

The business models of singularity mass production, length extension and thought simplification are all B2C. Moreover, each is limited to only part of the DIY identity value chain. And they all accept the DIY sovereignty of productive consumers; nudging against the interests of consumers is not part of their strategy. Their central resource is knowledge of cultural selection. They all promote cultural efficiency.

The term *culture industry* is usually reserved for commercial actors in artistic, musical and literary fields. It needs to be given a broader definition in QTC. It must be applied to whatever industry contributes to the work done in the sorting plant of culture. Fashion labels, retailers and the gutter press are as much a part of that industry as opera houses, educational TV programmes and artists. The term *identity industry* covers this idea more broadly and accurately: whatever contributes to improving cultural efficiency belongs to the identity industry.

Postmodern business models make use of vector components of cultural selection. Table 13 summarises their differences. Both singularity mass production and length extension make use of the *Ordering Law* (H$_4$): The order shown in the phylogram is superior to singletons and chains. Singularity mass production furthermore makes use of the *Singleton Law* (H$_3$), following the example of the art world, it integrates singletons into phylograms.

Length extension and singularity mass production collide in the sorting plant of culture. This is because singularity mass production in phylograms exposes their suprema to the danger of being devaluated by length-extending fashion. This business model therefore strives to evade this danger by offering editions. Under the impact of length extension, singularity mass production turns into a risk-opportunity strategy: it exploits the opportunities of cultural selection (H$_3$, H$_4$), but at the same time defends itself against the cannibalising effect of the length extension business model, with the continuous production of new qualities. Length extension, on the other hand, can only succeed against whatever already exists with the broadside of continuously new fashions. But with this it also cannibalises the fashion which it had previously put on the market itself. Singularity mass production also confronts the short-lived nature of length extension. Singularity mass production and length extension stand in dialectical opposition.

Table 13: Postmodern business models.

Identity Industry	
Business Model	*Cultural Selection*
Singularity mass production	• Singleton Law (H$_3$) • Ordering Law (H$_4$)
Length extension	• Ordering Law (H$_4$)
Simplification of thought	• Polytomisation Law (H$_9$)

These counteracting forces push length extension into the niche of short-lived consumer goods with brands such as *Benetton, Zara, H&M* and singularity mass production into the niche of longer-lasting consumer goods, with companies such as *Swatch* and *Rosenthal. Absolut Vodka*, the brand that succeeds with its singularity production (the packaging) amongst a market for short-lived consumer goods (spirits), is the exception to that rule.

Simplification of thought sets in where the other two business models fail to enhance cultural efficiency: at the polytomisation of the world of objects (H9).

Singularity mass production creates knots, length extension perpetuates them. Thought simplification works on this legacy and transforms it.

Culturally Dynamic Time

For the philosopher Jean-François Lyotard, the terms *modernism* and *postmodernism* refer not to the sequence of societal states, but to the state of objects and styles *in* society. An object (which he calls a work) is either in the state of modernism or postmodernism. All objects always change their state of being in the same sequence: from the postmodern state to the modern state. A new object must first be postmodern before it can become modern. Postmodernism, understood in this way, is modernism in the nascent state.

Lyotard's stance is reflected in QTC in Figures 11 and 12 in connection with the concept of over/undercoding. New objects from other style groupings are at first unfamiliar to the mainstream, but end up being assimilated by it as familiar ones. Hence, an object is postmodern in the early stages of its transformation, when it is familiar only on the fringes of society, or also to one of the special groupings II or IV, but not yet to the mainstream. An object is only modern in the final stage of its transformation, when it is familiar everywhere. In QTC, Lyotard's transformation of objects from postmodern to modern is therefore the syndromic effect of their undercoding to overcoding; or, in Scitovsky's view, the change from stimulation and inspiration to monotony and boredom; or, in Barber's words, from slow/difficult/complex to fast/easy/simple; or, from the standpoint of cognitive psychology, from slow to fast thinking.

According to Lyotard, if we distinguish between modernism and postmodernism not at the level of society but within the world of objects, then we always find two types of objects – those in the state of postmodernism and those in the state of modernism. The culture-changing function of industry is to transfer objects from a state of postmodernism to a state of modernism. The work of creative departments and the goal of branding and advertising are directed towards the steady creation of modernism and the elimination of postmodernism. The postmodern industry ensures that Lyotard's modernism does not disappear. It industrialises the process that moves from undercoding to overcoding of objects, from stimulation and inspiration to monotony and boredom, from slow/difficult/complex to fast/easy/simple, from slow to fast thinking.

Time *as such* does not exist. Instead, there only exist alternative time concepts for the before and after. The thermodynamic time of physics regards every closed system as striving towards a state of greater disorder. This thermodynamic time arrow (the only time arrow known to physics) is matched by QTC's culturally dynamic time arrow. The world of objects strives for ever greater monotony, for what is easier and simpler, so that it becomes more and more ingrained by fast thinking. The industry can do nothing other than be part of this journey and turn it into a business model. This throws new light on the practice of trend scouting: it nourishes culturally dynamic time.

The Ecological Footprint

Besides its infantilising effect, consumerism is also criticised for taking too high a toll on nature. The continuous pursuit of more of everything, or the compulsion behind this, is claimed to harm the biosphere and thus the very existence of human life. The many facets of this criticism can be reduced to a simple thermodynamic effect. Photosynthesis (including its fossil legacy) delays the steady return of solar energy into space by temporarily storing it. This enables the input of physical work which is necessary for the preservation of all life. The biosphere develops and sustains itself by means of this work. Its order, diversity and complexity are a direct result of this entropic delay. The human species uses some of this available physical work for its own sustenance, in competition with the needs of the rest of the biosphere. If the human species claims too much for itself, the rest will suffer. The surface area of the Earth would then have to be larger in order to preserve the existing order, diversity and complexity of the biosphere. The (positive) difference between the necessary hypothetical and the actual size of the Earth is referred to as the human ecological footprint. The criticism of consumerism is directed at this ecological footprint and culminates in the appeal for consumers to exercise self-restraint and reduce their footprint.

This criticism of consumerism broadsides the consumer, as portrayed by the orthodoxy. A utility-maximising positive-quantities consumer strives for ever larger quantities of specimens of all types in their goods basket. The material throughput necessary for +*consumption* and the physical labour required for the production, distribution, consumption and disposal of quantities generate thermodynamic costs at every stage of the value chain, from cradle to grave. The orthodoxy's consumer can therefore be nothing but a thermodynamic cost driver that contributes greatly to the unsustainable human ecological footprint. Does this ecological criticism of consumerism concern the o/+*consumer*? Not to the same extent, at least. It must be qualified for at least three reasons.

First, in o/+*consumption*, relative to other consumers, restraint is just as goal-oriented as augmentation. Only interpersonal and group differences in consumption matter. The logic of an elective affinity abolishing style peripheries in its common style (*Nucleation Law*, H_{10}) is a winning logic of renunciation. Likewise, an object that is shown in all individual styles of an elective affinity contributes nothing to individuality. In objective function (13) there is a built-in incentive for the qualitative unbundling of individual and common styles. The slackening of stylistic differentiation (H_{17}), promoted by unbundling, is a hypothesis not only on the limits of social evolution but, in its underlying mechanism, also on asceticism: duplication of displayed qualities is not rewarded in the style system. This propensity limits the thermodynamic costs of *o/+consumption* to those physical object specimens (few compared to orthodox consumption) that are still needed to generate the system of social distance and individuality in the style system.

On the other hand, the thermodynamic costs of *o/+consumption* are driven up by the *Quality Law* (H5), because more and more qualities in the style system need a demonstrable specimen. Moreover, the *Up-to-Dateness Law* (H_6) prevents old qualities from being discarded completely. The propensity to asceticism based on quality is counteracted by the equally inherent propensity to limitlessly create more qualities. The goods basket of the *o/+consumer* is thrifty, their goods *type* basket, however, is lavish. This ambivalent effect *of o/+consumption* on the thermodynamic costs is contrasted by the unequivocal cost-driving effect of the more-of-everything propensity of orthodox consumption.

Secondly, in the objective function of the orthodoxy, quantities of material things are the arguments of utility. Each of them contributes to thermodynamic costs. The greater the consumption utility, i.e. the more of everything that is consumed, the higher the thermodynamic costs. In objective function (13), however, there is not a single physical thing. The arguments of happiness – social distance and proximity – are concepts of the inner world of the productive consumer, based on (concepts of) qualitative differences in consumption, which show up in the orderings of the world of objects, $(X, \square)$, that is, in the structures, $\{\circ, |, \mathrm{m}\}$, and which are moderated by culture, $\square$. Only in the background does there exist the tangible material (chapter 1), as the only thermodynamically effective 'substance', of which all these 'dreams' are made.

QTC's non-material bias contrasts with the material bias of the orthodoxy. Orthodox theory overestimates the thermodynamic costs of consumption, whereas QTC underestimates them. In reality, where the idea of the ecological footprint takes hold, consumption of quantities and qualities go hand in hand. It is therefore necessary to work out the systematic thermodynamic conceptual differences between the orthodoxy and QTC.

Third, the orthodox theory of consumption is one concerning the relation-ship between human being and thing, while QTC is concerned with the relation-ship between humans and humans. The difference is that, in the orthodoxy, communication is a secondary issue, whereas in QTC it is the main concern.[10] In QTC social distance and proximity are communicated by means of consumption and produced by means of communication. The lack of communication in the orthodoxy and its presence in QTC have thermodynamic consequences. The question is whether there are components of communication that do not result in (measurable) thermodynamic costs. At least these components of *0/+consumption* must be spared the ecologically motivated criticism of consumerism.

Mathematician Claude Shannon offers a fundamental proposition to answer this question.[11] Two components of communication need to be distinguished: the engineering component and the semantic component. The engineering compo-nent includes the coding of information on storage media, their storage, archiv-ing, transmission and decoding. It is part of the thermodynamic system – all en-gineering tasks can only be done by the input of physical work. Therefore, they increase entropy. However, the semantic component, the meaning of communi-cation, which follows encoding and decoding, has no measurable thermody-namic costs.

For example, if you heat an oven by burning a sheet of paper (storage me-dium), it emits the same energy whether it contains parts of the *Canterbury Tales* (meaning) or what you are reading at this very moment. Likewise, the physical work embodied in Gutenberg's lead typesetting is independent of what is com-municated by it. If I write you the SMS "Max is sick again" and you receive and read it, the thermodynamic costs of this digital communication are the same, whether you interpret it as an appeal for sympathy or as a warning that that nui-sance Max is up to his tricks again. The semantics of communication is situated in the context of the communication, not in its engineering component. Think-ing slowly costs a lot of my energy, but it makes no measurable thermodynamic difference which stored memory I recall, what exactly I analyse, interpret, syn-thesise.

---

10 Even in orthodox signalling economics, which is the most communication-centred branch of in-formation economics, the communication process is de facto irrelevant. By design, communica-tion is regarded as successful if the signaller has invested sufficiently in signalling. Whether the interpretation of the signal by the addressee coincides with the intended one of the signaller is tacitly ignored.

11 Shannon 1948.

Shannon's epistemological interest was in information theory. Biochemist Antony Crofts applies Shannon's distinction between the engineering and semantic components of communication to the entire biosphere, from DNA to human culture.[12] A distinction should be made everywhere between the engineering and semantic components of communication. And everywhere, the meaning of communication arises solely from its context. For instance, the context of the chemical coding and storage of information in DNA, he claims, is Darwinian evolution.[13] The metabolic synthesis of DNA (engineering component) creates measurable thermodynamic costs. However, these costs are sequence independent. Just as the thermodynamic costs of Gutenberg's lead typesetting are sequence independent. However, it is precisely the sequence of chemical molecules in DNA that encodes a specific semantic content (much like the sequence in lead typesetting). This sequence results in the phenotype of an organism, epigenetically transported and translated. However, according to Crofts, its meaning only arises in the context of Darwinian evolution. Crofts concludes that the semantic component of communication does not in principle – epistemologically, for the time being – result in any measurable thermodynamic costs anywhere in the biosphere, including in human communication.

If you follow Shannon's and Crofts' line of argumentation, you can declare the entire semantic component of the communication brought about by *0/+consumption* as thermodynamically neutral. This part of *0/+consumption* does not contribute to the ecological footprint. The work of the productive consumer done in the sorting plant of culture has as its input the world of objects, X, and the thermodynamically neutral sorting instruction from culture, $\square$. The world of objects thus ordered, $(X, \square)$, in the ordering structures $\{\circ, |, ⋔\}$, is the output from the sorting plant. It is thermodynamically neutral as well. The 'work' done in the sorting plant of culture is physically no work, but culturally essential. Of all the "Yes to this, no to that!" decisions, only the "Yes to this!" decisions, reflected in demonstrable specimens, create thermodynamic costs. For the sake of

---

12   Crofts 2007. He uses the term 'information' for what is generically better covered by the term 'communication'. Communication requires an active recipient of information, equipped with a degree of freedom in decoding, whereas information does not need this in a narrow (sender-focused) interpretation of the term. However, Crofts repeatedly points out that information also requires interpretation as part of the overall transmission process. He thus uses the term 'information' in the sense of semantically effective communication.

13   Yet, Darwinian evolution is still too narrow a context, even for the semantic component of DNA. It must be extended to the nature-culture context. For example, race is genetically underdetermined, it only gains its meaning in a cultural context (cf. Marks 2013).

completeness, so does the energy consumption of the fast and slow thinking of the productive consumer. Combined with the frugality of their goods basket, but also with the lavishness of their goods-type basket, the productive consumer presents itself as a more complex subject than the one the orthodoxy delivers to the ecologist's pillory.

Brand (Equity) and Ecology

Brand equity is an intangible asset of a firm; inventories, factories and other production facilities, distribution infrastructure, etc., are tangible assets. For some firms, brand equity is the most valuable asset. In QTC it is derived from two factors. First, from the scaling of the market in which the brand succeeds (mass versus niche market), and second, from its brand function and brand position in the style system. (More on this in the last chapter.) In the style system, the meaning of a brand is determined within the context of all other brands. Just as – taking a classic analogy from semiotics – a dictionary entry can attain meaning only relative to all other entries.

In QTC, a brand can be understood in its initial appraisal as another object from the world of objects: as a thing (e.g. a logo) with a meaning that is used for communication. Like any meaning in the Shannon/Crofts sense, brand meaning does not belong to the thermodynamic system. For example, there is no known technical process by which a meaning such as 'advancement through technology' (the meaning proposition for *Audi* by *Audi*, as opposed to BMW's 'joy of driving') could be thermodynamically converted into better acceleration or ultimate speed. This is not a joke! Different brand meanings *per se* simply do not cause different thermodynamic costs, whatever they may be. It is only the engineering component of brand communication that generates thermodynamic costs – construction, design, distribution, promotional material and its coding at customer touchpoints, etc. The ecological footprint of industry is not affected by the meaning of its brands *per se*. In conclusion, it is only the scale factor of brand equity (number of specimens shown, geographical reach of advertising campaigns and presence, number of customer touchpoints, etc.) that influences its ecological footprint.

It can therefore be postulated that, with constant industry scaling, an increase in the brand equity of a company (or industry as a whole) does not increase its ecological footprint. The perception of the ecological responsibility of industry takes on a new dimension in QTC. Not only are ecological responsibility and corporate success not mutually exclusive in the brand dimension of business, they simply have nothing to do with each other.

The question arises as to how firms can foster this ecological transformation. The following questions outline a path to that destination. What business are we in? When gastro, event, clothing, mobility firms, etc., give the answer "in the style communication services business", they are on the right track. Where in the style system is our brand currently positioned? This question is more comprehensive than the standard question, "Who are our customers?" (the young, elderly, etc.) and addresses more subtle points such as the exact position of the current clients in the style system and their specific communicative environment there. What *local* restrictions does the style system impose there? What are our competing brands *there*? How can we valorise the semantic component of our communication service *locally* in the style system? And what is our optimal *global* position in the overall style system?

Alongside conventional reduction of the thermodynamic costs of the engineering component, the outlined path opens up the potential for systematic, ecologically compatible growth for brands. They only need to know one more thing: what communicative needs do consumers have in the style system? This is the subject of the last chapter.

Chapter 10
The Added Value of Becoming

"If you tell the truth, it's bound to be found out sooner or later."

"The play was a great success. Only the audience flopped."

"I have learned that it is not what I do that is wrong, but what I become as a result of my doing."
Aphorisms attributed to Oscar Wilde

The organisational theory of economics is based on Ronald Coase's 'make' versus 'buy' question: which inputs are better produced as part of the organisational form of the firm and which are better bought from the market.[1] From this efficiency criterion, economics derives its forecasts as to where in the value chain the boundary between the firm and the market is drawn.

For QTC issues, Coase's question must be broadened. We must also ask which parts of the identity value chain are produced by the consumer themself, which parts are produced for them by other productive consumers outside the market, and which parts they buy on the market from the identity industry. But there is still another question preceding these: which parts of the value chain can in principle be produced by which economic agents. Conceived exclusively in conventional terms – in terms of goods, brands, labels and advertising – only trivial answers result. To gain more substantive answers, one must advance to the core of the DIY identity: the creation of social distance and proximity by *0/+consumption*. Because

---

1   Coase 1937.

being is produced by communication through consumption. The organisation of the value chain of the DIY identity is the topic of the final chapter.

With the output of this value chain, the style system informs us about identity: about the collective identity of each elective affinity and the individual identity of each of its members. Everyone can find out about their own identity and that of everyone else. But how does the style system distinguish being from pretence? For at the beginning of identity there is only stylistic volition, which must still be transformed into being by 0/+consumption. The style system must separate the wheat from the chaff. To this end, it generates two types of information. From 0/+consumption, which is the consumer's input for their DIY identity, the style system filters out information about the consumer's volition, which it then processes into information about their being. Thus, the style system establishes two paths to human being: first, the path from volition (0/+consumption) to being, which is identical to it. Second, the path from volition (0/+consumption) to pretence and from pretence to a being different from volition. So, everyone ends up with an identity, even though it is not always the desired one. Oscar Wilde's aphorism about the link between doing and being succinctly highlights this communication-interpreting function of the style system.

If the style system were not capable of this triage, it could not persist. Individual volition alone would determine being and any 0/+consumption would mediate it. Instructions to the sorting plant of culture would be obsolete, the clustering of individual styles (0/+consumption) to common styles would not transport information about individual being, and no elective affinities could be inferred from individual styles. The unconditional society would end in social arbitrariness. This is only prevented by the triage work of the style system. It is the sole disciplining force. The possibility of deviating from volition is the disciplining contingency.

This triage turns culture into the key process of the economy, because the style system not only mirrors the social but is also an incentivising institution. In the style system, consumers have an incentive to steer clear of pretence. Whoever doesn't heed this ends up, as predicted by Oscar Wilde, if not in their very own world, then at least having to live with the wrong consequences of their doing. By staying clear of pretence, on the other hand, the being that is identical to volition is sooner or later revealed. It is by setting this incentive that the style system safeguards its existence.

Signalling and Sign Transformation

0/+consumption is a signal by which we communicate our being. It is necessarily *communicative* because being that is identical to our volition depends on the resonance of our audience. Thus, *0/+consumption* is the 'speech' in which communication takes place.[2] By this speech-like function of consumption, the style system as an economic institution, is tied back into semiotics. Thus, semiotics offers insights into the process of communicative consumption.

A signal is expression, which semiotically appears either as representation or exemplification (chapter 2). As the constitutive element of the individual style, a specific *0/+consumption* is the only means of expressing, *ceteris paribus*, a specific individuality within the elective affinity. Semiotically, the signal of individuality is therefore *representation* and not exemplification.[3]

In contrast, with objective function (13), a signal of social distance is, in itself, *exemplification*. This is because any supremum of an individual style that belongs to the core of the common style of one's elective affinity, could be replaced by any object as yet unshown by anyone, having the same distancing effect. With a world of objects never being fully absorbed by the style system, there are therefore interchangeable signals that produce precisely the same social distance in an exemplifying manner.

Each of these two forms of expression are assigned to a different argument of being: representation is assigned to individuality within the elective affinity, and exemplification is assigned to the distance of the elective affinity from the social whole. Thereby, the style groupings in Figure 11 differ from each other also in terms of the applied semiotic signalling technique: groupings I/IV signal identity mainly by exemplification, and groupings II/III mainly by representation. Figure 14 shows this relation.

---

2   Baudrillard 1968.

3   Any bilateral exchange of 0/+consumption with another member of one's own elective affinity
     would generate the same individuality in an elective affinity of two. Therefore, the statement
     applies only ceteris paribus, for given individual styles of other members of the elective affinity.

Figure 14: Semiotic transformation of 0/+consumption signals.

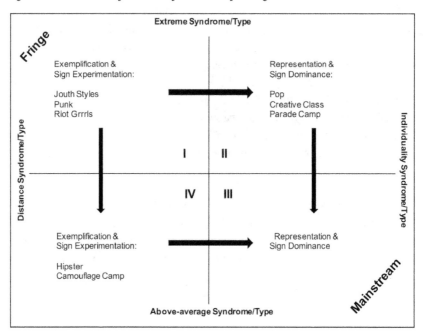

Signals in the distance syndrome are semiotically exchangeable stylistic exemplifications. In the individuality syndrome they are non-exchangeable representations. In the assimilation process of style innovation into the mainstream, a second transformation of the codes used in signalling takes place. In the transition from grouping I to grouping II and from grouping IV to grouping III, sign experimentation is replaced by sign dominance. In the semiotic transformation process, experimental exemplification on the fringes of society has become a sign-dominant representation, once the innovation has reached the mainstream. Signals of identity now convey a widely understood message.

 Experimenting with signs for the purpose of exemplification is more viable than for the purpose of representation, as there are many options for the use of objects for exemplification but not for representation. Sign experimentation is therefore more widespread in groupings I/IV than in groupings II/III. Therefore, in the mainstream, signs contain little experimentation. As in the pop and parade camp, unmistakable, dominant signs are set in the mainstream: corporate attire and luxury labels in the mainstream, the symbols of popart in pop, and the signs of the drag queen in parade camp. Sign dominance is typical for signals of the mainstream, sign experimentation is typical for signals coming from the fringes of society. But also, the hipster world is experimenting with constantly new exchangeable excavations from the repository of consumerism. Just as camouflage camp does with its eternal replacement of what was once the green carnation in the buttonhole of Oscar Wilde's jacket.

The transformation syndrome of innovation thus includes the transformation of signs. The assimilation of objects in grouping II is coupled with the loss of their experimental character, which they still had in grouping I. The same goes for the transition from grouping IV to grouping III. In the mainstream, all style innovations are ultimately marked by dominant signs, leaving no doubt about the representativity of the object. It is this sign dominance, with which the innovation is now endowed, that gives mainstream consumers the confidence they need for accepting the innovation. Nobody any longer concludes that someone is a punk simply because they show a stylistic element of punk; nobody is taken for a riot grrrl when they wear *Dr. Martens* boots with a dirndl at Oktoberfest. As a result of this process, *0/+consumption* as a signal of the mainstream has lost all its communicative ambivalence, even if it contains elements from a fringe style. With it, membership in the mainstream can be shown beyond any doubt, and in it one's own individuality is shown without any risk of misunderstanding.

Therefore, an integral part of all business models of the identity industry is the elimination of communicative ambivalences of all innovations brought to the mainstream. Design, advertising and the management of customer touchpoints serve a clear semiotic purpose: *the transformation of exemplifying sign experimentation into representational sign dominance*. This sign transformation is the semiotic key to the industrial opening up of the mainstream for innovations from the societal fringes.

QTC thus also offers an economic access to epistemological issues in semiotics. From the point of view of QTC, sign transformation is not an autonomous process (a sign of an older sign of a still older sign). It is a creative component of *gestalt*, for shaping the social in a forcefield generated by the objective function (13). Communication takes place in the social, signs serve the purpose of communication, but they develop different powers depending on their position in the style system.

Semiotics of Being and Having

In Saussure's view, being is the significate and *0/+consumption* is the signifier. Therefore, in QTC the *signal*, a term used in the orthodoxy, refers to the same idea as the semiotic term *signifier*. Social proximity as a constituent component of being is encoded in the signal/signifier as representation, social distance as exemplification. QTC thus offers semiotics a case where the same signifier, o/+consumption, can signify different significates with different codes.[4*] This is caused by the near and distant vision of the productive consumer, as elaborated in chapter 3, which in the semiotic model is the referent responsible for interpretation. The significate of social distance to other elective affinities is generated through the psychological lens that makes the comparable disappear. The significate of individuality in one's own elective affinity is generated through the lens that makes the incomparable invisible.

In the semiotic 'signifier-code-significate' model, a significate can be deduced from the signifier/signal only after each object is assigned a code. From a semiotic point of view, o/+consumption is not only a subset from the world of signifiers but also a corresponding subset from the world of codes. In o/+consumption, as the representation of individuality, all codes that convey incomparability disappear. And as an exemplification of social distance, all codes that mediate comparability disappear. This is to say, in the semiotic interpretation of o/+consumption, each signifier has two codes. The perspect manager of the productive consumer activates one or the other, depending on the situation, i. e. whether they are working on social distance or proximity. Hence, by activating different codes, one and the same signifier – o/+consumption – can exemplify and represent different significates – social distance or proximity. This implies that the communicative function of the style system is not based on the speech-like property of o/+consumption per se, but on two alternatively activated code systems born in it.

The two signifiers Western suit and barong tagalog, for example, contain codes that conveyed fundamental differences, such as in the country's history. When activated they exemplified the distance between 'Americanists' and Filipino nationalists. But each of these garments exist in a thousand nuances whose codes, when activated, represented individuality within the respective elective affinities. Therefore, it is not o/+consumption per se that establishes identity, but the codes in it that activate different significates.

Being and pretence can now be conceived semiotically. In pretence the consumer permits the audience's perspect manager to activate dormant codes in the individual's o/+consumption against its will. The consumer must therefore learn that their actions, by way of communication, turn them into something that they

---

[4*]   The (mathematical) functional relationship between the determinant 'o/+consumption' and the variable 'identity' is therefore not bijective. Only the representation of individuality is bijective, the exemplification of social distance is not.

do not want to be. In being, on the other hand, there are only those codes dormant in *0/+consumption* that, when activated, lead to the correspondence of desire and being. The truth contained in the *0/+consumption* is found out sooner or later by virtue of the codes it contains.

In the orthodoxy, by contrast, being always comes from the communication of the possession of quantities. Communication is expensive, and the consumer communicates only because their possessions are not yet known to the audience. Its signalling utility is a *being* that nourishes itself on a *having* that is now also known to others. *Having* means larger endowment with resources – more money, power, intelligence, education – the larger quantity of which is spent on the acquisition of such goods, for which poorer but equally prudent people would never waste their scarcer resources. From the orthodoxy's point of view, these consumer goods thus signal a being that poorer consumers, for good reasons, regretfully renounce. Only those who already possess will buy the signal. The orthodox signalling of *having* thus leads to an alignment of wanting and being only for those who possess. Those who do not *have*, are and remain what they have always been. Therefore, the underlying position of the orthodoxy is that only those rich in something actually signal by consuming, and the rest of society wisely refrains from doing so. One of the main differences to the orthodoxy is that, in QTC, all consumers signal their being with their *0/+consumption*.

The orthodox *signalling of having* needs no codes, or only the crudest ones. The signifier is the well-known high price of the signal, which is only bought by someone who has a lot. And where the high price is not common knowledge, it is a crude code in the signifier, from which the high price can be directly deduced – exquisite materials, expensive addresses, luxury labels, etc. In contrast, in QTC's *signalling of being*, identity is signalled by length and width as gained from complex *0/+consumption*. In comparison, signalling of having is like a single catchword that is called out to you. *Signalling of being* is like a thick book that needs to be read.

Creative versus Conservative Signalling

Signalling of being and signalling of having also differ in the direction of encoding. Signalling of having encodes in a backwards direction for the purpose of future signal utility. It refers to something that has always been there: upbringing, money, power, advantageous genes. It is not creative, nothing new can arise from it. It merely reveals.

Its conservative effect is not inherent in the orthodoxy's signalling theory of having, but is implicit in the socio-economic context in which it is embedded. The utility from signalling of having preserves the initial endowment differences: advantageous genes combine with advantageous genes (dating), power is nourished by power (network), money protects (ability to assert one's own interests) and good upbringing perpetuates itself by means of better educational prospects. The signal safeguards and magnifies what was already present as favourable endowment. Thus, with signalling of having, pre-existing differences in endowment are perpetuated. It has a conserving effect.

Signalling of being, on the other hand, encodes in the forward direction for the purpose of a future signalling utility. It refers to something that is not yet there and can only arise after the signal is given: socially shared identity acquired by means of communication. Signalling of being is creative. Each new signal creates a new identity, which can only emerge in this way.

But even in the most unconditional society, where everyone has the same initial endowment, identity is not unconditional: it requires the proper *o/+consumption*. Although every individual can afford any consumption, this entails opportunity costs. Showing a particular *o/+consumption* deprives the individual of all other possible identities. The signalling utility of *o/+consumption* is the specific being that corresponds to volition. The signalling cost is the associated renunciation of all other possible modes of being. The signal, *o/+consumption*, is unconditional, but the being that the signal implies is not.

Stylistic Engagement

The different encoding directions of the signalling of being versus having call for different types of codes. The signalling of having encodes "I am able!", the signalling of being encodes "I am engaged!" The backward-directed signalling of having encodes invisible endowment in visible consumptive ability: what one is able to consume – expensive watches, cars, etc. The forward-directed signalling of being encodes in *o/+consumption* stylistic engagement – engagement in an elective affinity and in one's own individuality therein. Those who don't show it remain in limbo between elective affinities. The overall contour of *o/+consumption* encodes engagement. It is not "Yes to this and that!" that creates contour, but the more salient "Yes to this, no to that!"

By showing contour, *o/+consumer* stereotypes emerge in collective interaction: in clothing sporty, playful, classically conservative, elegantly fashionable, staid, retro, bling. The industry supports the contours of these style stereotypes with its design styles for every consumption need. No contour and thus no engagement is shown by those who mix stereotypes arbitrarily. Engagement is shown by those who show their version of a consumer stereotype or even invent a new one. The coding in the signalling of being is therefore not to be found in the number of signs of the goods type basket, but in its stylistic contour (or the absence thereof). One can formulate the essence of the DIY identity as follows: Identity arises from signalling of being, signalling of being encodes stylistic engagement, and stylistic engagement manifests itself in a style with a contour. Consumer stereotypes therefore do not result from a lack of consumer imagination nor from a compulsion exerted by capitalist forces, but from the need to communicate being in a clear and distinct way by means of style – which is possible with visible engagement in a stylistic cause.

Since stylistic engagement can only be decoded from an aesthetic point of view, aesthetics covers increasing aspects of everyday social life. It has become a central driver of happiness. By now, successful business models are built on an in-depth knowledge not only of culture as a process *per se* (Table 13), but also of the aesthetic codes and schools that culture generates. Management studies is increasingly becoming a humanities discipline.

With stylistic engagement as code, clearly distinguishable clusters emerge from the sorting plant of culture. Individuals choose a goods type basket that shows contour: length and width of individual styles can be easily assessed aesthetically. Individuals with an engaged individual style consequently end up in elective affinities with a clearly distinguishable common style. The style system only gains contour as a result of the signalling of being.

Not every signalling of being automatically brings about contour. Where it is missing, such as within the mainstream, a large cluster emerges that can only be clearly distinguished from other clusters (groupings) as a whole. The lack of stylistic engagement within the mainstream turns it into a mixed-up soup.

Signalling Typology and Signalling Cascade

By accounting for endowment differences in the incipient DIY identity, QTC bridges the gap to the orthodoxy, in which endowment determines everything. Insofar as endowment is not observable *per se*, it must be signalled if the individual wants to derive a benefit from it. In that respect, QTC follows the orthodoxy. Hoewever, in the orthodoxy, only an advantageous endowment opens up the opportunity for signalling. In QTC everyone (with any endowment) has to establish their identity by signalling. But an advantageous endowment offers the chance for additional benefit.

With the additional argument of non-observable endowment in the objective function

$$U_i = U[Distance, Individuality, Endowment]$$

the signal *0/+consumption* now contains two pieces of information. It informs about identity and about additional happiness-relevant endowment. If the individual has no such endowment, *0/+consumption* merely informs about identity. In this operationalisation, endowment is identity-neutral in the following sense. The signal *0/+consumption* shows the addressees the identity-defining elective affinity and individuality, and for the identity thus established, the signal offers an additional endowment-dependent social advantage.

In the mainstream, coolness is such a social advantage (Figure 13). When everyone wishes to be cool, but not everyone can be cool – otherwise no one would want to be it – coolness must come from something that not everyone can do. The introduction of endowment into QTC broadens the theory of coolness contained therein (chapter 8). Coolness does not increase individuality in objective function (13), but is a socially advantageous characteristic of the self, which shows itself in the individual style. Making this characteristic visible generates signalling utility: being appreciated, admired, etc.

Creativity is an endowment that not everyone has at their disposal to the same extent. With creativity as input, style innovation is easier to achieve. If it is missing, the individual style must be more strongly oriented towards role models. Creativity turns consumers into style leaders (Table 8 and 11). It is not directly observable. Like the volition that exists before showing, it must be signalled. As part of being – "I am creative!" – its coding must refer to something that does not yet exist and can only come into existence by signalling: *stylistic autonomy*.

Figure 15 maps the signalling of style leadership in the semiotic and the corresponding signal-economic model. In the individual style (signifier/signal), norm violation is encoded as representation. However, new rules for the sorting plant of culture are also exemplified. The primary meaning (denotation) of the *0/+consumption* of style leadership is: "The rules are different!". Its secondary meaning (connotation) is stylistic autonomy. It is associated with stand-out (distanced or extreme) coolness. From the point of view of signalling economics, the audience deduces from associative stand-out coolness a creativity that is not observable *per se*. From then on, as a reputation, creativity confers a signalling utility.

Figure 15: Creativity signalling.

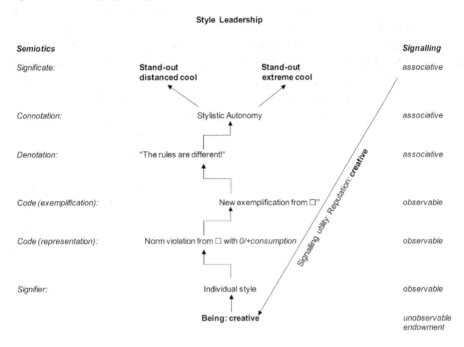

Norm-breaking in connection with a new exemplification in individual style conveys to the audience that new rules exist in the sorting plant of culture. This in turn conveys the association of stylistic autonomy as either stand-out distanced coolness or stand-out extreme coolness. Coolness, in turn, signals the not directly observable characteristic "I am creative For non-creative individuals, the costs of exemplification exceed the signalling utility.

In the style system we also find savants with a special endowment. Their knowledge of why the style system is the way it is (*know-why*) places them as intermediaries between the style leadership and its followers. This knowledge is not observable and, as *having*, must be encoded backwards in spoken and written signals that refer to *stylistic authority*. This knowledge resides in individuals who make a name for themselves as critics, curators, journalists, bloggers or vloggers, or in intermediary businesses – fashion and lifestyle magazines or culture channels – that employ people endowed with it. I will argue further on that consumer brands themselves can also take on the function of savants, namely by encoding in their advertising their stylistic authority. This signalling is mapped out in Figure 16.

Whilst style leaders themselves do not have to claim role model status for their stylistic activities, intermediary savants give innovations precisely this spin. The denotation of their know-why signalling is: "The rules are indeed different!" On its own, this does not confer a signalling utility. Only its association with stylistic authority as the significate and the resulting reputation turns their signalling into success.

Savants do not only exist in industry and the freelance professions; consumers can also be savants. Their knowledge of culture liberates them from the compulsions of fashion. In contrast to style leadership, consumer savants are, however, in need of endorsement from an authorised source – admiration alone is not enough. These authorities are professional style guides and industrial intermediary savants (style consultants, brands) that 'certify' the knowledge of the consumer savants.

Figure 16: Know-why signalling.

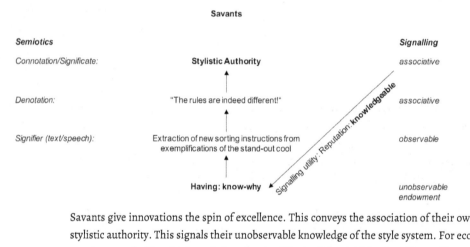

Savants give innovations the spin of excellence. This conveys the association of their own stylistic authority. This signals their unobservable knowledge of the style system. For economic agents lacking this knowledge, the signalling costs exceed the signalling utility.

Style followers are uncreative. Hence, in their DIY identity they are stylistically productive but not autonomous. Their agency is also heterogeneous. Some recognise style trends sooner than others. This is *per se* an unobservable part of their being: "I am sensitive to cultural selection!" It must therefore also be signalled. Like the encoding of creativity, this encoding refers to something that can exist when the signal is sent, at the earliest: *stylistic trendiness*. It is encoded by speed – to show something before others do is the code. Figure 17 illustrates this early-bird signalling. Its special feature is the encoding of both norm violation and norm compliance. It is norm violation from the point of view of the stylistic rear-guard, their out-group, which forever fails to jump on a trend in time. It is norm compliance from the point of view of the savants, whose stylistic authority is fully acknowledged by the early birds. The connotation of the individual style of early birds is stylistic trendiness, the significate is fit-in coolness. Their reputation for always being up-to-date gives the fit-in cool ones their signalling utility.

Figure 17: Early-bird signalling.

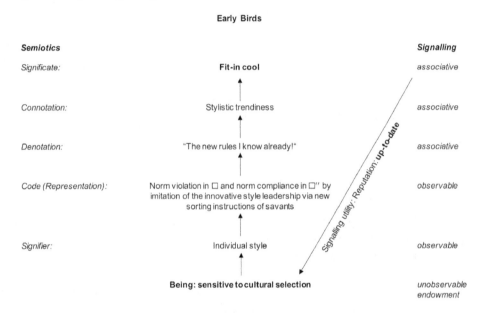

Norm violation from the point of view of the rearguard, and norm compliance from the point of view of the savants (by early imitation of the examples from the style leadership and by following the guidances of the savants). This conveys the association of stylistic trendiness, which in turn is associated with fit-in coolness. This signals the sensitivity to cultural selection that is not directly observable. Individuals lacking this sensitivity can only be up-to-date at too high a cost.

Early-bird signalling introduces an ambiguity. The recognition it receives from the stylistic rearguard offers signalling utility. However, it also signals stylistic dependence on the style leadership (either directly on the leadership itself or on the identity industry). Their early-bird signalling is only a full success to the ex-tent that the signallers manage not to receive or notice resonance from the style leadership. Early birds will therefore tend to avoid direct contact with style leaders and prefer to be guided by intermediary savants whose business model guarantees them positive feedback.

Figure 18: Actively uncool signalling.

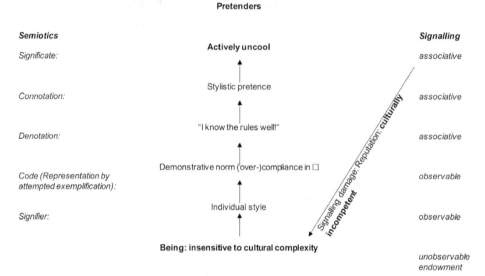

Demonstrative (non-ironic) norm compliance by means of overinvestment in brands and labels conveys the association of stylistic pretence and signals stylistic incompetence instead of the intended stylistic competence.

In the style system there are also those whose signalling completely fails but still has an effect. They are insensitive to the complexity of culture, the mastery of which they (like the early birds) actually want to signal. But in fact they send out the signal "I am culturally insensitive!" Their signalling is mapped out in Figure 18. It encodes demonstrative (over-)compliance with the norm, whose denotation is "I know the rules well!" but whose unintended connotation is one of stylistic pretence – as a matter of fact, the style shows that the rules are not mastered. The individual style signifies uncoolness. But it is not uncool in the sense of being old-fashioned, boring, predictable, which the signal giver does not even try to avoid. It is uncool due to a failed visible effort – it is actively uncool: active posing instead of living one's habitus (Bourdieu), active in the strenuous "keeping up with the Joneses" (Veblen), active in the restless fashion attitude, active in the showing of *having* where everyone already knows it or nobody cares anymore. Signalling utility is lacking, but signalling damage is present. By way of pretence, a being is signalled that is not identical to volition.

The style system does not eradicate pretence, because it is not itself threatened by its existence. It merely provokes a resonance that makes those among the pretenders who are capable of learning learn, and leaves behind those who are incapable of learning, to their own detriment. The character of *Geri Weibel* in Martin Suter's short story collection *Business Class* addresses precisely this type of signalling.

Whoever is uncreative, unpretentious and trend insensitive is an unconditional style follower. Their being – "I am!" – is encoded in *0/+consumption* merely as a reference to being nested in a common style. The significate is the membership in an elective affinity with a maintained individuality therein. The signalling utility is affiliation. Figure 19 shows this case.

Figure 19: Unconditional signalling.

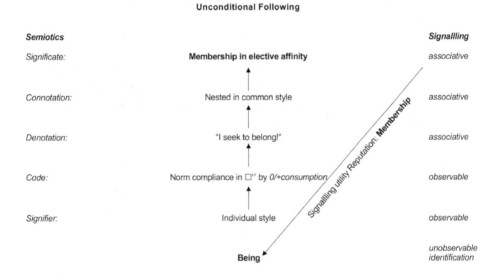

Compliance with the norm set by the style leadership for 0/+consumption is a necessary and sufficient condition for membership in an elective affinity. This is the reference case discussed in detail in Parts I and II.

Unconditional signalling is the reference case against which every signalling of endowment is compared. As the reference case of successful compliance with the norm, unconditional signalling renders the sender uncool. However, this is passively uncool signalling. Visible fruitless effort is lacking, as is a violation of the norm. Thus, it does not trigger any undesirable resonance. Volition and being become one. Style followers signal largely unconditionally. The only precondition is their 0/+*consumption*.

In the style system we also find actors with an extra amount of the accumulated. This is an endowment advantage that is not observable *per se* but has to be made visible by means of signalling of having. This is the orthodox reference case. The encoding is backwards-directed. The signal does not create, but instead reveals autonomy. However, it does not reveal stylistic but rather social autonomy. Figure 20 maps out this signalling type.

The orthodox reference case is well received by coolness research, which identifies power as one of the causes of stand-out coolness.[5] Just as with the stand-out cool style leaders, norm violation and autonomy are encoded in this signalling of having. But their denotation is not "The rules are different!" as in the creativity signalling of style leadership, but "Your rules do not apply to me!". Consequently, its connotation is not stylistic but social autonomy – the autonomy of those whose endowment lends them power.

Power *per se* is as invisible as endowment. But in order to be effective, power does not have to be exercised, it is enough if it is shown. This is exactly what the power signalling of having serves to do. It makes power visible in stand-out power-autonomous coolness that gives a damn about "your rules". The scamp who is the only one in the office who breaks the dress code and smokes, and the professor who is always late for class, show this pattern.

---

5   Bellezza, Gino and Keinan 2014.

Figure 20: Power signalling.

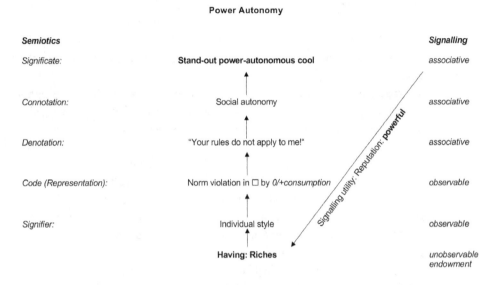

Norm breaking in an individual style conveys the association "I don't care about your rules". Thus it does not exemplify new rules but represents social autonomy as stand-out power-autonomous coolness. This signals the not-directly-observable endowment with power-creating resources. For individuals lacking these resources, the costs of breaking the norm are higher than its signalling utility.

Ostentatious Russian consumption does not necessarily have to be understood as actively uncool, pretentious signalling by the nouveau riche, who are still un-familiar with Western rules. In the logic of Figure 20 it can be understood as power signalling. In a vacuum of state power and security in the transitional pe-riod after the collapse of the Soviet Union, in which the protection of property and family had been a private matter for some time, power signalling demon-strated the ability to protect one's own rights.[6] In this example, it is also apparent that signalling is dependent on culture. One and the same individual style, which functions as power signalling in Moscow, may become an actively uncool signal during winter holidays in the Alps. In the end it is the audience that makes the signal.

As remnants of modernism, patricians cling to the style system. Their having consists of tradition, which they signal not with luxury but by stylising austerity.

---

6   Lindquist 2002.

The *Nucleation Law* (H_{10}) provides the lever for this. Given decreasing marginal utility of social distance and individuality, the withdrawal without replacement of objects from the periphery of the common style only increases happiness if individuality is sufficiently large. Therefore, individuality, which remains invisible to out-groups behind closed doors, can still be signalled. Figure 21 maps out this case.

Patricians are the *o-consumption* champs in the style system. They show by not showing. It is not exposure that creates signalling utility but hiding. They hide what they have accumulated, the world of objects they show is sparser than that of (much) poorer consumers, and yet they communicate who they are. Austerity signalling replaces the vitreous individual in DIY identity. As a bonus, withdrawal from the vitreous society beckons, which they can afford. Patricians do not live behind walls behind which luxury is visible and show no pomp when they leave them. One example is the so-called 'Basler Daig' in the swiss city of Basel – old patrician families with enormous wealth, who lead a modest existence in public. Patricians are not formed spontaneously by an elective affinity, because the signifier is not the individual but the common style. Only the knowledge of the shared tradition, present in the style system, makes them exist as a group.

Figure 21: Austerity signalling.

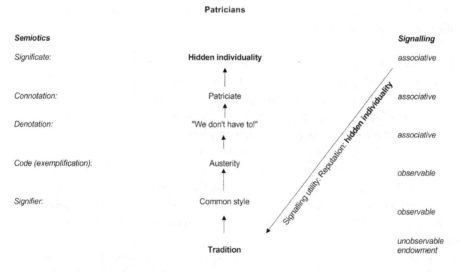

The advantageousness of removing objects from the periphery of the common style requires a minimum of individuality (Nucleation Law H_{10}). Individuality can thus be signalled by a frugal common style and makes the vitreous individual redundant.

The style system thus accommodates seven different signalling types, whose properties are summarised in Table 14. The backward-directed encoding of the power and austerity signalling cannot create anything new but only reveal what exists. In this sense of creation, both are unproductive. All other signalling types are productive. Know-why signalling creates a role play in the style system, all others create a being through the resonance they trigger. Only the creativity signalling of style leadership is stylistically innovative. The other productive signalling types are only imitatively productive. Apart from actively uncool signalling, all of them provide signalling utility and establish a correspondence between volition and being. Actively uncool signalling inflicts signalling damage by creating unwanted *being*, which is why it is the only one that is not self-stabilising. Individual experience perpetuates all other signalling types.

Table 14: Signalling typology.

		Signalling Properties				
		Endowment	Direction of Coding	Denotation	Connotation	Significate
Actant- and Signalling Type	Style Leadership: Creativity Signalling	Creativity	forward	"The rules are different!"	Stylistic autonomy	Stand-out distanced/ extremely cool
	Savants: Know-why Signalling	Know-why	forward	"The rules are indeed different!"	Stylistic authority	
	Early Birds: Early-bird Signalling	Sensitive to cultural selection	forward	"I already know the new rules!"	Stylistic trendiness	Fit-in cool
	Style Following: Unconditional Signalling	Being	forward	"I seek to belong!"	Nested in common style	Uncool membership in elective affinity
	Pretenders: Actively Uncool Signalling	Insensitive to cultural complexity	forward	"I know the rules well!"	Stylistic pretence	Actively uncool
	The Power-Autonomous: Power Signalling	Having	backward	"Your rules do not apply to me!"	Social autonomy	Stand-out power-autonomous cool
	Patricians: Austerity Signalling	Tradition	backward	"We don't have to!"	Patriciate	Hidden individuality

For style innovation and its diffusion from the fringes of society into the mainstream, power signalling, austerity signalling and actively uncool signalling are redundant. The first two create nothing and the actively uncool signalling is a communicative disaster. Only creativity signalling, know-why signalling, early-bird signalling and unconditional signalling by the style followers are conducive to the diffusion of style innovation.

The abstraction by the orthodoxy (for which only the rudimentarily modelled signalling of *having* exists) from the plurality of signalling types blocks the view of how they interact. They collaborate in the signalling cascade of the diffusion of style innovation, which is sketched in Figure 22.

The signalling cascade starts with new exemplifications from the style leaders and culminates in the being of the unconditional followers. In between is the signalling of the savants and the early birds. Savants take up the exemplifications of the style leaders' creativity signalling and condense them in their know-why signalling into new rules for the style followers. They are first followed by the early birds. Their signalling is associated by the unconditional followers with stylistic trendiness. This gives unconditional followers the assurance that the style innovation is nested in the common style of their own elective affinity. Innovation thus diffuses into their common style.

In the cascade of signalling types, the 'baton' changes hands at increasingly later stages of signalling. Between the style leadership and savants it occurs in the observable section of signalling. Between savants and early birds it occurs later on the denotative level, and between these and the unconditional followers it occurs on the even later connotative level of the signal. It is the connotation of imitation that is needed to create and preserve the identity of the unconditional followers in their elective affinity.

Figure 22: The stylistic signalling cascade and industrial transfer.

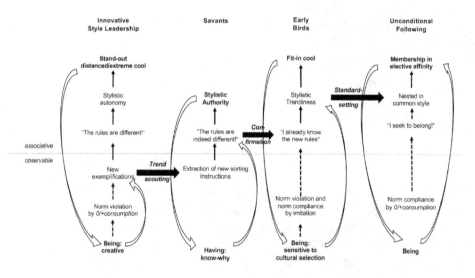

Industrial Transfer and Scaling

The signalling cascade offers a new, information-economic view of industry. The transformation of fringe innovations into mainstream innovations, as outlined in Figures 12 and 14, is accommodated by the identity industry. It transfers meaning from one actor/signalling type to the next. With this transfer, it closes the gaps in the signalling cascade left open by the productive consumers (Figure 22).

Their trend scouting in grouping I identifies new exemplifications and presents them in the form of experimental designs to the style groupings II and IV (Figure 11). Savants then filter out of them new rules for the mainstream. As stylistic authorities *vis-à-vis* the fit-in cool in grouping III, they confirm that their imitations are the current proof of their understanding of the rules. The services of savants, which are often part of the identity industry themselves (fashion and lifestyle magazines, feuilletons, paid influencers, etc.), consist of trend consolidation by trend confirmation. The fit-in-cool ones alone do not have a broad enough impact to establish their compliance with the rules as the new standard for the unconditional followers of grouping III. This is where the identity industry assists in setting standards by means of brands for the mass market. What began as an exemplification of stylistic autonomy in grouping I has ended as a new standard for belonging in grouping III: time and again, fit-in coolness is positioned as a standard for the whole.

Industrial transfer is increasingly scaled up along the signalling cascade. Niche products and niche brands are positioned in the style groupings I, II and IV. When the final standard is set for the unconditional followers of formation III, the identity industry is scaled up to the size of the mass market. In the information-economic perspective of QTC, the identity industry therefore does not consist of a juxtaposition of niche and mass market firms, but the former are the foundation of the latter. In terms of information economics, the business model of the mass market is fed from the business model of niche markets.

Brand Groupings

Brands are signs associated with things and services. The o/+consumption – "Yes to this, no to that!" – includes o/+consumption of brands/signs. Just as there are objects that belong to a common style and those that do not belong to it, brands/signs belong to a common style (in-group brands) or not (out-group brands).

QTC predicts that consumers prefer in-group brands in their individual style and avoid out-group brands. This is empirically substantiated.[7] The *o/+consumption* builds a nexus between self and brand (*self-brand connection*). The self-brand connection turns the brand into an instrument of self-categorisation (see the psychology of the objective function in chapter 5). If an individual affiliates with skinheads and discovers that skinheads are wearing *Dr. Martens* boots, they also want to show *Dr. Martens* (in-group brand). If they find out that skinheads are not wearing *Birkenstock* sandals, they will avoid this brand (out-group brand). Brands can therefore be positioned in the style system.

Like product differentiation, brand diversity is an output of the *Quality Law* (H_5) of cultural selection. The plethora of brands is traditionally explained by economies of scale and cost reduction (house of brands). Instead, QTC predicts that same plethora by the increasing variegation of the world (H_{18}).

Figure 23: Brand groupings.

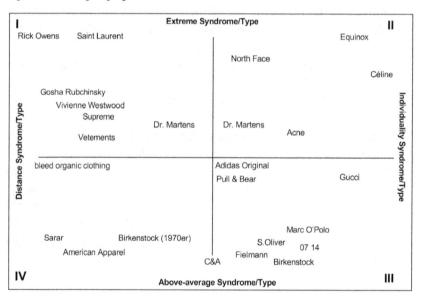

The example of apparel and accessory brands illustrates the brand positioning of an entire consumer goods industry in the style system. Brands are positioned in the style groupings and make up corresponding brand groupings. Within a grouping, brands also differ in

---

7   Escalas and Bettman 2005.

their relative position. Viewed from the midpoint, the more distantly a brand is situated, the stronger its grouping-specific characteristics.

Figure 23 positions apparel and accessory brands within the groupings of the style system. Brand are assigned to whole groupings but not to specific elective affinities. This is because brands can belong to the periphery of several common styles, and because it is in the interest of a brand owner to reach a larger clientele. With this, QTC offers a new logic for the classification of brands.

C&A with its non-committal slogan "Good prices, good everything" serves as a reference case for the positioning of brands in Figure 23. With this message, the brand positions itself in the stylistically indeterminate area between the motive of social distance and individuality. It does not present potential friction for people who avoid the extreme. Positioned this way, C&A addresses a maximum number of customers.

(The other) mass market brands are positioned in grouping III. They serve the demand neither to show social distance (the *what*) nor to operate with means of the extreme (*how*). In contrast to C&A, they focus more on individuality and/or use (slightly) more extreme means. *Fielmann* with its barely provocative eyewear designs is positioned horizontally next to *C&A*. With its slogan "Everyone is beautiful" it promises natural individuality to those who entrust themselves to the brand. With the slogan "Real fashion for real people" (2015), *S.Oliver* serves the motive of individuality more strongly. However, its fashion stands out just as little as *Fielmann* glasses. *Birkenstock*, "Simply good" (1984) or "Comfort with every step" (2012), occupies a position in the same range. With its slogan "More than normal" and entirely normal accessories that can be personalised with proper names, the leather accessory brand *0714* is oriented towards the least daring individuality. *Marc O'Polo*, with its highly combinable range of products in many different but always monochrome colours, also lacks any potential for conflict or provocation. With slogans such as "Take it easy! Simple cuts and subtle colours for a relaxed look", it provides almost unlimited interchangeability and therefore hardly any individuality that really stands out.

Grouping III also includes brands that serve consumers on the borders of neighbouring groupings, and address more specific market segments. Typical for luxury brands, *Gucci* targets a highly individualised clientele with some affinity for the extreme, but within strictly controlled limits. Exclusive brand collaborations, for instance with the iconic *Novembre Magazine*, which posts the anti-aesthetic "Ugly Look", take the *Gucci* brand to the boundary of grouping II, where individuality and the extreme types fuse together. *Adidas Originals* collaborates via social media with hip hop stars from grouping I (Old School) and grouping II

(New School). Thus, it positions itself in their neighbourhood and at a certain distance from the mainstream, from which the brand originated and to which it still belongs. Similarly positioned is the teenage-focused brand *Pull & Bear*, whose everyday fashion displays rebellious slogans such as "Revolutionary girl" or "I refuse to become what you call normal".

Formation II contains brands like *Acne, North Face, Céline* und *Equinox*. Here, brands are more strongly charged with the extreme. However, the motive they serve remains that of individuality. *Acne* has cult status among digital nomads and in the creative class. The penchant for the extreme is served with extravagance, which nevertheless remains combined with basics. *Acne* thus remains in the immediate vicinity of brand grouping III. The outdoor brand *North Face* serves and glorifies the performance cult, in the extreme experience of nature, and under extreme weather conditions. The aim is not to widen social distance, but build an individual sporty and active lifestyle. The cult brand *Céline* positions itself way off the beaten track of fashion, combining extreme individuality with the aesthetics of modern art. It presents itself in campaigns that break radically with the high-gloss aesthetics so typical of the industry. *Equinox* targets self-optimisation on the basis of the potential that resides within oneself. The brand slogans "It is not fitness, it is life" and "Commit to something" heroise passion and top performance.

Brand grouping IV contains brands that avoid the extreme, but sublimate social distance from the mainstream. *American Apparel* was regarded a hipster brand. Despite the mass-market products sold, the brand positioned itself at a distance from the mainstream by its carefully cultivated nimbus of political (sexist) incorrectness. *Birkenstock* was an alternative lifestyle brand in the 1970s, unobtrusive as it is today, but at a moderate distance from the mainstream. *Sarar* is a Turkish apparel brand whose style can be described as Western, but also old-fashioned, compared to Western standards. Like all mainstream mass brands, it does not stand out, but in its backwardness in fashion it allows ethnic affinity to be shown in a non-rebellious way. Grouping IV also includes eco-brands that mark distance to the ecological footprint of the mainstream, without radically rejecting its underlying lifestyle. Many have their ecological footprint certified (GOTS, Fairtrade, etc.), and a tendency to go to the extreme is mostly limited to consistent renunciation in one or a few dimensions of the footprint. *Bleed Organic Clothing* is an example of the edge to the extreme. The brand offers vegan 'leather' clothing made of cork.

Grouping I includes niche brands that mark social distance by means of the extreme. The streetwear brand *Supreme* draws on the aesthetics of punk, hip hop and the skateboard style. With its origin in downtown Manhattan, the staff was made up exclusively of members of the countercultural underground. It represents a group of brands that also includes *Vivienne Westwood*, whose objects were initially directly inspired by the fringes of society and were also consumed there. Initially, these were community brands created by and for members of fringe groups.[8] The more successful ones became commercial brands for a larger clientele. *Gosha Rubchinsky* manifests a post-Soviet countercultural chic of trackpants, shaved heads, bomber jackets and football scarves. It appeals to fashionistas who use the stylistic ruptures of this antiaesthetic to mark distance from the Western standard. Like *Saint Laurent*, *Vetements* is not a brand created by and for fringe people. In exclusive shops and with extremely expensive products, they attract a financially strong clientele. *Vetements* presents subcultural codes in streatwear that irritates and provokes. It provokes with slogans like "May the bridges I burn light the way" and irritates with garments showing logos of industrial companies or state organisations. Mass styles of the subordinate work and office world are thus debunked. Individuality is suppressed, only conveyed in the connotation of the luxury label. *Saint Laurent* over-stylises the codes of the social fringe by means of androgynous monochrome aesthetics. It is reminiscent of punk, goth and rockabilly. It promotes a provocative heroin chic. It is a brand for the extremely successful (rock stars, etc.), whose success allows them to live a life of luxury outside the bourgeois norms. Codes cannot be outdone in the extreme (extremely black, extremely skinny, extremely sexualised). *Rick Owens* shows a rebellious, masculine, monochrome avant-garde aesthetic with allusions to minimalist art. Extremely expensive, with extreme stylistic features (extremely black, wraparound clothes, naked skin) and references to Japanese aesthetics, it moves its wearers to the stylistic brink of Western society.

Dr. Martens is an example of an attempt to position a brand in two style groupings. Like *C&A*, which is positioned indeterminately between these groupings, *Dr. Martens* aims at tapping the markets in groupings I and II. However, with the slogans of 2014 "Stand for something", "We stand for non-conformity" and "I stand for being an individual", the brand does not remain undefined between groupings I and II but rather explicitly within both.

The migration of *Birkenstock* from grouping IV (in the past) to grouping III (today) makes it clear that brand position is temporary. The brand positions in Figure 23 show the state of the style system at the time this book was written. It can change. Just as culture remains dynamic, from which the style system is shaped.[9]

---

8   Füller, Luedicke and Jawecki 2008.

9   I thank Ella Lu Wolf for the compilation of the empirical brand findings.

Figure 23 contains an interesting analogy. In the style system, brands are positioned in groupings, such as they are in the groupings of brand gender. The concept of brand gender covers brands without gender (e.g. *Amex*), those with a decidedly feminine gender (*Dove*), a masculine gender (*Harley-Davidson*) and a distinctly androgynous gender (*Walt Disney*). The brand equity of brands without gender is lower than that of brands with gender; and the brand equity of androgynous brands, which show decidedly feminine as well as masculine traits, is higher than that of purely masculine or feminine brands.[10] *C&A* remains stylistically undefined between the distance and individuality types, just as *Amex* remains undefined in the gender space. The other brands are distinctly positioned in the style system, like *Dove* in the gender space; and *Dr. Martens* is positioned variously in style space, as is *Walt Disney* in gender space. An interesting question that is not pursued further concerns the connection between the position of a brand in style groupings and brand equity.

Cascade Position and Brand Erosion

Brands are not only assignable to different brand groupings in the style system. They also occupy different positions in the signalling cascade. There, brands are lubricants of style innovation in the communication process outlined in Figure 22.

Mass market brands like *C&A* or *Walmart* ("Save Money. Live Better") address a clientele that is not interested in style leadership, but in value for money. Whatever kind of aesthetics mass-produced objects offer is okay. *C&A* and *Walmart* address the unconditional style followers. With the slogan "Every little helps", *Tesco* aims for a down-to-earth identity that is nourished by the little things in life and that follows the masses step by step. *Birkenstock* advertisements feature average people and slogans such as "In my Birkenstocks I have warm feet and feel really good". *S.Oliver's* slogan "Real Fashion for Real People" is aimed at people for whom trend-signalling is unimportant. The high street chain *Zara* assumes the role of standard-setter for unconditional followers in the fast fashion segment. It recklessly copies designs from high-fashion brands like *Céline* and presents them as the current fashion standard. They are all brands of unconditional following.

Other brands are positioned among the early birds. *Pull & Bear* conveys the current trend to its teenage clientele with corresponding slogans on the apparel.

---

10   Lieven 2017.

Adidas Originals collaborates with hip hop stars in influencer marketing, giving customers the confidence to keep up with the trend. *Acne* attracts the attention of culturally sensitive consumers with eye-catching cuts and patterns, which are made widely visible in extravagant shops. Trends are 'loudly' conveyed. *North Face* addresses the same need with the slogan "Innovation for firsts". This way, brands convey fit-in coolness. Sometimes this is done by highly specialised signalling services. For example, the apparel brand *Oscar de la Renta* addressed a culturally demanding clientele in its brand cooperation with Sotheby's, when auction items were presented together with the fashion brand. With Sotheby's reputation as experts in art and culture, the brand was given the reputation of having expertise in fashion. In contrast, *Volkswagen* bluntly positioned itself and its customers as early birds with their slogans "Often copied, never matched" (2013), "You can have followers even without Twitter" (2013) and "Always one leap ahead". Slightly more subtle is "A sign of things to come" (2017) by *BMW*. In this way, brands try to elevate their clientele to a position closer to the beginnings of the style innovation value chain.

Other brands strive to lend their customers the aura of savants. This requires them to position themselves at least at savant level in the signalling cascade, so they can instruct their knowledgeable clientele on equal terms. The slogan of watch brand *Pulsar*, "Tell it your way", does not only convey individuality but also superior knowledge. *Cartier* follows the same path with "The art of being unique". It replaces knowledge only with superior cultural skills. "For people who do not go with the times" (2007) of the watch brand *Carl F. Bucherer* orients the savant, who knows why trends and fashions need not be followed. And the business model of the structured sales organisation *CMB* (Colour Me Beautiful) conveys precisely this 'know-why' from savants for savants: under *CMB*-guidance, customers self-revise their identity by determining their 'individual' colour type ("I am a brown-haired Winter type"). This gives them the confidence of standing above fashion.[11]

Lastly, there are brands that seek to impart the aura of the stylistic autonomy of style leaders to their customers, no matter what their preconditions for it may be. The oxymoron "Begin your own tradition" (2015) of the *Patek Philippe* traditional watch brand legitimises norm-breaking ("Begin your own …") by certifying its bourgeois innocuousness ("… tradition"). With "In the centre of the hurricane there is always stillness" and "Absolutely wrong for so, so many people", *Porsche* also insinuates stylistic autonomy. With "Never follow", "Follow your own rules" (both 2006) and "You'll want to follow yourself" (2012) by *Audi*, as well as with

---

11   Grove-Whight 2001.

"Unlike any other" (2006) by *Mercedes*, *Porsche* is faced with competition not only on the road but also on the same position of the signalling cascade. *BMW's* oxymoron "Return to a new era" (2017) leads towards stylistic autonomy in a clever way. "Return ..." helps the clientele out of the hamster wheel of fashion, and "... to a new era" positions the brand as a fixed, fashion-independent guiding star.

BMW is an example of how brands sometimes, perhaps deliberately, fail to clearly position themselves in the signalling cascade. "Return to a new era" is from the same campaign as "A sign of things to come." Overarching the set of slogans, the signalling of style leadership as well as that of the early birds is nurtured here. Early birds are thereby brought closer in their self-perception to style leadership. But what applies to the brand grouping position also applies to the cascade position: it is not fixed, it can change over time.

As remuneration for their services, companies receive a share of the signalling utility that their brand engenders. The greater this signalling utility for customers is, the greater the brand's margin. The signalling utility of creativity signalling is greater than that of early-bird signalling, and that at the very end of the signalling cascade is least. Brands that position themselves at the beginning of the cascade (*BMW*) tend to generate larger margins than those in the middle (*Volkswagen*), and these in turn larger margins than those at the end (*Lada*). The hypothesis therefore is that the closer the brand is positioned to the signalling cascade's beginning, the greater its brand equity (as a share of the company value). Therefore, *ceteris paribus*, all brands wanted to be at the beginning of the cascade. But a trade-off with the positioning costs distributes the brands across the entire cascade. Because positioning at the beginning requires greater cultural capital in marketing than in the mass market further down the cascade. Moreover, the volume is larger towards the end.

Brands can also lose their cascade position against their will. The car brand *Opel* is an an example of brand erosion. Positioned similarly in the market to BMW in the 1960s, the company was stripped of resources after the takeover by *GM*, and slid further and further towards the end of the signalling cascade. Today, brand equity is low compared to that of *BMW*. QTC offers a dual logic of brand positioning: in the static logic of brand groupings (Figure 23), and in the complementary dynamic logic of the style innovation process (Figure 22). A brand is always positioned in both.

Mass market brands position themselves in the signalling cascade as standard-setters. On the boundaries of grouping III, however, brands already position themselves for people with greater cultural capital, i.e. for early birds or even style autonomous people. Thus, the brand grouping of the mainstream offers a wide range of signalling utilities: from the low signalling utility of the passive uncool, to that of the fit-in cool, to the signalling utility of savants and the (almost) stand-out cool. In grouping IV, brands are found that aim for autonomy from mainstream consumption patterns (*Bleed Organic Clothing*). Typically, they present themselves in sporadic stylisation. In grouping II one can find brands for the trendy as well as for the style autonomous. In grouping I, there are only brands for the style autonomous. But here the autonomy is that vis-à-vis the whole value system of the mainstream (*Gosha Rubchinsky*). Accordingly, stylisation promised by brands is not selective, but total. At the extreme end of style groupings I and II, brands (*Rick Owens* or *Equinox*) aim for extreme stylistic autonomy.

Brand Upgrade and Stylistic Ship Wrecking

Style curation by use of brands does not guarantee consumers signalling success. The risk of pretence, triggering signalling disutility and arising from actively uncool signalling with brands, is unavoidably built into the signalling cascade. Style followers can be guided in their stylisation by brands that position themselves in the signalling cascade, prior to their target customers' signalling aspirations. Brands want to present themselves at least as savants to wannabe early birds, and to wannabe style leaders they can only present themselves as style leaders. Brands that do not possess this potential face a problem. They must upgrade themselves in the signalling cascade to be able to promise signalling utility to their target customers.

Active uncool signalling with brands can take two forms. First: someone fails in signalling with a brand that in and of itself could have been successfully applied. Culturally insensitive, the consumer applies useful material incorrectly. Failure follows due to the brand *user's* lack of cultural capital. Second: a consumer fails in using a brand for signalling because the brand cannot deliver what it promises. Those who think of themselves as early birds with their *Golf GTIs* run the risk of failing due to a brand upgrade, which may seem all too obvious to the audience. Here, failure follows due to a lack of cultural capital on the parts of both the brand user and the brand *owner*. Successful signalling with brands requires cultural competence on both sides of the market, which many brands (their marketing) miss. Not only for consumers, but also for the industry, the menacing pretence lurks between volition and being.

The Size of the Mainstream

The scaling of the style system can be understood as preference-driven and exogenously given (orthodox view) or as endogenously determined. The signalling
cascade of style conveys endogenous understanding. It is not a larger number of
consumers, with exogenous preferences for a mainstream existence, that makes
the mainstream a mass market, but the natural economies of scale at the end of
the cascade. All other brands in the style system deliver *pro bono* services to the
brands at the end of the cascade. If we take costs into account, this transfer results in a cost advantage for the recipients. We can now define the mainstream
in two ways: in terms of quantity it is the exogenously large mass of consumers;
in terms of signalling it is the endogenously large group at the end of the cascade.
With the second definition, the mainstream becomes large through the cost advantage in marketing, which it passes on to consumers and thereby attracts
them.

Different positions of brands in the cascade show the division of labour in the
identity industry. Even if all brands wanted to be positioned at the end of the cascade for reasons of scale advantage, some will continue to position themselves
closer to the beginning in order to gain a USP in terms of signalling. Define brand
equilibrium in the style system as (stable) distribution of brands over the signalling cascade. In brand equilibrium no brand wants to take a different position:
some occupy the mainstream and the rest occupy the remainder. The scale advantage of mainstream brands lets more brands appear in the mainstream and
fewer brands in style groupings I, II and IV. What applies to the distribution of
consumers also applies to brands: the concentration of brands in the mainstream
is endogenous.

Customer Touchpoint Management

The identity industry's customer touchpoint management is suited to brand
grouping. You will find outlets of brands, that mediate the transformation from
grouping I to grouping II/IV, in backstreets (in subcultural milieus). Outlets of
mediator brands between groupings II/IV and III are found in sidestreets (hip
neighbourhoods that were formerly backstreets). And the large number of
brands for the mass market (grouping III) are found in mainstreets and urban
peripheries. Exclusive shopping districts combine niche brands of the mainstream and highly stylising brands from groupings I/II.

As style innovation spreads from the fringes to the mainstream, customer touchpoints undergo a change along the way: from cheap to expensive and from uncontrolled to controlled. On the mainstreet the goods on offer may be cheap (supermarket), but the property is not. In the supermarket as well as in the luxury boutique, customer experience is planned down to the last detail. In contrast, fewer and fewer well-planned customer experiences are delivered, at less and less specially designed customer touchpoints, closer to the source of style innovation.

This organisation of customer touchpoints can be understood as a resource-based strategy: with lower purchasing power in the fringes, customer touchpoints increasingly focus on functionality. The store reflects the purchasing power of the surrounding milieu. QTC offers a different logic. The fringes of society are stylistically made up of the distance type and the extreme type. Outlets that signify distance from the symbols of both commerce and the establishment, respond better to this customer need than the commercial symbolism of standardised outlets. Uncontrolled shopping thus becomes a valuable customer experience in itself.

Well-designed outlets of brands mediating between groupings I and II/IV have already mitigated this lack of control. Criticism of commerce is mixed together with professionalism and openness for different customer segments, so that it becomes a borderland for the fringe which still can enter it. This customer segment adds authenticity that attracts customers from groupings II/IV. Well-designed outlets of brands that mediate between groupings II/IV and III are already beyond all serious criticism of the establishment: the Che Guevara cap and the Palestinian scarf now only have meaning in fashion. Customer experience is now evidently a management concern, outlets let customers sense that they are being guided. This serves the need for stylistic self-assurance of the mainstream following.

Outlets of brands for the fit-in-cool show the symbols of shamanism, evidence of the very presence of savants, and it is precisely here that the trend is occuring. Exclusive shopping districts push the control of customer touchpoints to the limit. This way, they provide their specific target customers with an experience that leads them towards the desired signalling. It assures customers with little cultural capital of purchasing the right signal.

Brands like *Saint Laurent* and *Rick Owens* from brand grouping I are presented in luxury stores that are totally untypical for style grouping I. They combine the two stylistic worlds; of the extremely distant from the mainstream, and of luxury that is so closely associated with it. Stylistic fringe existence is presented as the *luxury of stylistic autonomy*. The contradiction between fringe and luxury is thus dissolved. With brands like *Saint Laurent* and *Rick Owens* and their outlets, the identity industry accomplishes the greatest possible stylistic fusion of the values of the social fringes and the mainstream. The transformation and path of innovation through the style system is minimised: with even more extreme aesthetics than the original, distance-marking innovation is transported directly into the cathedrals of consumerism.

Brand as Mediator

The productive consumer must signal clearly and avoid ambiguity, contradiction and uncertainty in their communication. However, the cultural encounters between the style groupings (Figure 12) are full of incongruities. Thus, between groupings I/IV and II/III there is the tension between what is extreme and what is above-average. Between groupings I/II and III/IV there is tension between the dominant motives of distance versus proximity. And between groupings I and II/IV there is tension between potential conflict and peaceful coexistence. Consumers have no inherent advantage in moderating these cultural encounters. They avoid this no-man's-land and the associated risk of getting trapped between groupings. It is precisely at these interfaces that the industry has a comparative advantage over the DIY of consumers.

Brands are sometimes positioned as neutral in the cultural no-man's-land, neither clearly right nor wrong, neither clearly this nor that. In Figure 23, *C&A* and *Dr. Martens* are examples thereof. Another example, *Club Med*, offers an escape from the routine of everyday life, and at the same time offers the comfort of everyday life. And *McDonald's* offers efficiency, affordability and predictability, while at the same time offering leisure and pleasure. Likewise, *Carrefour* emphasises the essentials with private labels while enhancing the shopping experience by building hypermarkets with bistros and art exhibitions.[12] Unlike consumers, brands can prosper in the indeterminate zone. Not in the indeterminate zone between two cultures, but in a stylistic contact zone where all consumers still share the understanding of the same symbolic language.[13]

Therefore, brands are useful mediators/moderators between style groupings. Contradictions between groupings are encoded in one and the same brand, but never the contradictions in life *per se*. This way, each individual can find the meaning that suits their DIY project in the biotope of brands, without getting

---

12   Heilbrunn 2005.

13   Berthon, Pitt and Campbell 2009.

caught in the indeterminate zone between groupings. Just like everyone at *McDonald's* decides for themselves, whether they are there for the sake of efficiency or fun.

'Brand per se' Signification

It is time to semiotically embed the brand more broadly. The interpretation of a brand so far has been as a signifier that tells something about something else, which thereby becomes a significate.[14] In cultural encounters, however, brands as signifiers not only speak about something else, but also about themselves: As a *brand per se*, a brand is also its own significate, tantamount to system conformity and assimilation capacity. Brands demonstrate that they and whoever displays them are innocuous. Whoever displays brands demonstrates that they accept the commercial game, that they are not (any longer) hostile to it. The brand as a signifier of itself, the *brand per se*, attests to the user system conformity and ability to assimilate innovation.

The *brand per se* is like a quality seal on a product, which certifies hygienic, health or ecological safety. Its very existence as a commercial icon deprives the brand of some of the irritating aggressiveness that may still exist in the thing itself. *Dr. Martens* are boots worn by skinheads. But they are not skinhead boots. As a brand, *Dr. Martens* absorbs part off their symbolic menace. As a significate, the *brand per se* becomes the ideal mediator between the style groupings. Downstream, it creates trust and confidence, taking the edge off irritation between groupings. Style innovation diffuses more rapidly through the style system when it carryies the seal of the *brand per se*. Irritation caused by something creepy is transformed by the *brand per se* into fascination in the creepy.

The link between the signifier *brand* and the significate *brand per se* is encoded by the market. Brands have passed the test of the market (until further notice). They were born out of commercial thinking and are perpetuated by commercial thinking. After all, brands are not given away for free (in things), they are sold and bought. The exchange anchored in the market thus becomes a meaning-giving ritual. Market success is the code that turns the brand as significate into a seal. The thing bearing the brand is not so strange, provocative, repulsive or garish that it would cause the brand to fail in the market. Those who display brands know that they are not left out, even if they initially encounter incomprehension or resistance with their innovation. Market sociology stresses the complex

---

14   Baudrillard 1968; McCracken 1986.

interplay between culture, the social and the economic,[15] which acquires a further facet in the *brand per se*.

The Cultural Foundation of Economic Activity

The function of the identity industry, highlighted in QTC, is to help shape culture. This is its function because the productive consumer is working on the transformation of culture. One of the first in management science to recognise the culture-shaping effect of industry was Grant McCracken.[16] In QTC we find his propositions in a deepened form.

> "The groups responsible for the radical reform of cultural meaning are those existing at the margins of society, e.g. hippies, punks ..."

The most stylistically innovative consumers are those in style grouping I in Figure 11.

> "Such groups invent a much more radical, innovative kind of cultural meaning than their high-standing partners in meaning-diffusion leadership."

The creative units of industry fall far behind them in their innovation impact. In the cascade of cultural encounters from the fringes to the mainstream, industry only takes an assisting role (Figure 12).

> "[C]ultural meaning in a hot, western, industrial, complex society is constantly undergoing systematic change."

Figure 12 shows the path through society that meaning takes. And Figure 14 shows the change it is undergoing on this path.

> "The fashion system serves as one of the conduits to capture and move highly innovative cultural meaning."

---

15   Zelizer 1988.

16   McCracken 1986, all citations from p. 75–76.

The business models summarised in Table 13 show that the culture-changing industry is not limited to fashion in the narrow sense. They also show how exactly the identity industry as a whole is participating in this change.

McCracken's much quoted article, however, leaves the content of the change of meaning completely open – what was before and what exists thereafter remains unspecified. He describes the process of change of meaning (semiosis) merely as a process *per se*. In contrast, with cultural selection (Table 12), QTC lends a concrete direction to the change in meaning. The culture-transforming industry is not able to alter cultural selection. It can only strengthen, sublimate and accelerate its effects.

Grant McCracken has shown marketing the way to postmodernism. He has opened eyes to the fact that the creatives of industry work at the melting rim of culture. According to him, they unite existing cultural categories (time, space, age, gender, etc.) with consumer goods in advertising, labels and brands. Viewers/readers are thereby encouraged to recognise a similarity between the two. That way, goods with initially unknown properties are assigned those from these cultural categories. The transfer of meaning from the culturally institutionalised world into consumer goods is complete when the viewer/reader recognises a correspondence between the world and consumer goods.

So, in the end, 'crystallised history' emerges again: eventually, the consumer good, as an object with a meaning that it did not have before, has once again become part of culture as 'crystallised history'. It has thus become part of that phenomenological world from which the creatives of the industry once again extract their codes for new advertisements/labels/brands. Old signs (advertisements/labels/brands) 'produce' new signs (advertisements/labels/brands) in this semiotic sense.

McCracken leaves no doubt about the indispensable role of consumers in this transfer and production process.

> "It is worth emphasising that the viewer/reader is the final author in the process of transfer."[17]

The productive consumer is the all-important agent in this process. Yet, McCracken's homage to the productive consumer takes place in the maximum model of corporate agency. The consumer is only productive at the very beginning of the process as a provider of ideas from the fringes of society, and as the

---

17   ibid., p. 75.

final author, at the very end of the 'writing process'. In between, the value chain is controlled by industry.

QTC counters this with an inverse production depth of the consumer. It goes right down to the very foundation of any potential meaning: the information that we, the productive consumers, read from signs in our environment. But not everything we perceive is information. As the anthropologist Gregory Bateson put it, information is a difference only if it makes a difference. But the most basic information we can extract from our environment are basic differences between two objects (dissimilarity), and basic differences in and between ensembles of objects (diversity). It is only from these differences in our outside world, perceived from our inner world, that additional meanings arise in the further value-added process. These are dissimilarities and diversities based on comparability or incomparability (length versus width), social distance (diversity as width) and social proximity (diversity as length), which we collectively produce by consuming, and with which we collectively create and curate our social identities.

This is the cultural foundation of economic activity. A microeconomic theory – which starts from *having* and develops a theory of the relationship between human being and things with quantities and prices – does not do it justice. Neither does a marketing theory, which in B2C is tied to the myth of the *industrial controllability* of brands, products and services. The Mecca of marketing practice is not the nudging of consumers in shopping situations but the cultural moderation of the identity-do-it-yourself value-added process. On this scientific foundation, the consumer goods industry turns into an identity industry, and becomes part of a cultural industry in a broader sense. And economics fuses with business administration, cultural studies and semiotics to form the cross-disciplinary field of *cultural economics and management studies*.

Bibliography

Akerlof, G.A. and R.E. Kranton (2000). Economics and Identity. Quarterly Journal of Economics 115 (3): 715–753. https://doi.org/10.1162/003355300554881

Akerlof, G. A. and R. E. Kranton (2010). Identity Economics – How our Identities Shape our Work, Wages, and Well-Being. Princeton, Princeton University Press. https://doi.org/10.1515/9781400834181

Aragon, J. (2008). The 'Lady' Revolution in the Age of Technology. International Journal of Media and Cultural Politics 4 (1): 71–85. https://doi.org/10.1386/macp.4.1.71_1

Arnheim, R. (1981). Style as a Gestalt Problem. The Journal of Aesthetics and Art Criticism 39 (3): 281–289. https://doi.org/10.2307/430162

Arnheim, R. (1995). Problems of Style – Foundations for a History of Ornament. The British Journal of Aesthetics 35 (5): 402–403. https://doi.org/10.1093/bjaesthetics/35.4.402

Ashmore, R.D., K. Deaux and T. McLaughlin-Volpe (2004). An Organizing Framework for Collective Identity: Articulation and Significance of Multidimensionality. Psychological Bulletin 130 (1): 80–114. https://doi.org/10.1037/0033-2909.130.1.80

Banzhaf, S. and J. Boyd (2005). The Architecture and Measurement of an Ecosystem Services Index. Washington, Resources for the Future.

Barber, B. (2008). Consumed – How Markets Corrupt Children, Infantilize Adults, and Swallow Citizens Whole. New York, W.W. Norton & Company.

Basili, M. and S. Vannucci (2013). Diversity as Width. Social Choice and Welfare 40 (3): 913–936. https://doi.org/10.1007/s00355-011-0649-8

Baudrillard, J. (1968). Les Systèmes des Objects. Paris, Gallimard.

Baudrillard, J. (2009 [1970]). The Consumer Society (La société de consommation). Los Angeles, Sage.

Becker, G.S. (1992). Habits, Addictions, and Traditions. Kyclos 45 (3): 327–345. https://doi.org/10.1111/j.1467-6435.1992.tb02119.x

Belk, R.W. (1988). Possessions and the Extended Self. Journal of Consumer Research 15 (2): 139–168. https://doi.org/10.1086/209154

Bellezza, S., F. Gino and A. Keinan (2014). The Red Sneakers Effect: Inferring Status and Competence from Signals of Nonconformity. Journal of Consumer Research 41 (1): 35–54. https://doi.org/10.1086/674870

Bengtsson, T.T. (2012). Learning to Become a ›Gangster‹. Journal of Youth Studies 15 (6): 677–692. https://doi.org/10.1080/13676261.2012.671930

Berger, J. and C. Heath (2007). Where Consumers Diverge from Others: Identity Signaling and Product Domains. Journal of Consumer Research 34 (2): 121–134. https://doi.org/10.1086/519142

Bergesen, A.J. (2000). A Linguistic Model of Art History. Poetics 28 (1): 73–90. https://doi.org/10.1016/S0304-422X(00)00012-7

Bergman, D. (Hg.) (1993). Camp Grounds – Style and Homosexuality. Amherst, University of Massachusetts Press.

Berlyne, D. (1971). Aesthetics and Psychobiology. New York, Appleton-Century-Croft.

Berthon, P., L.F. Pitt and C. Campbell (2009). Does Brand Meaning Exist in Similarity or Singularity?. Journal of Business Research 62 (3): 356–361. https://doi.org/10.1016/j.jbusres.2008.05.015

Bessis, F., C. Chaserant, O. Favereau and O. Thévenon (2006). L'identité sociale de l'homo conventionalis. L'économie des conventions, méthodes et résultats. F. Eymard-Duvernay. Paris, La Découverte. 1: 181–195.

Binski, P. (1990). The Cosmati at Westminster and the English Court Style. The Art Bulletin 72 (1): 6–34. https://doi.org/10.2307/3045715

Black, D. (2009). Wearing Out Racial Discourse: Tokyo Street Fashion and Race as Style. Journal of Popular Culture 42 (2): 239–256. https://doi.org/10.1111/j.1540-5931.2009.00677.x

Boast, R. (1997). A Small Company of Actors: A Critique of Style. Journal of Material Culture 2 (2): 173–198. https://doi.org/10.1177/135918359700200202

Boltanski, L. and L. Thevenot (2006). On Justification: Economies of Worth. Princeton, Princeton University Press.

Bothe, H.-H. (1995). Fuzzy Logic – Einführung in Theorie und Anwendungen. Berlin, Springer Verlag.

Bourdieu, P. (2010). Distinction. London, Routledge.

Braudel, F. (2011 [1980]). History and the Social Sciences: The Longue Durée. Cultural Theory: An Anthology. I. Szeman and T. Kaposy. Chichester, Wiley-Blackwell: 364–375.

Brewer, M. (1991). The Social Self: On Being the Same and Different at the Same Time. SPSP 17 (5): 475–482. https://doi.org/10.1177/0146167291175001

Bronk, R. (2009). The Romantic Economist – Imagination in Economics. Cambridge, Cambridge University Press. https://doi.org/10.1017/CBO978113 9166805

Budzanowski, A. (2017). Why Coolness Should Matter to Marketing and When Consumers Desire a Cool Brand: An Examination of the Impact and Limit to the Perception of Brand Coolness. School of Management. St. Gallen, University of St. Gallen. PhD.

Caballero, A. and M.A. Toro (2002). Analysis of Genetic Diversity for the Management of Conserved Subdivided Populations. Conservation Genetics 3: 289–299. https://doi.org/10.1023/A:1019956205473

Cevik, G. (2010). American Style or Turkish Chair: The Triumph of Bodily Comfort. Journal of Design History 23 (4): 367–385. https://doi.org/10.1093/jdh/epq028

Chan, C., J. Berger and L. Van Boven (2012). Identifiable but Not Identical: Combining Social Identity and Uniqueness Motives in Choice. Journal of Consumer Research 39 (3): 561–573. https://doi.org/10.1086/664804

Coase, R. (1937). The Nature of the Firm. Econometrica 4 (16): 386–405.

Costello, D. (2004). On Late Style: Arthur Danto's 'The Abuse of Beauty'. British Journal of Aesthetics 44 (4): 424–439. https://doi.org/10.1093/bjaesthetics/44.4.424

Crofts, A.R. (2007). Life, Information, Entropy, and Time: Vehicles for Semantic Inheritance. Complexity 13 (1): 14–50. https://doi.org/10.1002/cplx.20180

D'Arnoldi, C.T., J.-L. Foulley and L. Ollivier (1998). An Overview of the Weitzman Approach to Diversity. Genetics Selection Evolution 30: 149–161. https://doi.org/10.1186/1297-9686-30-2-149

Dawkins, R. (1989 [1976]). The Selfish Gene. Oxford, Oxford University Press.

Dawkins, R. (2005). The Ancestor's Tale – A Pilgrimage to the Dawn of Evolution. Boston, Mariner Books.

Delanty, G. (2011). Cultural Diversity, Democracy and the Prospects of Cosmopolitanism: A Theory of Cultural Encounters. The British Journal of Sociology 62 (4): 633–656. https://doi.org/10.1111/j.1468-4446.2011.01384.x

Dell'Era, C. (2010). Art for Business: Creating Competitive Advantage through Cultural Projects. Industry and Innovation 17 (1): 71–89. https://doi.org/10.1080/13662710903573844

Duhigg, C. (2013). The Power of Habit. New York, Random House.

Dundas, J. (1979). Style and the Mind's Eye. The Journal of Aesthetics and Art Criticism 37 (3): 325–334. https://doi.org/10.2307/430786

Eco, U. (1979). The Role of the Reader. Bloomington, Indiana University Press.

Elias, N. (1997). Über den Prozess der Zivilisation: Soziogenetische und psycho-genetische Untersuchungen. 2 Bde., Frankfurt am Main, Suhrkamp Taschenbuch Wissenschaft.

Elsner, J. (2010). Alois Riegl and Classical Archaeology. Alois Riegl Revisited – Contributions to the Opus and its Reception. P. Noever, A. Rosenauer und G. Vasold. Wien, Verlag der österreichischen Akademie der Wissenschaften: 45–57.

Escalas, J.E. and J.R. Bettman (2005). Self-Construal, Reference Groups, and Brand Meaning. Journal of Consumer Research 32 (3): 378–389. https://doi.org/10.1086/497549

Favareau, D., K. Kull, G. Ostdiek, et al. (2017). How Can the Study of the Humanities Inform the Study of Biosemiotics?. Biosemiotics 10 (1): 9–31. https://doi.org/10.1007/s12304-017-9287-6

Florida, R. (2002). The Rise of the Creative Class. New York, Basic Books.

Force, W.R. (2009). Consumption Styles and the Fluid Complexity of Punk Authenticity. Symbolic Interaction 32 (4): 289–309. https://doi.org/10.1525/si.2009.32.4.289

Fromm, E. (2005 [1976]). Haben oder Sein – Die seelischen Grundlagen einer neuen Gesellschaft. München, dtv-Verlagsgruppe.

Füller, J., M.K. Luedicke and G. Jawecki (2008). How Brands Enchant: Insights from Observing Community Driven Brand Creation. Advances in Consumer Research 35: 359–366.

Gaiger, J. (2002). The Analysis of Pictorial Style. British Journal of Aesthetics 42 (1): 20–36. https://doi.org/10.1093/bjaesthetics/42.1.20

Gaston, K.J. (1994). Biodiversity – Measurement. Progress in Physical Geography: Earth and Environment 18 (4): 565–574. https://doi.org/10.1177/030913339401800406

Genova, J. (1979). The Significance of Style. The Journal of Aesthetics and Art Criticism 37 (3): 315–324. https://doi.org/10.2307/430785

Girst, T. and M. Resch (2016). 100 Secrets of the Art World. London, Koenig Books.

Gollnhofer, J. (2017). The Legitimation of a Sustainable Practice Through Dialectic Adaptation in the Marketplace. Journal of Public Policy & Marketing 36 (1): 156–168. https://doi.org/10.1509/jppm.15.090

Graf, L.K.M. and J.R. Landwehr (2017). Aesthetic Pleasure versus Aesthetic Interest: The Two Routes to Aesthetic Liking. Frontiers in Psychology 8 (Artikel 15): 1-15. https://doi.org/10.3389/fpsyg.2017.00015

Greif, M., K. Ross, D. Tortorici and H. Geiselberger (Hg.) (2012). Hipster – Eine transatlantische Diskussion. Frankfurt am Main, Suhrkamp Verlag.

Gross, P. (1994). Die Multioptionsgesellschaft. Frankfurt am Main, Suhrkamp Verlag.

Grove-Whight, A. (2001). No Rules, Only Choices? Repositioning the Self within the Fashion System in Relation to Expertise and Meaning: A Case Study of Colour and Image Consultancy. Journal of Material Culture 6 (2): 193–211. https://doi.org/10.1177/135918350100600204

Haidle, M.N., M. Bolus, M. Collard and N.J. Conard, et al. (2015). The Nature of Culture: An Eight-Grade Model for the Evolution and Expansion of Cultural Capacities in Hominins and other Animals. Journal of Anthropological Sciences 93: 43–70.

Haselbach, D., P. Knüsel, A. Klein and S. Opitz (2012). Der Kulturinfarkt – Von allem zu viel und überall das Gleiche. München, Knaus.

Hebdige, D. (1988). Subculture – The Meaning of Style. London, Routledge.

Hecken, T. (2012). Pop-Konzepte der Gegenwart. POP. Kultur und Kritik (1): 88–107.

Heilbrunn, B. (2005). Brave New Brands – Cultural Branding Between Utopia and A-topia. Brand Culture. J. Schroeder and M. Salzer-Morling. London, Frank Cass: 103–117.

Heine, S.J. and E.E. Buchtel (2009). Personality: The Universal and the Culturally Specific. Annual Review of Psychology 60 (Januar): 369–394. https://doi.org/10.1146/annurev.psych.60.110707.163655

Hellman, G. (1977). Symbol Systems and Artistic Style. The Journal of Aesthetics and Art Criticism 35 (3): 279–292. https://doi.org/10.2307/430288

Hogg, M.A., D.J. Terry and K.M. White (1995). A Tale of Two Theories: A Critical Comparison of Identity Theory with Social Identity Theory. Social Psychology Quarterly 58 (4): 255–269. https://doi.org/10.2307/2787127

Holzer, D. (2013). How to Form a Taste for the Unfamiliar? – Preferences for an Undetermined Symbolic Component and the Contingency of Taste-Milieu Dilemmas in Middle-Class Shanghai. School of Management. St. Gallen, University of St. Gallen. PhD.

Hornsey, M.J. (2008). Social Identity Theory and Self-categorization Theory: A Historical Review. Social and Personality Psychology Compass 2 (1): 204–222. https://doi.org/10.1111/j.1751-9004.2007.00066.x

Howard, J.A. (2000). Social Psychology of Identities. Annual Review of Sociology 26 (August): 367–393. https://doi.org/10.1146/annurev.soc.26.1.367

Howard, S. (1981). Definitions and Values of Archaism and the Archaic Style. Leonardo 14 (1): 41–44. https://doi.org/10.2307/1574480

Humphries, C.J., P.H. Williams and R.I. Vane-Wright (1995). Measuring Biodiversity Value for Conservation. Annual Review of Ecology and Systematics 26 (November): 93–111. https://doi.org/10.1146/annurev.es.26.110195.000521

Irwin, K. (2001). Legitimating the First Tattoo: Moral Passage through Informal Interaction. Symbolic Interaction 24 (1): 49–73. https://doi.org/10.1525/si.2001.24.1.49

Jacquette, D. (2000). Goodman on the Concept of Style. British Journal of Aesthetics 40 (4): 452–466. https://doi.org/10.1093/bjaesthetics/40.4.452

Kadmon, R. and O. Allouche (2007). Integrating the Effects of Area, Isolation, and Habitat Heterogeneity on Species Diversity: A Unification of Islands Biogeography and Niche Theory. The American Naturalist 170 (3): 443–454. https://doi.org/10.1086/519853

Kahneman, D. (2011). Thinking, Fast and Slow. New York, Farrar, Straus and Giroux.

Kandinsky, W. (1973 [1926]). Punkt und Linie zu Fläche. Bern, Benteli Verlag.

Kidder, J.L. (2005). Style and Action – A Decoding of Bike Messenger Symbols. Journal of Contemporary Ethnography 34 (3): 344–367. https://doi.org/10.1177/0891241605274734

Kilpinen, E. (2008). Memes versus Signs: On the Use of Meaning Concepts about Nature and Culture. Semiotica 171: 215–237. https://doi.org/10.1515/'SEMI.2008.075

Kjeldgaard, D. and A. Bengtsson (2005). Consuming the Fashion Tattoo. Advances in Consumer Research 32: 172–177.

Koç, F. and E. Koca (2011). The Clothing Culture of the Turks, and the Entari (Part 1: History). Folk Life 49 (1): 10–29. https://doi.org/10.1179/043087711X12950015416357

Lancaster, K. (1975). Socially Optimal Product Differentiation. American Economic Review 65 (4): 567–585.

Landfester, U. (2012). Stichworte – Tätowierung und europäische Schriftkultur. Berlin, Matthes & Seitz.

Latour, B. (2005). Reassembling the Social: An Introduction to Actor-Network Theory. Oxford, Oxford University Press.

Layard, R. (2005). Happiness – Lessons from a New Science. New York, Penguin Press.

Lengbeyer, L. (2007). Situated Cognition: The Perspect Model. Distributed Cognition and the Will – Individual Volition and Social Context. D. Ross, D. Spurrett, H. Kincaid and L. Stephens. Cambridge, London, MIT Press.

Lezzi-Hafter, A. (2017). Dieser namenlose Künstler. Neue Züricher Zeitung. Zürich: 36.

Lieven, T. (2017). Brand Gender: Increasing Brand Equity through Brand Personality. London, Palgrave MacMillan.

Lind, G. (2010). Uniform and Distinction: Symbolic Aspects of Officer Dress in the Eighteenth-Century Danish State. Textile History 41 (1): 49–65. https://doi.org/10.1179/174329510X12646114289545

Lindquist, G. (2002). Spirits and Souls of Business: New Russians, Magic and the Esthetics of Kitsch. Journal of Material Culture 7 (3): 329–343. https://doi.org/10.1177/135918350200700304

Lipp, W. (2014). Kulturtypen, Kulturelle Symbole, Handlungswelt. Kultur-Soziologie. S. Moebius and C. Albrecht. Wiesbaden, Springer VS: 95–138.

Lotman, Y.M. and B.A. Uspensky (1978). On the Semiotic Mechanism of Culture. New Literary History 9 (2): 211–232. https://doi.org/10.2307/468571

Lyman, R.L. and M.J. O'Brien (2000). Measuring and Explaining Change in Artifact Variation with Clade-Diversity Diagrams. Journal of Anthropological Archaeology 19 (1): 39–74. https://doi.org/10.1006/jaar.1999.0339

Lyotard, J.-F. (2011). Answering the Question: What is Postmodernism?. Cultural Theory – An Anthology. I. Szeman and T. Kaposy. Chichester, Wiley-Blackwell.

Maffesoli, M. (2007). Tribal Aesthetics. Consumer Tribes. B. Cova, R. V. Kozinets and A. Shankar. London, Routledge.

Mainwaring, L. (2001). Biodiversity, Biocomplexity, and the Economics of Genetic Dissimilarity. Land Economics 77 (1): 79–83. https://doi.org/10.2307/3146982

Mankiw, N.G. and M.P. Taylor (2008). Economics. London, Cengage Learning EMEA.

Marks, J. (2013). The Nature/Culture of Genetic Facts. Annual Review of Anthropology 42 (Oktober): 247–267. https://doi.org/10.1146/annurev-anthro-092412-155558

McCracken, G. (1986). Culture and Consumption: A Theoretical Account of the Structure and Movement of the Cultural Meaning of Consumer Goods. Journal of Consumer Research 13 (1): 71–84. https://doi.org/10.1086/209048

Mesoudi, A. (2017). Pursuing Darwin's Curious Parallel: Prospects for a Science of Cultural Evolution. PNAS 114 (30): 7853–7860. https://doi.org/10.1073/pnas.1620741114

Metelmann, J. (2016). Pop und die Ökonomie des Massenoriginals: Zur symbolischen Form der Globalisierung. POP. Kultur und Kritik 8: 135–149.

Mick, D.G., J.E. Burroughs, P. Hetzel and M.Y. Brannen (2004). Pursuing the Meaning of Meaning in the Commercial World: An International Review of

Marketing and Consumer Research Founded on Semiotics. Semiotica 152 (1): 1–74. https://doi.org/10.1515/semi.2004.2004.152-1-4.1

Moffitt, J.F. (1979). A Historical Basis for Interpreting Styles of Late 18th- to Late 20th-Century Pictoral Artworks. Leonardo 12 (4): 295–300. https://doi.org/10.2307/1573891

Mohr, E. (2016). Punkökonomie – Stilistische Ausbeutung des gesellschaftlichen Rands. Hamburg, Murmann Verlag.

Müller, H.-P. (1992). De gustibus non est disputandum? Bemerkungen zur Diskussion um Geschmack, Distinktion und Lebensstil. Produktkulturen – Dynamik und Bedeutungswandel des Konsums. R. Eisendle and E. Miklautz. Frankfurt, Campus Verlag: 117–135.

Neer, R. (2005). Connoisseurship and the Stakes of Style. Critical Inquiry 32 (1): 1–26. https://doi.org/10.1086/498001

Néret, G. (2007). Gustav Klimt. Köln, Taschen.

Parmentier, R.J. (1997). The Pragmatic Semiotics of Culture. Semiotica 116 (1): 1–113.

Penney, J. (2012). 'We Don't Wear Tight Clothes': Gay Panic and Queer Style in Contemporary Hip Hop. Popular Music and Society 35 (3): 321–332. https://doi.org/10.1080/03007766.2011.578517

Perniola, M. (2007). Cultural Turns in Aesthetics and Anti-Aesthetics. Filozofski Vestnik 18 (2): 39–51.

Perry, N. (2010). The Ecological Importance of Species and the Noah's Ark Problem. Ecological Economics 69 (3): 478–485. https://doi.org/10.1016/j.ecolecon.2009.09.016#

Pesendorfer, W. (1995). Design Innovation and Fashion Cycles. American Economic Review 85 (4): 771–792.

Peterson, R.A. and N. Anand (2004). The Production of Culture Perspective. Annual Review of Sociology 30 (August): 311–334. https://doi.org/10.1146/annurev.soc.30.012703.110557

Phelps, E. (2015). What is Wrong with the West's Economies?. The New York Review of Books, 13. August.

Pountain, D. and D. Robbins (2000). Cool Rules. New York, Reaktion Books.

Prown, J.D. (1980). Style as Evidence. Winterthur Portfolio 15 (3): 197–210. https://doi.org/10.1086/495962

Rabinovitch-Fox, E. (2015). (Re)Fashioning the New Woman: Women's Dress, the Oriental Style, and the Construction of American Feminist Imagery in the 1910s. Journal of Women's History 27 (2): 14–36. https://doi.org/10.1353/jowh.2015.0024

Racinet, A. and A. Dupont-Auberville (o.J. [1869–1888 und 1877]). Die Welt der Ornamente – Vollständig kolorierter Nachdruck von ›L'Ornement poly-chrome‹ und ›L'Ornement des tissus‹. Köln, Taschen.

Rauser, A. (2015). Living Statues and Neoclassical Dress in Late Eighteenth-Century Naples. Art History 38 (3): 462–487. https://doi.org/10.1111/1467-8365.12147

Robinson, J.M. (1981). Style and Significance in Art History and Art Criticism. The Journal of Aesthetics and Art Criticism 40 (1): 5–14. https://doi.org/10.2307/430348

Roces, M. (2013). Dress, Status, and Identity in the Philippines: Pineapple Fiber Cloth and Illustrado Fashion. Fashion Theory 17 (3): 341–372. https://doi.org/10.2752/175174113X13597248661828

Saisselin, R.G. (1958). Buffon, Style, and Gentleman. The Journal of Aesthetics and Art Criticism 3 (3): 357–361. https://doi.org/10.2307/427383

Sarr, M., T. Goeschl and T. Swanson (2008). The Value of Conserving Genetic Resources for R&D: A Survey. Ecological Economics 67 (2): 184–193. https://doi.org/10.1016/j.ecolecon.2008.03.004

Schouten, J.W. and J.H. McAlexander (1995). Subcultures of Consumption: An Ethnography of the New Bikers. Journal of Consumer Research 22 (1): 43–61. https://doi.org/10.1086/209434

Schulze, G. (2005). Die Erlebnisgesellschaft – Kultursoziologie der Gegenwart. Frankfurt, New York, Campus Verlag.

Scitovsky, T. (1976). The Joyless Economy – An Inquiry into Human Satisfaction and Consumer Dissatisfaction. New York, Oxford University Press.

Shannon, C.E. (1948). A Mathematical Theory of Communication. Bell System Technical Journal 27 (3): 379–423. https://doi.org/10.1002/j.1538-7305.1948.tb01338.x

Shayo, M. (2009). A Model of Social Identity with an Application to Political Economy: Nation, Class, and Redistribution. American Political Science Review 103 (2): 147–174. https://doi.org/10.1017/S0003055409090194

Shusterman, R.M. (2011). Somatic Style. The Journal of Aesthetics and Art Criticism 69 (2): 147–159. https://doi.org/10.1111/j.1540-6245.2011.01457.x

Simmel, G. (1905). Philosophie der Mode/Zur Psychologie der Mode – Zwei Essays. Moderne Zeitfragen. H. Landsberg. Berlin, Pan Verlag.

Smith, T.S. (1974). Aestheticism and Social Structure: Style and Social Network in the Dandy Life. American Sociological Review 39 (5): 725–743. https://doi.org/10.2307/2094317

Spooner, B. (2010). Weavers and Dealers: The Authenticity of an Oriental Carpet. The Social Life of Things – Commodities in Cultural Perspective. A. Appadurai: 195–235.

Stets, J.E. and P.J. Burke (2000). Identity Theory and Social Identity Theory. Social Psychology Quarterly 63 (3): 224–237. https://doi.org/10.2307/2695870

Stigler, G. and G.S. Becker (1977). De gustibus non est disputandum. American Economic Review 67 (1): 76–90.

Stobart, J. (2011). Who were the Urban Gentry? Social Elites in an English Provincial Town, c. 1680–1760. Continuity and Change 26 (1): 89–112. https://doi.org/10.1017/S0268416011000038

Stuiber, P. (Hg.) (2012). Adolf Loos – Ornament & Verbrechen. Wien, Metroverlag.

Swindler, A. (1986). Culture in Action: Symbols and Strategies. American Sociological Review 51 (2): 273–286. https://doi.org/10.2307/2095521

Tajfel, H., M.G. Billig, R.P. Bundy and C. Flament (1971). Social Categorization and Intergroup Behaviour. European Journal of Social Psychology 1 (2): 149–178. https://doi.org/10.1002/ejsp.2420010202

Thaler, R. and C. Sunstein (2008). Nudge. New Haven, Yale University Press.

Turner, J.C., M.A. Hogg, P.J. Oakes, S.D. Reicher and M.S. Wetherell (1987). Rediscovering the Social Group: A Self-categorization Theory. New York, Blackwell.

Veblen, T. (1970). The Theory of the Leisure Class. London, Unwin.

Veenis, M. (1999). Consumption in East Germany: The Seduction and Betrayal of Things. Journal of Material Culture 4 (1): 79–112. https://doi.org/10.1177/135918359900400105

Vogt, L. (2008). The Unfalsifiability of Cladograms and its Consequences. Cladistics 24 (1): 62–73. https://doi.org/10.1111/j.1096-0031.2007.00169.x

Warren, C. and M. Campbell (2014). What Makes Things Cool? How Autonomy Influences Perceived Coolness. Journal of Consumer Research 41 (2): 543–563. https://doi.org/10.1086/676680

Wartovsky, M.W. (1993). The Politics of Art: The Domination of Style and the Crisis in Contemporary Art. The Journal of Aesthetics and Art Criticism 51 (2): 217–225. https://doi.org/10.2307/431388

Weitzman, M.L. (1993). What to Preserve? An Application of Diversity Theory to Crane Conservation. Quarterly Journal of Economics 108 (1): 157-183. https://doi.org/10.2307/2118499

Whittaker, R.J., K.J. Willis and R. Field (2001). Scale and Species Richness: Towards a General Hierarchical Theory of Species Diversity. Journal of Biogeography 28 (4): 453–470. https://doi.org/10.1046/j.1365-2699.2001.00563.x

Wilk, S. (1983). Titian's Paduan Experience and Its Influence on His Style. The Art Bulletin 65 (1): 51–61. https://doi.org/10.1080/00043079.1983.10788048

Wooten, D. and J. Mourey (2012). Adolescent Consumption and the Pursuit of 'Cool'. The Routledge Companion to Identity and Consumption. R. Belk and A. Runo. Routledge: 169–176.

Zelizer, V. (1988). Beyond the Polemics on the Market: Establishing a Theoretical and Empirical Agenda. Sociological Forum 3 (4): 614–634.

Zelizer, V. (2005). Culture and Consumption. Handbook Economic Sociology. N. J. Smelser and R. Swedberg. Princeton, Princeton University Press: 331–354.

List of Figures

Figures

Tables

Index

Social Sciences

kollektiv orangotango+ (ed.)
This Is Not an Atlas
A Global Collection of Counter-Cartographies

2018, 352 p., hardcover, col. ill.
34,99 € (DE), 978-3-8376-4519-4
E-Book: free available, ISBN 978-3-8394-4519-8

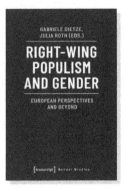

Gabriele Dietze, Julia Roth (eds.)
Right-Wing Populism and Gender
European Perspectives and Beyond

April 2020, 286 p., pb., ill.
35,00 € (DE), 978-3-8376-4980-2
E-Book: 34,99 € (DE), ISBN 978-3-8394-4980-6

Mozilla Foundation
Internet Health Report 2019
2019, 118 p., pb., ill.
19,99 € (DE), 978-3-8376-4946-8
E-Book: free available, ISBN 978-3-8394-4946-2

**All print, e-book and open access versions of the titles in our list
are available in our online shop www.transcript-publishing.com**

Social Sciences

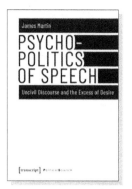

James Martin

Psychopolitics of Speech

Uncivil Discourse and the Excess of Desire

2019, 186 p., hardcover
79,99 € (DE), 978-3-8376-3919-3
E-Book:
PDF: 79,99 € (DE), ISBN 978-3-8394-3919-7

Michael Bray

Powers of the Mind
Mental and Manual Labor

in the Contemporary Political Crisis

2019, 208 p., hardcover
99,99 € (DE), 978-3-8376-4147-9
E-Book:
PDF: 99,99 € (DE), ISBN 978-3-8394-4147-3

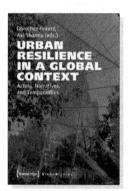

Dorothee Brantz, Avi Sharma (eds.)

Urban Resilience in a Global Context

Actors, Narratives, and Temporalities

October 2020, 224 p., pb.
30,00 € (DE), 978-3-8376-5018-1
E-Book: available as free open access publication
PDF: ISBN 978-3-8394-5018-5

**All print, e-book and open access versions of the titles in our list
are available in our online shop www.transcript-publishing.com**

CPSIA information can be obtained
at www.ICGtesting.com
Printed in the USA
JSHW020307270821
18208JS00005B/103